The Future
of the
World Motor
Industry

To Fenella

The Future of the World Motor Industry

Krish Bhaskar

Kogan Page, London/Nichols Publishing
Company, New York

Copyright © Krish Bhaskar 1980
All rights reserved

First published in Great Britain in 1980 by
Kogan Page Limited, 120 Pentonville Road, London N1 9JN

ISBN 0 85038 262 9

First published in the United States of America 1980 by
Nichols Publishing Company, Post Office Box 96, New York, NY 10024

Library of Congress Cataloging in Publication Data
Bhaskar, Krish N
The future of the world motor industry.

1. Automobile industry and trade. I. Title.
HD9710.A2B48 1980 338.4'76292'0904 80-12040
ISBN 0-89397-083-2

Printed in Great Britain by
The Anchor Press Ltd and bound by Wm Brendons,
both of Tiptree, Essex

Contents

Foreword

Michael Hinks-Edwards
Euroeconomics, Eurofinance

No book about the future of the world motor industry can expect to meet with complete agreement. Professor Bhaskar's book is appealing because of its scope. The global demand/supply picture for motor vehicles is crucially important in understanding the local changes which have taken place, and those which may be about to take place. In Britain in particular, too many of the efforts to 'steer' the motor industry have gone awry and been counter-productive, partly because of failure to take account of the global dimension. The British car industry experienced a sharp contraction in the 1970s: output has fallen by over one-third from the high point in the early 1970s, and sales of imported cars on the British market have rocketed. The conventional explanation for this state of affairs leans heavily on those much-publicized features of British economic life: low investment, low productivity and strikes. But these factors only accelerated the pace of change in the British motor industry's fortunes; they did not cause that change. Professor Bhaskar's book shows how and why change and contraction occurred.

As the rather tired joke has it, when two economists agree it is a miracle, but when three agree it is a disaster. In the case of Professor Bhaskar's book, there will be no miracle and no disaster. There is enough in the book — ranging from matters of detail through questions of interpretation to forecasting methodology issues — to keep economists arguing.

Data

Professor Bhaskar has drawn on many reputable statistical sources for his work, but no one knows the precise size of the world's stock of motor vehicles, nor the precise size of world annual production and sales. One of the main problems is that of double counting, but in certain areas of the world there is no counting whatever.

Another aspect of the data problem referred to in the book is the fact that it is becoming increasingly difficult to track the industry's development with the data and data concepts currently in use. In Europe, there are 'British cars' assembled in Belgium from parts made in Germany; 'Italian cars' with Brazilian-made engines; and 'Swedish cars' with a high content of British-made parts. There are Renault cars with Peugeot engines, Chrysler US cars with Volkswagen engines and Ford's transcontinental heavy truck, which is assembled in Holland from cabs, engines, gearboxes and axles purchased complete from companies located elsewhere in Europe.

At present, official statistics fail to convey the internationalization of the motor industry. In the 1980s, as motor industry internationalization increases, the gap between reality and the picture conveyed by official statistics is likely to widen, adding to the problems already facing motor industry statisticians.

Forecasting

The basics of car demand forecasting are simple. But moving from simple basics to forecasts necessary for business planning is far more difficult. Car demand forecasting starts on the car stock side. For a given (forecast) set of macroeconomic conditions and population size and structure, economists attempt to calculate how many cars are likely to be in use; the book explains the principles of the approach. This method has an in-built technical tendency to overestimate future levels of car ownership. Moreover, there are large numbers of cases where the standard theory of car ownership/demand forecasting cannot be applied, either because there are no data worth working with, or they will be irrelevant (eg in the centrally planned economies where the level of car ownership has nothing to do with the standard theory as applied in the West).

If the standard theory of car ownership has so many weaknesses as a forecasting tool, why is it still applied so widely? The answer is because no better alternative has yet emerged, and this should be held firmly in mind by readers of Professor Bhaskar's book. There is no unanimity on the question of the likely future growth of car ownership in the world. There is only a wide range of speculation and opinion. My view is that Professor Bhaskar's estimates are on the high side.

In the mature markets, where 80 per cent of the world's cars are bought and sold, demand forecasters have generally had an unhappy time in the boom-bust-boom years of the 1970s. The size of the annual new car market in developed countries is heavily influenced by the timing of replacement purchases (ie people buying new cars to replace existing cars which are generally passed on into the used car market), which is affected by a large number of factors.

For the 1980s, the general view is that the industry is likely to continue to experience large swings in demand for its products. This implies a premium on production and marketing flexibility as well as stepping up the forecasting effort to improve the ability to anticipate turning points. For those who would scoff at this as being a patently self-evident response to potential volatility in the market, it should be pointed out that it is easier said than done. Most forecasters have been wrong-footed on the performance of the German car market since 1974, but particularly in 1978 and 1979 when the predicted easing off in the pace of sales failed to materialize. By contrast, the Italian car market is still awaiting the post-1974 improvement in sales which other big European markets have already experienced.

The doubts raised over the validity of car ownership forecasting and the developed markets' experience of car demand cycles in the 1970s have created a state of confusion in motor industry forecasting. This confusion seems to be fostering a shift to more simple, pragmatic approaches to forecasting and planning. It remains to be seen whether these approaches will yield better results than those of the econometricians.

Energy

In the USA, cars and commercial vehicles account for nearly 40 per cent of total oil consumption; the figure is close to 25 per cent in Europe and just under 20 per cent in Japan. The world's cars and commercial vehicles are unlikely to be able to switch fuels to any significant extent in the rest of this century. How big a threat, therefore, is the oil/energy problem to the world's automotive industries in the 1980s?

Probably the most common assumption made about oil in the 1980s is that its price will go on rising in real terms, and that there will be intermittent economic crises as the world adjusts to future OPEC oil supply/price decisions. On this basis, car demand will be affected by constraints on economic growth in general, and swings in the cycle could be pronounced. But all the evidence since 1973 suggests that sharp increases in fuel prices have only a short-term deterrent effect on car demand. No one is quite sure how far fuel prices have to rise before having a lasting deterrent effect on car ownership, demand and use.

The price of fuel is not the only factor in the cost equation for car owners. Before 1970, new car prices in developed countries tended to rise more slowly than the average for prices as a whole. This trend was reversed after 1970, but we are not yet at the point where cars are being shunned by the market because of rising costs.

If the oil/energy problem has yet to produce a revolution in the demand for cars, its effect on the supply side has been dramatic. Before the oil crisis of 1973-74, no one would have forecast that the average American car of the 1980s would be similar to the medium-large models familiar in Europe and Japan now.

Supply

In 1968, Giovanni Agnelli, currently President of Fiat, forecast that by 1990 there would only be six or seven car makers left in the Western world. It is doubtful if, at the time, more than a handful of people cared much about the thoughts of Sgr Agnelli on the future of the world motor industry. Things are rather different now. What has happened since Sgr Agnelli's prophecy is that the stakes in the competitive battle to supply cars to world markets have been progressively raised, and with each new 'bid', some 'players' have dropped out — exactly as Sgr Agnelli predicted. For the 1980s, the stakes have been raised substantially. This time, the new 'bid' is called 'world component supply'.

A world component supply system has a highly important practical application in industrial politics. A car maker manufacturing vehicles in different parts of the world is faced with a barrage of different types of industrial policy, to say nothing of construction and use legislation. Policies governing the level of locally manufactured content in vehicles sold on developing markets and the associated import/export requirements can result in uneconomic production. But as physical controls (eg local content) are relaxed in favour of financial requirements (eg a net trade contribution of x million dollars from a given company's activities in the country concerned) new opportunities open up. Car makers can restructure and integrate their operations to meet local requirements at the same time as pushing up volumes on key items such as engines, gearboxes and certain sub-assemblies. The recently announced Fiat investment programme involving integration of its Polish, Italian, Spanish and Brazilian operations illustrates the application of world component supply strategy.

Rationalizing and integrating their component production for new ranges of cars for world markets, GM and Ford could wield an enormous competitive advantage in unit costs of production. The threat posed by the US producers is being taken seriously by the big European and Japanese car makers who cannot match the scale of output of Ford and GM, particularly in what are called the centre markets (ie North America, Europe and Japan).

The future

Most published long-range forecasts of world car demand and production do not differ widely, regardless of source. The consensus view now would seem to be that sales of cars in the world will grow annually at a little over 3 per cent to reach 45 million in 1990. These figures are down sharply on those circulating before the oil crisis of 1973-74. But whatever figure is put on the 1990 world car market, what really matters is what is behind that figure. How will world car sales be distributed market by market? Which countries will be supplying the world's demand for cars? What might be the pattern of world trade in cars? How will world car supply be divided company by company?

A world car industry dominated by eight major companies, with a consequent squeeze on the combined unit car output of the other manufacturers, is the most likely scenario. There is likely to be a substantial volume of international trade in basic components, but this will be mostly intra-company trade. Centre, new and fringe market trade in finished cars will decline. There will be a new breed of component suppliers, with companies such as United Technologies and Schlumberger who have bought into microprocessor technology, and Fujitsu, Hitachi, Mitsubishi, etc. Components might be one of the ways in which the Japanese automotive sector gets off the hook of being a national direct exporter. The 1980s will be a difficult decade for the Japanese if they continue to use direct exports as the springboard for growth. But the Japanese producers, particularly Toyota and Nissan, are likely to change strategy quickly in the early 1980s.

Since 1973-74, things have moved very fast in the motor industry. Frequently, events have overtaken forecasts, and will probably do so again in the 1980s. But this probability should not unduly affect what Professor Bhaskar has to say about long-range trends in the economics of the car industry and its markets. But on a number of important specifics, he, I and others who have held forth on the subject, will have to stand ready to eat our words.

Preface

This book attempts to cover the entire world motor industry, but attention is restricted to the study of motor vehicles (cars and commercial vehicles). Looking into the future is risky and the motor industry is especially difficult in this respect, and, by the time this book is published, events will perhaps have overtaken some aspects of the motor industry.

One area in which this is almost certain is the increasing merger fever now taking place around the world and especially in Europe. As the book went to press, Renault announced a link-up with Volvo's car operations. Not to be outdone Alfa Romeo wooed Nissan, the Japanese giant, but Fiat promptly responded and offered assistance to Alfa Romeo, self-interest being a more likely motive than jealousy. Whichever company succeeds in linking with the troubled government owned firm of Alfa Romeo is likely to find the association fraught with difficulties.

In 1975, a team of researchers, spearheaded by the author, completed a research project entitled *Alternatives Open to the UK Motor Industry: An Analysis and Evaluation*. The team included Alan Armstrong, Martin Slater, Garel Rhys, Andy Friedman, Glyn Barker, Tim Mawby and others. My interest in the motor industry continued. It became obvious that the UK's ailing motor industry was bedevilled by problems which could only be understood in a European and global context. An earlier book published on the motor industry was specifically concerned with the UK and the general European situation (K N Bhaskar [1979] *The Future of the UK Motor Industry* Kogan Page).

One of the foremost economists engaged in forecasting of the motor industry is Michael Hinks-Edwards of Euroeconomics, Eurofinance, Paris.[1] The high quality of Eurofinance's predictions and their careful analysis of world events has been a major influence on my thinking. I was fortunate in persuading Michael Hinks-Edwards to write a foreword to the book.

The only recent major study of the World Motor Industry and its future was a massive report undertaken by Business International[2] in a confidential multi-client research project. The report is contained in five volumes and is entitled *The World Automotive Industry to 1995*. The report contains projections of demand produced by a sophisticated computer model, and gives a fascinating analysis of the sociological and political factors affecting the world motor industry. I have been much influenced by the findings of this excellent study, which have particularly affected my views in Part 1. The conclusions of the report point to some key themes:

> Corporate management in the motor vehicle industry may easily underestimate the basic and probably turbulent nature of the changes in the business environment now taking place on a global scale. Even the most optimistic projections of the industry's future must consider the impact of explosive forces: a more radical industrial unionism; an important and affluent labour force; worldwide environmental and consumer movements and related governmental reactions; a new type of international competition, including government controlled or owned corporations; vast capital requirements to implement new technologies and many more.

The precise forecasting of events is impossible in the motor industry. All the predictions contained here must be taken as representative and a logical extrapolation of current events and trends.

Grateful thanks must be given to Richard Wainwright, Mike Lowcock, Anne Beech, Michael Hinks-Edwards, Fenella Bhaskar and many others who have helped me in the course of writing this book. In a project of this type, it is vital to have contacts in the motor industry; I thank them all and many of the ideas in the book are attributable to them.

One of the greatest problems in writing a book of this nature is the use of a variety of statistical sources. A note of these sources is provided at the end of the book. Another problem is that the argument depends, in part, on statistical projections: these should be treated as representative guides rather than precise forecasts.

Although I have had much help in writing this book, I must accept any responsibility for any errors, omissions or incorrect or inadequately analysed conclusions.

Krish Bhaskar
University of East Anglia

1. Eurofinance, 9 Avenue Hoche, 75008 Paris, France.
2. Business International. World Headquarters: 1 Dag Hammarskjold Plaza, New York, NY 10017, USA. General Headquarters: 12-14 Chemin Rieu/CH-1208 Geneva, Switzerland.

Part 1:
Introduction

Chapter 1

The Motor Industry: Economic Importance and Change

The world motor industry is facing a period of turbulent change, a transitional phase in the development of the industry which could radically alter its structure. Traditionally, observers and theoreticians have seen the industry in terms of a global divide between US (North America) and non-US producers, with the world's most prosperous market on one side of a gigantic trading fence and the rest of the world on the other. In this book we shall be arguing that theoretical constructs of this sort have outlived their usefulness, and that it is no longer possible to understand the workings of the motor industry in such simple terms. The fundamental changes now taking place demand a more sophisticated approach. We hope to supply this by placing the development of the industry in a cyclical context, demonstrating that producers and their markets move from infancy through an emergent phase to a state of fully-fledged maturity, which degenerates as they pass from maturity to senescence.

The transition is not a rapid one. Each phase in the 'life' of the industry could last for 10 or 20 years, the minimum period required under present conditions to construct plant and to develop and launch a new product. But we maintain that the changes, although gradual, are of such a magnitude that no one should underestimate their importance.

Superimposed upon this cyclical development are two major influences: environmental and consumer-oriented constraints dictated by the peculiarities of the local market, and the energy crises which seriously affected the Western world at the end of 1973 and again in 1979 following the internal upheavals in Iran. Energy is now of such importance that it dominates all other factors and may well lead to a worldwide homogeneity in the motor vehicle product. We return to this discussion in Chapter 2.

This book sets out first to describe the current state of the industry, identifying the mature, emergent and infant markets. The local market forces and the all-pervasive energy problem will be placed in perspective. We will consider how the industry has developed and how it functions, and we will examine the economic, political and social constraints affecting that industry. Finally, we will analyse ways in which cyclical shifts in production and demand could change one of the world's most important manufacturing concerns. Some will find our conclusions surprising, others may find them disagreeable, but no one concerned with the motor industry can afford to ignore them.

Global dimensions and infrastructure

Before we characterize the various mature, emergent and infant markets in greater detail, we must understand the inputs and linkages needed to sustain a viable motor industry and give some idea of the dimensions of the industry.

There are some 350 million vehicles in the world today, and almost 42 million vehicles were produced in 1978. This, however, is only part of the story. The industry demands a massive infrastructural network of related manufacturing and service industries. Figure 1.1 provides a schematic representation of the range of inputs needed. The primary commodities required include oil, oil by-products, chemicals, aluminium, lead, copper, iron, zinc, steel, glass, asphalt, concrete, paint and power. The motor industry is therefore dependent upon electricity generation, petroleum refining, crude oil and natural gas, coal-mining, various non-ferrous metals, iron ore mining, industrial chemicals, basic iron and steel production, glass, clay and concrete products, the construction industry, and the world's transport and distribution network. The industry generates further industry and employment through its fuel, oil and anti-freeze requirements and its demands on road construction, maintenance and repair.

The structure is daunting. Less developed countries are often unable to provide the necessary infrastructure to support an autonomous motor industry and must link in to a more advanced country's infrastructure by importing the necessary components or materials to maintain production. Although the motor industry is not the only manufacturing industry to require such a large range of inputs, its economic importance is enhanced by the scale of the operation and the number of services it requires.

An impressive measure of the importance of the motor industry can be seen in the number of jobs dependent, directly or indirectly, on that industry. When much of the industry is functioning well below capacity, as it is at present, figures for total employment can be misleading. It has been estimated, however, that under conditions of full capacity output about one million workers are directly involved in the production and assembly of motor vehicles in the US, 2 million in Western Europe (including some of the smaller specialist producers) and some 0.5 million in Japan. The worldwide total is about 4 or 5 million workers. But the motor industry is not confined solely to those who are concerned with the manufacture and assembly processes: there are 5 million people employed in the components manufacturing industries in Western

Figure 1.1 *Inputs to the motor industry*

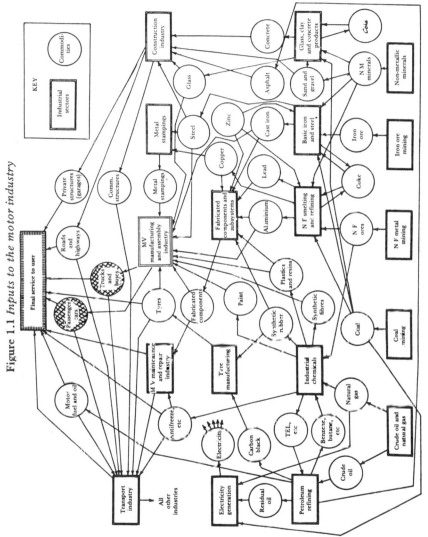

Source: The World Automotive Industry to 1995 Business International

Europe alone, and the world total probably exceeds 12 million. Moreover, there may be as many as 12 million additional workers involved in
distribution, sales, maintenance, repair, breakdown, petrol sales, etc
throughout the world, servicing the 274 million cars and 73 million
trucks and buses on the world's roads. A full account of employment
totals in the industry should also include some proportion of the
workers employed in the steel, plastics and oil refining industries, as
much of their output is produced for the motor industry. If one adds to
the list the civil engineers, personnel in the extractive industries, road
and building contractors and associated industries, it becomes apparent
that the motor industry casts an extremely wide employment net.
Allowing for a reasonably wide margin of error (and assuming full
capacity production) the motor industry employs 28-35 million people
directly, and another 60-100 million people *indirectly*. Two-thirds of
these are employed in the advanced economies, and Western Europe
alone accounts for some 42 million workers.

In economic terms, however, numbers are not as important as the
value of the output in any particular industry. To illustrate this point,
Figure 1.2 gives estimated values for input and output for a representative advanced country (the UK). Of the £2520 million output of the
motor vehicle manufacturing and assembly industry, some £1775
million was accounted for by the value of inputs (though this figure
may be an underestimate) giving an input/output ratio of 70 per cent.
The motor industry is a major industry, but it is also a heavily
concentrated industry. The major manufacturing firms are colossal: the
sales of the six largest firms account for a significant percentage of GNP
in the countries concerned. General Motors' (GM) sales in 1974, which
amounted to nearly $31 billion, were the equivalent of nearly one
quarter of the total UK GNP in the same year! As a general rule, motor
manufacturers' *per capita* output is usually high: in 1974 GM accounted
for nearly 2.5 per cent of the US GNP while employing only 0.5 per
cent of the national labour force.

Markets: a brief history

The range of inputs needed for viable motor manufacture explains why
the major producers (and the mature markets) are found in those areas
of advanced industrial development. But the existence of a mature
market begs the question: is it possible for a mature market to age even
further? A brief historical note on the development of the major
mature markets will provide the answer.

Immediately after World War II the world motor industry was
dominated by the USA, which accounted for 75 per cent of the world's
motor vehicles. The US share of world production has now fallen to less
than one-third of the total. By 1973, net US imports had risen to

Figure 1.2 *The UK motor vehicle industry: Estimated value of input and output (1974)*

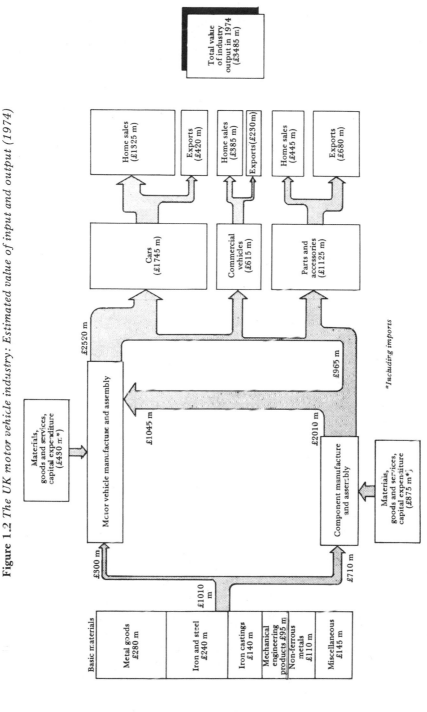

Total value of industry output in 1974 (£3485 m)

Home sales (£1325 m)

Exports (£420 m)

Home sales (£385 m)

Exports (£230m)

Home sales (£445 m)

Exports (£680 m)

Cars (£1745 m)

Commercial vehicles (£615 m)

Parts and accessories (£1125 m)

£2520 m

£965 m

Materials, goods and services, capital expenditure (£480 m*)

Motor vehicle manufacture and assembly

£1045 m

£2010 m

Component manufacture and assembly

Materials, goods and services, capital expenditure (£875 m*)

£300 m

£710 m

£1010 m

Basic materials

Metal goods £280 m

Iron and steel £240 m

Iron castings £140 m

Mechanical engineering products £95 m

Non-ferrous metals £110 m

Miscellaneous £145 m

*Including imports

Source: The Future of the British Car Industry CPRS Report

2.3 million, and the US producers now manufacture fewer vehicles than Western Europe as a whole and have a slower rate of production growth than any other major producer (see Figure 1.3). Rising import penetration in the US suggests that the major US producers − GM, Ford and Chrysler − have lost their momentum. They have certainly been dangerously slow to respond to the import threat; they have become lethargic. The industry as a whole is constrained by a battery of environmental and consumer imperatives in the form of safety measures and emission controls, most of which appear to be a function of advanced market maturity. The USA is still a major producer and its motor industry still the most profitable in the world, but some of the available evidence suggests that the US market is now in a decline and no longer in a position to reverse the downward spiral.

Whether this will continue is an open question. Despite a slow start, there is some evidence that the US producers are now reacting to business and governmental stimuli. Nevertheless the US market is, in effect, moving from maturity to senescence. In Figure 1.3 it can be seen that US and US-controlled production has risen at a slower rate than total world production, and US production has now almost reached the point of stagnation.

As the US share of world output falls, can other mature markets be identified? As argued in the next chapter, the motor industry is now centred around three core areas − North America, Western Europe and Japan − that are categorized as mature motor industries. Of these, Japan is the youngest, though it and Western Europe have developed rapidly since the 1950s and production has expanded dramatically. As world demand took off in the 1950s and 1960s, the character of the West European market was transformed from a collection of fragmented markets to a more closely integrated single market, though complete integration may be a slow process. Production levels in the area as a whole now show signs of fluctuation, a feature of a mature market. Japan, meanwhile, has emerged as a fully mature producer, with significant penetration of markets in both the USA and Western Europe. Japanese output has increased sixty-fold in the last 30 years, expanding its share of world production from less than one per cent in 1950 to more than 20 per cent currently. Japan spearheaded an unprecedented rate of growth in world production during the 1960s and early 1970s which was brought to an abrupt halt − even in Japan's case − only by the 1973 oil crisis, which created the most severe worldwide depression in motor vehicle demand in recent years.

Although motorists tend to blame the sharp and sudden rise in oil prices for the depression in the motor industry, a number of conflicting theories have been proposed to account for the slump. One suggests that the 1970-73 boom could have temporarily outstripped demand and saturated the market. Within a matter of years, the theory suggests,

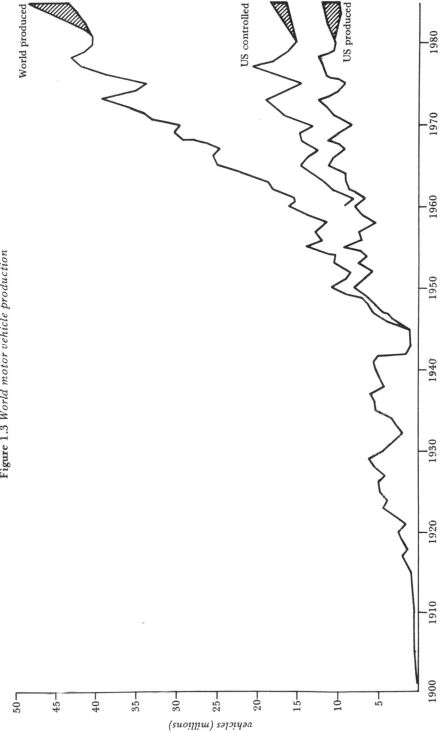

Figure 1.3 *World motor vehicle production*

demand will recover as the excess is absorbed. An alternative theory posits expenditure on private transport as a constant fraction of total consumer expenditure — in other words, the general public are only prepared to pay so much of their total income on travel. If the cost of keeping a car on the road increases (as, for example, the price of petrol rises), expenditure on other forms of travel decreases or fewer journeys are made. A third possible explanation considers the macroeconomic implications of the rise in oil prices, whereby many of the oil importing countries experienced a sudden and rapid deterioration in their balance of payments. To remedy the imbalance, steps were taken to reduce internal demand, a classic and usually effective remedy. The longer-term effect of such a solution, however, has been to dampen *potential* demand. It should, however, be remembered that although the quad-rupling of oil prices added some $30 billion to the balance of payments deficits of the eight major trading nations, this was in part recouped by unprecedented price increases which have nearly trebled the value of exports in the last six years. Nevertheless there is a clearly demonstrated relationship between sudden increases in oil prices (and scarcity of oil) and new vehicle registrations. We return to consider the oil crises and their effects on the motor industry in Chapter 3.

In all three of the major markets — the US, Western Europe and Japan — the cyclical development of the industry is clearly visible. The US now has to contend with the effects of inflation, slower growth, and a host of extra-market forces at a time when demand is falling and import penetration is rising. Western Europe appears to be teetering on the brink of old age. And Japan, so recently elevated to the ranks of the major producers, could yet be forced to step down in face of a challenge from a newer and more aggressive emergent producer. Slowly, the Big Three US producers are being edged out of major segments of their domestic market: the very factors which helped to boost production now hinder further growth. What is it, then, that promotes competitive-ness and boosts trade in the motor industry?

Trade and competitiveness

First, a brief word on the extent of international trade in the motor industry (see Figure 1.4). Total world production in 1978 was over 42 million vehicles (higher than the pre-oil crisis of 1973 figure) of which about one-third (13 million) were exported. The major trade was *between* the 'advanced' countries: North America is a net importer; Western Europe a net exporter suffering from rising import penetration; Japan primarily an exporter. The pattern of trade has changed dramatically in the last two decades: the 'oldest' of the mature markets — North America — now imports vehicles from both Western Europe and Japan. Western Europe, which was until recently the major exporter

Figure 1.4 *International trade flows of motor vehicles between mature markets*

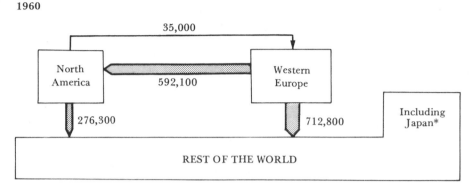

1960

Japan was not a major producer or a major market in 1960 and therefore has been included in 'Rest of the World'

1977

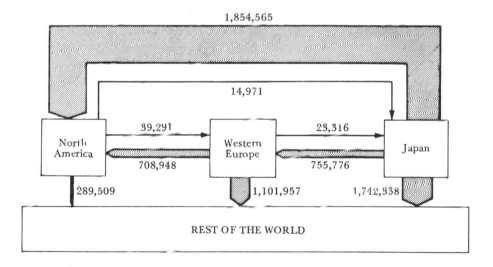

to North America, has now been forced to concede a major share of the North American market to the Japanese and to concentrate instead on trade within the Western European market, and to a lesser extent on trade with smaller markets elsewhere. Japan, on the other hand, has increased its volume of exports to compensate for a reduction in domestic demand.

What factors promote competitiveness? A competitive cost structure, whether achieved through economies of scale, a pool of cheap labour and/or the availability of cheap components, is critical. Moreover, a manufacturer must be responsive to changing patterns of demand and exploit those changes to maximum effect (through marketing expertise) if he is to remain competitive. Both factors are vital in a mature market, where producers are excluded from certain market segments, particularly at low volume levels because rising costs make them uncompetitive. Similarly, as a market matures *new* vehicle buyers form a smaller proportion of total vehicle buyers (most of whom are buying replacement vehicles). Manufacturers must chase after ever fewer new-car buyers, most of whom they will only attract through skilful marketing.

Generally speaking, trade is promoted because a producer is competitive within a certain market segment. Immediately after World War II, the UK and the USA dominated the export trade, but during the 1950s some of the standard US models were eclipsed in the domestic US market by a cheaper and distinctive European product, while US exports to Europe dwindled to almost nothing. At the time, European cars enjoyed a marked price advantage (European labour costs were significantly lower), but as European producers began to feel the effects of rising costs consistent with their more advanced industrial status they were in turn ousted in the US market by the Japanese, who were even better placed to supply a cheap basic car, the market for which they were also able to capture in Western Europe. European producers, fighting a rearguard action by the late 1960s to defend their traditional export market and segments of their own home markets, switched their marketing emphasis, concentrating on advanced engineering, speed and luxury, a tacit admission that they were no longer able to produce a cheap, basic car at a competitive price.

Clearly, as a market matures, costs increase and the product becomes more expensive. When it is no longer possible to produce a cheap, basic car competitively, manufacturers are obliged to change their product, seeking higher returns on up-market luxury models, but forgoing a large share of the domestic and export market in the process. Even if Western Europe does not become a net importer in the next 10 to 20 years, import penetration is certain to reach even higher levels and exports will continue to fall. Japan may also face competition from a newcomer even better equipped to manufacture inexpensive volume cars. By that time, one revolution of the cycle will have been completed.

Internal and extra-market forces

Independent of the apparently inevitable fluctuations in trade which will disrupt future patterns of supply and demand, a series of extra-market forces may cause even greater turbulence, particularly in the three major mature markets. To a greater or lesser extent, all three markets have been affected by similar changes. A growing interest in the recreational possibilities of increased leisure time is a characteristic common to all three areas, and, particularly in the US, has stimulated demand in certain sectors of the economy. We must also take into account changes in the composition of the population: a declining birth rate and a longer average life expectancy have created an aging population, increasingly dependent on state support. More money spent on care could mean less available for consumer durables, which may in the long term affect the pattern of market demand for motor vehicles, particularly if the concept of market saturation becomes a reality. It will be helpful to analyse this concept in the context of the mature markets.

In the US there is more than one vehicle for every two people; some observers maintain that densities of this sort are commensurate with a saturated market. Densities, however, can be misleading as we see if we examine changes in the patterns of demand affecting television sets. As the market for conventional black and white sets reached saturation level, an entirely new demand was generated by the development of colour TV. Growth was further extended by the introduction of portable and miniature sets. The development of new products is evidently vital in spinning out demand and avoiding (or at least postponing) market saturation. This applies equally to patterns of demand for private cars. There are, moreover, possibilities for further growth in 'mainstream' demand (demand for private cars, for example, as opposed to 'spin-off' demand for recreational vehicles) as mature markets show a tendency to prefer, and therefore experience a growth in demand for, larger cars with bigger engines. The economic recession and oil price rises have temporarily halted this demand but there is evidence to suggest that in both Western Europe and Japan the market for slightly larger cars still has considerable potential for growth. A reverse trend, reflected in a growing demand for slightly smaller cars, can be predicted for the US market, currently dominated by large cars.

An increasing emphasis on the 'quality of life', which is usually taken to mean the quality of the environment, will intensify efforts to combat the 'anti-social' aspects of the motor industry, eg pollution, congestion, etc. The essentially non-productive cost of dealing with these environmental hazards is a capital penalty that manufacturers will be obliged to meet. This same concern for the quality of life may extend to an increase in welfare provisions and to increased public spending generally, at the expense of other sectors of the economy. Similarly, continued urbanization (and the unacceptable levels of congestion which have in the past followed in the wake of urban development) will involve greater expenditure on improvements to urban facilities, again at the expense of other sectors of the economy and reducing economic growth.

The availability and cost of raw materials will also affect growth. Although the recent increase in oil prices has by now been almost completely absorbed, commodity prices will continue to rise as supplies are exhausted or depleted, or as the cost of extracting remaining, less accessible deposits increases. Depleted resources, moreover, will have to accommodate levels of demand equal to or probably in excess of current levels, as industrial growth in less developed countries accelerates. This will be further complicated by the distribution of resources: advanced industrial countries will find that the import cost of essential raw materials exacerbates existing balance of payments deficits, requiring deflationary measures and possibly involving the introduction of high import taxes and import quotas, all of which will act as a brake on growth.

The average number of working hours per year is likely to be reduced, occurring in the form of longer holidays, but the indications are that in the longer term an overall reduction in the length of the working week (to a four-day or a 30-hour week) will be widespread. To compensate for the inevitable fall in productivity, automation will be more widely introduced, the cost of which will be considerable.

Increased demand for resources and a world population explosion (now estimated at 3.5 billion people and rising to 5-7 billion by the year 2000 according to fairly conservative projections) will put inflationary pressure on all resources, but especially on food and basic commodities. The rate of inflation in mature markets will continue at its present high level and may even increase. Rising prices do not necessarily reduce spending, as consumers are capable of making rapid adjustments in their expectations, but bolder action on the part of governments to combat the effects of inflation may reduce growth (see Table 1.1).

This combination of increased expenditure on non-productive services, inflationary pressures and increased labour and production costs will inevitably reduce the rate of economic growth. Developed countries will be able to justify their economic status (and maintain their economic position) only by exploiting to the full their technological advantage. This would involve increased investment in education, research and development and a concentration of available resources on the capital-intensive, scale-sensitive, high-technology industries, such as telecommunications, electronics, computers, aerospace developments, chemicals and plastics. Governments, through protective tariffs, may resist the logic of this 'relocation', but radical alterations in the structure of world industry seem inevitable.

Government interference

Government intervention affects the whole economy, but it can also

Table 1.1 *GDP growth rates for selected countries 1950-70*

	Real GDP (%)	Real per capita GDP (%)
Belgium	3.9	3.5
France	5.1	4.8
Germany	6.3	5.6
Italy	5.4	5.9
Netherlands	5.1	3.8
UK	2.3	2.0
Denmark	3.7	2.5
Norway	4.1	3.7
Sweden	4.0	3.3
Switzerland	4.3	3.0
Canada	4.5	2.0
USA	3.6	2.1
Japan	9.6	7.7
Australia	4.5	2.3

depress or encourage demand in particular sectors through controls on production (supply) and the consumer (demand). The highly concentrated nature of the motor industry makes it particularly vulnerable to these types of government action. On the supply side, a concern with safety (through accident prevention) and a desire to reduce pollution levels (through control of emission levels and so on) have been the main areas of concern. Safety, for example, can be improved by restricting the lower and upper age limits of drivers and by penalizing drunken or dangerous drivers. Seat belts can reduce the severity of injuries received in motor accidents, and most of the developed countries have introduced measures encouraging or enforcing their use. The US and Japan have both introduced controls on emission levels, but further (and more severe) measures have been postponed, partly because of the oil crisis and the subsequent depression. Ford, one of the major US manufacturers, estimated that the adjustments necessary to comply with regulations of this sort added $284 to the $3392 cost of their smaller models between 1971 and 1975.

All of these regulatory measures affect demand and therefore growth. It remains to be seen whether governments can afford to add to the existing cost and price pressures when it becomes apparent that a more flexible approach may be necessary to 'preserve what is essentially a major income generator for their economies'. Governments in all three major markets have thus far shown a readiness to protect the industry, encouraging mergers (in Western Europe and Japan), restraining import competition through agreements or the imposition of controls and regulating the activities of both multinational and domestically owned companies. In recognizing the importance of the motor industry, governments have offered help in raising finance to companies in difficulty, but in return they have demanded the right to intervene in the affairs of those companies. At the same time, beleaguered managements have been obliged to negotiate more openly with an increasingly belligerent workforce, flexing new muscle and anxious to participate more directly in company affairs.

Production

Having examined factors external to the industry, we turn to the question of changes engineered from within. Predictably, perhaps, the discussion begins with the changing status of the workforce. In common with workers in many other sectors of industry, motor industry employees are finding it increasingly difficult to derive any worthwhile job satisfaction from the boring and repetitive tasks required on a high-speed assembly line. As their expectations rise, and are generally unmet, job dissatisfaction increases and with it a reluctance to identify closely with the interests of the employer and the company, or to see anything in their work relationship to indicate possible mutual interest. The puritan work ethic, in other words, has lost much of its appeal and most of its usefulness. To relieve the tedium of assembly work, improve working conditions and combat falling productivity, there will have to be major changes in manufacturing technology, involving the introduction of computerization and increased automation.

Technology

The advanced economies can only preserve their relatively high economic status through an increasing reliance on advanced technology. Most of the advantages of volume production and conventional motor vehicle technology are now widespread, and increasingly within the reach of the newer producers. To keep one step ahead, the established producers have to fund major research and development programmes, concentrating particularly on improvements in (and new concepts of) engine and propulsion systems, control and diagnostic systems and new materials.

PROPULSION SYSTEMS

The most commonly used propulsion system is the heat engine. Internal combustion engines of all types combust a working fluid (eg petrol) to convert heat into mechanical work, by means of a reciprocating or rotary mechanism. Some propulsion systems are used on a regenerative stored energy system (eg the electric car) usually requiring an electrical battery or a spinning flywheel. If a fuel cell could be developed to replace the battery, the relatively short distance capabilities of the electric car would be much improved. Work is currently in progress on the possibilities of a hybrid system in which an electric battery is supplemented by a heat engine.

Of the existing systems the current (Otto cycle) engine is probably capable of considerable refinements. The development of dual catalyst emission control systems, electronic ignition, electronically controlled fuel injection and stratified charge engines, possibly with a rotary mechanism, will all improve fuel consumption and reduce emission levels. The increasing use of aluminium and the development of advanced ceramic technology will extend the life of conventional engines.

VEHICLE DESIGN

Economy and safety considerations dictate changes in design: lighter car bodies and an improved anti-skid braking system are currently being developed. Aluminium alloys and plastics will be further developed and more extensively used, and there will be improvements in the aero-dynamic properties of body styling and in reduction of rolling resistance in moving parts. However, there are two clear and contradictory future possibilities for the motor industry in developed economies: the rising relative cost of cars could induce less design obsolescence (less emphasis on styling for its own sake) and extend model and engine life, or excessive competition could shorten model life as a range of funda-mentally similar products, differentiated only by the superficialities of styling, compete for a shrinking market.

TRANSMISSION

The move towards five-speed gearboxes will continue. If the US pattern is repeated, there will be greater demand for automatics despite the fact that European and Japanese engines are smaller in size.

MANUFACTURING TECHNOLOGY

So far, we have been discussing product developments; what of changes in manufacturing technology? To counteract falling productivity (which is based on our assumption of a shorter working week) and to alleviate the increasingly unacceptable tedium of semi-skilled assembly work, increased automation, through the flexible medium of semi-intelligent computerized robots, will mean a great increase in mechanization. The use of new materials and techniques will inevitably affect manufacturing processes as new technologies are geared for volume production. And finally, the manufacturing plant will face growing pressure to recycle waste products more efficiently.

Conclusion

The changes required by these new developments will be expensive, involving vast capital expenditure at a time of slower growth, recession and higher rates of inflation. In these circumstances, resistance to change is to be expected, but in the long run only those firms able to keep abreast of such changes will survive in the new world market. Before we can predict the outcome of such changes, however, we will consider the structure of the industry and examine supply and demand considerations in general terms. We will then analyse existing and future demand considerations in each of the producing areas and estimate the supply levels needed to meet that demand, taking the end of the twentieth century as an appropriate horizon for our projections on the grounds that a shorter time-scale would not necessarily reveal the cyclical nature of changes in the industry, while projections any further forward would be too speculative to be useful. The next 25 years promise to be a period of transition during which many traditional materials and technologies will be replaced and the wisdom of traditional marketing strategies will be seriously challenged. No major producing area will follow exactly in the footsteps of another; changes will be affected and modified in each case by conditions peculiar to the market in question, but throughout there will be similarities consistent with the evolution of a market from infancy through youthfulness to maturity and finally old age.

Chapter 2

The Motor Industry: Definitions and Typology

This chapter provides some basic definitions which are used throughout the book, constructs a typology of mature, developing and nascent industries, and examines the growth of the latter and their intrusion into the established markets.

Defining the Motor Industry

The product of the motor industry is extremely complicated and highly diversified. Figure 2.1 shows the structure of the automotive product. The market is split into three: cars, commercial vehicles (CVs) and components. The most uniform of all the products is cars. Even so cars are split into two distinctive types: volume and specialist. Specialist manufacturers include Rolls-Royce, Porsche, Volvo, Daimler-Benz and BMW. The market is further fragmented into sports and sedan. Volume manufacturers usually have to cover the model range from mini, small and medium to the large executive segments. Manufacturers who cover the range may also produce specialist sports and sedan models.

CVs are far less uniform. The small CV, usually built in large volumes, can be categorized into a number of distinct segments: car-derived vans and small vans, four-wheel drive vehicles (4 x 4s) and recreational vehicles (RVs). The USA, the home of the RV, has defined types such as motorhomes, pick-up covers, travel trailers, truck campers and camping trailers. The medium CV segment includes larger vans (called 'panel' vans) and small trucks often based on a panel van. The heavy CV segment spans an enormous range of vehicles from light trucks (over 3 to 4 tonnes carrying load) through to vehicles suitable for use in 'city delivery' and other types of distribution, inter-city and construction CVs (usually over 12 to 15 tonnes and under 250 HP engine), linehaul trucks (over 15 tonnes and over 250 HP engine) which are used on motorway/expressway journeys and finally vehicles designed to take heavy loads (dubbed as 'heavy conventional') together with buses. In addition there are the bus and special purpose vehicles[1] which have some commonality with the larger trucks.

1. Refuse lorries, fire engines, oil tankers, etc.

Figure 2.1 *The automotive product range*

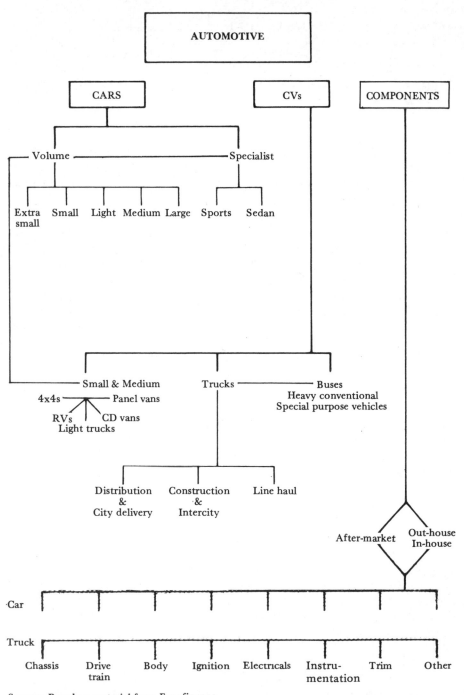

Source: **Based on material from Eurofinance**

The components market is a vast segment covering original equipment and after-market (to service the existing vehicles on the road). Some component manufacturers are completely independent, but many are part of the motor vehicle manufacturing concern. The book does not cover the components sector nor does it deal with motorcycles and motorbikes. In the maturer markets such transport forms a minority or luxury transport segment, although in less developed countries it is more important.

Distribution

Once a motor vehicle has been built it is sold through a vast distribution network. Distribution can either be through a single tier where the motor vehicle manufacturer deals direct with the retailer or through a multi-tier system. In the latter, the manufacturer will deal with a distributor, who is in effect a wholesaler (but usually a retailer too); the distributor then deals with a number of dealers. In the event of a problem, (eg insufficient supply of vehicles or persistent mechanical faults on a new model) the dealer cannot communicate direct with the manufacturer but must go through the hierarchy (ie via the distributor). The multi-tier system is most common in Western Europe but because of its drawbacks the system's popularity is in decline. If vehicles are in short supply it is the distributor who gets the lion's share of the cake. If there are problems with a new model, communications from the dealer via the distributor back to the manufacturer can be tortuous.

The function of a retailer is not just to sell new cars. Most of his work is connected with other activities: fuel retailing and other forecourt services; used-vehicle retailing; routine repair and maintenance of vehicles, crash repair, bodywork and painting; spare parts and components sales; and offering information and advice; and general retailing of goods and components that may be purchased at a garage or service station. Recently conventional garages have found significant portions of their market snatched away from them by fast specialist retailing outlets who will, for example, fit exhaust systems while you wait. Another trend is the move of retailing services to hypermarkets, the extra distance travelled being outweighed by the additional discount obtained. This book, however, does not specifically cover distribution systems or attempt to extrapolate these trends to predict the shape of the future network.

The evolution of the motor industry

The motor industry's most rapid growth, which will never again be repeated, was during the 1945-73 period. The motor industry began in the 1890s, and by 1900 production had risen to nearly 10,000 units, mainly in Europe and the USA. The one million unit mark was achieved in 1915 and production increased rather unsteadily to 6.3 million in 1929. This figure was not surpassed until the end of World War II, for the economic recession of the 1930s had a dramatic effect on motor vehicles, reducing production to 1.9 million vehicles in 1932.

The world location of the industry has gradually shifted, reflecting the growth of the industry through its technical cycle from early technical evolution, to engineering production, to 'conveyor belt' mass production and finally to 'robotic' production. Western Europe dominated motor vehicle production up to about 1905. North America then took over with large-scale production techniques and a society geared to motorized transport. Figure 2.2 traces the shares of major producers over the period 1900-75; total world production over time was shown in Figure 1.3. North America's dominance began to wane before World War II, and once Europe had recovered from the aftermath of the war, it began to make rapid inroads into North America's share of world production. Other groupings, including Eastern Europe, Australia, South Africa and parts of South America followed, though slowly and tentatively. Asia (mainly Japan) was late to begin production (in the late 1950s) but has since grown phenomenally.

The mature producers and diffusion

The post-war period has essentially seen a wider diffusion of manufacturing. Table 2.1 shows the relative sizes in the world car industry today together with an export profile, which may change significantly over the next decade.

Table 2.1 *World motor vehicle production by major region in 1978 (with % of production exported)*

Area	Motor vehicle production (millions)	Percentage of production exported*
North America	14.5	1.9
Western Europe	12.8	14.5
Japan	9.3	49.6
Communist Bloc	3.3	6.1
South America	1.6	—
Rest of the World	1.0	—

* To outside region (ie excluding intra-regional exports)

From Table 2.1 it can be seen there are three core areas: North America, Western Europe and Japan. North America is the most mature followed by Western Europe; Japan is the youngest and perhaps most aggressive of the mature producers. Certain common attributes can be

Figure 2.2 *Share of world motor vehicle production by major regions since 1900*

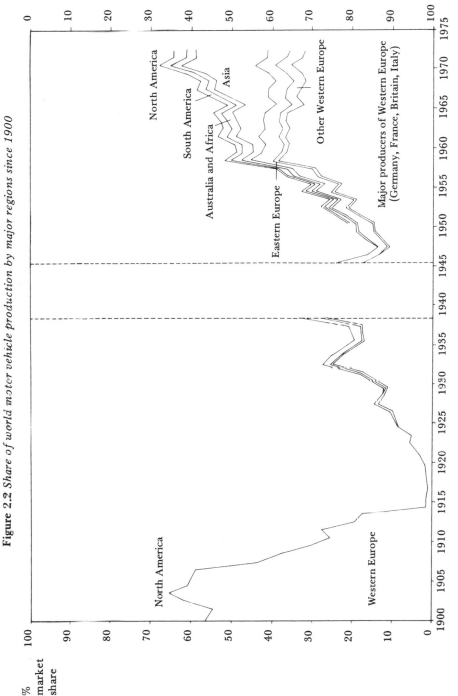

Source: Bloomfield, Gerald (1978) *The World Automotive Industry* David and Charles

defined for mature markets and are analysed in this and the next two chapters.

Apart from the mature producers there are two minor (but steadily growing) production centres — the Communist Bloc[1] and South America — which may develop into mature producers. The rest of the world production is small: it can be subdivided into the Middle East, the old colonies of South Africa and Australia, and some infant producers. Of these the Middle East with its oil resources looks the most promising, although there are no true production capabilities as yet (ie its plant is assembly only). Some of the infant producers (eg Korea and Taiwan) are near the take-off stage, others have established a manufacturing presence but show no signs of growth as yet (eg India and China).

Market development and the producer

A mature market has several distinguishing features. It has a large number of vehicles in use (vehicle parc) and each year some of these vehicles will be scrapped (eg worn out or crashed beyond economically justifiable repair). Each year newly manufactured vehicles will be sold on the market and the number of the new vehicle additions to the vehicle parc (vehicles in use) will be sufficiently large to support a viable motor vehicle manufacturing industry. Demand, throughout the book, is defined as new additions to the stock of vehicles, and is synonymous with new registrations of motor vehicles. The term 'total registrations' is equivalent to vehicle parc. Supply is defined as the additions to the vehicle stock supplied by manufacturers.

A mature market will have its own mature motor vehicle producers, and the evolution of a producer from infancy to maturity is a fascinating aspect of the motor industry. Motor vehicle manufacturing technology, in its simplest form, can be established anywhere in the world (although the existence of an industrial infrastructure helps). With an increasing scale of output producers can become sufficiently competitive to start exporting to other markets.

The most mature market will export little but will own subsidiaries in newer markets which in turn may export elsewhere. North America, for example, exports little but owns substantial foreign subsidiaries elsewhere. Western Europe has undergone a metamorphosis from the 'exporting' stage to transferring local assembly to other regions. Japan, the newest of the mature markets, still relies largely on exports to generate sufficient output so that it can benefit from scale economies.

Mature producers have usually followed an established pattern. There is one fundamental axiom of the motor industry: the larger the output, the cheaper the product, and the motor industry is an example of an

1. Defined as Eastern Europe, Yugoslavia, Albania and the USSR.

industry where the economies of scale seem endless (see Chapter 4). A mature producer starts life by exporting from domestic plant through import/export agencies and branch offices to other markets. The next stage is to transfer local assembly to the export markets, to protect the local market or take advantage of lower labour costs in export markets.

An infant producer is born initially by means of local assembly, with the degree of locally-made content rising from body pressings, through to a range of mechanical components and finally manufacture of the power train (engine, gearbox, clutch and other points of the transmission). The infant producer may mature by exporting to other regions.

There are a number of ways in which the newer producers can develop. The local assembly stage must involve the cooperation of a mature producer. However, once the 'local assembly with increasing local content' stage has been reached there are several ways in which the motor industry may proceed. All involve a degree of protection of the local market, thereby closing what was an 'open' market for the mature producers: the only way to get a foot in the closing door is to be one of the cooperating manufacturers setting up the local assembly facilities. Hence there is often an international race by manufacturers to set up local assembly facilities — sometimes prior to real need and not economically justifiable — to maintain a presence in the market before it becomes 'closed'.

One standard way of proceeding is illustrated by the Japanese model. With protection and government encouragement and financial support, a number of local assemblers began to manufacture their own product. The government did not allow the mature producers to own or control the indigenous manufacturers. The industry grew, gained the necessary economies of scale and began exporting. The important feature of the Japanese development model is that growth through exports was a major objective of the indigenous producers. The Communist Bloc and the Middle East are developing mainly along these lines. Of the infant producers, South Korea and Turkey (though very different in many ways) have followed the Japanese example and have indigenous manufacturers.

The second model of development is typically seen in South America. Local assembly and the transference to local manufacture is entirely owned and controlled by the mature producers. The distinguishing feature between this development model and the Japanese model is the motivation to grow through exports. In South America, exports are negligible or on a *quid pro quo* basis: the mature producers seem to have little or no motivation to export to other markets. The reasons are obvious. The mature producer will either be supplying an export region from domestic production or will have established local assembly/manufacturing facilities in the export market. Either way the South

American model can be contrasted with the Japanese model in terms of slower development and few, if any, exports. Productive capacity expands simply to meet the needs of the domestic market. Examples of newer producers following this pattern of development are Australia, Taiwan, nearly all Africa, and many of the developments in the Far East.

Western Europe's growth was a mixture of indigenous and foreign development, and occurred when the world industry itself was very young and competition among the mature producers was non-existent as North America was the only mature producer. But Western Europe soon began to compete effectively with US producers on world markets, and to accommodate the rapidly expanding level of domestic demand.

Dominant producers

North America's early lead has been caught up by Western Europe. Japan's growth seems all set to catch up with and overtake the other two mature producers. Whether Japan will make it or not is one of the questions which will be discussed later. Hegemony in world motor manufacture appears to be ephemeral and, indeed, in addition to the protectionist policies favoured by some trading nations, there are various reasons why a mature market cannot maintain its dominance. First, stagnation in demand may occur in a mature market as the market becomes 'saturated' with the commodity. A static demand, with cyclical fluctuations, is not a recipe for expansion. Second, as the market matures, so labour and other costs (eg land) rise: newer producers operating from low cost bases find they can undercut the more expensive products. Japan, for example, has had great success in exporting cheap basic products to the mature markets. Rising import penetration and the success of newer producers in export markets are standard characteristics of a mature market.

Will Japan, as it matures further, be supplanted by one of the new producers, perhaps South America or the Communist Bloc? The way in which new producers develop is discussed in Part 3. Different regions will follow different development models, but one factor does emerge: the stranglehold on the industry exerted by the multinationals in all three mature markets seems to be increasing and it is becoming more difficult for a new producer to emulate the Japanese development model.

Chapter 3

Demand

There are a number of myths concerning demand for motor vehicles. For example, contrary to some informed opinion, there seems to be no practical limit to car demand given sufficient energy and other resources. In the USA there is one car for every two people. The concept of a saturation level, in the abstract, for cars is a myth, as is the notion that cars do not naturally belong in cities. Cars are essentially an urban phenomenon and the determinants of the transport requirements which are transmitted into demand for cars are closely related to the geographical distribution of human activities that constitute an urbanized area. A third myth concerns alternative transport media. As cars become more popular, congestion increases within cities and this leads to the conclusion that urban development is incompatible with reliance on travel by cars. However, if left to market forces there are clear signs that quite the reverse happens: the resulting process of 'automobilization' that typically occurs in urban life is accompanied by the decay of alternative transport media.

For many throughout the world today cars are not a luxury, though car densities differ according to the level of income and wealth of a country. We will therefore look at the socio-economic factors influencing vehicle densities.

Socio-economic factors

At a subsistence level of demand there is no need for transport of any kind. At a slightly higher level of economic activity farming remains the major occupation in rural areas, though not all of the produce is consumed by the farmers themselves and surplus is exchanged for farm equipment, seeds or livestock and other domestic commodities. Farmers depend heavily on animal-drawn transport in the initial stages of development, but subsequent development and commercialization may necessitate the use of small trucks as transporters of surplus produce to the local market

Urbanization increases the need for transportation. The lifestyle becomes more complex: work patterns are more complex, and the much wider range of leisure, sports, cultural, political and social activities and personal interactions all involve more random patterns of physical movement.

In urban lifestyles the most important single reason for local travel is the need to get to and from work. The two journeys, to and from work, account for nearly half of all daily urban 'person trips'. Other important categories are shopping trips, social trips, trips between home and school, business trips and trips involving the movement of goods. The most important generators of local travel are the home, the place of work and places of commercial activity. Figure 3.1 illustrates the relative importance of these various activities and shows how trips with different purposes are distributed by the time of day. The information contained in the figure is typical of any large city in the world. Whilst home-to-work and work-to-home trips are strongly concentrated in the early morning and late afternoon rush hours, other trips belonging to other categories are more evenly distributed over the day.

Business and financial services and retail trade activity produces the highest density of trip-ends. They must therefore be located in places having a high degree of accessibility and are therefore concentrated in the central business district and along major transportation routes. A city needs a high-density central core precisely for the purpose of accommodating activities of a type that naturally attract and generate a large number of trips.

Industrial and extractive activity on the other hand is more dispersed because of land requirements for industrial plant sites, but still requires proximity to major transportation facilities. Residential areas are normally distributed more or less symmetrically around the central business district on land that is not required for activities needing greater accessibility.

Of the rival forms of transport to a motor vehicle, many are generally located along corridors of intensely developed land with at least one terminus located within the central business district. However, the use of most mass transit systems is heavily concentrated in rush hours, whereas private car traffic is distributed more uniformly than any other mode throughout the entire urban area. The car has flexibility by means of its freedom from fixed routes and schedules. This flexibility enables the car to conform more closely than any other mode to the overall distribution of trip-producing activities except in 'core' areas in most of the industrialized world.

The need for transport

Public transport in towns serves little more than a commuter role. As an American observer noted 'the capacity for meeting peak loads without breakdown is far in excess of the average capacity of the system.' This pattern of extremely heavy use at only two periods of the day places

Figure 3.1 *Hourly distribution of automobile person trips (by purpose) in Washington DC (1955)*

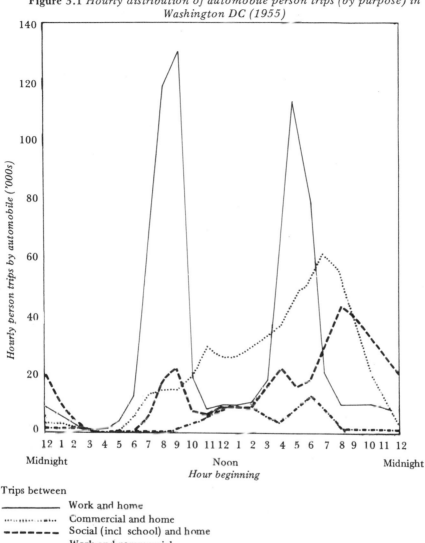

Trips between

———————— Work and home

⋯⋯⋯⋯⋯⋯ Commercial and home

— — — — — Social (incl school) and home

—▪—▪—▪—▪ Work and commercial

Source: Business International

enormous strains on the system and increases the likelihood of malfunction or breakdown. Dissatisfaction with the service, coupled with the greater convenience of travelling in comfort from door to door, leads to a change from public system to private car which has been observed in most of the advanced countries.

People who have the choice usually prefer to do their travelling by private car whenever this is a realistic option, see Table 3.1. This is primarily because of the advantages of privacy, flexibility and cleanliness,

Table 3.1 *Why some commuters prefer cars to public transit*

Reasons cited[1]	Sample[2] (%)
Trip is faster	70
Waiting time too long for public transit	35
Do not like transfer	35
Greater route flexibility	30
Lower (out-of-pocket) costs	10
Enjoy driving	10
More comfortable	25
Car is useful for after-work trip	20
Poor accessibility of public transit	15

1. In European conditions the relative percentages might be altered;
   trips are not always faster by cars, whereas transfers, flexibility,
   comfort, accessibility and after-work trips become more important
2. Since informants were allowed to give multiple reasons, the
   percentage total exceeds 100

Source: *The World Automotive Industry to 1995* Business International

although social status can play a role where private cars are scarce and therefore symbolic of personal success or importance. Furthermore for many kinds of trips, particularly in low-density areas without public transportation services, cars are the only convenient means of transportation available. There is also an inertia factor to consider: once the initial purchase of a car has been made, there is a natural tendency to use it even when other means of travel are actually available.

The 'automobilization' of an urban society has typically been accompanied by the decay of public transport services and facilities. People's preferences for flexibility, coupled with the high cost of public transport systems, has led to the marked tendency for expenditure on public transport to decrease over time. Figure 3.2 shows how this decay has occurred for a few selected countries.

An important consideration from the consumer's point of view is the percentage of total consumption (private consumer expenditure) spent on transport and communication. There appears to be a maximum expenditure limit of 15 per cent in most of the advanced industrial countries, with a sharp distinction drawn at the lower end of the scale between rural and urban areas. In India, for example, urban populations are prepared to spend much more (relatively speaking) on transport than their rural counterparts (eg over 5 per cent as compared with one per cent). In the advanced industrial countries, nearly 80 per cent of all expenditure on transport is accounted for in the purchase, maintenance and operating costs of private vehicles. In less developed countries, the reverse is true — a far higher proportion is spent on public transport. However, there is a marked tendency for expenditure on public transport to decrease in relative terms over time (as shown in Figure 3.2) consistent with a country's economic growth.

Figure 3.2 *Private expenditure on public transportation as a fraction*
of private expenditure on transport and communications

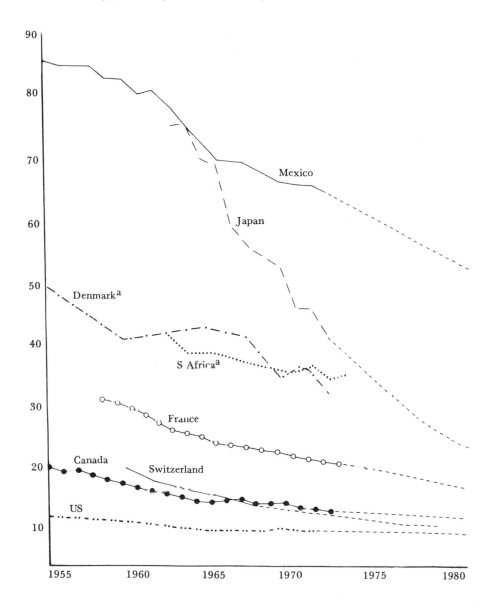

a   Public transport and communications expenditure as a fraction of private transport and
    communications expenditure

Source: Business International

The impact on urban development of increasing accessibility by motor vehicles comprises various conflicting forces. The process of automobilization is sustained by the operation of a feedback loop: investment in a transportation infrastructure increases accessibility, which leads to new high-density land development and increased trip-generation, and eventually increases demand for new transportation facilities. Thus, the construction of a new motorway linking the central business district with a sparsely populated peripheral area usually results in rapid residential and commercial development adjacent to the new road. This in turn increases traffic on that road which adds to the congestion problem in the central business district. The obvious conclusion is that high-density urban development is ultimately incompatible with total reliance on travel by private car. Practical steps to inhibit private cars from using streets in city centres are becoming increasingly common in developed countries, especially in older cities.

In most countries the urban/rural patterns of interactive infra-structure, lifestyle complexity and occupational interaction are similar. Thus in most countries the rates of ownership of automobiles are higher in urban than in rural areas, though the distinction is less distinct in more developed countries. Whereas the urban ownership rate is 20 times the rural rate in India, it is only six times the rural rate in Venezuela and less than three times the rural rate in Italy. The distinction becomes even more blurred in the USA, but an analysis of this situation is deferred until Part 2.

We may now formally analyse the determinants of the demand for motor vehicles bearing in mind that the urban/rural distinction is extremely important.

Basic constituents

There are, in effect, two types of demand: replacement and new demand. Replacement demand is the number of vehicles which have been or are about to be scrapped (a move which may be dictated by prevailing economic conditions or a number of other factors). The meaning of replacement demand must not be confused with the day-to-day decision about people replacing their vehicles; it is concerned with the replacement of the entire stock of vehicles. Replacement demand normally exactly matches the number of cars which have been scrapped, including scrappage caused by accidents but mainly through vehicles wearing out or proving uneconomic to maintain. Such replacement demand comprises numerous separate decisions: a businessman replacing his car every two years, a blue collar worker buying a new (to him) used vehicle, a student scrapping a vehicle and buying another 'old heap' to replace it. New demand creates a growth in the number of vehicles on the road (the vehicle parc). This is directly affected by economic conditions, although the decision to acquire a car for the first time could also be influenced by the availability of satisfactory alternatives. In more prosperous countries, car ownership is preferred to reliance on public transport and it is reasonable to assume that developing countries will follow this trend unless government policy decisions attempt to reverse it.

On the whole, the demand for new, privately owned cars reflects (a) the income levels *per capita* (and income distribution); (b) the relative price of cars; (c) running costs; (d) the availability of hire purchase and other finance costs or restrictions affecting payment over time; (e) the size of the car driving population and changes affecting it; (f) the availability of suitable transport alternatives; and (g) consumer preferences (expressed in terms of convenience and flexibility) associated with car ownership. Other considerations affect the level of demand for CVs although it is difficult to generalize as the CV market is enormous and the model range spreads from light trucks to giant articulated lorries designed almost exclusively for motorway travel. Certainly, the growth in industrial activity and the alternatives available within any one area do affect new demand, and the consumer's preference for convenience and flexibility applies with equal force in the CV market. In general there appears to be a close relationship between the level of *per capita* income of a country and the density of vehicle ownership.

In both sectors, however, replacement demand is more sensitive to the state of the economy as a whole and to the position of that economy within a trade cycle, be it boom or slump. 'Tight' money, high interest rates and restrictive HP rates can effectively defer the decision to scrap or replace an existing car when the higher running costs associated with an older vehicle are seen as less of a penalty than the capital outlay required to purchase a new one. We will now consider in greater detail the effects of both types of demand in specific cases.

Theoretical summary of demand

Table 3.2 summarizes statistics on car and CV densities and income levels in a number of regions. It can be seen that car density levels vary widely, and it is therefore necessary to examine some of the factors affecting relative density. Car demand appears to be an urban phenomenon. Table 3.2 shows that regions with a high proportion of densely populated urban areas are also those regions boasting a higher 'cars to people' ratio.

But just as the requirements of urban living create the demand for a convenient and flexible alternative to over-used public transport systems, an increasing reliance on private transport brings with it problems of congestion and pollution which may in the longer term inhibit the use of private cars in those same areas. Another important

Table 3.2 *Vehicle density by region 1977*

	Number of cars per 1000 people	Number of CVs per 1000 people
Mature markets		
North America	501	126
Western Europe	249	29
Japan	164	103
Minor markets		
Eastern Europe	32	20
Central & South America	48	17
Near East	17	11
'Old colonials' (Australia, New Zealand and South Africa)	203	57
Infant markets Oceania (excluding Australia and New Zealand)	12	7
Africa (excluding South Africa)	8	4
Far East (excluding Japan and China)	3	2

Source: Automobile International

factor in determining demand is the level of income within a particular country. The specific relationship between car density levels and the level of income in a country is graphed in Figure 3.3. High car density levels (which for our purpose will be considered as the number of cars per thousand people) suggest a high level of *per capita* GNP, although the Communist Bloc countries are a significant exception, with car densities there lower than might be expected for the given income levels. Elsewhere, car densities form a rather deceptive cluster at the top end of the scale (high income levels) which conceals wide variations in density within that relatively narrow band (because the data in Figure 3.3 is graphed in log scale). At the lower level, however, discrepancies between income levels and car densities are more noticeable. Although Korea and Morocco, for example, have similar income levels, car densities in the two countries do not compare. The same point could be made in a comparison of Kenya and Nigeria. To put it another way: Korea, Nigeria, Zaire and Indonesia have similar car densities despite marked differences in their respective income levels.

These discrepancies suggest at least one plausible explanation: that in areas where a potential but largely dormant demand exists (ie where at least one of the conditions necessary for the creation of demand, a high income level, is already in being), deliberate policy decisions have inhibited that demand. In Eastern Europe, for example, governments have until recently taken deliberate measures to suppress demand

Figure 3.3 *Relationship between car density levels and level of income using 1975 data*

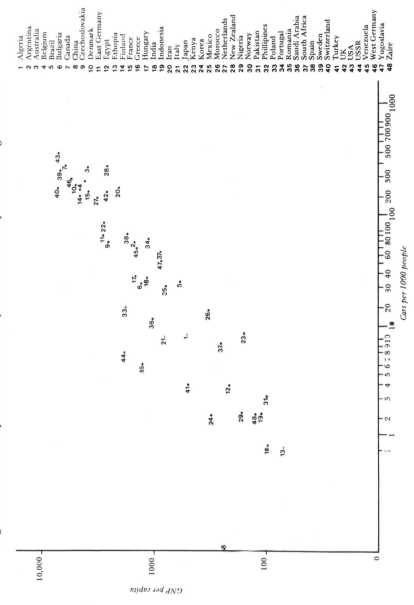

although there is now some indication that restrictions are being eased. Further East, Communist China is only now relaxing her previously intransigent hostility towards Western technology and consumer durables. In the Middle East, the near feudal conditions prevailing have suppressed demand, but increasing prosperity will probably act as a force for change.

There is an important distinction between institutional demand and private demand. Below the $500 to $750 GNP *per capita* levels (US $ at 1979 values) much of the demand for cars is institutional, ie to accommodate government officials, company requirements, embassies, etc. Above the $750 GNP *per capita* level, demand becomes more widespread among the middle income groups. Only with income levels in excess of $2000 to $3000 will car ownership spread throughout all income groups within any one country.

Car densities can also vary widely at the top end of the scale. Western Europe and Japan, for example, are unlikely to overtake (or even equal) the US level for the very simple reason that they do not have the *space* to accommodate such densities. Australia is far more likely to follow the US pattern, for obvious reasons. At the lower end of the scale, those countries with lower income levels may not have a sufficiently advanced road network to make car ownership a particularly attractive (or even useful) proposition. Although this argument has had a 'chicken or egg' flavour in the past, there is now much evidence to suggest that car ownership *is* sufficient to create the demand for roads. At the moment, however, poorer countries, confronted with the dauntingly expensive prospect of a major road construction programme, may well decide that it is easier (and probably simpler) to restrain or suppress demand. Obviously, restricting car purchase in this way can limit the demand for more, or better, roads.

Once a certain level of car density has been established the car parc necessary to meet the level is defined. For example a country with a population of 100 million people and a car density level of four persons per car would require a car parc of 25 million vehicles. This can then be used to yield a forecast of both the replacement and new vehicle demand. A 'rule of thumb' that 25 million vehicles will yield an annual replacement and new demand equal to one-tenth of the car parc yields a projected level of new registrations of 2.5 million vehicles.

The above methodology is used in the following chapters to predict demand for cars. More sophisticated forecasting methodologies were not considered appropriate for the long-range projections considered here. The basis for the prediction is to project both population and car density levels in the future. This yields an estimate of the projected car parc which is used to derive a forecast of the level of new car registrations. Because the projections are long-term ones, a range is often provided and sometimes it proved necessary to divide the future into a number of scenarios, where major decisions affect projections in dramatically different ways.

In less developed countries the average age of a car is often longer than in a developed country where repair costs are higher in relation to the capital cost of the vehicle. On the other hand less developed countries may be expected to have a faster rate of growth of new demand. For the most part it is assumed that the two forces cancel each other out. However each individual market is considered on its own merits.

CV demand

Until now, we have been discussing demand for cars only, and we now turn to the CV market. Table 3.2 shows that variations in the pattern of CV demand differ from that of cars. CV demand reflects the level of industrial activity, the possible alternatives to road transport and the sort of commodity to be transported. The CV market is highly fragmented, and specific factors affect demand in the various segments of the CV market. The small volume end of the CV market includes the recreation market which becomes increasingly important with market maturity. This segment of the market is more dependent than others on general economic conditions.

In the early stages of development (industrial or agrarian) it is not unusual to find that the demand for CVs is far greater than the demand for private cars. Roads are frequently the only major transport network available, and the capital expenditure required to construct an equivalent rail network is usually prohibitive. As countries prosper (and industry develops), patterns of CV demand change, moving up the scale from small, relatively versatile trucks capable of operating in rough terrain, through to, at the top end of the market, articulated lorries designed for peak performance on highly developed motorway networks. In those areas where motorways have been established, industries already dependent on road transport show a tendency to relocate closer to motorway rather than rail networks, thus increasing the likelihood of a continued reliance on CVs and perpetuating their use. Where motorway and rail infrastructures exist in tandem (usually in more developed countries), the choice between road and rail is usually dictated by the commodity to be transported. In most of the extractive industries, for example, raw or semi-processed materials are more suitably transported in bulk carriers of one sort or another, whereas the fabrication and distributive industries generally prefer road transport. In less developed countries, however, where there is often no alternative to road haulage, there is a greater dependence on road transport and a much more varied demand for CVs, irrespective of the commodity to be transported.

The forecasting methodology for future CV demand is broadly similar to that for cars but is subject to many more specific influences such as the size of the CV, the alternatives to road haulage and prevailing local circumstances.

General influences

We now turn our attention to more general influences affecting demand including alternative modes of transport.

Road networks

Road networks play an important part in determining the level of demand for both private cars and CVs. It would be helpful at this stage to examine their importance (and their future development) in greater detail.

Very little *new* road construction is expected to take place in developed countries over the next 20 years. In urban areas, indeed, it is possible that existing road systems may even be reduced in an effort to combat congestion and to improve the environment. In less developed countries, however, a number of studies have projected rapid growth, stressing an increase in the number of roads but pointing out that, unless additional finance can be obtained, there is little likelihood that the quality of existing roads, many of which are unpaved, will be much improved. On the other hand, some less developed countries will benefit from the completion of the major international motorways (Pan-American, Trans-Amazon, Trans-Asian) which are expected to become more or less fully operational within the next two decades and which represent the most important of the existing plans for road development and expansion.

Alternative methods of transport

Variations of demand are also affected by the existence of alternative forms of transport. Where pipelines, waterways and rail and air services exist they are frequently used as more suitable (or more convenient) methods of transport for goods and commodities. Tables 3.3 and 3.4 summarize relative costs and give the percentages of total goods transported by road, rail and water (excluding pipelines).

Although pipelines and waterways have increased their relative shares of total commercial traffic in recent years (and, in the case of pipelines, could be further developed to increase this share), rail, air and urban transport systems are the most widely used and the most viable alternatives to road transport for both commercial and private purposes. Since 1960, railways have increased the overall volume of

Table 3.3 *Energy requirements of alternative freight transport modes*

Mode	BTU/ton-mile	Ratio (to pipelines)
Pipelines	450	1.0
Waterway	540	1.2
Rail	680	1.5
Road	2340	5.2
Air	37,000	82.0

Source: *The World Automotive Industry to 1995* Business International

Table 3.4 *Modal split in regions (1962 and 1972)*
(percentages of total ton-km, excluding pipelines)

	Road (%)		Rail (%)		Water (%)		Total (bill ton-km)	
	1962	1972	1962	1972	1962	1972	1962	1972
Western Europe	45	61	42	29	13	10	625	980
North America	27	28	51	50	22	22	2060	2710
Eastern Europe	6	8	88	86	6	6	2000	3470
Developing Countries	41	51	59	49	- -	—	280	490
Total	22	25	65	64	13	11	4965	7650

Source: *The World Automotive Industry to 1995* Business International

traffic (cargo and passenger, although passenger use has declined in Australia and the USA) despite the fact that they captured a smaller share of total traffic. Profits, however, have been low or non-existent, although few countries have resisted the idea or the fact of public subsidy, partly, it must be assumed, because of the public service role which seems to be characteristic of most rail networks. Most countries are now conserving or improving their railways to improve the facility; modest growth has been predicted for rail networks in the future as containerization and high-speed passenger travel are more widely introduced. These improvements, together with the energy-efficient aspect of rail transport, make it a more attractive proposition for the future than it is at present. Air transport, particularly long-distance passenger transport is not, however, expected to benefit from any subsidy, and any further growth in air transport's share of total transport is highly improbable, given recent increases in air transport costs.

From the passenger point of view, the choice available for urban travel must include existing (or developing) *non-automotive* systems: rail transit (metro or underground systems) and the older surface systems (trams, buses etc). Rail transit systems are expensive to install but usually receive government support in an attempt to alleviate the problems of intra-city and commuter travel. Many more metro systems have been built or contracted for in the last few years, although rising installation costs will probably inhibit further growth. Surface systems have been in existence in many cities for several decades, particularly in Western Europe. For some years, their use declined as commuters switched to private car transport, but a reverse swing can be detected. In Paris, for example, the volume of bus traffic *increased* in 1974 after years of decline. It is possible that other surface systems, such as the virtually moribund trolley and tram systems, or the bus service, will experience a similar revival in passenger use in most of the developed countries with the exception of Japan, where *per capita* car ownership is relatively low and will continue to rise at the expense of public transport. In less developed countries, public transport will continue to be the only available form of transport.

Relative motor vehicle costs

Having examined some of the alternatives to motor vehicles, let us now turn to the likely effect that increases in the cost of acquiring and operating cars and CVs may have on demand. It is argued in subsequent chapters that there will be increasing pressure in established markets for the relative price of cars and CVs to increase, although this could be offset to some extent by the availability of relatively low-cost vehicles produced in the newer manufacturing areas. Rising energy and oil costs and increasing labour costs are all likely to have an impact on relative running costs. The effect this will have on demand is less certain. Some theories suggest that in fact these increases might affect the choice of car (particularly engine capacity) but would have only a marginal effect on overall demand. Cars would continue to provide transport but individuals might control costs by reducing the frequency and length of journeys. This could well apply to passenger cars but it can hardly hold true for CVs. Stringent attempts to make better use of CV transport might convince some firms to dispense with part of their CV fleet, but piecemeal reductions of this sort are unlikely to have much of an impact on overall demand. The same could well apply to fleet cars.

An overview

Having examined most of the factors that could affect future growth in demand for new cars, it may be concluded that such growth will be slower in the future than it has been until now. The demand for CVs will be affected by increasing competition for the haulage market from alternative forms of freight transport, although it should be remembered that the high capital cost of constructing new systems (rail, pipeline, etc) in a world facing increasing capital shortages could limit the development of practical alternatives where none presently exists. Where road and motorway networks already exist they will continue to be used: the introduction of larger and more specialist CV models and ranges could increase the intensity of that use. In passenger transport, although demand will increase more slowly in developed countries, it is unlikely that there will be an actual fall in demand, as the car has become firmly entrenched as a primary form of private transport.

Saturation levels

There has been much discussion of the concept of a saturation level for cars. Proponents of the saturation theory posit a maximum limit of vehicle ownership. Such a limit may exist ultimately and vehicle ownership may gradually approach it, but whether this limit will be reached in the foreseeable future is open to question. Figure 3.4 illustrates this concept; some of the more mature markets are showing signs of vehicle ownership tailing off as if approaching some limit. Interestingly, this limit may well be different for differing regions; US vehicle ownership's saturation limit may be substantially above that of the UK.

In theory and assuming a source of cheap energy to power motor vehicles, there is no reason why a vehicle ownership limit should ever be reached in the most mature markets (see Part 2). Even if such a saturation level were proved to exist there would still be a demand for new vehicles consistent with the replacement of worn-out vehicles. A saturation level of demand is therefore defined as the point at which replacement and maintenance expenditures consume all available funds. However, one popular misconception is that market saturation occurs approximately at the point when the number of cars equals the number of eligible drivers. This is manifestly incorrect as one driver may own several vehicles. Multiple car ownership is well-established in the USA and shows no sign of diminishing. In fact multiple car ownership is clearly a function of personal incomes as shown in Table 3.5.

Future patterns are likely to see the emergence of a recreational vehicle (typically a truck), a commuting car (easier to park, cheap to run yet comfortable in traffic jams), a luxury sporting car, a car for shopping trips and a family outing car. Such market segmentation is further analysed in Part 2. Car ownerships in the USA have now reached record proportions and there seems to be no sign of ownership levels declining. On the other hand a future administration, by interfering with natural forces, may succeed in nearly reducing sales to the replacement of existing stock only (ie saturation level). We have already noted that city planners are aware of the problem of better roads producing greater congestion in the central business district. Although the extent to which a car is used in cities may be gradually reduced this does not

Figure 3.4
Motor vehicles in use in selected countries over time

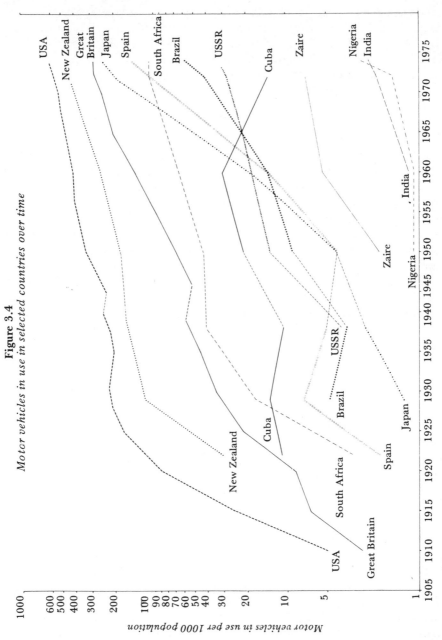

Motor vehicles in use per 1000 population

Source: Bloomfield, Gerald (1978) *The World Automotive Industry* David & Charles

Table 3.5 *Multiple car ownership in the USA (1974)*

Income US $	Proportion of households owning:	
	One or more cars (%)	Two or more cars (%)
under 3000	46.2	6.2
3000 – 4999	64.2	8.8
5000 – 7499	79.4	15.6
7500 – 9999	88.3	23.1
10,000 – 14,999	93.9	54.9
15,000 – 19,999	96.7	50.1
20,000 – 24,999	97.4	60.1
25,000 and over	97.2	67.2
All households	83.8	32.7

necessarily mean that car ownership levels will be drastically affected. People will still own cars but will commute by a public transport system.

For simple economic reasons, new demand (as opposed to replacement demand) is inevitably determined by the economic growth of a country and the relative costs of vehicle ownership. Unless a mature market can achieve high growth rates and maintain vehicle costs at a low rate, growth in vehicle ownerships must slow down. Since it is unlikely that the USA, the most mature market, can achieve either of the above it is likely that vehicle ownerships will grow more slowly but this is *not* to say that they will necessarily reach a saturation level.

Oil crises

The 1973-74 and 1978-79 oil crises have had a significant impact on demand. Not only is the high price of fuel a deterrent to using a vehicle but the question of whether fuel can actually be obtained (regardless of price) has a further dampening effect on the demand to drive. However, this is not necessarily transmitted through to long-run demand for motor vehicles. Even if fuel is rationed, a consumer may still wish to own a car and enjoy the benefits of whatever motoring he is allowed. A commuter may be persuaded to switch from a private car to a public mass transit system, but this does not mean that he will not use his car in the evenings and weekends. Scarcity of fuel may lead to even more segmentation matching the right vehicle to the right need in order to maximize the benefit of the available fuel supplies. One could counter this by arguing that the hiring of vehicles (instead of ownership) will increase and that the number of multi-car families will be reduced: in essence a better utilization of vehicle stocks would be achieved. In reality, demand for vehicles may be dampened by inadequate energy resources but to a smaller extent than might be expected. Even this analysis assumes that vehicles will not become more efficient and that alternative energy sources will not be found; the assumption adopted in this book is that they will.

Why then have both recent oil crises had a significant impact on demand for vehicles? A clue to this mystery was given in Chapter 1. It is not so much oil itself as the reaction by governments to the oil crises and the consequent deterioration of the balance of payments. Increases in oil prices have a direct effect on costs and this can affect economic growth. Some forecasts predict that the impact on growth of the 1978-79 oil crisis will not be fully eroded before 1985. Governments tend to over-react to the oil crises by deflating their economies over and above the direct oil price effect, in the belief they can correct the impact of the oil price increases on their balance of payments. This can lead to a loss of business and consumer confidence which may take two or three years to overcome. Finally the economic equilibrium may be further upset by inventory adjustments. Businesses will typically underestimate the extent of the post oil crisis downturn and will involuntarily build inventories. The subsequent adjustments of production will further delay the economic recovery.

Size and type of vehicles

The differences between developed and less developed markets in the type of demand for vehicles is fairly marked. Less developed countries demand the cheapest possible type of utility car for private individuals (although firms and government agencies may have a more luxury-oriented demand) and a general-purpose utility CV of a medium size for use on poor narrow roads and capable of being maintained by semi-skilled people without specialized tools or training. Developed countries, by contrast, will increasingly use more specialized trucks and buses. Many distinct submarkets have evolved, ranging from long-distance, high-speed haulage through small pickups and vans to special electric vehicles that operate in the aisles of warehouses or in mine tunnels. Body types also evolve into highly specialized forms eg concrete mixers, refuse compactors, liquid-fertilizer spreaders, refrigerated tanks, etc. Many CVs are, in effect, movable machines. This trend will continue and become more pronounced in the future. Buses, too, range from simple utility type (airport or school buses) through double-decked or articulated urban transit buses to long distance touring buses. This product differentiation is characteristic of a mature industry and a large diverse economy. It also requires large, integrated producers capable of manufacturing common components on a mass scale.

On the car side, developed countries produce higher performance and more luxurious cars. Again product differentiation has resulted in a more specialized vehicle. The emphasis for developed countries must clearly be on maintaining a technological advantage through accelerated research and development, since existing motor vehicle technology is now widespread and production economies of scale are now accessible to some low-wage countries. Alternatively an essentially urban car perhaps electrically driven might be developed for urban use. This is further discussed in Part 2.

Conclusion

Private consumption expenditure on transport is unlikely to rise beyond 15 per cent of income, although in very advanced countries the decay of expenditures on public transportation may be reversed. Higher fuel costs in the future may only succeed in a tendency to restrict the use (not necessarily the purchase) of vehicles.

North America has the most dense level of vehicle ownership. The West European markets are likely to move towards the North American vehicle ownership rates but by that time the North American vehicle ownership will have increased. Similarly Japanese rates will approach West European levels. Other developing markets will have vehicle density levels consistent with the national income of that economy.

In those areas where demand has until now been artificially dampened or where income levels are expected to rise rapidly (the Middle East and parts of South America perhaps) demand for cars will continue to grow. CV demand will also see further expansion in those developing countries with no feasible alternatives to road transport. In poorer countries, however, any increase in the relative price of cars will effectively prevent the take-off in the growth of demand for some time to come, although the demand for CVs will keep pace with industrial and agrarian development in those areas.

In Part 2, we examine in greater detail those major advanced countries where demand for vehicles may be waning and approaching (but not actually reaching) saturation point. The development of newer markets will be discussed in Part 3.

Demand is significant because of the effect it has on promoting supply and thus on the indigenous production of motor vehicles. Either due to artificially dampened demand in the past or to currently rising economic status there are now three major emerging markets: the USSR and Eastern Europe, parts of South America and parts of the Middle East. Rising demand in these three areas may ensure the development of an indigenous motor industry and our attention is focused on this in the next chapter.

Chapter 4

Supply

The three major mature markets (within which the major producers operate) are the US and Canada. Western Europe (principally France, Italy, West Germany and the UK), and Japan. All of the major US car firms and some of the largest European manufacturers such as VW and Fiat have distributed production and assembly plant throughout the world. Production figures for the world's leading manufacturers are given in Table 4.1.

Table 4.1 *Production by some of the largest manufacturing groups (In millions of cars for 1978)*

	North America	Europe*	Japan	Other	Total
GM (including Isuzu)	7.7	1.2	0.4	0.6	9.9
Ford (including Toyo Kogyo)	4.4	1.5	0.9	0.4	7.2
Toyota (including Daihatsu and Hino)	—	—	3.3	0.2	3.5
Chrysler (including Mitsubishi but excluding Chrysler Europe)	1.9	—	1.0	0.3	3.2
Nissan/Datsun (including Nissan Diesel and Fuji)	—	—	2.7	0.2	2.9
PSA Peugeot-Citroen (including Chrysler Europe)	—	2.5	—	0.2	2.7
VW Group	0.04	1.7	—	0.7	2.4
Renault (including American Motors and Volvo)	0.4	1.9	—	0.1	2.4
Fiat (including Seat)	—	1.8	—	0.1	1.9
BL and Honda	—	0.75	0.75	0.15	1.6

* Includes only UK, France, Belgium, West Germany, Italy and Spain

A number of international groupings have been formed: GM and Isuzu (Japan) have been combined as have Ford and Toyo Kogyo, and Chrysler and Mitsubishi. These links into Japan by major US motor companies are all minority shareholdings; Mitsubishi is by far the strongest of the partnerships. Similarly British Leyland (BL) and Honda are aggregated because of their trading arrangements. Fiat is linked with Seat in Spain. The two largest Japanese companies have also spawned domestic links. The reasons for these links are explained in Part 2.

The newer or emergent producers are to be found primarily in the countries of the Communist Bloc, the Middle East and South America, all areas of strategic marketing importance because they have expanding domestic markets and are in close proximity to much larger mature markets. The old colonial producers (South Africa and Australasia) are not expected to make any significant contribution to growth of the motor industry as a whole, although there are some countries whose motor industries are either non-existent or in their infancy who could emerge as major producers in the future.

The groupings as shown in Table 4.1 have been rapidly reforming since World War II. Mergers, takeovers and collapses have been accelerated by the onset of the oil crises endemic to the 1970s. There is every sign that this transformation will continue during the 1980s, as recent speeches by leading personnel in major manufacturers indicate. Estes of GM: 'We intend to go out and get him (Ford) and we are going to pass him; that is our objective (in Europe).' Bourke of Ford has replied that '. . . ears are going to be ripped off in the fight.' Sauzay of the French Industry Ministry (echoing the war theme): 'Fiat cars will one day be for sale. The French should take it; if not, they could be encircled by the Americans.' And Colin Hill, of BL, on the European car manufacturers: 'If we do not hang together . . . we will each hang separately.'

From these quotes it can be seen that the world motor industry is a highly competitive, aggressive industry where failures, takeovers and mergers are rife. The rationale for this is the concept of economies of scale: the larger you are the more profitable your firm is. What factors contribute to the development of a viable car industry?

Economies of scale

Economies of scale are vital in determining minimum viable size for a volume car producer. There are two principal ways in which the average costs of producing vehicles varies with the level of output, and it is important to make a clear distinction between them. First, if a factory with given machinery and staffing levels is producing fewer cars than it is designed for, the fixed overheads must be spread over a smaller volume, resulting in higher unit costs. This variation is essentially a short-run phenomenon, and must not be confused with the second variation — long-run economies of scale. In the latter, the management (starting more or less from scratch) can decide on the best size of factory and the best type of machinery to install. For the moment, we are more concerned with estimating the way unit costs vary with the *designed* output of the various types and scales of plant available, ie considering what sort of output the producer should set out to achieve in order to benefit from maximum economies of scale. Only when that has been decided and plant built with the necessary productive capacity, does it become susceptible to the short-run variations in unit cost caused by actual production falling below the levels for which the plant was designed.

For example, in Figure 4.1 two cost curves relating to two factories of different optimal sizes are given. If output is only at level x, the smaller factory has lower costs.

Figure 4.1 *Short-term variations in unit costs*

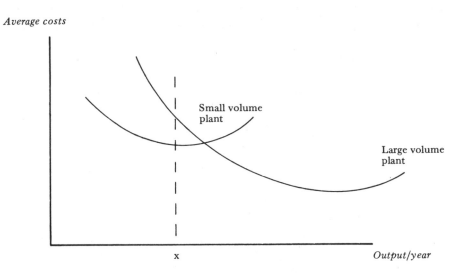

Another important factor is that many of the fixed costs are in fact initial ('one-off') costs associated with a particular model (eg design and development, special tools required, etc) which are incurred only once in the 'lifetime' of a model and must be spread over the total lifetime model output.

Production processes in the motor industry

Prior to the production process, there are a number of vital stages such as market research, product planning, styling, design engineering and testing. Such functions occupy a significant element of total costs; for example, parts (such as a wing mirror) have to be designed to meet safety requirements for up to 50 different countries, often with differing safety specifications. Consequently these centres can employ up to 5000 or more highly qualified (and highly paid) personnel. Obviously there are substantial economies of scale gained by spreading such fixed design costs over a large volume of production. Testing too costs substantial sums: for example, if all engines are required to be tested by a dynomometer (for one hour) this may work out at some 50-60 'dynos' for a 200,000 engine a year capacity plant. At $¼ million per dyno, this adds up to $15 million simply to meet one (future) US Federal requirement.

The operations normally carried out within a large 'integrated' car plant can be divided into four areas. First, there are the foundry operations, where the engine and transmission components are cast, usually in grey iron or aluminium. During the machining operations, the rough castings are machined to the tolerances required, culminating in the assembly of complete engines, gearboxes and axles. The body panels of the car are pressed or stamped from sheet steel using massive presses fitted with the appropriate dies. These three processes precede the assembly operations: the pressed body panels are fitted together in jigs and welded (body assembly); the complete body is then painted and moves on to the trim and final assembly lines, where interior and exterior fittings are added and the mechanical units (engine, gearbox, axle) are installed. At the end of the line, the car is given a short test drive and then driven off to await delivery. All the assembly operations (body and final assembly) are carried out on a moving production line (see Figure 1.2).

Many of the assembly processes undertaken by hand in the past have now been automated, the most common form being a programmable specialized robotic arm generally used in welding operations during the body assembly stage. Japanese plants tend to be the most automated with the USA not far behind.

In most cases, car firms work a two-shift, 16-hour day, five days a week and output per year figures are quoted on this basis. Three-shift working would give better utilization of facilities in theory, but in continuous flow production processes it is necessary to have off-shift maintenance time, and the greater flexibility in being able to work overtime in periods of high demand is convenient.

At each of the four stages of production, specific economies of scale particular to the operation in question can be achieved, and these are now examined.

FOUNDRY WORK
Although the available evidence varies, it is widely thought that using modern flow-line techniques there are economies of scale to be achieved in producing up to one or two million engines a year.

Figure 4.2 *Car design and production*

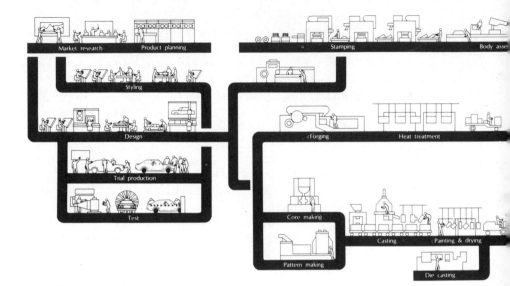

ENGINE AND TRANSMISSION MACHINING

For the manufacturer, a reasonable range of engine types and capacities is an important (and desirable) factor. There appears to be a minimum requirement of about 250,000 units per year of one basic engine type. There are further advantages to be gained from higher outputs or by grouping two or more different engine lines in one plant. As a manufacturer will want to cover the full range of engine capacities, he will require two or three basic engines, which will entail a plant capable of producing between 500,000 to one million engines overall per year. Because the costs of design and development are large, and the investment in specialized tools for production equally so, the usual practice is to spread this cost over as long a lifetime as possible. The manufacture of gearboxes and axles is similar to that of engines, with perhaps only marginal economies to be achieved. This area too has become highly automated; the use of automatic and specialized equipment is now the norm throughout all mature markets.

STAMPING

Presses are arranged in lines and sheet steel is passed down a line of presses; the required form is produced by a series of blows from different dies. Rate of output and the total lifetime output of a particular model are again important variables. The process is capital intensive, involving three items of capital expenditure which must be

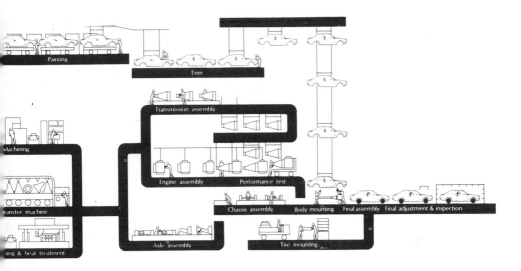

Labels within figure: Painting, Trim, Transmission assembly, Machining, Engine assembly, Performance test, Transfer machine, Chassis assembly, Body mounting, Final assembly, Final adjustment & inspection, ing & heat treatment, Axle assembly, Tire mounting

Source: The Global Datsun Family: A Guide to Nissan Motor Company

spread as thinly as possible over each car: the presses, very expensive but with a long life (20 years) and not specific to any particular model; the dies, less expensive and with a shorter life, but specific to the model; and the design and development costs of the body (obviously model-specific).

Ideally, each press should operate continually with the same dies, as changing dies is expensive and time-consuming. However, at the rate that presses currently in use are capable of working, this would require a volume of nearly 2.5 million identical units per year; die-changing, therefore, is inevitable. The optimal length of press runs between die changes is determined by trading off the costs of holding the greater stocks of finished panels entailed by longer runs. Few manufacturers achieve even 50 per cent utilization of their presses, and die utilization must be much lower, which means that the cost per car off the presses and dies is twice as high as it could be. It is obvious that large economies from better press scheduling could be obtained from greater volume. Our conclusion would be that there are significant economies to be gained right up to the output of 2 million identical cars per year.

ASSEMBLY
Assembly operations are probably least susceptible to significant economies of scale. The work is comparatively labour intensive (although

this is rapidly changing), with many workers only requiring screwdrivers or spanners. There are some large automatic pieces of equipment, such as the multi-welders performing several welds simultaneously on some large sub-assemblies, but most welding is done by hand or by programmable robotic arms (more than 95 per cent of the 4000 welds on some cars are made by automatic equipment in some US, Japanese and Italian car plants). Although automatic equipment is expensive, it is more reliable and consistent than its manual equivalent, can deal with a variety of model mixes, and can be programmed for a redesigned model quickly, efficiently and without any costly changes to transfer lines (ie conveyor belts or track) or retraining programmes. In most factories, painting is also carried out by fully automatic processes although examples of painting by hand can be found. The most expensive item, however, is the transfer line itself. Scope for further automation using microprocessor controlled robotic arms linked to a central computer exists. Some European countries (eg the UK) have yet to catch up the Japanese and US norms. Judging from the high profits of the latter two countries, automation must be considered vital; to centre one's production process around manual assembly seems to be courting disaster.

The optimum speed of an assembly line is determined by three main factors: the capacity of the large automatic machines, the tasks assigned to the robotic arms, and the efficient use of workers along the line. Each worker stands at a particular point along the line, with the necessary tools and stocks of components performing one or more jobs on each car as it passes. To increase output, the line must move faster, and either each worker must do his set tasks faster, or the number of tasks per worker must be reduced and additional workers brought in. The latter requires a longer line and more space, and uses up stocks of components faster, requiring either larger stocks or quicker replenishment. Reducing the number of tasks per worker increases efficiency: time is saved by fewer tool changes, picking up fewer components, etc and, through repetition, the worker becomes exceedingly proficient. As speed increases, however, he must spend more time moving between cars and this, together with the cost of extra components and space, places limitations on the maximum speed.

Most writers are in agreement that the optimum rate of production for assembly is 200,000 to 300,000 cars per year, corresponding to an hourly rate of 60-80 cars. Although some US and Japanese plants have higher rates these are probably impracticable given European attitudes to production line work. Although the US practice is to have one long fast-moving track, the majority of British manufacturers seem to prefer two slower lines, which probably does carry some cost penalty.

Other economies

Thus far, we have dealt only with technical economies of scale at plant level, but there are other areas in which economies can be achieved, mainly concerned with spreading central business overheads. There are always slight economies to be gained in specialization of management function, but the major administrative problem even in small motor companies is the avoidance of diseconomies of bureaucracy rather than the attainment of further economies.

A more important function in which there are economies of scale to be achieved is in product development and design. Specialization in different aspects of design has always been fruitful. Faced with a plethora of safety regulations changing from day to day and from one country to the next, it is important to assign specialists in the various fields to ensure that one's cars remain saleable in as many markets as possible. A large design staff can prove expensive, but it is really the key to achieving all possible economies of scale: the demand potential of most models falls below the ideals of least-cost production but good design can offset this disadvantage to some extent by standardization of components between models. With skilful adaptation, engines, gearboxes, suspensions, trimmings, pressings, etc can all be used to a greater or lesser extent in different models, but it takes a concerted design effort to achieve this level of standardization. Most equipment used in the car industry is specific to a particular model. A firm which is in a position frequently to change models is better able to gain the cost-saving advantages of new technology.

Diseconomies of scale

Economies of scale, brought about by an increase in size, carry with them potential diseconomies of scale. Simply because of the sheer number of people involved, there is the possibility of a loss of effective control. Greater automation and increasingly specialized equipment could prove insufficiently flexible in an industry increasingly vulnerable to considerable fluctuation in demand and the consequent risk. And, finally, size brings with it even greater barriers to effective management/ worker communications. These are not inevitable penalties (consider, for example, the experience of large American corporations already operating on a larger scale), but they must be taken into consideration. The most important diseconomy, and the one which has been suggested as an effective limit to the size to which firms could grow is the problem of organization and administration. The larger the firm, the greater the number of hierarchical levels and the wider the span of control. Information flows between different levels are longer and the internal communication network vastly greater. The increase in the transmission of information generates 'simple control loss' as well as 'compound control loss', which also involves communication lines. The direction of the enterprise becomes partly the responsibility of partisan management who are likely to exploit discrete opportunities to advance their own individual and functional interests. In other words, they may pursue personal goals which are not readily or necessarily identical with the goals of the company as a whole. Moreover, further losses in control may occur through communication biasing.

The US producers have reacted to such administrative diseconomies by developing a multi-divisional organizational form which recognizes quasi-autonomous 'natural decision units'. Even with this type of organization, however, the size at which diseconomies are incurred is simply moved up to a larger scale. GM, for example, must find it exceedingly difficult to analyse discrepancies between observed results and internal performance standards into first, inadequacies or deficiencies in the control mechanism and second, failure of the market to conform to management expectations.

The extra information flow and the accretion of hierarchical levels also mean that the perception of problems is slower and that more time is needed to pass alternative solutions through successive stages and levels of committee. In practice this means that the company not only becomes slow to perceive the problem but also slow to react to it. Once a decision has been made, it must be implemented on several organizational levels. Monitoring whether or not the decision has produced the desired results may itself be a slow process and one in which the feedback loop is further complicated by other changes in the corporation.

Overall

Leaving aside organizational and administrative diseconomies it would appear that the possibilities of achieving economies of scale are never really exhausted in the motor industry. Larger scale production, up to two million identical units per year for example, will always confer some advantage, but the most significant advantages are to be gained at lower scales. There is widespread agreement that individual models should be produced at levels exceeding 200,000 per year, and that ideally a firm should have an overall output of not less than one million cars per year. Individual engine types should also be produced at rates of at least 300,000 per year, so that a firm with an output of one million overall could cover the whole capacity range with three types (see Table 4.2).

Automation increases the assembly plant size to about 0.5 million and increases the minimum efficient size with respect to costing and machining. The enormous design requirements of pollution controls and

Table 4.2 *Estimates of minimum efficiency scale*
thousand units pa

	Casting	Machining	Stamping	Assembly	1 Model	Overall Complete Model Range
Pratten[1]	1000	250	500	300	500	1000
Rhys[2]	200	1000	2000	400	—	2000
White[3]	small	260	400	200	400	800
University Study Group[4]	1000– 2000	400– 1000	500+	200– 400	200+	1000+ with small economies thereafter

1. Pratten, C F (1971) *Economies of Scale in Manufacturing Industries*
2. Rhys, D G (1972) *The Motor Industry: An Economic Survey*
3. White, L J (1971) *The Automobile Industry Since 1945*
4. University of Bristol Motor Industry Research Group

energy conservation have shifted the minimum efficient size of a world-wide company from one million units per year to in excess of 2 million units. Below this level, a manufacturer will not be able to weather the storm over a long period; there are some exceptions such as specialist manufacturers and Japanese producers who were launched in a period of buoyant demand but these companies have yet to experience a static market coupled with further energy crises and fiercer international competition.

A firm operating at this sort of level would be too large to fit on one site, and operations would have to be split between several sites. Body assembly, paint, trim and final assembly on a particular model should be carried out together, because of the high costs involved in transporting assembled bodies. Transport of unassembled panels is less expensive, and the location of the pressing plant is therefore less crucial. Engines and power train (engine and gearbox) components are easier and cheaper to transport, and the production technology involved is also very different, so there is no particular need to have these plants on the assembly sites. The same would apply to other gearbox and axle production. Other small components produced internally may have their own plants to be integrated with others of a similar nature, depending on circumstances.

It is difficult to quantify the cost penalties of operating on a smaller scale, but, as an example, the cost of producing only 250,000 units per year over a four or five year model life has been estimated at between 6 and 20 per cent, a very considerable difference in cost. The cost penalties of producing a model range over a similar period become progressively steeper with levels of less than 100,000 units per year. As Adam Smith said: 'The division of labour is limited by the extent of the market.' Thus, the extent to which economies of scale can be used in the executive and luxury segments of the market are limited, though Daimler Benz no doubt benefits from its model runs of greater than 100,000 quality cars per year. A reasonable volume for a car classed in the executive luxury market segment is around 100,000 to 200,000.

It would be difficult to quantify when organizational and administrative diseconomies in multi-divisional firms like the US multinationals start to occur. All that can be said is that some of these companies are now probably suffering from just such diseconomies. Companies which are not organized in a multi-divisional form can develop scale diseconomies at relatively low volume levels. For example, it is claimed by some that British Leyland was suffering from similar diseconomies at only 1.3 million vehicle capacity.

In short, the major producers are running out of steam. Because they operate, for the most part, in mature markets, they are obliged to develop and manufacture products geared specifically to those markets, only to find that their products are not necessarily saleable elsewhere. Just as price becomes critical in certain sectors of the market, the major producers must contend with rising labour and component costs, both of which effectively bar them from manufacturing a cheap basic car. Carefully balanced scale economies are disrupted as size itself threatens to become a major diseconomy. We have seen that size is critical in the motor industry, but we must now concede that there is an upper limit, beyond which size is a major liability. It would appear that size alone, and the growth that it implies, is no certain guarantee of continuing profitability.

Oligopoly and control

Why have firms sought to grow and thereby attain economies of scale? The motor industry is fiercely competitive: price *and* product acceptability are paramount. If a rival can produce an acceptable product at a lower cost then the higher-cost producer may face a struggle for survival. The only way of ensuring that costs are competitive is to expand to achieve the major scale economies. This is why the Japanese have been so growth-oriented; each extra unit exported has made available extra scale economies which have reduced unit costs and thereby increased profits on all production. Of the major producers, only Western Europe as a region has a much more fragmented industry, for which local nationalism and the lack of a fully integrated regional structure are to blame. In global terms, the conditions needed to achieve scale economies have produced a highly concentrated industry, closely resembling a macro-oligopoly (ie a worldwide oligopoly). Ford, for example, is one of the two largest manufacturers in each of six of the world's major motor producing countries (see Table 4.3).

Table **4.3** *Concentration of production*

Country	Number of producers accounting for 80% or more of production	Companies	Approximate historical % of total production
US	3	GM, Ford, Chrysler	90
Japan	3	Nissan, Toyota, Toyo Kogyo	80
West Germany	4	Volkswagen, Ford, Daimler Benz, GM	80
France	2	Renault, Peugeot-Citroen	80
UK	3	BL, Ford, Chrysler	85
Italy	1	Fiat	90
Canada	3	GM, Ford, Chrysler	90
USSR	5	Zhigulf, Lada, Moskovitch, Zaporozhet, GAZ	90
Spain	5	Seat, Ford, Renault, Chrysler, Peugeot-Citroen	95
Brazil	3	VW, Ford, GM	90
Sweden	1	Volvo-Saab	100

Ownership and control under these conditions are largely a question of the extent to which companies are publicly or privately owned and, if the latter, the extent to which privately owned companies are *domestically* owned. Most major producers are privately owned, but only a few of them are domestically owned and operated concerns. Of the top 10 firms (all with a potential production capacity in excess of one million vehicles) only two (British Leyland and Renault) are wholly state owned. In VW ownership is divided between the state and private sectors; two others (Peugeot-Citroen and Fiat) maintain close links with their respective governments and it is anticipated that those links will be further strengthened in the future. European firms show a tendency to be state owned (or to be subject to state intervention), which is not the case in either the USA or Japan.

We will be arguing later that the possibilities of any extension of foreign ownership in mature markets would appear to be strictly limited. Greater uncertainty exists in considering future prospects for less developed markets. On the whole, the prospect of establishing foreign-owned subsidiaries in those areas is remote, given the ever-present threat of nationalization, although cooperation between companies already operating there and various experiments in partial co-ownership are increasing.

Finance

There has been a marked tendency towards consolidation in the industry, but how have the largest of the major producers fared in terms of finance and profitability? Table 4.4 summarizes sales, assets and net income for the major manufacturers, and Table 4.5 charts two profitability ratios for the various firms.

Table 4.4 *Sales, assets and net income for largest firms producing motor vehicles 1973*

Company	Country	Sales (US $'000)	Assets (US $'000)	Net Income (US $'000)
GM	US	35,798,289	20,296,861	2,398,103
Ford	US	23,015,100	12,954,000	906,500
Chrysler	US	11,774,372	6,104,897	255,445
Volkswagen	Germany	6,412,056	4,792,851	73,071
Daimler Benz	Germany	5,590,817	2,161,425	97,527
Toyota	Japan	5,547,425	3,696,562	277,807
Nissan	Japan	4,883,494	5,059,173	150,985
Renault	France	4,655,696	1,818,269	12,902
Mitsubishi	Japan	4,133,189	7,290,506	66,189
Fiat	Italy	4,074,914	3,173,144	450
British Leyland	UK	3,827,248	2,403,444	68,802
Peugeot	France	2,820,157	1,820,876	72,782
Citroen	France	2,560,644	389,404	12,262
Volvo	Sweden	2,064,017	1,924,053	56,552
American Motors	US	1,739,025	712,955	44,526
Toyo Kogyo	Japan	1,675,276	2,334,088	34,562
Honda	Japan	1,399,552	1,180,428	43,318
Saab-Scania	Sweden	1,243,069	1,131,711	28,552

Source: Company reports

One of the most startling conclusions to emerge is that profitability in the period covered (a boom period for motor manufacturers) was conspicuously mediocre. Only companies operating in North America, Sweden, Japan and Germany showed even marginally healthy profits, and in Germany even VW's performance was disappointing. Since the early 1970s, the profitability of these markets has waned. Table 4.6 shows how profits have fared since 1973. Of particular interest is the performance of GM in real terms; even in 1978, a record year for unit sales, real profits actually fell. The financial results for 1979 and 1980 promise to be poor for nearly all companies (even the specialist manufacturers whose profits were largely unaffected by the 1973 oil crisis are likely to feel the pinch this time). It is apparent that the major producers in 'mature' markets are experiencing difficulties, and it is to this we now turn.

Even in a boom year profitability is uncertain, which makes it even more important to gauge the effect of a poor year on the industry. Two factors in particular affect profitability: the capital intensive nature

Table 4.5 *Comparison of car manufacturers profitability ratios 1970-73*

	Return on shareholders' funds (%)[1]	Return on capital investment (%)[2]
GM (West Germany)	19.1	28.1
Peugeot (France)	19.4	20.7
Ford (West Germany)	17.9	22.3
Nissan (Japan)	15.5	15.5
Toyota (Japan)	15.4	21.6
Volvo (Sweden)	15.0	17.6
Daimler Benz (West Germany)	11.6	26.2
BMW (West Germany)	11.6	21.3
Chrysler (France)	7.2	11.0
Ford (UK)	5.9	10.2
British Leyland (UK)	5.6	10.6
Volkswagen (West Germany)	4.2	11.2
Fiat (Italy)	− 1.5	2.6
Renault (France)	− 3.6	6.1
Citroen (France)	− 5.5	2.4
GM (UK)	− 8.4	0.6
Chrysler (UK)	− 9.6	0.5
GM (worldwide)	15.4	17.6
Ford (worldwide)	12.5	12.3
Chrysler (worldwide)	5.6	4.6
American Motors (worldwide)	− 1.3	2.0

1. Return on shareholders' funds defined as profits *after* interest and tax divided by shareholders' investment

2. Return on capital employed defined as profits *before* interest and tax on the total capital employed in the business

Source: Company reports and *The Future of the British Car Industry* CPRS

Table 4.6 *Net profit after tax for some major manufacturers (in millions of US $)*

	1973	1974	1975	1976	1977	1978
GM	2398	950	1253	2903	3338	3508
Ford	907	361	323	983	1673	1589
Chrysler	255	− 52	− 260	423	163	− 205
Toyota	333	191	235	486	570	567
Nissan	202	92	255	416	394	400*
PSA (Peugeot-Citroen)	—	35	61	310	272	300
VW	159	− 390	− 76	485	202	277
Renault	12	8	− 120	133	48	100*
Fiat	29	43	4	148	136	130*
GM (at 1973 $)	2398	856	1035	2266	2448	2391

* Estimate

Source: Company reports

of the industry in general, and the effect of a drop in demand on those
companies operating in a mature rather than a developing market. To
take the first point: whilst the larger US producers operate on a break-
even capacity possibly as low as 50 per cent, in Western Europe and
Japan the figure is more likely to be in the region of 60-70 per cent.
From this, it is clear that a small drop in sales creates a much larger fall
in profits. For example, GM's US production dropped from 6.5 million
vehicles in 1973 to 4.7 million in 1974, but profits fell from $2.4 billion
to less than $1 billion in the following year. Even in 1973, the profits
for most of the major companies (with a few notable exceptions) were
disappointingly low: Table 4.4 reveals that of all the major companies
Ford, GM and Toyota were the most profitable. Ford's performance
was particularly impressive as even the company's subsidiaries in
Germany, Canada and the UK showed profits on their individual
operations. Chrysler and GM, however, have not enjoyed the same
success with their subsidiaries (with the exception of Opel in Germany
which has shown consistently good profits). Part of the problem in
Europe is quite simply the enormous concentration of firms in the
region. Total European capacity to produce cars and CVs far exceeds
any possible demand within the market. In order to survive, the weaker
firms have been obliged to find other sources of finance to subsidize
their operations, usually through a direct approach to the government
concerned (British Leyland and the old Chrysler UK are obvious
examples), and occasionally through change of ownership or merger
(eg Peugeot-Citroen). A third possibility exists — increased cooperation,
rather than competition, between firms. This possibility will be
considered more fully in Part 2.

Growth rates

With the exception of the low growth achieved in the UK, even the
lowest growth rates recorded by European producers have been nearly
double the highest rate of growth in the US and have exceeded the
highest rates of growth in Canada. The Japanese, however, have
experienced by far the largest increase. If both Nissan and Toyota, for
example, continue to grow at their present rate (20.5 per cent and
19.3 per cent respectively for the period 1954-73), home-based
production of these two companies could exceed GM's US-based
production within the next decade — an astonishing possibility. Japan,
a newer producer and now a major one, has grown faster than producers
in the long-established mature markets and will probably continue to
do so, although the rate of Japanese growth could slow down as the
motor industry in Japan produces a more sophisticated (and therefore
more expensive) product. Traditional export markets for Japanese cars
will increasingly resist higher levels of Japanese imports, just as some of

the newer producers (eg Spain and Brazil) begin to compete in the markets which have thus far provided growth opportunities for Japan. New producers would at that stage be in a better position to exploit the advantages of lower labour costs in manufacturing cheap, basic cars but even if their growth rates increase dramatically, they are unlikely to surpass the Japanese rate in the foreseeable future. Nevertheless, Japan's export markets will be eroded and import penetration in Japan itself is likely to rise.

It remains to be seen whether or not the existing multinationals will be able to participate in the growth of capacity in the newer producing areas (as they are at the moment in both Spain and Brazil) or whether they will be displaced by the establishment of new, home-based firms, as appears to be the case in Iran and Korea. At the moment, the pendulum has swung in favour of home-based firms, often with government approval and aid.

Corporate strategies

The major manufacturers have adopted a variety of measures in response to the slow or minimal growth and mediocre profitability of recent years. Marketing strategies have been evolved to cope with falling demand in domestic markets, usually based on (1) the export of domestic production, and (2) the establishment of plants in foreign locations, either as self-sufficient manufacturers or sub-assembly plants dependent on imported supplies of certain components (eg power train). The US 'big three' (GM, Ford and Chrysler) have adopted strategy 2 for most of their West European operations; a few of the 'domestic' European firms (Fiat, Renault, Daimler-Benz, Volkswagen) have also located plants abroad, although to a very limited extent (see Table 4.7). Japanese producers by and large have followed the export strategy (1 above) although a small number of Japanese plants, assembly only, have been established abroad.

The Japanese strategy is at the moment the most successful: exports account for over 50 per cent of production, which brings Japan into line with other (West European) producers in terms of export share and places her far ahead of the USA, which is not a major exporter. Moreover, the trend is for Japanese exports to increase (although there may be upper limits) while West European exports to non-European countries diminish. The USA and most of the West European market (taken country-by-country and as a whole) are suffering from increased import penetration.

Of those European producers who have pursued, or are about to pursue, a 'foreign plant location' strategy, both Volkswagen and Volvo (although lack of finance has temporarily halted Volvo's plans) are now building assembly plant in the USA, and returning a few chickens to

Table 4.7 *Marketing strategy by manufacturer in 1973*

Manufacturer	Total production	Domestic sales (%)	Exports (%)	Foreign sales of subsidiaries abroad (%)
GM	8,683,800	75.0	—	25.0
Ford	5,871,028	64.2	—	35.8
Chrysler	3,449,831	57.2	—	42.8
Toyota	2,087,133	65.0	34.5	—
Volkswagen	2,281,000	27.1	45.6	27.3
Nissan	1,996,427	63.8	36.2	—
Fiat	2,178,231	44.1	27.3	28.5
Renault*	1,328,324	45.9	24.3	29.8
British Leyland	1,012,488	52.4	20.5	27.1
Mitsubishi	562,932	83.7	16.3	—
Peugeot	761,870	52.0	48.0	—
Daimler-Benz	547,617	48.2	44.7	7.1
Volvo	272,632	22.9	48.7	28.4
BMW	197,446	50.9	49.1	—
Saab-Scania	106,372	67.3	62.7	—
Toyo Kogyo	739,172	53.5	46.5	—
Honda	355,016	79.1	20.9	—
Isuzu	217,753	72.5	27.5	—
Suzuki	243,734	98.3	1.7	—

* 1972 figures

Source: The World Automotive Industry to 1995 Business International

roost! The Volkswagen decision to locate abroad is a particularly interesting one, reflecting the mix of economic and political motives which influences such decisions. Labour costs in the USA, for example, are expected to be lower as German wage rates now exceed US levels; the market potential is greater as cars assembled within the USA will not carry import duties or be penalized by import controls, and US-assembled Volkswagens will avoid the exchange rate difficulties of adjusting to a Deutschmark apparently in a state of perpetual revaluation.

Future strategies will depend on a number of possible developments. If, for example, the industry worldwide polarizes into low-technology and high-technology sectors, this could persuade producers in the mature markets to concentrate their efforts on high-technology production while affiliates or subsidiaries in low-cost developing areas produce low-technology volume cars. Certainly there will be changes in the economic *status quo*, as wealth accrues to the resource-rich developing countries, nearly all of whom are anxious to establish their own motor manufacturing capability. Capacity, however, would almost certainly exceed demand if there were a sharp increase in the number of producers. This would endanger newly established industries and increase the likelihood of drastic government intervention, such as defensive nationalization, to maintain employment. Few manufacturers are prepared to risk such eventualities and most will prefer less direct involvement, although in doing so they face the prospect of virtually identical models re-exported to their traditional markets at lower cost and in direct competition with their own product (which has in fact been the case with the Polski Fiat).

Those companies within the industry who have felt that greater diversification would contribute to the profitability of their operations appear to have selected one of four options: to diversify into other activities and operations closely associated with transportation (motor cycling, insurance, motor finance, etc); to produce other forms of transport indirectly linked to their existing enterprise (eg locomotives, buses, ships/tankers); to manufacture other capital goods (tractors, earth-moving equipment); or to branch out into the production of other consumer durables (air-conditioning units, radios, refrigerators). Of the products mentioned in each category, it is immediately clear that they are either complementary (radios), competitive (buses), or require similar technologies to those already in use. In Table 4.8 the proportion of these 'non-automotive' sales to total sales is given company by company, and it is apparent that the US manufacturers are generally less diversified than the larger Western European firms.

Table 4.8 *Extent of diversification in 1973*

Manufacturer	Non-automotive sales	% of Total
GM	$ 2255 billion	7.4
Ford	$ 1975 billion	8.6
Nissan	¥ 14.5 billion	1.1
Chrysler	$ 383 million	3.3
American Motors	$ 205 million	10.2
Fiat	L 401 billion	16.9
Citroen	Fr 952 million	3.0
Peugeot	Fr 1766 million	14.1
British Leyland	£ 56 million	3.6
Mitsubishi	$ 3290 million	65.7
Renault	Fr 4732 billion	29.4
Volvo	Kr 1866 billion	20.8
Saab-Scania	Kr 1079 billion	19.9
BMW	DM 469 million	18.0

Source: Company reports

Of the Japanese firms, Nissan began as a motor vehicles manufacturer and later joined forces with Fuji heavy industries. Mitsubishi, principally a heavy industry company, diversified in the opposite direction and is now the most diversified of all the major vehicle manufacturers. In fact, in view of the opportunities (and the financial and technical resources) that apparently exist, it is surprising how little diversification there is in the industry as a whole. Companies in public ownership, it is true, have no reason to diversify, and for privately owned companies the uncertainty of obtaining finance in the future might act as a deterrent, but these two factors alone do not provide a satisfactory explanation for the lack of diversification.

The possibilities of relocation are now severely limited, and diversification into non-automative manufacture seems to offer only limited growth potential. If the major producers are unable to boost or sustain growth, they must become increasingly vulnerable to market pressures. Increased liberalization of trade barriers (eg within the Common Market, the US-Canadian agreement, the Andean Pact), higher levels of import penetration in the North American and European markets by the Japanese producers and possibly some of the newer producers, and the prospect of increased competitive pressure from non-automative companies, such as Westinghouse in the USA, who are anxious to exploit the market potential for electric cars, further threaten the future success of established manufacturers.

The major manufacturers in the most mature markets (North America and Western Europe) are experiencing a new set of difficulties consistent with old age. Many of the factors which contributed to the development of the major producers now appear to limit possibilities for further significant growth. The companies concerned now suffer from major *diseconomies* of scale: they are too cumbersome to respond rapidly to fluctuations in demand, and the cost of labour and components in the mature markets has made volume production of cheap basic cars no longer viable. The major producers are being pushed out of certain significant market segments, having to concentrate on products which are by and large specifically geared to the most mature markets and which are unacceptable or too expensive to be sold in significant quantities elsewhere. This is happening at a time when overall demand in the mature markets has fallen dramatically, and patterns of supply to markets elsewhere are undergoing a rapid transformation.

Trends in the supply of motor vehicles

Motor vehicles have for the most part been produced in and supplied to those areas capable of supporting the highly developed technology required and with a market large and affluent enough to sustain a healthy demand. Both Japan and Brazil developed their motor industries in response to the growth of such a market. In recent years, however, the pattern has begun to change as a new factor — government action — brings greater influence to bear on the supply of motor vehicles. Relatively new industries in South Korea and the Middle East, for example, were virtually created at the behest of government. Further development in other areas will increasingly depend on the extent (or lack) of government support and possibly government initiative. The existence of an adequate infrastructure, in terms of component and supply industries, could also enhance, or in its absence restrict, further possibilities for growth.

The world's largest producers have become multinational, not only by establishing subsidiaries in the major industrial countries, but also by seeking locations for new manufacturing facilities in less developed countries where labour costs are significantly lower. But the advantages of low labour costs must be weighed against the disadvantages of their lower productivity and of their more limited market potential.

For leading producers this balancing of factors has created a dilemma: in the countries that have become mass consumers of automobiles, the automotive industry has contributed heavily to the economic development and standard of living that makes such consumption possible; but the high standards of living in these countries have made the compensation demands of automotive workers increasingly difficult to satisfy. Particularly in those countries where high automotive productivity and high standards of living have been long established, automotive labour costs have risen and, in some cases, labour-management conflicts have escalated, to the point where the traditional institutional forms of the industry have been severely shaken, and new assumptions about the role of labour in the industry have begun to emerge (this is further discussed in Part 2). However, the traditional approach to the problem of exporting production overseas is one which may no longer be possible. Therefore a crisis point has arisen.

At the same time, less developed countries have an incentive to create their own motor industries. Now that the technology for producing motor vehicles is spread throughout the world, it is often the aim of an emerging nation, which considers it has a large enough market to support a motor industry, to encourage growth in that sector. It is precisely because an enormous industrial infrastructure is necessary for a motor industry that governments are keen to see their motor industry developing. Once an industry is established, the number of supplying firms required and the total employment generated is vast. Moreover, in general, despite the existence of assembly lines, the labour content in assembling motor vehicles and motor components (with some exceptions) is high. Although the reaction of the USA and Japan (but, surprisingly, less in Europe) is to substitute intelligent (ie computerized) robotic equipment for conventional labour in routine assembly and manufacturing tasks, cheap labour in less developed countries is sometimes less expensive. Moreover, the Western nations themselves face a problem. If the machines take the place of man, what will man do to find gainful employment? We return to the socio-economic problems of the mature markets in Part 2 where we will also consider the ways in which the mature producers will respond to the changes now threatening them. The emergent producers are considered in greater detail in Part 3. In each case, we will first analyse demand for the various markets and then consider various estimates of the supply needed to meet that demand. In the conclusion, Part 4, we will attempt an overview of the major trade flows that could result.

Part 2:
Mature Markets and Producers

Chapter 5

The Mature Markets:
An Overview

This chapter introduces the mature markets and deals with issues common to all three. All are experiencing problems and the next decade promises to see a number of fundamental changes.

Product differentiation

Up to the 1970s, the North American, West European and Japanese product, particularly the car, grew along different lines with distinctive features dictated by local market conditions. North America, which has plentiful land and thus far adequate energy resources, designed powerful and bulky products. Meanwhile Europe, where space is at a premium and with little domestically produced oil, developed small, fuel-efficient, high-performance and technically rather sophisticated products. The Japanese, confronted by the same constraints as the European producers but wishing to follow the North American pattern, gave birth to a hybrid vehicle, a European-size North American vehicle (complete with gaudy tail lights!). One of the things to be investigated is whether this degree of product differentiation will continue.

Demand

We must re-examine the characteristics of demand in a mature market. Although vehicle ownership will increase, growth will be slower than in the past. Growth in new registrations will either be small or non-existent. Some of the mature markets will have seen their all-time peak demand. Consistent with the stagnation in demand, there will be a greater degree of cyclical variation in the demand.

Cars

Figure 5.1 shows the relative sizes of car market for the three mature markets. The North American market oscillates the most, the Japanese market, the youngest mature market, the least. The demand for all the markets has begun to taper off; the North American market is closest of all to saturation; Western Europe has entered the saturation phase and

Figure 5.1 *Car demand and supply in the mature markets*

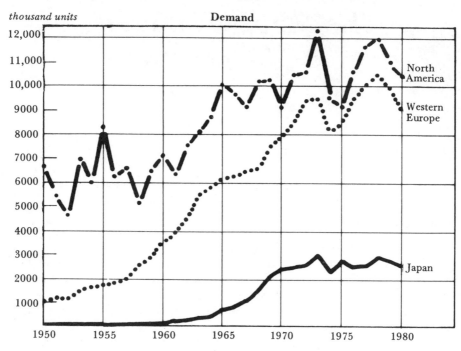

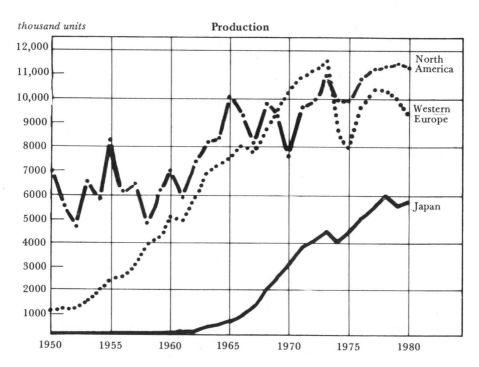

Japan is just about to enter it.

CVs

Figure 5.2 shows the relative positions of the CV market for the mature producers. Of interest is the phenomenal increase in recent demand in the North American market. This reflects the demand for recreational vehicles in their broadest sense, including four-wheel drive vehicles, motorhomes, pickups and the RVs themselves (vans converted to the highest standard of luxury, with bars, hi-fi, picture windows, air-conditioning, etc providing a comfortable and spacious mode of transport with excellent visibility). The 1978-79 oil crisis saw demand for these vehicles evaporate overnight in 1979. Western European conditions are different. With space at a premium, there is insufficient room actually to house RVs. Regardless of the oil crisis, it is unlikely that Western Europe would ever develop the same market potential. Otherwise European and American conditions are similar. Figure 5.2 attempts to calculate North American CV demand without RV demand (a wide definition has been used, since registrations of RVs in the USA using a strict definition only catches a small proportion of CVs bought by private households with recreational activities in mind). The discrepancy between Western Europe's and North America's demand can be explained by the greater distances to be covered in the USA and the greater number of alternatives to road transport in Europe.

Although Japanese CV ownership seems significantly higher than in North America (minus the RVs) and Western Europe (see Table 3.2) demand is mainly for vans. Japan has not developed a complex motorway network and the great bulk of goods are transported in small CVs. In North America and Western Europe, maturity has led to the more efficient transport of goods involving large haulage trucks capable of traversing motorways at high speeds. It is doubtful whether Japan will ever completely catch up with the other mature markets because of the lack of space and the prohibitive cost of motorways. On the other hand, the integration of all the three markets will put pressure on Japan to move towards a transport mode that is more similar to that of the other mature producers.

Production

Figures 5.1 and 5.2 show vehicle production for the mature producers. Production in North America was soon overtaken by the growth of demand, and North America was a net importer of cars from 1952 onwards. Western Europe's production exceeded demand; the region was the chief net exporting region until Japan toppled Europe from this position by eclipsing its export markets and import penetration

Figure 5.2 *CV demand and production in the mature markets ('000s)*

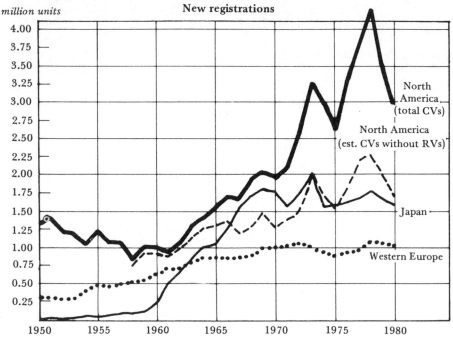

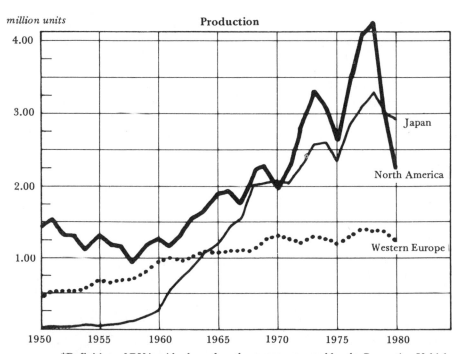

*Definition of RV is wider here than the narrow one used by the Recreation Vehicle Industry Association

into the domestic market. Japan's growth has been most spectacular; supply and demand for cars were in balance until the late 1960s, when car production took off. Whereas Europe had exported up to one-third of its production, Japan now exports about half its car production.

CV production in North America has just kept ahead of demand, implying that North America is a net exporter of CVs. Western Europe is a net exporter. Japan's production, as with cars, matched demand until the late 1960s, but Japan has since exported a more significant share of its output than Western Europe.

Ford and GM are planning to introduce a standardized worldwide model range designed at international centres. Each company will, in the 1980s, produce about seven or eight standard models (see Table 5.1).

Table 5.1 *Standard car model sizes in the 1980s*

Model	Ford's European classification	Example
Extra-small	A	Fiat Ciro, Renault R2, Ford and GM entries in 1985
Small	B	Ford Fiesta, VW Polo, GM entry in 1981-83
Light	C	VW Golf (Rabbit), GM 'T' car, Ford Erika
Medium	C/D	Ford Cortina/Taunus
Large	D	Ford Granada, Chevrolet Citation
Executive	E/F	Mercedes, Jaguar, large BMWs
US intermediate		Down-sized version of current US range
US standard		Down-sized version of current US range

Local market characteristics can be catered for by adapting the model, which may be regarded as forming a basic design concept, on which modifications can be made. Some models may not be sold in certain markets. For example, the largest models may be reserved exclusively for the North American market but this is unlikely. The 4 or 5 smallest models will be used throughout the world. Sub-assemblies and power trains will become standardized and will be used on several models. To give an example of the enormous economies of scale open to GM and Ford, the most widely used model will probably be produced in more than 2 million units a year, while the average annual production for every other model will be around one million. Moreover, from 1980 onwards, GM will standardize on some four or five petrol engines and two diesel engines; Ford will follow suit.

A similar process is occurring with CVs, especially in the small and medium segments. In the heavier CV sector, economies of scale are not so important.

Economies of scale and the small CV producer

Much of the CV industry in the mature markets (except in Japan) has evolved a highly efficient structure, which involves even the larger firms in buying out a high proportion of requirements, and a specialized CV sector which concentrates on pure assembly, with any manufacturing being done by techniques appropriate to low annual output volumes. As a result, even large-scale manufacturers have bought out items such as gearboxes and axles from even larger-scale component makers, while the small-scale specialists are able to enjoy external economies of scale.

By keeping their assembly operations at a high degree of efficiency, the small firms have survived and prospered by being able to purchase diesel engines, axles, gearboxes, cabs, as well as the usual bought out items such as electrical components, from large-scale suppliers who themselves incur the cost and risk of high capital investment in manufacturing equipment.

The manufacturers and their location

Table 5.2 demonstrates how the major components are spread across the three continents, and gives a rough guide of their likely capacity in each area.

Table 5.2 *Major manufacturing companies and distribution of estimated capacity in mature markets 1980 (millions of motor vehicles)*

	North America	Western Europe	Japan
GM Group			
GM (US))	8	—	—
Opel/Vauxhall)	—	1+	—
Isuzu)	—	—	0.2
Ford)	5	2	—
Toyo Kogyo)	—	—	1
Chrysler)	3	—	—
Mitsubishi)	—	—	1
PSA Peugeot-Citroen	—	3	—
VW	0.4	2	—
Renault and Volvo)	—	2+	—
AMC)	0.5	—	—
Fiat	—	2	—
British Leyland)	—	1	—
Honda)	—	—	1
Nissan Group	—	—	3
Toyota Group	—	—	4

Only Ford and GM are truly spread across all three markets. The European manufacturers have, by and large, adopted a less federal policy to the other mature markets, though VW's assembly plant in the US and the link-up between British Leyland and Honda are notable exceptions. Japan, the youngest of the three markets, has been the most passive in the pursuit of international liaisons.

Oligopoly and control

A feature of all the mature markets is an increase in concentration. AMC in the US has forged links with Renault in Europe; Chrysler has sold its European subsidiaries to PSA Peugeot-Citroen and is currently courting a possible partner, perhaps Mitsubishi (Chrysler US owns a 15 per cent stake in this Japanese company); GM and Ford are actively expanding their European subsidiaries at the expense of British Leyland, Fiat and VW. GM and Ford will also try to increase their grip in the Japanese market; GM currently owns a share in Isuzu and Ford in Toyo Kogyo.

Some of the groupings shown in Table 5.2 will discontinue, and others will form. At the time of writing, British Leyland was rumoured to be about to collapse (yet again!). It is by no means certain that Chrysler US and Mitsubishi will continue their association; other possible partners include VW and PSA Peugeot-Citroen. So the situation is fluid and the types of relationships discussed in the next four chapters are illustrative only.

Finance and economies of scale in the mature markets

The financial performance of a company depends on maintaining production at high capacity levels in all plants and reducing costs. The former depends on shrewd marketing and meticulous product planning. The latter depends on the cost of labour (about 12 to 20 per cent of total costs, reduced by increased automation but this necessitates far higher capital costs), labour relations and economies of scale. There are two issues at stake: first whether a company can generate sufficient profits to finance new model development in the long run and, second, whether the vast capital expenditures can be generated in the short run from profits and/or raised externally. For Chrysler US the answer to the second question is no; for Ford US the answer is that the profits earned from its successful European subsidiaries will finance the capital expenditure for the US parent company. Whether this dependence is wise is discussed in Chapter 6.

A firm's survival depends on its ability to be competitive and efficient. A comparison of the (after tax) returns on sales provides a valuable insight into the profitability and efficiency of the motor car manufacturers. These are shown in Table 5.3 and provide an object lesson on the importance of economies of scale. In the US, the largest company is operating most profitably, and the smallest operates the least profitably. In Europe the same pattern emerges; GM, Ford and VW are the most profitable (apart from 1974 for Ford). Fiat, although large, is suffering from excess capacity. Daimler-Benz makes its high return from specialist cars and CVs. Renault is government owned and does not necessarily pursue the profit objective. PSA Peugeot-Citroen includes the combined results of three independent companies for the most part. Even for the specialist producers, Daimler-Benz (the largest) out-performs the others and Volvo (the smallest) performs least well. A similar pattern emerges in Japan.

Table 5.3 *After tax return on sales 1973-78 (%)*

	1973	1974	1975	1976	1977	1978
Japan						
Honda	3.1	2.7	1.0	1.3[1]	2.9	4.2
Nissan	4.1	3.3	1.3	3.0	4.2	3.6
Toyo Kogyo	1.8	1.0	*	1.8	1.8	3.8
Toyota	6.6	3.9	3.6	5.8	5.8	5.4
European						
Ford in Europe	3.2	*	1.4	5.1	7.0	7.5
Daimler-Benz	3.9	3.7	4.1	5.2	5.8	5.9
GM (Opel/Vauxhall)	4.0	*	0.4	5.8	4.3	4.8
BMW	5.0	1.4	2.6	3.9	3.7	3.4
VW	2.5	*	0.7	3.6	4.1	4.4
Fiat	0.6	0.7	0	1.7	1.6	1.4
British Leyland	1.7	*	*	1.2	*	*
Renault	0.2	0.1	*	1.4	0.4	0.4
PSA Peugeot-Citroen	1.8	*	*	3.1	2.5	2.6
Volvo	2.8	0.9	0.3	0.6	1.0	1.3
US						
GM (worldwide)	6.7	3.0	3.5	6.2	6.1	5.5
Ford (worldwide)	3.9	1.5	1.3	3.4	4.4	3.7
Chrysler (worldwide)	3.0	*	*	2.7	1.0	*

* indicates a negative return
1. Six months only

Source: Company reports

Management decision areas

The management of the major motor manufacturers have an extremely difficult task. As the firm grows to gain technical economies of scale scale, so the possibility of organizational diseconomies arise. In the difficult situation ahead for these firms, management will take decisions in a number of important areas. These are now discussed to provide the reader with an insight into a managerial viewpoint when considering the mature markets.

Model policy

To design and spend up to $1 billion or more on unique expenditure for a model range, implies that a range which does not sell well can be a severe drain on the financial resources of a firm. Since all the major companies will cover at least four or five segments of the market in the 1980s and the model life is between three to seven years, each firm will introduce some 10 to 30 models during the next decade. A mistake on one model is serious; two mistakes may be disastrous. Any firm can have bad luck in its marketing strategy, consumer surveys, clinic tests, and so on. Current strength is no guarantee of future strength: VW demonstrated this by its rapid change in fortunes, turning a loss into adequate profits by switching from the Beetle to the current model range.

Capacity

Management must plan ahead and decide whether any additional capacity is required. The installation of additional capacity at an existing site will take some two to five years to plan and implement; a greenfield site takes nearer five years. Management, therefore, has correctly to predict demand and, if necessary, expand capacity to cope. A mistake in this decision process is also costly. Extra capacity may provide additional economics of scale but unused extra capacity can be less profitable than a smaller, but fully utilized, capacity.

Having decided to install additional capacity, the next problem is where to install it. Most companies are influenced by a number of standard spatial and geographical factors. Some less usual factors which are currently important in mature markets are given below.

1. Political considerations play an increasingly important role in the location decision, since governments can make or break motor vehicle manufacturers.
2. Local and/or state governments will be eager to attract new capacity to their area, in order to reduce unemployment. Currently in Western Europe, a manufacturer can expect competitive bidding among governments to provide up to 50 per cent of the capital investment and working capital of new plant.
3. The extent to which a market may become closed, if the manufacturer does not generate public goodwill by providing employment, is a classic condition found in Western Europe.
4. The availability of good labour which is willing to undertake repetitive

tasks. Alfa Romeo's Naples factory has always been unprofitable, and some analysts believe that the cause lies in a labour force which is temperamentally unsuitable. Motor companies often tap the trained labour force in areas where iron and steel work have been recently closed.

Production technology

Another central question is the type and style of production technology to be used in a firm. The four types of technology employed in the production of cars are considered below.

1. *Conventional.* The conventional assembly line or conveyor-belt process workers are restricted to the performance of a single relatively simple task, such as spot welding the joints of a car sub-frame, which makes few demands on the worker and can quickly become routine and monotonous. Job satisfaction in assembly line work is low. Workers find it hard to identify their task with the finished product, while employers suffer from a rapid labour turnover and a lowering of standards as the work is performed with little care or concern.

2. *Unit working.* Unit working is an arrangement whereby small groups of workers are involved in problem solving and production work at a number of different stages in the manufacturing process. Demarcation is minimal, thus allowing all members of the group to engage in the tasks that the group as a whole decide upon, with the aim of increasing job satisfaction through stimulating the workers' interest and involvement and by encouraging worker interaction. When problems arise the workers involved are encouraged to discuss them freely and arrive at their own solutions. In theory, unit working could be the answer to the motor manufacturer's prayer: increased worker involvement and enhanced job satisfaction should improve quality and reduce absenteeism. It has been introduced to a limited extent in a number of industries in Sweden where production line methods were previously used. Saab, for example, opened a new engine assembly division in 1971-72 based almost entirely on unit working, while Volvo's Kalmar car assembly plant (opened in 1973-74) has also adopted the unit working approach.

3. *The Robotgate system.* Fiat has developed a system called the Robotgate system. This system involves the use of trolleys (as opposed to the traditional assembly lines) which move automatically over the floor guided by a series of invisible magnetic tracks. The course which trolleys take on the shop floor depends on the computer controlled instructions which they are given. The welding machines can be programmed to sense the particular model on the trolley and the appropriate welds can be made without human

intervention.

4. *Assembly line plus robotic arms.* This system uses the standard assembly line method but has programmable robotic arms to emulate the work of humans. The welding mechanism is positioned at the end of a mechanical arm which is controlled by a microprocessor (which may be linked to a central computer), and the arm probes in and around the body shell making welds at various instructed places.

The conventional system does not work well in the mature markets. Educated workers do not respond well to boring and repetitive tasks. However, the unit working experiment has not succeeded either: productivity is low, absenteeism is high, extra capital equipment is required, and the process is only suitable for low volume work. It appears that even Volvo and Saab have moved away from the unit working system to the last of the four technologies. The third technology is by far the most technically exciting, but in pure financial terms it is too expensive to be competitive. Each trolley is very expensive and unless there is one trolley continually passing through a gate, plant utilization is low. It could be made economically viable but this would require further development work. The fourth technology, which has become standard in Japan, is by far the most economical. In most mature markets, a DCF appraisal of replacing a conventional assembly line with this newer technology system would, in a wide variety of circumstances, be positive.

The advantages of automation are several. First, boredom for the remaining workforce is lessened and the character of the work becomes more skilled and varied. Second, there is greater flexibility of production. Traditionally, each assembly line and supplying transfer lines contain much equipment which is fixed to only one type of vehicle. Each production line is geared to a particular model. In periods of low demand for that model the production line runs at below capacity. If demand is higher for the model than the capacity of the production line, the excess demand cannot be switched to another line because it will not have the appropriate machinery. The new process allows a production line to take several models (with each product simply having a separate programme in the robot's computer). The increased flexibility means that a firm should be able to match patterns of demand more closely than in the past. The third advantage of the new production system is that it will reduce capital expenditure in assembly plants (but not pressing or power train plants) by about 60 to 80 per cent, because it will no longer be necessary radically to alter transfer lines and other fixed equipment which is specifically tied to certain models. The computer controlled equipment (mechanical arms, trolleys, etc) could simply be reprogrammed and, if necessary, adapted.

Labour relations

Labour relations in the motor industry have followed different routes. In general, car workers are well organized and potentially powerful: a stoppage by a small number of workers on an assembly line may halt an entire plant, other plants supplying the first plant, and component manufacturers supplying the car manufacturer. There is good reason to believe that this power is abused in some of the mature markets.

The North American market is dominated by the United Automobile Workers (UAW) Union, an efficient and technically competent organization, employing teams of economists and finance specialists. The UAW has in the past tried to pitch its wage claims for the maximum amount a company and the industry can afford. Only one firm is usually singled out for a strike, and the bargain struck from that confrontation will set the industry norm in what is a legally binding contract. There is some reason to believe that the UAW will adopt a more enlightened and benevolent attitude to industrial relations in firms in trouble (ie Chrysler and AMC).

In Western Europe anarchy does seem to reign: poor work practices, union negotiated overmanning, absenteeism running at 20 per cent plus, wildcat strikes, strikes for political ends, demarcation disputes, anti-modernization disputes, anti-managerial disputes and so on. British Leyland has lost more than 300,000 vehicles, or 40 per cent of its planned output, through industrial relations disputes in a single year. The UK's and Italy's records for labour relations are poor; Spain's is not good, Benelux is mixed, France is mixed (Renault poor, Peugeot-Citroen good), and West Germany is good. Trade unions are usually fragmented across the region and are drawn upon nationalistic lines. Ford's recent experience highlights the fact that labour organizations can also spread international tentacles; trade unions in the UK, Belgium, Spain and Germany are beginning to think of taking concerted action. However, a strike for all the employees in one country is easy to arrange; a strike across national frontiers has proved a much more difficult proposition. Companies whose production facilities are spread across countries in Europe seem to have had a better strike record.

Japan's legendary labour force must be a major asset for the firms producing there. The Japanese worker has a history of discipline and loyalty. Absenteeism and labour turnover rates are low. The unions are, in general, company based and negotiate for hours of work, holidays, fringe benefits and bonuses. In the stagnant climate ahead, it will be interesting to see whether the Japanese worker will become more militant.

Marketing and distribution

One of the areas of management decision must be in the distribution network used by the company. This was especially important when PSA Peugeot-Citroen was formed with three sets of dealer networks (Peugeot, Citroen and Chrysler Europe). British Leyland took the decision to slim its network after its formation in 1968 (see Chapter 7), whereas PSA Peugeot-Citroen is thinking of retaining all the dealers from the three separate groups. One of the most crucial variables in the mature markets will be retail outlets. Why? It can be argued that up to 80 per cent of a change in market share for cars can be statistically explained by the change in the number of retail outlets. For CVs the relationship is less strong but still significant.[1] This partly explains the fall in British Leyland's share of the domestic market. If outlets are lost or cast aside in a merger, they will start to sell another manufacturer's products. On the other hand, to set up a distribution network from scratch is time-consuming and expensive. Retail outlets, in the future, may be cherished by manufacturers and there is a tendency in Western Europe for companies to develop multi-franchises (ie sale of two or more manufacturers' products).

In terms of marketing, the mature manufacturer must be able to offer a range of products. Each model will be offered with a range of engines, and in a number of different standard forms (eg with or without a tailgate, two or four doors, coupe/saloon/estate, etc). Management's task will be to see that there are no gaps in the product range (which may be exploited by competitors) and that each feature in a car is priced and passed on to the customer.[2]

Raising of finance

One vital condition for a company to survive will be to generate sufficient profits to plough back into the company to finance the vast capital expenditures that competition in the 1980s will demand. If the profit budget is insufficient to finance a competitive level of expenditure, external capital must be raised.

Competitors

Management will be keeping a close eye on competitors. Any action taken by another competitor will be carefully scrutinized and analysed. If it is seen as a sensible or profitable course of action, it will probably be followed or countered by action in some other area. This atmosphere of 'what's he doing now' will lead to conditions where knowledge of

1. See Bhaskar, K N *op cit* p 368.
2. Current European marketing attitudes are discussed in Bhaskar, K N *op cit.*

competitors' actions is gained in advance by means of formal or informal actions, and collusion and cartels across international frontiers may develop.

Chapter 6

North America

This chapter treats the USA and Canada as one major producing unit and as a single uniform market. In all significant respects, the Canadian market closely resembles that of the US, but on a smaller scale. The population is smaller and car densities are marginally lower. It is reasonable to assume that future developments in the Canadian market will correspond more or less exactly to trends prevailing in the USA. The Canadian market and industry is dominated by the USA and some of the factual material presented in this chapter is provided for the USA only (as typical of the North American market).

Demand and the distinguishing features of the North American market

Cars

The North American market is the largest and richest in the world (see Table 6.1), shaped by a demand for a standard American car which has evolved over the last 50 years in response to the requirements of an increasingly affluent market.

The North American car was substantially differentiated from its rivals prior to the 1973 oil crisis. In general terms the 'standard' American car was longer (about 230 inches) and wider (80 inches) than its foreign counterpart, with a wheelbase of 124 inches and powered by a large V8 engine coupled to an automatic transmission, giving a 'soft' ride, but disadvantaged by poor instrumentation and unimpressive cornering and braking. As prices rose, the range of optional and standard fittings available increased to the point where US buyers are used to choosing from an array of over 40 options (either standard or to order). Such options include air-conditioning, trip computers, astroroofs, lock-up torque converters on automatic transmissions, power brakes, power seats, power windows, speed regulating devices, white sidewall tyres and so on.

This past commitment to a specific type and size of car (even allowing for variations in design and specification from one model to the next) was a peculiarly North American phenomenon, reflecting the particular requirements of the US motorist and his environment.

Table 6.1 *The North American market*

Population (m) 1976		
US	215	
Canada	23	
Total	238	

GNP per capita in 1976 (US $)		
US	6996	
Canada	7341	

Vehicle Parc in 1977 (m)		
	Cars	*CVs*
US	110	28
Canada	9	2
Total	119	30

Densities		
People per vehicle		
US	2.0	8.0
Canada	2.5	11.5
Vehicles per 1000 people		
US	500	125
Canada	400	87

New Registrations (m)		
1973 US	11.35	3.03
Canada	0.95	0.24
Total	12.3	3.27
1977 US	10.75	3.47
Canada	0.95	0.33
Total	11.7	3.8

Production (m)		
1973 US	9.7	3.0
Canada	1.2	0.4
Total	10.9	3.4
1977 US	9.3	3.4
Canada	1.2	0.6
Total	10.5	4.0

Handling and manoeuvrability, for example, are low on the list of priorities in a country where cars are required to do little more than travel in more or less straight lines across a network of well-surfaced motorways. Speed limits, overall, are low and until recently petrol was relatively inexpensive. Low density housing developments, characteristic of urban areas in the USA, provide ample accommodation for a larger car. The American 'standard' car was ideally suited, in marketing terms at least, to the needs of the US motorist and to the motoring conditions in which he could expect to operate. Although domestically produced 'compact' or 'sub-compact' cars enjoyed a brief (if spectacular) success, they were marketed more or less as an afterthought, a slightly frivolous addition to the market, rather than a serious challenge to the hegemony of the standard vehicle.

GOVERNMENT REGULATIONS

The US government has set fuel consumption targets of 21 mpg by 1980, rising steadily to 27.5 mpg by 1985. Manufacturers are compelled to comply with these limits which are assessed under a corporate average fuel economy programme (CAFE). In some respects, these fuel consumption targets co-exist rather awkwardly with the more controversial emission control measures. In 1977 permitted levels were 1.5 HC/ 15 CO/ 2.0 NOx and the government has requested that by 1985 these should be reduced to 0.41 HC/ 3.4 CO/ 0.4 NOx, although there is every chance that this target will either be relaxed or postponed. Debate centres on the stipulated reduction in NOx, which US manufacturers claim would be almost impossible to achieve. In addition, noise abatement and safety measures have been extensively revised and enforced with greater stringency in recent years. Safety regulations already demand conformity to certain standards (ie measures to protect the driver from steering column injuries in the event of a collision) and more radical safety proposals are the subject of continuing debate, as in the case of measures to improve occupant crash protection and the imposition of passive restraint standards such as the air bag. Whether or not these particular measures are enforced, there is little doubt that US manufacturers will in future be confronted with an increasing maze of regulations, controls, and statutory safety requirements.

In the 1980s the main regulations will be imposed by the need for fuel economy (the CAFE programme). To achieve the CAFE targets, which impose an average fuel economy for all a manufacturer's cars (starting with 18 mpg in 1978), the US car will have to undergo a radical alteration A drastic reduction in size, front-wheel drive, and the use of lightweight materials: aluminium, magnesium, plastics, high elastic limit steel and other compound materials. To achieve a more efficient combustion and ignition control, both carburization and ignition will be computerized.

MARKET SEGMENTS

With the advent of multiple car ownership, in the period following World War II, 'up-market' trends were counterbalanced by an unanticipated growth in demand for a lower priced small or popular car for use as a second car by families already owning a larger standard model (about 33 per cent of all households own more than one car). In acquiring a second car, consumers deviated from the standard car norm, choosing a vehicle geared to specific needs (such as non-commuter local travel from home to shops and schools) and perhaps even adapted to specialist recreational uses for which the standard car no longer seemed the most appropriate choice. This change in the pattern of demand can be most clearly seen in Table 6.2; the group 2 vehicles (incorporating minibuses, lightweight trucks and similar models) were one of the few market segments to register a consistent growth in demand in the otherwise depressed period following the 1973 oil crisis.

Table 6.2 *US truck sales by gross vehicle weight 1972-78*

| Total sales in '000s | Gross vehicle weight | | | | | | | | Total |
	Group 1 <6000 lbs	Group 2 6001-10,000 lbs	Group 3 10,001-14,000 lbs	Group 4 14,001-16,000 lbs	Group 5 16,001-19,500 lbs	Group 6 19,501-26,000 lbs	Group 7 26,001-33,000 lbs	Group 8 >33,001 lbs	
1972	1532	562	58	11	26	172	33	121	2514
1973	1843	717	48	2	18	218	39	145	3029
1974	1616	640	22	3	12	196	29	139	2657
1975	1204	896	23	1	9	156	23	85	2397
1976	1285	1440	51	14	7	149	21	92	3058
1977	1218	1903	61	12	6	153	27	129	3509
1978	1143	1408	55	15	3	147	39	153	3963

Source: *Automobile News*

Although the standard car accounted for most of the car sales in the US, the US market has been showing signs of greater diversification. In the 1950s, standard car (defined as a wheelbase of over 118 inches) sales accounted for over 70 per cent of the market, but since then there has been a proliferation of sub-compacts (less than 100 inch wheelbase), compacts (with a wheelbase between 100-111 inches), intermediates (marginally smaller than the standard car, with a 112-17 inch wheelbase) and the luxury and speciality market (which includes the Cadillac and the Chevrolet Corvette). Figure 6.1 shows the effect of this diversification on sales and summarizes the market share acquired by newer, non-standard models in recent years. Although the so-called standard car is still an important part of the US market, it is no longer the only model of any significance. The US market is developing a more 'European' concept of model diversity and car market segments. Figure 6.1 illustrates the steady growth in the small-car market and the gradual erosion of the overall demand for the standard car.

The impact of the government regulations and the 1979 oil crisis is

Figure 6.1 *US automobile sales by size class (% excluding imports)*

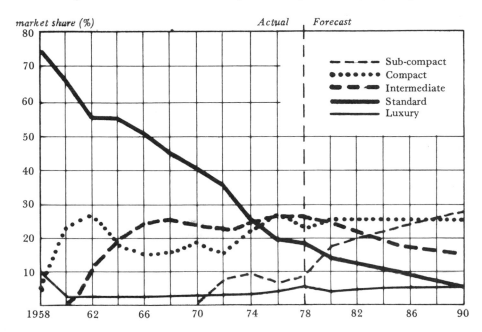

forcing manufacturers to reduce their cars in size as well as placing pressure on consumers to opt for a smaller vehicle. In fact the traditional market classes of sub-compact, compact, intermediate, standard and luxury may have little relevance to the future. Some of the down-sized cars of one market segment may be smaller than the old versions of smaller segments. At the moment large European cars such as the Jaguar and Mercedes 'S' class are classified as compacts. In the analysis of future car segments it has been assumed that the compact and sub-compact segments will still cover the major European car sizes. Although uniformity across the mature car markets will occur, the North American market will retain a market segment of larger cars partly through habit and partly through nostalgia (eg the large cars will be rolled out on official state business).

MATURITY OF THE MARKET

With over 120 million vehicles on the road, the North American market is the most mature of the major car markets, a fact which to a large extent determines the nature of demand. New car demand (which would enlarge the car parc or quite simply increase the number of cars on the road), accounts for only a small proportion of total annual sales of new vehicles. Replacement demand, however, currently running at a level of between 6 and 9 million cars per year, represents the most important single sector of the market. Might this account for the disconcerting variations in the level of demand which are unquestionably a feature of the market? (see Figure 5.1). A number of economists (such as Milton Friedman) argue that fluctuations of the sort to be observed in the US car market are primarily the result of economic mismanagement in general and money mismanagement in particular, an inept and potentially disastrous market facsimile of the economic excesses of the 1930s. Few economists would take exception to the theory as it applies to the events of the earlier decade, but critics contend that market conditions have altered radically in the intervening years and that the analogy is contentious and perhaps meaningless.

As an alternative explanation it has been suggested that the vacillations in demand currently affecting the motor industry can only be understood in terms of the character of a market in which replacement demand predominates. As the market matures, the element of replacement demand increases. A market dependent on replacement to this extent is peculiarly vulnerable to a pattern of fluctuating demand, as the demand itself is inherently unstable. 'Replacement decisions' (to acquire a new vehicle as a replacement for an existing one) can in most cases be conveniently postponed should consumers decide that replacement costs are too high. A number of other factors, economic conditions in general, availability of credit, etc, could effectively postpone or defer the decision. Perceptible but unforeseeable variations are therefore to be expected.

The American consumer will be subjected to two new influences. First, the government will dictate to the consumer what he can buy through the CAFE programme. Since the pressure is on the manufacturer, his pricing policy must be such as to encourage purchase of the economy model. As James Schlesinger, as US energy secretary, said: 'American drivers think that the Declaration of Independence gives them the right to consume 60 per cent of the world's gasoline.' To increase car running costs is unpopular but to deny the use of a car totally would be certain death. Future US governments have their hands tied. Second, the price of oil in real terms must increase. As energy becomes more scarce, international pressures of supply and demand will increase the real price. US governments will be unable and unwilling to protect the US consumer from the impact of these price increases. This will force the US consumer to move towards a smaller car.

The market segment that will be most popular will be the one which spans the five basic car segments of the European market (sub-compact and compact). Intermediate and standard cars will be produced but they will become much more of a speciality purchase. These trends are shown in Figure 6.1. Thus the trend will be to smaller cars but the car manufacturers will also move the market segments downwards. Hence the new GM X-body (Chevrolet Citation) is much smaller than previous compacts. This down-sizing of the market segments will still not be able to stop the fall off in the intermediate and standard segments.

THE FUTURE

Even taking a pessimistic view, it must be recognized that there are still markets to be tapped in the US. Greater product diversification should stimulate demand in different segments of the market judging by the potential growth in demand for recreational vehicles. But changing consumer tastes will be reflected in a more critical approach to cars. The notion of 'stylistic obsolescence' will be considered insufficient reason for abandoning one car in favour of another and, much longer model runs will become a permanent feature of the US market. In other respects, much more will be demanded by way of technological improvement, to make motoring easier and more comfortable (which might involve the introduction of an auto-pilot mechanism of some sort), and to simplify servicing and maintenance requirements in an effort to combat the effect of inevitable price rises. Existing model ranges will be radically revised to accommodate greater diversification of demand, and there may be far greater emphasis on the importance of engineering innovation, particularly in the import sector. VW, for example, is already basing its marketing strategy on the concept of engineering excellence, and it is to be expected that the high reputation for quality engineering already enjoyed by import models will encourage higher levels of technology throughout the US industry.

Commercial vehicles

Two features of the commercial vehicle market in North America differentiate it markedly from the private vehicle sector. In manufacturing terms, it is clearly less concentrated. Whereas the bulk of car production in the USA is accounted for by the big three, CV production is spread across the CV subsidiaries of large engineering concerns, CV output from the large car producers, and specialist independent producers, a feature common to most of the 'mature' producers. Although the CV divisions of Ford, GM and Chrysler are clearly the largest of the CV manufacturers, the independent producers account for a not insignificant 20 per cent of the market. Second, unlike the private car sector, the CV market has shown steady growth in recent years (see Table 6.3). This is in part due to the fact that until the 1960s American operators favoured the high-speed petrol engined vehicles rather than the diesel engined CVs more widely used in other CV markets. Petrol was relatively inexpensive (which tended to offset the high petrol consumption of the US vehicles), and higher speeds produced greater mileages per day and

Table 6.3 *US new truck registrations*

	Total ('000s)	4 x 4 Vehicles ('000s)	Recreational vehicles ('000s)
1961	919	147	63
1962	1069	120	80
1963	1244	137	119
1964	1362	137	151
1965	1529	146	193
1966	1610	151	220
1967	1518	154	244
1968	1776	162	483
1969	1889	175	514
1970	1790	162	472
1971	1993	225	549
1972	2514	297	748
1973	3029	404	753
1974	2657	481	529
1975	2397	480	552
1976	3058	674	656
1977	3509	824	745
1978	3963	973	589

Source: *Automotive News*

hence greater labour productivity, at a premium when labour costs were high. Improvements in diesel engine design and the need to control fuel costs as petrol prices rose worked to the relative disadvantage of petrol engined CVs, but has clearly enhanced the growth potential in the heavy and medium weight sectors for a diesel engined alternative.

At the heaviest end of the CV market, sales are substantial and increasing, as large trucks have become one of the main forms of inland transport. The market is, however, volatile. Patterns of demand are changing significantly at the other end of the scale, and demand for lightweight CVs acquired for non-commercial purposes (broadly defined as recreational/pleasure uses) is growing rapidly. This we have already alluded to in an earlier consideration of the private vehicle market. Given the extent of their impact on CV sales, however, their importance should not be underestimated. The total US market for CVs in 1978 exceeded the previous 1973 peak by only some one million vehicles. The market is heavily distorted by the demand for recreational vehicles. The medium and heavyweight segments of the market amount to less than 0.5 million vehicles. In Europe, growth in the heavy sector of the market stimulated demand for medium and heavy trucks, and by comparison the heavy end of the US market is not vast. Since the highway network in the US has been well developed for some time, demand for heavy vehicles has been spread over a longer period. Although demand is modest, the heavy CV parc is large. New registrations are mainly replacement, although there may be some further growth if business is transferred from the ailing US rail companies.

CV demand has experienced similar vacillations to that of the car market (see Figure 5.2). Although the market still has potential for further growth in *new* demand, successive oil crises may have choked off this demand. A downward trend in the 1950s (explained in part by the successful introduction of heavier trucks with haulage capacities frequently in excess of immediate needs), was followed by a period of slow growth accelerating in the 1960s. The 'non-commercial' demand for recreational and lightweight utility vehicles began in the late 1960s and accelerated in the early 1970s in spite of an overall downturn in car demand, and there is no reason to suppose that demand in that sector has peaked. There has been a perceptible shift in all of the CV weight categories away from all-purpose utility vehicles and towards more 'use-specific' vehicles (both lorries and buses), catering for the particular needs of a wide range of specialist submarkets. These vary from vehicles designed for specific operations in the building and construction trades, in mining or for indoor warehouse use, through to armoured trucks and cars and high-speed inter-city buses covering a vast range of specialized options.

The manufacturers

Although import penetration of the US market is rising, the bulk of car production is accounted for by the domestic output of GM, Chrysler and Ford with three relatively minor exceptions, American Motors (AMC) (which manufactures the Rambler), Checker (which concentrates on producing taxis) and VW. In all other respects, the big three dominate the market – a singular achievement.

At the turn of the century, there were probably about twelve viable manufacturers in operation. This number had risen to more than 80 by the 1920s, but in the 1930s fell to fewer than 30. By 1950 only 13 firms were still functioning and, in the first years of the decade, the last of the remaining four small independent producers disappeared. Nash and Hudson merged to form AMC (1954) and Studebaker and Packard also joined forces (see Figure 6.2).

Cars

Soon after its formation, AMC tried to increase its market share by launching the compact car. Hopes of monopolizing trade in that particular corner of the market soon vanished. Other US firms were quick to market their own compact models, hoping to exploit the potential of unfamiliar territory and uneasily aware of the success of smaller imported cars, arriving for the first time in significant numbers.

Figure 6.2 *Key mergers and acquisitions of the*
US motor vehicle manufacturers

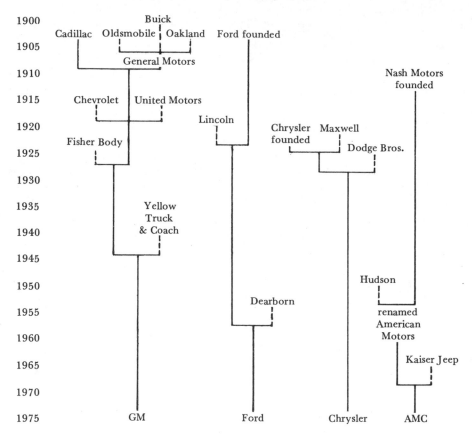

Source: *The World Automotive Industry to 1995* Business International

In some respects, this first excursion into 'small car' country was an aberration, but two points of interest invited comment: first, it offered a stay of execution for AMC and Studebaker Packard, neither of whom could hope to compete successfully in the mainstream market; and, second, when the big three launched their own compact models (backed with massive marketing campaigns), the drop in demand for imported cars was sudden and dramatic, and only VW's idiosyncratic offering survived unharmed.

By the late 1960s, however, all of the big three compact models had been transformed, either enlarged and upgraded to an intermediate size, or extensively restyled, as was the case with the Mustang. Lacking the necessary resources in both volume output and capital to finance the annual facelifts indulged in by the larger firms, the two smaller firms were forced out of the race. Studebakers' market collapsed and AMC declined. Faced with no real competition, the larger standard car consolidated its share of the US market, and any residual enthusiasms for a smaller mass market car vanished. In 1970, however, smaller cars were being imported at the rate of over one million a year and rising, a potentially damaging incursion into a previously safe market. The US producers could not ignore the problem, and this time it was far more serious. Their response was immediate and Ford's Maverick was the first of the new generation of compacts.

MARKET SHARES

Throughout the 1950s and 1960s, GM's market share remained fairly steady at between 40 and 50 per cent of the total market. The market shares of the major manufacturers for cars are shown in Table 6.4.

Table 6.4 *US market shares for cars (%)**

	AMC	Chrysler	Ford	GM	Imports (including VW)	Japanese imports	VW
1960	8.5	14.4	27.3	42.3	7.5	—	—
1961	7.5	11.6	29.2	45.4	6.3	—	—
1962	7.6	9.3	26.6	51.6	4.9	—	—
1963	6.7	12.3	25.2	50.9	4.9	—	—
1964	5.3	12.9	25.2	51.2	5.4	—	—
1965	4.1	15.3	26.2	48.7	5.7	—	—
1966	3.1	15.6	26.3	48.4	6.6	—	—
1967	2.7	15.7	25.2	48.7	7.7	—	—
1968	3.0	17.0	22.0	48.7	9.3	—	—
1969	2.7	15.2	24.3	48.0	9.8	—	—
1970	2.7	15.2	24.1	46.0	13.2	3.0	7.2
1971	2.8	15.4	26.2	40.4	17.2	5.7	5.4
1972	2.8	14.4	25.2	45.4	14.1	6.0	4.5
1973	3.2	14.3	24.5	44.7	15.2	6.7	4.2
1974	4.0	13.9	25.1	43.8	15.1	6.9	3.8
1975	3.6	12.6	24.1	42.6	19.2	9.9	3.2
1976	2.7	13.3	23.8	46.9	14.4	9.2	2.1
1977	1.7	11.0	22.7	46.4	18.3	12.1	2.4
1978	1.4	10.2	22.9	47.7	17.8	12.0	2.3
1980†	1.5	11.0	23.0	50.0	20.0	12.0	3.0
1985†	1.5	9-11	22-24	40-47	20-27	13.0	2-4
1990†	1.5	8-11	21-25	35-47	20-34	10.0	2-4

* In volume terms

† Representative forecasts

Source: Automotive News and author's estimates

In the 1920s and 1930s Ford was the market leader but the company was slow to adapt and lost ground (and a large section of the market) to the more flexible strategy of GM. Ford and Chrysler both remained highly competitive throughout the 1930s although neither could wrest the market lead from GM in that period. In the 1950s however, Chrysler went into a relative decline, enabling both Ford and GM to consolidate their respective positions in terms of market penetration. By the 1960s GM's share was established at between 45 and 50 per cent, reaching the upper limit when either Ford or Chrysler produced an unsuccessful range. Relative market shares altered once again as, experiencing marketing and financial difficulties, Chrysler's share of the US market fell to 12 per cent in 1959 and to less than 10 per cent in 1962. Ford, which suffered some losses in 1958-60 with the unsuccessful Edsel range, had recovered its position by 1962. GM's lead remained firm at 50 per cent. In the period 1962-67, however, the balance changed once more as Chrysler recovered dramatically, capitalizing on its as yet untarnished reputation for reliability and superior engineering, and enlarging its market share once again to 18 per cent. In the face of renewed competition, GM was nevertheless able to retain a market share in excess of 45 per cent in 1960-70. These figures, however, convey only the total market picture. When further broken down for large and small car segments, they reveal a number of interesting variations in performance and suggest several potential weaknesses.

In 1962-70 both Ford and Chrysler performed well in the lower price ranges, together accounting for 55 per cent of total sales and output. In the middle and upper ranges, however, GM accounted for a disproportionately large share of sales, gaining 80 per cent of the total. This heavy bias towards the top end of the range proved something of a liability in the early 1970s, as the market shifted to smaller cars. The consequences were more serious for GM than for its principal competitors, although a continued concentration in the standard and intermediate ranges suggested that GM were slow to revise model policy in the light of these events. Ford's share has been stable at 20 to 25 per cent, a good performance reflecting the success of Ford's marketing policies and, until recently, an increased sensitivity to changing consumer tastes. GM's market share declined in the mid-1970s, but has since improved markedly and seems set to return to 50 per cent. Ford, owing to a mistake in its marketing strategy (discussed below), held steadily to 25 per cent in the early 1970s but has declined in recent years. Chrysler's fortunes, however, appear to have deteriorated once more. Financial difficulties have made it impossible for the company to compete in the potentially highly profitable sub-compact market, and a half-completed factory has been sold off to VW. Conversely, AMC benefited from the revival of interest in smaller cars in the mid-1970s. However, once the US big three had reacted to these changes, albeit half-heartedly, and the Japanese import machine began to work, AMC's market share began to drop dramatically and has fallen beyond the point of redemption.

Recent events have shown that GM can produce a European type product, the front wheel drive X-body (eg Chevrolet Citation/Oldsmobile Omega). Consequently its market share is now climbing towards the magic 50 per cent once again. But GM's strengths could also be weaknesses; in boom periods, its position at the top of the larger car market would greatly improve company performance, but in periods of slump, despite the existence of a complete GM model range, it might experience an even greater reduction in its market share. Ford's has been declining and heading for 20 per cent (though now seems stuck around 22 per cent). Chrysler's share is again 10 per cent and the company may become a permanent pensioner. AMC's survival depends on Renault. Meanwhile attention is focused on whether VW, now it has become a small-scale indigenous assembler of cars, can re-establish its market share at its former level — a doubtful proposition. Japanese imports are around 12 per cent and this may be near their politically safe maximum limit.

MARKETING STRATEGIES AND MODEL POLICY

A distinctive feature of the US market is the widespread use of the concept of badge engineering whereby several identical models, differentiated only in terms of minor styling details, can be marketed under separate names. Both Ford and Chrysler have three brand names, reserving one for more expensive models and using the remaining two to market 'parallel' models. GM have a range of five brand names in all, one of which is reserved for a luxury model. The rest are spread throughout the various market segments. A complete list of 1979-80 models is supplied in Table 6.5.

Of the big three only Chrysler has had no sub-compact, but this is due to change shortly. GM, on the other hand, offers a choice of no fewer than six models in the compact range. GM also has six models in the intermediate range, which is also well covered by the other major producers. AMC produces nothing in the standard range, and GM is poorly represented in the low quality standard class, with better coverage in the high quality standard segment. Chrysler's Imperial, previously their only luxury car, is no longer manufactured. And in the remaining speciality car segment GM offers the Corvette, allegedly a sports car.

Of the major producers, Ford's marketing strategy could have been described as the most lucid, although recent strategy has been totally misjudged. The company is split into three divisions: Ford, Lincoln and Mercury. The Lincoln division is in direct competition with GM's Cadillac. Ford and Mercury produce more or less identical models, with

Table 6.5 *Model line-up of US manufacturers (1979)*

	Sub-compact	Compact	Intermediate	Standard	Luxury
AMC	AMX Spirit	Concord Pacer			
Chrysler Dodge	Omni	Aspen	Diplomat Magnum	St Regis	
Plymouth	Horizon	Volare			
Chrysler			LeBaron Cordoba	Newport New Yorker	
Ford Ford	Pinto	Mustang Fairmont Granada	LTD II Thunderbird	LTD	
Mercury	Bobcat	Capri Zephyr Monarch	Cougar XR7	Mercury	
Lincoln				Versailles Continental Mark V	
GM Buick	Skyhawk	Skylark	Century Regal	LeSabre Electra	Riviera
Chevrolet	Chevette Monza	Camaro Citation	Malibu Monte Carlo	Chevrolet	Corvette
Oldsmobile	Starfire	Omega	Cutlass	Delta 88, 98	Toronado
Pontiac	Sunbird	Firebird Phoenix	Le Mans Grand Prix	Pontiac	
Cadillac					Seville Eldorado de Ville Fleetwood
VW	Rabbit (Golf)				

an up-market emphasis on the Mercury range. The smallest in the range is a US equivalent of the ultra-compact Fiesta. Ford has recently been losing market share and this can be attributed to their model and overall strategy. Ford's strategy has been wrong for several reasons. It seems that the American management was unwilling to follow the successful strategy adopted by the company's apparently more astute European management. Front-wheel drive cars are being introduced during the 1980s, and there are no new power trains yet dedicated to producing the type of fuel-efficient performance now demanded by the US customer. For example one would have expected the new US Mustang/Capri to have had a new power train rather than modifying existing products. Worse still the model range may be too dense in conventional compact cars (eg the Mustang, Fairmont and Granada) rather than in down-sized compact cars. However, on the credit side, in 1977-78 Ford's production in the US was running at its highest levels since 1965.

Chrysler, who have not enjoyed a spectacular success in marketing in recent years, have based their policy on three brand names: Chrysler, Dodge and Plymouth, with the Chrysler division concentrating on models in the high standard and sporting coupe segments, and Dodge and Plymouth, following the pattern of the Ford/Mercury parallel operation, producing virtually identical ranges in the compact and sub-compact ranges. To cover these ranges Chrysler imported products from their European subsidiaries and from their Japanese associate, Mitsubishi. This reliance on non-US products to bolster the bottom end of Chrysler's range has contributed to their current problems. Chrysler US now has a sub-compact which was developed for the European market (the Omni-Horizon). Since Peugeot-Citroen purchased its European subsidiary, Chrysler US can no longer spread development costs over a greater volume.

The marketing strategy governing GM's five divisions — Buick, Chevrolet, Oldsmobile, Pontiac and Cadillac — suggests a rather less logical approach, but one that aims for higher levels of market penetration. Although Cadillac is clearly aimed at the luxury market, Chevrolet output is apparently split between models intended for the lower end of the standard segment and a strong 'brand' identification with 'sportier' models (such as the Corvette). The traditional images associated with the other badge names have been modified by the new range of models. Oldsmobile was rather taken by surprise with the runaway success of its intermediate 'Cutlass' in the latter part of the 1970s. Pontiac's model range fell midway between the cheaper sports models more closely identified with the Chevrolet range, and the heavyweight Oldsmobile standard range. Evidently, each of the four non-luxury GM divisions (excluding Cadillac) produces a model spread covering most of the major marketing categories, launching more or less identical models in direct competition with each other and with the other major producers. Though slow to move, the giant GM has now flexed its muscles and has responded to the worldwide challenge facing the company. GM now appears to be the only indigenous manufacturer which is successfully producing smaller, purpose-built energy-saving cars with adequate performance and specification.

COMMONALITY OF COMPONENTS AND ECONOMIES OF SCALE

Many of the models within each range are based on common components to a greater or lesser extent, enabling all three of the major manufacturers to exploit the possibilities of vast economies of scale, basing a proliferation of models on a standard body shape often with virtually interchangeable body panels. All three producers have geared production to take full advantage of this commonality. In fact, this rather understates the position, as interchangeability can be exploited not only within categories but also between them.

Superimposed on this desire to maximize economies of scale within the USA, is the desire to obtain maximum economies of scale throughout the world. Ford's small car, the Fiesta, will be produced both in the USA (with some modifications) and Europe. GM, although slow to meet European standardizations has now set the lead by designing its cars as worldwide models. GM's philosophy is to produce a worldwide concept design which individual countries can tailor to their individual needs. An example of this is the 'T' car which is marketed as the Chevette in the US, Opel Kadett in Germany, Chevette in the UK and Isuzu in Japan. Although this car is to be replaced by a more modern front-wheel design, it illustrates GM's approach.

What of Ford? Apart from the Fiesta, the replacement Escort of Ford Europe (codenamed Erika) will also oust the Pinto. However this raises something of a dilemma for Toyo Kogyo, which is planning its own model in this segment (the P221). Again in the compact segment the US design centres are busy reworking the Fairmont/Zephyr range, Toyo Kogyo is planning a replacement to the Montrose, and Ford Europe is planning a more modern equivalent (front-wheel drive) Taunus/Cortina for the early 1980s. A similar duplication of effort occurs in the next market segment: US, European and Japanese design centres are planning replacements for the Granada/Monarch, European Granada (a down-sized version of the US product) and 929/Cosmo respectively. However, a car for the segment below the Fiesta will be produced on a worldwide scale. Ford no doubt will have to take some painful steps to cut down this duplication. It is not obvious that the US design centres will win through since they do not have a good record for producing acceptable worldwide cars.

Chrysler can no longer achieve large economies of scale in the smaller market segment since much of its capacity has been sold off to generate finance. AMC's link-up with Renault will not yield immediate benefits (although some economies will be achieved in the medium term), and VW has just ventured into its first US assembly facility.

PRODUCTION

Car production figures for North America are shown in Figure 6.3. Despite record imports GM achieved its most consistently high production during 1976-78. Ford achieved a production volume similar to that of 1972-73. Ford and GM were slightly stretched because of the resurgence of demand, particularly in the RV sector. Nevertheless an analysis of the individual US and Canadian capacities indicates that neither Ford nor GM were working at quite full capacity in all plants in 1977-78.

Figure 6.3 *North American car production*
by manufacturer (millions of cars)

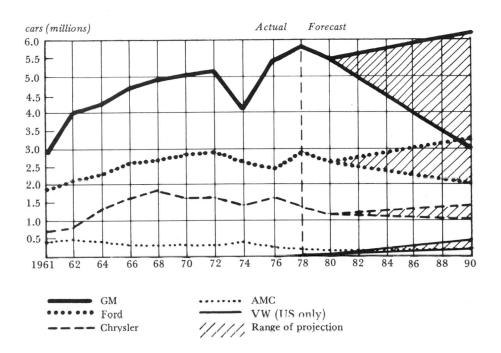

Commercial vehicles

Unlike the car industry the CV industry is characterized by a much larger number of producers at the heaviest end of the market. There are a number of smaller US manufacturers such as Brockway, Diamond Reo, FWD, Kenworth, Mack, Peterbilt and White, all of which have a production capability of 30,000 or less, mainly concentrated at the heavier end of the CV market. International Harvester has an appreciable top-end range but also produces a lighter CV range. In the lightest end of the market GM, with Chevrolet and GMC (Truck and Coach Division), are market leaders. Ford, Chrysler (Dodge and Plymouth) and AMC (with its Jeep range of vehicles) all produce significant numbers, and GM also produces a medium to heavy range of vehicles.

The most surprising feature is the dominance of the smaller and lighter end of the market by the US big three. AMC has a safe marketing niche with its Jeep. International Harvester's presence in this sphere is also rather surprising. In the company's links with European countries

(Seddon-Atkinson in the UK and DAF in the Netherlands) it has tended to concentrate on the top end of the market, and its strength in the USA has also been the medium and heavy market sectors. In 1974, International Harvester produced more heavy CV vehicles than Ford and GM combined, but this is less startling than it appears and there are 10 other significant companies (eg Mack, White etc) which together produce more than International Harvester, and a number of other smaller companies (Divco, Hendrickson, Oshkosh, etc). Although there are fewer economies of scale at the top end of the CV industry it is curious that the CV industry is so much less concentrated than the car industry. The individual tailoring needed to meet the special requirements of customers might explain this phenomenon. There are also fewer economies of scale to be gained in truck manufacture, as many of the components are bought from component manufacturers and the product's potential audience is much smaller.

The US market has relied far less heavily on imports in the supply of its domestic CV market. A combination of factors has helped to protect the US market. First, it is less easy to transport heavier vehicles across oceans. Second, despite having an extremely fragmented heavy section of the industry, the incomparable highway network protects the US market. Third, the USA has always been, hitherto, a pacesetter with both the move towards large trucks and, at the other extreme, the lightweight recreational vehicle.

Market shares are shown in Table 6.6. It must be remembered that rapid growth in the RV market distorts the shares for those manufacturers with no RV product. Chrysler and AMC have done well in the RV and four-wheel drive areas respectively. Ford and GM have maintained their combined share around 70 to 75 per cent, with GM taking some 40 per cent of the market.

By the 1990s import penetration will inevitably increase as the mature market becomes more uniform. In the early 1980s this will take the form of increased Japanese pick-up and more sales by European producers, which will take an increasing share of the medium to heavy truck segments. Whether International Harvester (together with its European subsidiaries) will be able to hold its own is debatable. The European importers which have been most successful are Mercedes-Benz, Magirus-Deutz and Volvo.

PRODUCTION

Table 6.7 shows CV production by manufacturer. While GM and Ford have been growing steadily, Chrysler's growth has been phenomenal, which made the collapse of the CV and RV markets in 1978 and its affect on the company all the more disappointing. AMC's production is entirely in the four-wheel drive area, while White, Mack and International Harvester are specialized CV producers. It is interesting to note

Table 6.6 *US market shares for CVs (%)*

	GM	Ford	Chrysler	AMC	International Harvester	Mack	White
1965	44.9	31.2	7.6	2.8	9.7	0.9	1.2
1966	43.5	32.4	7.5	2.7	9.7	0.9	1.3
1967	43.9	32.6	6.7	2.6	9.9	0.9	1.2
1968	42.8	35.2	7.8	2.2	7.9	0.8	1.1
1969	42.9	36.0	6.9	1.9	7.3	0.8	1.1
1970	38.2	37.2	7.7	1.9	8.0	1.0	1.0
1971	39.7	35.2	8.0	1.8	7.9	0.8	0.9
1972	38.9	34.2	10.7	2.0	7.5	0.8	0.8
1973	39.8	32.9	10.7	2.3	6.6	0.8	0.9
1974	39.3	32.6	11.0	3.7	6.1	0.9	1.0
1975	41.1	31.2	11.8	3.6	4.6	0.6	0.6
1976	42.8	31.0	13.1	3.5	3.3	0.5	0.5
1977	40.3	32.4	13.2	3.6	3.1	0.7	0.6
1978	40.5	33.2	11.7	4.1	2.9	0.7	0.6
1980*	40.0	33.0	10.0	2.8	5.0	1.0	0.9
1990*	38.0	32.0	8.0	2.5	3-6	1-3	1-3

* Representative forecasts

Source: Automotive News

Table 6.7 *North American CV production by manufacturer ('000s)*

	GM	Ford	Chrysler	AMC	International Harvester	Mack	White
1961	447	356	71	124	154	19	9
1962	525	401	102	86	157	26	14
1963	628	458	121	110	180	28	16
1964	682	496	149	121	179	27	14
1965	825	607	160	109	185	27	20
1966	818	651	170	103	183	33	20
1967	755	570	159	119	182	26	18
1968	925	802	191	121	159	31	20
1969	941	834	181	95	173	33	25
1970	1034	952	342	108	227	24	28
1971	1032	787	222	85	198	22	20
1972	1071	964	352	108	228	25	28
1973	1399	1114	401	132	228	32	34
1974	1254	1053	387	135	194	32	36
1975	1638	849	345	135	117	13.5	29
1976	1526	1050	526	154	127	22	25
1977	1522	1367	581	187	131	27	34
1978	1798	1516	582	218	141	19	37
1980*	1000	700	250	130	150	20	30
1990*	800- 1400	600- 1000	200- 300	100- 150	100- 200	20	30

* Representative forecasts

that heavy CV production, as represented by these three companies, was severely affected by the 1973 oil crisis and had still not recovered at the time of the 1978-79 oil crisis. Both International Harvester and White had production figures below their 1967 levels. Both Mack and White wish to improve their range which is entirely in the heaviest market segment; Mack is importing Renault products in the medium truck segment, and White is negotiating with MAN to do exactly the same. Hence the potential increase of market shares shown in Table 6.6.

Corporate strategy

Thus far we have characterized the US market as a mature market confronted with unfamiliar pressures and highly volatile shifts in the pattern of demand which affected the whole of the industry and made a fundamental reappraisal of strategy a matter of urgent concern for all involved. For 30 years, the market balance has been in favour of the market leader, GM, but its dominance no longer seems assured. GM's corporate strategy, once so successful, was apparently unable to respond to the challenges and international pressures facing the US manufacturers. However, the latest range of models by GM and its attempt to produce seven basic worldwide models cannot be faulted. Whether GM will be able to continue its dominance is a thorny question. GM has never been able to sustain its periods of responsiveness. Its US design centres seem to fall into a malaise, but now that its vehicle designs are produced by international centres this may not happen. The company has also tried to establish a firmer control over its worldwide subsidiaries.

How, and why, has GM's policy failed in the past? To answer that question is also to arrive at a fuller understanding of the complexities of the US industry and the market within which it operates. GM's model range spreads across the market, with a blanket coverage in nearly all segments, but with a much heavier concentration on the larger standard models at the top end of the scale. 'Style' leadership, a corporate priority in achieving maximum market penetration, is reinforced by annual design revisions ('style updates') and major model changes every three years, launched to the accompaniment of a barrage of publicity. Customers are persuaded to 'trade up' from lower price ranges to higher, and tight control is imposed on the dealer network through exclusive franchise arrangements. Manufacturing costs are regulated (and minimized) by exploiting all possible economies of scale and by vertical integration, with a strong emphasis on interchangeability of components ('inter-model commonality'). The rate of technological change has been slow and carefully controlled, to secure a maximum economic life from major plant investments.

In common with Chrysler and Ford, GM has used economies of scale to confer slight price advantages, minimizing profits on the most competitive models and relying on the sale of optional extras or the much more lucrative trade in luxury models to claw back higher profits. When applied to sales of a standard car, the formula is highly profitable. Small car production, however, presents different cost problems, and GM have been slow to find a solution. The difficulty centres on the fact that the cost of final assembly work represents a fixed cost per unit which remains constant regardless of size. In other words, small cars are, in relative terms, more costly to produce because of the higher percentage labour content, which is particularly important in an area with generally high labour costs. At the top end of the market GM enjoys a virtual monopoly with most of the benefits of near-monopoly pricing. But to market a small car, GM must compete at low price levels (and possibly with a price disadvantage) against aggressive and efficient foreign producers. This helps to explain GM's tardiness in reaching a decision on their role in the small car sector.

In all probability the policy of rapid model changes will be abandoned by GM and by the rest of the US industry in favour of greater style stability, better engineering and improvements in quality control. As a marketing device, model changes were successful in the short term. In the longer term, they wasted resources that could have been spent on legitimate improvements rather than purely stylistic ones. Furthermore, model 'instability' created a vacuum in the market for a more reliable, less aggressively styled vehicle in some sections of the market, which VW and other European producers were quick to recognize and to exploit. American producers will now have to work hard to recover lost ground and wasted time.

GM and monopoly

GM enjoys a virtual monopoly in some sections of the market. The company's monolithic structure has troubled a succession of congressional committees and federal administrations anxious to preserve free enterprise and wary of any monopolistic activities in the motor industry. IBM, another US giant, has already suffered the effects of a prolonged anti-trust investigation, and for years it was rumoured that GM had gone to extreme lengths to preserve a semblance of competitive trading in the motor industry, so that it might avoid a similar fate. To survive and operate profitably the company contrived an impressively 'competitive' profile, while (so legend goes) bailing out competitors in difficulty and consolidating an inconspicuous near-monopoly at the highly profitable upper end of the market. If GM had lost its dominant market position, the danger of anti-trust investigations would have vanished with it, removing any constraints on the pursuit of a more aggressive marketing stance in an attempt to win back some of the territory conceded to importers in recent years. However, GM's dominant position is for the moment assured and it is, accordingly, in GM's interest that Chrysler US is saved. Another compelling reason is that a weak domestic Chrysler US is a better neighbour for GM than a more aggressive foreign owned Chrysler US. Hence GM's willingness in 1979 to discount Chrysler's debtors up to the value of $230 million.

Ford

GM is undeniably a well-run firm with a strong bias towards generating profits, but Ford has a different set of objectives dictated from the top. Henry Ford II has until recently run the firm on a tight but professional rein. Because his company is underdog to GM, growth and expansion are more important to him than pure profits. Since the US market has little growth potential, Ford's expansion has occurred outside the USA, particularly in Western Europe where Ford dominates GM. Ford has, however, been slow to adopt a common model policy with its European and other subsidiaries, but the company is expected eventually to integrate its model policy both in North America and Western Europe. Integration of model plans with Toyo Kogyo must also be a major objective but there still seems a long way to go. Henry Ford II has now handed formal control over to Caldwell and W C Ford, and this means that Bourke and Caldwell, who were so successful in Europe, now have effective control. It may however be too late for them to overcome some of Ford's more serious problems in the US market.

Chrysler

Chrysler's sale of its foreign subsidiaries in Europe and elsewhere removed the last straw that may have made Chrysler viable. Its development costs can no longer be spread over a volume of over 2 million cars whereas worldwide model runs of GM and Ford may exceed 2 million. The short-run crisis for Chrysler in 1979 ended with a mixture of government aid ($1.5 billion), private finance and help from GM; together this provided the shortfall needed. This will mean that Chrysler can survive until 1980 at least. What will happen then depends on the finance required by Chrysler, and to shed light on Chrysler's plight we examine its present financial problems.

FINANCE

In Table 6.8, the profit after tax (net income) figures are shown for the US big three. These figures include the profits from all their subsidiaries. GM's profit dived in 1974 but otherwise this giant seems to have performed well. Ford was hit hardest and for the longer period by the 1973 oil crisis. Ford's European subsidiaries have been so profitable

Table 6.8 *Profits after tax for the US manufacturers*
($ million)

	GM	Ford (total)	Ford* (excl European operations)	Chrysler
1970	609	516		0
1971	1936	657	637	84
1972	2162	870	680	220
1973	2398	907	655	255
1974	950	361	382	−52
1975	1253	322	192	−260
1976	2903	983	427	423
1977	3338	1673	628	163
1978	3508	1589	700	−205
1979†	1000	250	−1000	−1100
1980†	2500	1000	0	−500
1985†	4000	2500	1250	250
1990†	3500	1000–	250–	−500–
		2500	1250	0

* Estimates
† Representative forecasts

Source: Company reports and author's estimates

that it is worth analysing the non-European profit contribution for Ford, and in this light, Ford's profit performance has not been so robust. Chrysler's performance was poor throughout the 1970s. Despite a forecast dip in profits in 1980, profitability should reach peak levels (at 1979 prices) for Ford and GM in the mid-1980s. However, in the absence of greater economies and substantial new equity, Chrysler is still only marginal.

By 1990 international competitive pressures and the increasing severity of successive oil crises will once again dampen profitability. Without external support Chrysler will collapse. GM can survive but at a lower level of profitability. Ford's circumstances are rather special and they will be explained below. Profitability will fall because of increased production costs of an even newer range of technology for the 1990s. In addition, all the companies will have to service increased debt charges consequent upon raising new long-term debts to pay for that new technology. And there will be increased competitive pressure which will trim profit margins throughout the mature market. Chrysler's position is such that, without capital expenditure to develop new models, the company will probably gain an insufficient market share to generate profits.

The wide forecast range of Ford is a result of the following dilemma. Ford is not willing to raise debt to finance the new range of US cars (whereas GM is). Instead it will finance the programme out of profits derived from its European companies. Ford US, which was expected to lose $1 billion on its North American operations in 1979, currently makes insufficient profits to finance the new technology, and if the highly profitable Western European subsidiaries fail to yield the expected profits the US parent company cannot implement its new models and will become uncompetitive in North America.

Table 6.9 shows cashflow (defined as retained profit plus depreciation and amortization), capital expenditure and the increase in working capital for GM, Ford and Chrysler. If the raising of new external finance is to be avoided, cashflow must finance both capital expenditures and the increase in working capital. The scenario for all companies involves high capital expenditures in the 1980s slackening off somewhat during the middle of the decade but increasing later. Continued inflation will also require continual increases in working capital. The figures in Table 6.9 are merely illustrative. Chrysler will have to look for external finance for all its capital expenditure. GM will require large sums of external finance in 1980 when the company requires cash for the new US models *and* for a major expansion abroad.

By 1990, the introduction of further new technology will require additional external finance. GM, when it could not meet its capital expenditure and working capital requirements from its profit budget, raised additional long-term debt in the mid-1970s and may do so again.

Ford require additional expenditure of around $1.5 billion and may require anything between $0.5 to $2.5 billion in 1990. If Ford does not raise external finance either the European or the US model programme must suffer. Ford already seems to have sacrificed some European expansion to pay for new US models. Either way, without external finance, Ford will suffer. At the moment the company is still obeying shibboleths established by the Ford dynasty, such as the dictum that Ford does not borrow money. If it does not change this axiom it will become substantially less profitable, and this chapter assumes that it will raise external finance. With Ford's expertise in producing worldwide models, the company has the management capability and structure to be more profitable per unit of sale than GM. GM is aware of this and its remedial action may be successful.

Importers

Recovery from the debacle of the 1961 compact counter-attack has been slow but sure for importers, and they can now boast a substantial and still rising market share (see Table 6.4). Until very recently, import models were on the whole cheaper than any US equivalents, which certainly contributed to their success, although the proposed 1980 prices suggest that the gap has narrowed. European cars enjoyed an enormous technological advantage in the small-car sector; to European buyers, for example, a car manufactured in Europe was clearly preferable

Table 6.9 Cash flow, capital expenditures and working capital requirements for the
US big three manufacturers ($ billion)

	GM			Chrysler			Ford		
	Cash flow*	Capital expenditure	Increase in working capital	Cash flow*	Capital expenditure	Increase in working capital	Cash flow*	Capital expenditure	Increase in working capital
1972	2.6	1.8	0.6	0.5	0.3	0.2	1.5	1.2	0.2
1973	2.9	2.1	0.6	0.6	0.6	0.2	1.5	1.5	
1974	1.7	2.6	-0.7	0.2	0.5	-0.2	1.3	1.5	-0.2
1975	2.6	2.2	0.9	0	0.4	-0.3	1.1	1.0	0.2
1976	3.5	2.3	1.2	0.8	0.4	0.4	1.3	1.1	0.6
1977	3.8	3.6	0.1	0.4	0.7	0	2.5	1.8	0.7
1978	4.8	4.6	0.3	0.1	0.7	0	2.5	2.5	0.1
1980†	3.5	6.5	3.5	-0.2	2.0	0.3	1.5	2.5	0.5
1985†	6.5	5.0	1.0	0.8	1.5	0.1	3.0	2.0	0.3
1990†	5.5	6.5	1.0	0	2.5	0.3	2.0–4.0	4.0	0.5

* Cash flow is defined as net income plus depreciation and obsolescence, and amortization of special tools less dividends
† Representative forecasts

Source: Company reports and author's estimates

to an equivalent US sub-compact because of its superior engineering, quality and durability. That the American product is so obviously lacking in this respect is a considerable disadvantage, especially at a time when even the usually inert American buyer is showing a renewed interest in the possibilities of greater value for money and fuel- and cost-effectiveness. But there is no reason to suppose that these short-comings are insuperable obstacles and US design teams are aware of new priorities. In this respect, the market performance of the GM Chevette is of particular interest, as the car is virtually European in conception and is made throughout the world (including Japan).

In yet another respect, the US producers have been slow to adjust to the possibilities of the small-car market, and have hitherto persisted in their mistaken belief that a small car could only be marketed successfully as a cheap car. European and Japanese producers have disregarded this theory and the recent growth in the luxury small-car sector should encourage US firms to follow the import example with a more positive approach to the wider potential of the small-car market. The 'if-its-small-it-must-be-cheap' connection in the mind of the American manufacturer might also explain an apparently insignificant but probably critical oversight − the question of performance. In any comparison with an equivalent import model, US sub-compacts and compacts are considered to be underpowered, a factor which added to the attractions of imported models.

As the market changes and US producers adopt a more combative approach, some of these conditions will no longer apply and importers may lose most of their 'product' advantages. VW's recent experience provides a useful illustration in this respect and stands as a cautionary tale on the dangers of complacency.

In the 1960s, the German firm enjoyed an enormous labour cost advantage. The hourly German rate was less than half the US rate, and this, together with a favourable exchange rate, made it possible for VW to market the Beetle in the US at an exceptionally competitive price. Exploiting the dual advantage of a cheap basic product and an obvious price advantage, VW successfully penetrated the US market, exporting more than 500,000 cars a year (over 60 per cent of the company's total exports) to the US and reinforcing their market position with a flexible, independent and highly efficient network of sales franchises offering VW dealers a 4 per cent profit on turnover per outlet, a rate double the US dealer average.

By the mid-1960s, however, higher German wages and a less favourable exchange (which by 1979 gave DM2.07 : $1 compared with DM4 : $1 in 1967) reversed the comparative cost advantage. The car itself seemed to have lost much of its novelty and most of its appeal. It was an outdated product. Other importers launched a wave of successful marketing campaigns and offered more attractive models. Too costly, too old-fashioned and too uncompetitive for comfort, the Beetle went into a rapid decline.

Two points emerge from this brief account of the sudden turnabout in VW's position, both of which shed some light on the character of the import market in the US and on the nature of recent changes affecting it. First (and disregarding for the moment the particular circumstances of the VW reversal), it should by now be obvious that import success is confined to particular sectors of the market, principally the sub-compact and the luxury segments, in which imported models offer a product simply not available from domestic manufacturers. In the late 1970s, import sales in the sub-compact/compact market (which included most of the sales for Toyota, Datsun, Honda, Mazda, Colt, Subaru, VW, Renault, Fiat and PSA Peugeot-Citroen) reached a figure in excess of one million cars, with a further 500,000 cars sold in the luxury market. Comparing these figures with the 1971 totals in each category (approximately 1.2 million compact/sub-compact and 300,000 luxury model sales), it is at once apparent that the pattern of demand for luxury/speciality imports shows signs of a healthy and probably continuing growth, unless the US producers react to this growth by producing directly competitive products.

A further comparison of import performance illustrates an important change in the composition of the import market. In 1971 most of the import market (excluding imports from US-owned European subsidiaries) was accounted for by the sales of only three firms, VW, Datsun and Toyota. Four years later, all of the Japanese producers had entered the market, with varying success. Of the European manufacturers, VW (now including Audi) had been joined by Volvo, Mercedes-Benz and British Leyland, which together accounted for a significant proportion of total import sales, with other European firms enjoying steady sales on a rather smaller scale.

What of the future for the US import market? As we might expect there is little evidence of a consensus on the probable developments. One theory suggests that there is a 'natural' and fairly constant import share of between 1.5 million and 2.5 million cars per year. Once import sales have stabilized at this level and extensive dealer networks to support sales at or above the lower limit have been established, they should remain largely unaffected by changing patterns of demand, experiencing no significant reduction in sales in an otherwise depressed market, but with little prospect of other than marginal gains during periods of peak demand.

A second theory places greater emphasis on the growing nonconformity of the US market, suggesting that greater diversity is at odds with the manufacturers' need to gain maximum benefits from economies of scale in order to remain competitive. If the conventional wisdom on economies of scale is to be applied, one might expect to see a reduction in the number of different models available within each range, and possibly the disappearance of some ranges altogether. The net result would almost certainly be a more limited choice from any one manufacturer. Even if all three of the major US manufacturers acted in concert, dividing responsibility for different sectors among themselves, they could not hope to satisfy the increasingly diverse requirements and tastes of the US consumer. The fragmented character of future demand could provide a basis for the continued presence of import models in the US market, if only to supplement the apparently unavoidable homogeneity of the US producers.

In many respects, the first theory would seem to be the more realistic. The US manufacturers are beginning to show that they can produce small European cars, in fact the same cars that are successfully being sold in Europe. If the US product is indistinguishable from the European and Japanese product and through greater economies of scale the price is competitive, the import share may fall. Inertia, the first theory, and to a lesser extent the satisfaction of the proliferation of consumer tastes will probably ensure that the import share does not fall. On the other hand VW's presence as an indigenous manufacturer may change the ground rules, though this is unlikely.

Some commentators contend that US manufacturers could still recover the ground lost to imported models with the introduction of a US-produced small car (which would be marketed and produced throughout the world), citing the events of 1961 in support of their argument. Certainly, the introduction of the compact models was almost overwhelmingly successful in countering import penetration and reducing it to more acceptable levels, but the rules which then governed the success of the compact strategy no longer apply. The importers have greatly strengthened their position in the intervening years, consolidating and expanding a comprehensive network of retail outlets and establishing a firm foothold in the market. And, as we have seen, the advantages of a switch to small-car production are far from clear: any large-scale changeover would certainly involve particular technical problems for US manufacturers, a disability which would lessen their chances of making an immediate impact on the highly competitive small-car sector. Finally, unless the US firms can acquire a large share of the sub-compact market, they will not be able to generate economies of scale at levels commensurate with those achieved by, say, the Japanese, who currently produce nearly one million units of their more popular models. In the absence of similar or even better scale economies the competitive strength of the US small-car production would be seriously undermined.

Future prospects for US manufacturers in the small-car market are thus not encouraging, but it would be wrong to assume that non-participation in one market sector is necessarily a sign of weakness.

A strong case could be made for conceding defeat in one direction and making much stronger moves in the opposite direction, towards the upper and middle ranges[1] of the market where US manufacturers can legitimately claim a certain competitive advantage.

In considering various aspects of the import market, and its effect on domestic producers, it appears that US firms have not been particularly successful in importing foreign-made cars from their wholly, or partly, owned subsidiaries abroad. In 1975, for example, Ford's marketing campaign for the Capri II focused on the 'German craftsmanship, Italian flair and thrifty gas mileage . . .' and made no mention of the fact that the 2.8 litre engine could out-perform the fastest models in the Mustang and Maverick range, offering higher speeds and better handling at roughly the same price as its two principal competitors ($5000 for the Capri II Ghia 2.8 litre, compared with $4900 for the two-door Mercury Monarch Ghia). But quite apart from this sort of undersell, there are more cogent reasons for the tardiness of US firms in dealing with what are, in effect, their 'own' imports. In a perfectly legitimate sense, the issue is one of conflicting loyalties. There is no guarantee that sales of their 'own' import models will not have an adverse effect on domestic sales, simply shifting productive capacity away from the US to subsidiary operations located overseas. Furthermore, US firms reason that if a large enough market existed (strong enough, say, to sustain a fairly steady demand in excess of 300,000 cars per year) and if AMC were not in a position to compete for a share of that market, there would be every reason to begin production of a US-manufactured small car (presumably using European prototypes) in preference to relying on further imports of an identical model. Some commentators therefore believe that these factors coupled with GM's massive $15 billion capital budget for the last quinquennium of the 1970s will lead not only to a substantial reduction in import penetration but also an increased market share in other major markets and (just possibly) increased exports from the US.

CV imports have already been discussed. Import penetration is likely to increase but to a lesser extent than with cars. Interestingly, the process is being helped by White and Mack.

The question of captive imports is now dead, killed by the CAFE programme in which the automotive unions persuaded the US government to exclude non-US produced vehicles in the corporate average fuel consumption figures. If a company imports cars these are not included in the CAFE figures and so cannot contribute to the company's average consumption figures.

---

1. Upper and middle ranges in worldwide terms would be in the current compact range of US cars.

Exports

Excluding exports to Canada, US manufacturers export very little, preferring instead to establish more or less autonomous manufacturing subsidiaries abroad. These subsidiaries are considered in greater detail in subsequent chapters, but a number of points arising from this policy of locating abroad can be more usefully considered within the context of our present discussion.

Locating production in foreign countries is likely to be fraught with difficulties, as companies are increasingly obliged to participate in discussions with various 'host' governments suspicious of the activities of multinational companies within their borders. The threat of government intervention or, in extreme cases, nationalization cannot be lightly dismissed. In some areas (eg Western Europe) scope for further expansion of any significance no longer exists. Japan offers promising possibilities for continuing development, and US firms are already well represented in South America, a new and rapidly developing market. Taking a rather pessimistic view, there would seem to be scope for some further growth in particular areas, but this would be the exception rather than the rule. The policy of exporting capital, rather than investing it at home, which has long been a hallmark of the US motor industry, might soon have to be reconsidered.

The US big three's reaction to domestic import penetration has been the development of worldwide models. In order to reap the maximum economies of scale it may only be feasible to produce the top end of the car range from the US. In this case US exports may increase, and it would make more sense to export the new luxury and intermediate size Cadillac (the Seville) to the richer European and other world markets rather than produce a 'rival' product in these other markets (in which production is found to be low and therefore costly). The other side of the coin is that some small cars may for similar reasons be produced in Europe (eg Ford Fiesta) and imported into the US, though the CAFE programme is currently preventing such a strategy.

Projected consumer market

In the summary projections given in Table 6.10, it has been assumed that the combined populations of the US and Canada in 1990 will be greater than 270 million, and that the number of cars per 1000 of the population will increase very slightly to a maximum of around 550. A strong case can be made for accepting that demand by 1990 will be mainly replacement demand. Similarly, there is widespread agreement that by the turn of the century, most of the labour force in the US will be working a four-day or 30-hour week. More leisure time will strengthen the demand for recreational vehicles. Nevertheless the higher

Table 6.10 *Projection for year 1990 for North America*

Population		271 million
	Cars[1]	CVs[2]
Vehicles per 1000 people	550	100
Vehicle parc (m)	149	27.1
Vehicle life (years)	14	12
Projected replacement demand (m)	10.6	2.3
Actual replacement demand, allowing for some non-replacement (m)	9—10	2.0
New registrations (m)		
Booms	11.5—13.5	2.5—3.0
Slumps	8—10	1.5—2.0
Average	9.5—11.5	2.0—2.5

1. Includes battery urban cars which will come into use in the US around 1985

2. Includes RVs

cost of fuel will dampen the RV markets; the giddy days of the 1970s will not be repeated. Rough projections suggest a car parc for North America (US and Canada) of approximately 150 million by 1990, with a CV parc of 27 million vehicles, although by that time it will be more difficult to make a clear distinction between the two. The annual demand for estate cars (station wagons) in both the US and Canada has already reached one million and potential demand for recreational vehicles is much greater. In order to satisfy the RV requirement, cars will be made more versatile and adaptable to various uses (commuting, shopping, journeys to school, camping, holidaying, etc). The North American market, because of its geographical extent, will support a greater RV demand than Western Europe or Japan, but it will not reach the 2 million plus units achieved in 1977 78. Conventional car demand will on average be 9-11 million, fluctuating according to the general economic climate.

One could take exception to projections of this sort on the grounds that the figures are too high, and that not even the US market could realistically expect to reach a parc of that size, but there are good reasons for accepting it as neither less plausible than slightly lower projections, nor at variance with the prevailing conditions of a saturated market and the low growth trajectory along which the US car industry is moving. Even if car ownership remained absolutely static, or if the combined US/Canadian population grew even more slowly to only 250 million, it would still be possible to achieve a car parc of 125 million vehicles.

Future production

Part of the difficulty in producing a convincing projection for the North American market is quite simply the problem of its size. Any developing country with a viable motor industry will be anxious to export vehicles in order to reach higher economies of scale than those dictated by domestic demand alone. In their eyes, the North American market will have much to commend it: a one per cent market share involves the sale of over 100,000 vehicles. Thus, by the turn of the century it is possible that many of the newer producers will be clamouring for a foothold in the American market.

One can arrive at alternative scenarios for the American market by introducing the import share as an adjustable variable, but in doing so allowance must be made for the fact that high import penetration applies pressure in a number of different ways. A high market share in the US market, for example, would place the importer in a better position to determine the price of smaller vehicles, forcing US manufacturers to comply with prices fixed by pressures *beyond* and not *within* the market. Were US firms to fall out of line (as they have in the past), import penetration would increase. Price alone, however, is not the sole factor in maintaining a competitive position within the market; considerations of advanced technology, superior engineering or a general reputation for high quality are all likely to play a more central role in determining the competitive potential of a car in the future.

Within the US market, imports could play an important part in accommodating the cyclical fluctuations inherent in a market nearing saturation. If US production is geared to reach capacity output at a point rather below peak demand, for example, in boom periods excess demand would be met by a corresponding rise in imports. In theory, US capacity could stabilize midway between the extremes of high and low demand, maintaining full production during periods of depressed demand and stockpiling surplus output as a hedge against return to a more buoyant demand, but the prohibitive holding costs and high interest rates involved would make this impractical. At the moment, total annual North American capacity is about 16 million vehicles, of which 12 million are cars. Small-scale improvements to existing plants (achieved through the judicious use of automation, for example) could expand annual output to 17 or 18 million.

Changing labour attitudes will also have some effect on future trends. The boring and repetitive nature of assembly work will eventually provoke a demand for greater job satisfaction. To improve matters and appease an increasingly intractable workforce, efforts could be made to relieve the tedium. Demands for an improvement in working conditions will be harnessed to an equally vociferous lobby agitating for shorter work periods. The introduction of a four-day or 30-hour week is a common industrial goal, and there is no reason to assume that car workers will be less than forceful in demanding it as of right.

In summary, most of the probable developments touched on suggest formidable difficulties for the motor industry in the future. Massive capital requirements will be needed to comply with statutory safety and anti-pollution measures, to fund an accelerated research and development programme, to facilitate technological improvements, to finance the installation of automated plant, and to introduce and market a more diversified model range. At the same time a decline in profitability will be further accentuated by greater import penetration, heightened international competition, higher labour costs and a volatile market. Certainly, the golden age is over. What shape will the US motor industry assume in the future? To answer the question, three scenarios are now presented (see Table 6.11). For the sake of convenience, projections for the CV sector have been excluded.

Scenario 1 specifics an import level of 1.5 to 2 million vehicles, and with no, or a modest, expansion of existing productive capacity in the US. Scenario 2 posits a higher level of import penetration, at 25 to 30 per cent of the total market, within which US firms remain competitive. In Scenario 3 GM and Ford fail to compete effectively and import levels run at a much higher level. In all three scenarios, Chrysler's position is problematic. The company now faces a major financial crisis because economic depression has been contemporaneous with an unsuccessful model range. Moreover it needs to spend at least $1 billion a year to meet emission standards, the CAFE programme, and produce attractive small cars. Although GM and the US government may help Chrysler, there can be no doubt that a merger with another major manufacturer is now certain. The most likely manufacturers are Mitsubishi (which has bought some of Chrysler's overseas subsidiaries and in which Chrysler has a 15 per cent stake), VW (which supplies engines for Chrysler's smaller range) and, less likely, PSA Peugeot-Citroen (which took over Chrysler Europe and in which Chrysler has a 15 per cent stake). An oil-rich country (perhaps Saudi Arabia or Libya) might acquire Chrysler US, or a group of manufacturers might act in concert to take over the company. A foreign-owned Chrysler could then be operated as an overseas subsidiary, supplying larger cars for export to the manufacturer's domestic market.

Although Ford's performance in the US seems disappointing, we believe that Ford will get it right in the early 1980s just as perhaps GM is 'coming off the boil'. This assumes two things: first, that Ford wins the fight with GM in Europe and, second, that Ford's management in the US is less rigid. The latter implies a more responsive model policy and the willingness to raise funds externally if required.

AMC, although not necessarily an unprofitable concern, is too small to finance a research programme in its own right, but it could use

Table 6.11 *Scenarios affecting North American car producers*

	Capacity 1980	Scenario 1 US manufacturers competitive. Low import share		Scenario 2 US manufacturers competitive with higher import share (25–30%)		Scenario 3 GM fails to be technologically competitive resulting in higher market share of importers	
Import Share Range		1.5 – 2 million units a year		25%		30 – 45% Higher in slumps	
		Boom	*Slump*	*Boom*	*Slump*	*Boom*	*Slump*
US and Canadian demand for new registrations		13m	9m	13m	9m	13m	9m
US Production by 'US' Firms (millions)							
GM	6.5	6.2	4.1	5.2	3.6	4.4	3.0
Ford	3.3	3.2	2.3	3.1	2.0	3.0	2.0
Chrysler	2.1	1.4	1.0	1.3	1.0	1.1	0.9
AMC	0.6	0.2	0.2	0.2	0.2	0.2	0.2
VW	0.3	0.2	0.2	0.3	0.3	0.3	0.3
		11.2	7.8	10.1	7.1	9.1	6.4
Less Exports (outside US and Canada)		0.2	0.4	0.4	0.4	0.2	0.4
		11.0	7.4	9.7	6.7	8.9	6.0
Imports		2.0	1.6	3.3	2.3	4.1	3.0

bought-in components. AMC could then survive as an assembly operation, using bought-in components to produce specialist models with a limited but assured market appeal. On the other hand, as a 'prestige' division AMC would offer an attractive investment opportunity to, say, a resource-rich company, or for one of the US component manufacturers wishing to diversify into the motor industry. AMC's products gradually lost market acceptability as the three big US manufacturers started to produce products closer to AMC's previous model strategy. This led to a sudden crisis for AMC. The actual course chosen was a link-up with a European manufacturer, Renault. The choice was odd since Renault is government owned. Renault has now arranged a distribution chain through AMC's outlets as well as having access to AMC's four-wheel drive products. Renault's CV products dovetail neatly with those of AMC as Renault has no four-wheel drive and AMC has no other models to offer.

VW's newly-acquired US assembly plant will begin to assemble components supplied from Germany and, increasingly, from Brazil. Both Chrysler and AMC have concluded agreements with VW to purchase VW engines and, if these arrangements arc successful, they might persuade VW to establish an engine plant in the US capable of supplying US requirements and an assembly plant within easy reach of the US market, say in Mexico.

Scenario 1 (optimistic for US producers). Scenario 1, with a low import market share of 1.5 to 2 million units is the most optimistic of the three proposed scenarios. It assumes that Ford will maintain a market share of 25 per cent, based on domestic production. Ford's US operation will have very little in the way of spare capacity, except when operating at less than full capacity during periods of depressed demand. Over the whole trade cycle, Ford produces much smaller profits than hitherto, generating high profits during peak demand to offset virtually non-existent profits (or possible losses) incurred during periodic slumps.

GM would also find profitability severely reduced, although it might see higher profits from some of its unrelated subsidiaries, particularly from finance and computer interests.

The export levels of Japanese producers may be overtaken by producers operating in low-cost developing countries, although the overall import level would not be high enough for any one manufacturer to justify establishing assembly plants within the US. If Chrysler can get the finance it needs and the company's model range is an unqualified success, and assuming only a minor depression in the trade cycle, Chrysler might survive but only by a very narrow margin. The odds are against its survival without a more permanent link to another manufacturer. The numerical values given in Table 6.11, however, assume that during a market depression a *foreign-owned* Chrysler exports part of its production to the owner's 'home' country.

Scenario 2 (moderately pessimistic for US producers). A much higher import level is assumed and the market share remaining to the US firms suggests that even with the benefits of automation both Chrysler and GM might have to consider plant closures. Ford might avoid closures by using the parent company as an export 'staging' post or by using existing US plant to produce high-technology components for export to Ford plants overseas. Assuming that profitability in Ford subsidiaries remains at a high level, the company may find it necessary to subsidize or support the US operations for short periods during severe depressions. There is less certainty that GM will be able to draw on financial reserves from its European subsidiaries, as their continued profitability is by no means assured, particularly in the case of the GM Opel concern in West Germany. In this scenario, as in the previous one, GM might rely more directly on maintaining profitability in the company's non-motor industry interests, which could play an even more crucial role in sustaining GM as a viable concern.

With overall import penetration at this higher level, it would be feasible for both Toyota and Datsun to establish assembly facilities within the US, although production figures for both of the Japanese firms appear as imports only in Table 6.11.

Scenario 3 (extremely pessimistic for US producers). Ford's position deteriorates slightly; Chrysler's position, resting on the twin assumptions of foreign ownership and plant closures, remains more or less unchanged; GM, however, has undergone a radical change. In Scenario 2, GM was still in a competitive market position, but increased automation and higher productivity dictated a further concentration of manufacturing plant. In Scenario 3, despite heavy expenditure, GM would not be in a position to compete even with a greatly reduced market share of certain segments of the small-car sector. This would create a further imbalance in market share and could increase import penetration. At these higher levels, Toyota and Datsun, as well as VW, could all support small-scale assembly plant within the US, using components imported from the respective parent countries.

In an extreme case, GM may find itself seeking increasingly large amounts of external finance, but in such an eventuality the company's requirements would be far in excess of any finance available on the capital market. To avoid collapse, the US government might intervene or a foreign manufacturer might offer a trade-off: finance in return for a share in ownership or a negotiated exchange in kind. In a less extreme case, GM could avert a threatened crisis if effective measures were taken to retrench, in which case GM would probably seek to streamline reasonably viable operations and hive off those sectors with doubtful profitability to any interested buyer. More optimistically, there might still be a sufficient margin from the profitable non-motor industry divisions to subsidize the company's car division, at least in the short term.

GM is a company with an indisputably impressive track record and is currently one of the most profitable companies in the world. It is difficult to see how it could find itself in distressed circumstances without taking effective action to avoid the degree of difficulty envisaged above. But GM's faultless pedigree will provide no guarantee of immunity, and to a greater or lesser extent GM, in common with the rest of the motor industry, could experience a degree of discomfort in the more difficult periods of recession in the next 20 or 30 years.

Of the three scenarios, VW does best in Scenarios 2 and 3. In Scenario 1 it just holds on to its market share of 2 to 3 per cent, with AMC, Ford and Chrysler holding their own against VW. In Scenario 2 and 3, the US companies fail to introduce the new technology in a way that appeals to the consumer. Hence VW with an acceptable product increases market share and productive capacity.

When we examine Ford's prospects as they might be affected by the assumptions of Scenario 3 a different picture of the company emerges: Ford is smaller and more flexible. It has already adapted successfully to the exigencies of international small-car production (in Europe), and therefore enjoys an immediate advantage over GM. Ford subsidiaries are already established in low-cost labour areas, and should provide Ford with an assured source of supply for cheaper components. All of which suggests that Ford could survive in all three scenario conditions. But all projections must be treated cautiously and any one of the crises threatening its giant rival could have an equally disastrous effect on Ford.

A counter argument to our pessimistic analysis of GM would emphasize the company's massive capital spending budget, its development of worldwide cars, its ability and willingness to raise new capital and its international marketing strategy. These may place GM on a surer footing, and some commentators believe that this will lead to the reassertion of GM's traditionally dominant position in the world. But such measures may be too late to counteract worldwide developments, such as the growth of low-cost, small-car oriented foreign competitors, which the US big three are powerless to control. Such a feeling of impotence must be strange to these companies which have been traditionally omniscient and omnipotent, but they will not concede their power without a struggle, and the next decade promises to provide an interesting spectacle.

Commercial vehicles

The implications for the car market can, broadly speaking, be applied to the light end of the CV market, though to a lesser extent. Import penetration has not been significant. There will still be a smaller RV segment of the market which will remain protected and lucrative, unless the Japanese break through (which they have done in the four-wheel drive segment).

The same is not true of the medium and heavy sectors of the CV industry. The fragmented structure of the industry is now less concentrated than both the European and other producing areas. It is inconceivable that all the 10 small significant producers will remain in their current form for the next four decades. There are four possible outcomes: collapse, merger among themselves, merger with a non-US company, or takeover by the US big three (or perhaps International Harvester). All four are likely to occur. Ultimately there may exist only two or three independent producers of heavy CVs, the others having merged with one of the major companies (US or non-US).

One expects International Harvester to survive as it draws its strength partly from agricultural equipment and vehicles for which demand shows no sign of abating and, indeed, will increase as population expands, the Third World develops and agriculture in developed countries becomes more intensive. However, International Harvester's performance in the CV marketplace has not been good. Content with locational diversification into Europe, its production is at 1950 levels. Whether the company will want to fight in an increasingly aggressive arena is an open question. It may choose to withdraw into the relative safety of the agricultural and other specialized markets. Such rationalization will only occur in an economic downturn coupled with increased import penetration. This may become significant when for example the rationalized European CV industry finds itself nearing a saturated European market and launches a major export drive in the US. Even then the US may be able to combat such a drive by changing the type or size of the vehicles at its top end. Such a defence however costs money which may in itself provoke moves to rationalize the US CV industry. Both Mack and White are developing European links, and International Harvester already has substantial stakes in European CV companies. This seems to indicate that the CV industry like the car industry will spread across the frontiers of the mature market.

Demand for RVs is likely to decline: with higher real fuel prices, the cost of running RVs must choke off some demand and, unless real fuel prices recover to their 1977-78 levels, the RV industry will not recover to its former levels. The future for the rest of the North American CV industry, despite the fundamental structural changes likely to occur, is rosier than that of the car industry, principally because of the special market developments of the US. Import penetration will rise, but it takes longer for importers to establish a CV reputation. Moreover, the experience from Western Europe indicates that fleet buyers tend to buy their domestically produced product, purchase price being less important than reliability, running costs, the availability of parts and driver acceptability.

Chapter 7

Western Europe

The West European market ranks second to the North American market in terms of size and maturity, although it may possess a higher overall potential demand. But three features differentiate the West European from the US market. First, car density levels in the North American market are twice as high as prevailing European levels and correspond more closely to the concept of a saturated market. However, the European market could, conceivably, reach saturation at a much lower density. Second, West European productive capacity is highly fragmented, with a total productive capacity greater than that of the North American industry. In recent years, however, the substantial and highly lucrative West European exports to North America have been challenged by the Japanese producers (discussed in Chapter 9). Third, the Japanese have made similar and equally successful inroads into the West European market itself.

These three factors — diminishing exports, rising import penetration and a fragmented industrial structure — create a less than healthy environment, and the 1973-74 oil crisis accentuated the problems. There is the additional threat of an increased import challenge from the Communist Bloc countries. Thus far the national governments and principal producers in Western Europe have failed to achieve a satisfactory long-term solution to their problems, if indeed there is one.

How are we to decide which countries fall within the Western European sphere and which do not? Membership of the EEC or EFTA, although probably a precondition, would be too narrow a definition, as in both cases future expansion in the number of member countries is highly probable. EEC trading links will almost certainly expand to cover a much wider area in the next 10 years. Countries such as Spain with associate status at present can reasonably expect to graduate to full membership in the near future. And where existing affiliations are more difficult to determine, the possibility of further integration into West European economic affairs is regarded as the most relevant criterion.

For our purposes a Western European country, within or beyond the confines of either EFTA or the EEC, is a country with close economic ties to markets within West European countries. Spain, Portugal and

Greece obviously meet these criteria and must therefore be considered as West European in character. Turkey, midway between Europe and the Middle East, is problematic in a geographical and economic sense. The situation is further complicated by unresolved hostilities between Greece and Turkey. Traditionally, the intimidating presence of the USSR on the Turkish border fostered a close identification by the Turks with Western Europe. Should Russian attitudes change, however, there is no evidence to suggest that Turkey would resist the possibilities of friendlier relations with her immediate neighbour. On balance, it would appear that Turkey, with a much lower *per capita* GNP, corresponds in so few respects to the West European norm that it should be excluded from our discussion in this section, and is discussed in Chapter 15.

Yugoslavia is an even more difficult case. Under Tito, Yugoslavia has been the only one of the COMECON countries to pursue a policy of strong trading links with EEC countries, but it seems likely that in the future the USSR will exert much greater pressure on the Yugoslavs to follow a less independent line. Yugoslavia will, therefore, be considered at greater length as one of the Communist Bloc countries in Chapter 11.

Although Western Europe has thus far been referred to as a single market, its historical development has been as a collection of individual markets. This distinguishes Western Europe from either North America or Japan, where the market has been much more homogeneous. The integration of the Western European market only became a fact with the development of the EEC which lowered tariff barriers. This development was only fully achieved during the 1970s and now pervades to countries outside the EEC, although by 1990 most of the countries within our Western European definition should have joined the EEC formally or informally.

Because of their size and relative insignificance we have excluded Cyprus, Gibraltar, Iceland, Malta, the Channel Islands and Monaco, which, with a combined population of some 1.5 million, support a total vehicle parc of only some 0.5 million.

The West European market

The West European market ranks as the second largest in the world, with a total population of some 344 million in 1977 and an average *per capita* GNP of $4903 in 1976. A summary of some of the relevant statistics is provided in Table 7.1. Figures 5.1 and 5.2 showed the development of the European market. Unlike the North American market, growth in the European car market has proceeded without any serious disruptions; the downturns of 1974 and 1975 were the first to occur since the 1950s. The CV market is rather different, with total sales figures concealing a dramatic change in the composition of demand

Table 7.1 Economic statistics for Western Europe

Country	Population		Per capita market prices 1976 ($)	GNP Growth rates		Vehicle parc 1977 ('000s)		Persons per vehicle in 1977	
	1976 (millions)	Growth rate 1970-76 (%)		1960-73 (%)	1966-76 (%)	Cars	CVs	Cars	CVs
West Germany	61.5	0.2	6451	3.7	3.2	19,180	1454	3	42
Italy	56.2	0.8	2723	4.3	3.1	15,900	1255	4	45
UK	55.9	0.1	3550	2.4	1.5	14,790	1913	4	29
France	52.9	0.7	5859	4.7	4.1	16,250	2410	3	22
Spain	36.0	1.1	2663	5.8	4.6	5282	1048	7	34
Netherlands	13.8	0.9	5892	4.1	3.8	3768	364	4	38
Belgium	9.8	0.3	6371	4.3	3.9	2738	325	4	30
Portugal	9.7	1.2	1500	7.4	3.4	999	205	9	47
Greece	9.2	0.7	2322	7.3	5.5	496	233	19	39
Sweden	8.2	0.4	8043	3.0	2.3	2881	178	3	46
Austria	7.5	0.2	4823	4.4	4.3	1828	171	4	44
Switzerland	6.4	0.4	8246	3.0	0.6	1864	152	3	42
Denmark	5.1	0.5	6803	3.9	2.9	1338	256	4	20
Finland	4.7	0.4	5351	4.5	4.1	1033	142	5	33
Norway	4.0	0.6	6400	4.0	3.9	1023	148	4	27
Ireland	3.2	1.2	2367	3.6	3.2	552	61	6	52
Total	344.1		4903*			89,922	10,315	3.8*	33.4*

* Average

reflecting a trend towards larger and more specialized vehicles.

Average car densities in Europe have now risen on average to a record four persons per car, evidence of the growing maturity of the market. As this process continues, one would expect to see a greater similarity in the behaviour of the Western European market and its North American counterpart, particularly in the pattern of cyclical fluctuation in demand. As the economic stature of the EEC increases, Europe may more closely resemble a single integrated community than it does at present, strengthening the argument for observing developments in Western Europe in terms of the precedent established in North America.

Increasing maturity within any market implies a market approaching saturation, wherein demand is for the most part replacement demand and is therefore inherently unstable. If the adverse experiences of individual countries are excepted, Western Europe *as a whole* has had little experience of the sort of downturns which affected the US market in 1958, 1966 and 1970, but Europe may soon experience the effects of cyclical demand fluctuations and will have to adapt accordingly.

A saturated market could, however, occur at a much lower car density level in Europe than North America. Alternatives to private transport in Europe are more fully developed and more frequently used than in the US, and could be even further extended. The suburban sprawl so common in the US (where it has made public transport systems almost worse than useless), has no European equivalent, suggesting that more favourable conditions for a viable public transport system still exist in Western Europe. Further, the very obvious fact of lack of space militates against a comparable growth in European demand for recreational and utility vehicles of the type familiar in the US. There will be some growth in demand for vehicles of a specifically 'recreational' type, but it will be on a much smaller scale than in the US.

In stressing the similarities between the European and North American markets, one should not overlook the differences. Whereas the American car buyer has, for the most part, been content with the ubiquitous standard car, the European market has always demanded a far wider choice. The 'European' market is still a confederation of smaller national markets, each with certain idiosyncracies making for pluralism in demand. Traditionally, West Germany and Sweden have been accustomed to a larger car, and, conversely, the French prefer a smaller car and the Italians favour vehicles which are smaller still. Now, however, there is a tendency to greater uniformity, continuing the dominance of a much smaller car — the European equivalent of a US sub-compact or compact such as the VW Polo or Ford Fiesta — as the major market segment in the 1980s or early 1990s. Recent trends towards larger engined cars appear to have been halted by the successive oil crises.

As cyclical fluctuations in demand become a more noticeable feature in the European trade cycle, they may be accompanied by swings from larger cars to smaller models in recessions, a move already apparent in the USA. This would be something of an innovation in European demand trends, though there is already some evidence of such a switch in the pattern of demand during the 1974-75 and 1979-80 downswings in Europe.

There is some indication that, prior to 1973-76, there was a long-term trend towards larger and more powerful cars. Table 7.2 illustrates the trends in the size of cars. The tendency through the 1960s and 1970s was towards larger cars but the oil crisis of 1973-74 produced an adjustment back to small cars, followed by some readjustment as the real price of oil fell in the mid-1970s. The 1978-79 oil crisis and the long-term trend in oil prices will see a more permanent switch to smaller, more fuel-efficient cars. In the longer run, it is likely that, as in the US, the larger-car segments will suffer permanent damage and there will be a more diversified range of demand across the market. However, this must be qualified by noting the highly developed market for luxury and 'executive' cars. These cars need not necessarily be physically large (eg BMW Series 300), but their price and specification places them in the executive car class. In the future the area which will suffer most damage is the medium-car segment (eg Cortina/Taunus, etc).

There is also a dramatic difference in the type of CV and the development of CVs in Western Europe. We have already noted that Western European conditions make demand for recreational vehicles at US levels impossible. But there has been a switch away from vans to medium and heavy trucks. The USA had established an excellent system of motorways capable of taking giant trucks. Apart from Germany, the building of an equivalent network in Europe is a recent phenomenon, and Western Europe's road system, taken as a whole, is still far short of the North American system. Consequently, the 1950s and early 1960s saw a greater demand for vans and smaller trucks, which gradually evolved into a demand for heavy long-haulage CVs designed for motorways. The heavy CV segment reached a peak in the early 1970s of around 30 per cent, but its share slightly declined in the late 1970s. Table 7.3 shows the trends in the CV market segments. (Table 5.2 shows total Western European CV demand.) One noticeable feature of Western European demand is the relative stagnation of CV demand, which may be explained by the move towards trucks with higher carrying loads. The higher the carrying capacity of a CV, the fewer CVs required to transport a given volume of products.

This brings us to the third analogy with the US. Until now, Europe has been a net exporter to territories and markets abroad. As saturation conditions approach, there is a natural tendency for this traffic to be reversed, producing import penetration at much higher levels and at

Table 7.2 *Car segments in Western European market share* (%)

Year	1960	1965	1970	1973	1974	1975	1976	1977	1980*	1985*	1990*
Segment share											
Extra-small	10	8.0	6.5	5.7	6.1	4.9	4.5	4.5	5.0	6.0	7.0
Small	29	22	20.5	16.9	22.0	20.8	20.9	23.0	25	23	23
Light	30	33	27.6	26.8	25.4	26.1	23.7	22.7	24	23	24
Medium	12.4	13.9	20.3	24.5	22.7	22.9	25.6	24.2	23	22	20
Large/executive	10.8	18.1	18.1	17.5	15.6	17.3	18.0	18.6	16	19	20
Luxury	7.8	5.0	7.0	8.6	7.3	7.3	7.5	7.2	7.0	7.0	6.0

* Representative forecasts

Table 7.3 *CV market segments in Western Europe*

Broad segments	1973	1978	1990*
Segment shares (%)			
Car derived vans (light)	25.3	25.4	24.0
Panel vans (medium)	45.2	47.2	45.2
Trucks and heavy CVs (heavy)	29.5	27.4	30.8
Volume (in '000s)	1175	1183	1300

Expansion of heavy segment	1973	1978	1990*
Segment shares (%)			
Light truck (over 3.5 tons)	14.7	19.3	16.2
City delivery	35.1	34.6	30.0
Inter-city and construction (over 15 tons, under 250 hp)	24.1	16.8	17.0
Linehaul (over 15 tons, over 250 hp)	10.3	15.9	24.4
Heavy conventional)			
Buses)	15.8	13.4	12.4
Other)			

* Representative forecasts

peak acceleration during periods of downswing in the trade cycle. The reasons for this will already be familiar from our discussion of a similar phenomenon in the US. The net effect is a growth in demand for a cheap, basic vehicle of the sort that only low labour cost countries can hope to produce profitably. At the moment, Japan is in a position to exploit a number of advantages in this respect, and some new producers may be in a similarly advantaged position in the future.

Market by market survey of demand

Cars

The four largest markets in order of importance are West Germany (1978 car registrations were 2.6 million), France (1.9 million), UK (1.6 million) and Italy (1.2 million). Table 7.4 shows the fluctuations in demand in each of the major national markets within Europe over the last few years. The largest single market is in West Germany, where demand rose very sharply towards the late 1960s. Since then demand has remained static, suggesting that consumers were perhaps a little over-optimistic in gauging their needs and their resources, and simply bought too many cars. Most observers agree, however, that the potential for further growth in the West German market has not been completely exhausted, and this was borne out by demand reaching record levels in 1978. But the West German industry may be in for a shock, for it is

Table 7.4 Western European new car registrations by country ('000s)

Year	West Germany	France	UK	Italy	Spain	Netherlands	Belgium	Sweden	Austria	Switzerland	Finland	Denmark	Norway	Portugal	Eire	Greece
1958	691	620	554	209	35	56	95	147	55	68	12	40	21	7	22	2
1959	828	595	664	253	40	77	110	169	55	70	18	60	21	8	25	3
1960	970	670	806	381	50	101	140	160	70	105	24	80	31	16	28	4
1961	1095	751	740	492	69	120	134	181	78	110	33	79	44	18	29	6
1962	1209	958	783	635	83	146	146	197	85	124	41	94	42	18	32	8
1963	1271	1100	1019	952	91	182	174	231	90	128	52	74	48	19	37	5
1964	1343	1106	1203	830	127	226	201	258	96	134	82	97	55	20	41	12
1965	1518	1111	1138	887	159	304	235	275	111	139	101	82	56	34	43	16
1966	1507	1210	1048	1015	251	213	231	208	121	146	79	98	60	36	39	20
1967	1357	1231	1143	1162	290	264	238	176	122	153	66	95	65	38	40	20
1968	1425	1240	1104	1168	310	335	270	213	131	168	48	91	65	42	40	25
1969	1841	1366	965	1218	378	350	311	226	101	192	84	117	99	55	52	30
1970	2107	1297	1077	1364	399	432	301	203	127	211	92	108	70	60	54	32
1971	2152	1469	1286	1435	433	403	266	198	195	235	75	104	81	73	52	37
1972	2143	1638	1638	1470	506	432	336	221	222	259	101	92	75	78	64	39
1973	2031	1746	1662	1449	595	430	341	226	187	239	118	122	89	79	74	42
1974	1693	1525	1269	1281	576	404	336	260	167	202	96	79	90	88	61	32
1975	2106	1482	1194	1055	572	450	365	285	185	190	117	116	103	84	52	59
1976	2312	1858	1286	1188	620	508	421	313	225	204	92	152	127	98	70	68
1977	2561	1907	1324	1228	663	552	429	241	296	234	90	141	145	76	82	98
1978	2664	1945	1592	1216	654	585	424	201	158	272	81	133	78	53	106	116
1979*	2500	1985	1700	1350	700	540	395	215	205	250	85	130	110	45	95	130
1980†	2200	1800	1480	1400	725	550	420	275	230	240	90	130	120	65	100	90
1985†	2400	2300	1750	1700	1100	650	500	300	250	290	125	165	170	150	150	150
1990†	2300	2200	1600	1600	1200	500	400	250	200	200	100	125	100	200	200	250

* Estimates
† Representative forecasts

unlikely that new car registrations will again reach the giddy heights of 1978. We return to considerations of the future in the next chapter.

France has had a more stable growth in car demand, assisted by a French government anxious to establish France as a major world force in the automotive industry. It has succeeded, but at a cost. French demand lagged behind that in West Germany in the 1960s but caught up in the 1970s. Elsewhere, while the French market has shown remarkable consistency, the Italian market has been adversely affected by the problems of the Italian economy in general in the 1970s. Although this is not a bar to further growth, it does suggest that any future increase in demand will be minimal. Demand in the UK market has been extremely volatile in recent years, partly the result of the economic demand management policies espoused by a succession of Labour and Conservative governments in an attempt to curb demand in the face of a chronic balance of payments crisis. Moreover, during the 1960s when demand really took off for Germany and Italy, the UK was performing poorly, for political as well as commercial reasons.

Spain, Portugal, Eire and Greece, where car densities are the lowest in Europe, have shown consistent growth; although the increase in demand in Spain and Portugal may not have matched the expectations of the manufacturers who installed capacity in those countries in the late 1970s. The Benelux countries enjoyed remarkable growth in the 1960s and modest growth in the 1970s. Austria and Switzerland have had modest growth.

The Scandinavian countries (Sweden, Norway, Finland and Denmark) must be singled out for special attention as they are the exception to the European rule. In these countries the market showed signs of considerable cyclical fluctuations in demand in the 1960s and 1970s, with virtually no overall growth during that period, the classic symptom of a saturated market. Car densities in Denmark are rather low, however, with five persons per car, suggesting that the Danish market has not yet reached saturation level. The depressed market in 1974-75 further distorted the picture, but it would be premature to dismiss the possibilities for further growth within Denmark.

Apart from the UK and Italy, whose economies are both weak, most of the European countries (eg West Germany, France, Benelux, Sweden, etc) had record car registrations in the mid-1970s, demonstrating that the healthy parts of Europe had recovered from the oil crisis of 1973-74. The recovery from this led some countries into a boom which required dramatic deflationary action in 1978; hence Portugal, Norway, Finland and Austria suffered large drops in new car registrations in that year.

CVs

Table 7.5 presents CV demand in much the same way and suggests an

Table 7.5 Western European new CV registrations by country ('000s)

Year	West Germany	France	UK	Italy	Spain	Netherlands	Belgium	Sweden	Austria	Switzerland	Finland	Denmark	Norway	Portugal	Eire	Greece
1958	78	109	187	28	11	15	12	14	10	5	8	17	9	6	4	3
1959	86	101	210	31	13	21	14	15	10	5	10	24	10	7	4	4
1960	101	124	247	46	17	23	19	15	13	6	17	28	11	7	4	5
1961	118	121	245	62	29	29	19	16	13	9	28	27	11	7	5	6
1962	121	133	213	70	34	29	20	15	12	12	23	29	11	7	5	6
1963	127	143	233	87	44	31	21	16	13	11	11	26	10	6	6	6
1964	130	159	257	64	60	35	21	18	13	11	13	33	11	6	6	7
1965	131	145	265	53	80	33	21	20	13	9	16	29	10	9	8	5
1966	127	158	240	60	88	36	21	19	12	9	18	32	11	11	7	9
1967	111	152	225	78	93	33	21	18	12	9	21	30	12	11	7	9
1968	123	167	244	86	82	39	21	17	11	10	10	31	13	13	8	8
1969	145	223	257	91	80	41	25	18	12	11	17	36	16	15	10	9
1970	165	208	257	85	78	47	25	19	16	13	23	25	16	16	10	11
1971	163	227	257	79	75	43	24	17	16	14	21	25	20	15	10	12
1972	149	249	283	81	87	40	24	16	20	17	12	32	22	20	9	13
1973	138	270	300	83	101	43	26	17	15	18	13	49	12	25	10	15
1974	108	253	237	101	101	40	23	17	14	15	14	24	11	21	8	22
1975	109	206	220	76	94	37	21	17	12	8	14	30	12	18	7	24
1976	137	293	209	95	93	42	24	19	18	8	14	45	14	21	8	29
1977	138	298	225	112	101	43	26	20	19	11	13	35	17	33	10	26
1978	156	300	256	98	104	47	29	17	19	14	12	23	14	29	13	33
1979*	150	280	250	100	110	40	22	17	16	13	11	25	15	30	10	30
1980†	120	250	225	95	100	42	23	18	18	10	12	30	15	36	11	33
1985†	150	300	250	110	120	45	25	19	19	15	14	35	18	41	14	35
1990†	150	280	265	120	130	40	20	17	18	12	12	27	15	35	10	30

* Estimate
† Representative forecasts

even more volatile pattern than that of car demand, with the UK and France as the two principal markets. Despite a higher overall volume in the 1970s, the French market has a large van segment; the medium and heavy truck segments of the two markets are comparable. Lower levels of demand in West Germany and Italy reflect the fact that both countries have access to alternative forms of transport, principally by rail or water networks. We have already noted that in all four markets there has been a steady growth in demand for larger CVs capable of transporting a larger volume of goods on the major road networks. Greater CV demand is to be expected in Spain, Portugal and Greece, developing markets where ever-increasing loads must be transported in small or medium size trucks over indifferent roads, and where no alternative haulage systems exist or, if they exist, lack sufficient spare capacity. As a whole, however, the European CV market already displays the pattern of cyclical fluctuation in demand characteristic of a saturated market, a development much in evidence in Belgium, Eire and the Scandinavian countries. These countries have shown no growth since the middle 1960s and (despite a switch in the pattern of CV demand) must be close to saturation. Some, but not all, of this stagnation may be due to a change in the size of CV demanded.

If the CV market has indeed reached saturation levels, it would have been almost impossible to predict such an outcome on the basis of the North American experience, as CV densities in Europe are still low by North American standards. To arrive at saturation at such a significantly lower level could be explained by the availability of well-developed transport systems as an alternative to road haulage. The highway/motorway network itself is underdeveloped by North American standards and there is a possibility that the average journey length is shorter, so that for any given quantity of goods to be transported a smaller truck fleet would be required. And the potential for further growth in the 'non-commercial' CV sector in Europe is far smaller than the evidence of the North American market might suggest. Overall, further growth in CV demand is expected to be of minimal significance, although slight growth in certain sectors, mainly at the heavier end of the market, may occur.

In terms of product range, the European CV market, like the car market, shows greater overall diversity than the US CV market, although coverage at the extremes of the scale (the heavy goods vehicle sector and the utility/recreational sector) is marginally thinner. However, given the rather different nature of road haulage requirements in Europe, omissions of this sort are more than compensated for by the diversity of the product range in the intermediate sectors.

Production

Cars

The fortunes of the various countries within Europe have changed dramatically as shown in Figure 7.1. In the 1950s, the UK dominated Europe but, while the demand management policies of the government hit UK manufacturers repeatedly during the 1950s and 1960s, France and Germany enjoyed more or less uninterrupted growth. Even in 1964, the UK production exceeded that of France and could have kept pace with West German progress but in 1964 a Labour government was voted into power. The party's doctrine of public ownership led to an unsympathetic view of the concept of private ownership of car production which damaged the motor industry. When demand recovered under the Conservative government of the early 1970s, it recovered too quickly and the UK manufacturers, after six years of stagnation, could not expand; the increase in demand simply sucked in imports. Meanwhile, this increase in demand produced complacency among the UK manufacturers; since they could sell everything they could produce, they were not encouraged to think of new products or efficient production. The 1973-74 crash hit the UK at a time when complacent

Figure 7.1 *Western European car production*
by major country

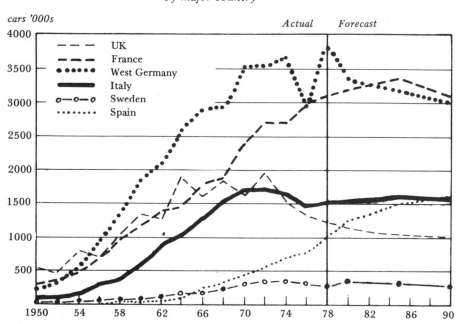

UK manufacturers were not in a position to respond imaginatively. It is unlikely that production will ever reach the 1972 peak again; it has been permanently lost to other European countries.

West Germany and France have been conducting an interesting battle as to production superiority. By 1970 the West Germans had established a clear lead, partly due to VW exports to North America. With the full support of the French government, French manufacturers persisted and production has steadily increased and may outstrip West Germany in the future. One of the problems experienced by West Germany is that success breeds a healthy exchange rate; a rising exchange rate makes exports more expensive in foreign markets which dampens demand.

Political uncertainty and interference has caused setbacks for Italy similar to the UK experience. A novel feature of the Italian scheme is the Italian government's insistence on taking car production to green-field sites in areas of high unemployment; for the most part these strategies have failed and we discuss their failure in the next chapter.

Sweden's growth was stunted in the mid-1970s due to some extent to insufficient scale economies. Spain's growth has been remarkable and the country is set to overtake both the US and Italy and become the third major producing country in Europe. Belgium, the Netherlands, Portugal and Finland do not manufacture cars in large numbers. Belgium is especially important in assembling KD kits from the UK, France and Germany. Ford's production from its Ghent plant in Belgium raises an interesting statistical problem; with sourcing from both the UK and Germany, and with the Belgium plant only assembling the product, most statistical sources do not credit Ford with the production of some 300,000 Cortinas a year. Certainly all the US statistical sources get it wrong, and this may explain why the GM bosses were unaware of the rate at which Ford were expanding in Europe.

CVs

The pattern found with car production is broadly repeated with CV production. Figure 7.2 shows CV production for individual countries: UK production has suffered even more dramatically than with cars, whilst France has overtaken a more sluggish West Germany. Italy's CV production has shown some growth, unlike its car industry, and Sweden and Spain have also grown, while the Netherland's production has remained static. These absolute figures must be carefully interpreted as there has been a switch in production from small to large CVs consistent with the changing pattern of demand. Interestingly, the sum of the UK and French production has remained roughly consistent. In terms of European production, the French have simply successfully captured part of UK production. French production remains buoyant, although

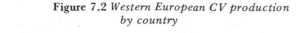

Figure 7.2 *Western European CV production by country*

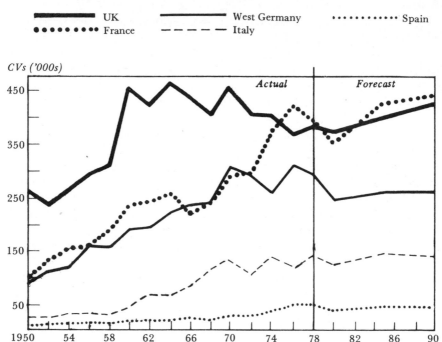

the CV producers are currently experiencing some difficulties.

The manufacturers

There are 12 major European manufacturers, 10 of which are indigenous to Western Europe. The other two are Ford and GM; Chrysler was represented but has been taken over by PSA Peugeot-Citroen and Chrysler Europe's products have been brandnamed Talbot. Table 7.6 gives capacity levels, majority ownership and the market segments to which output is directed for each of the major European firms.

A feature of the European market is state ownership; British Leyland, Renault and Alfa Romeo are state controlled, and Fiat (through Seat), Volvo and VW have an element of state ownership. Although North America has just come to grips with state aid for the motor industry, in Europe this has been a feature for some time. PSA Peugeot-Citroen and Volvo have received direct government aid, and Ford, GM, Fiat and Saab have received indirect aid (such as special capital investment grants).

Concentration

As with North America, market maturity goes hand-in-hand with an increased concentration of the industry. There were over 150 integrated motor manufacturers in France in the 1920s, with at least 40 firms of comparable size in the UK, and more than 30 in Italy. By the 1950s the number of French firms had dropped to just over 40, with 20 in the UK, 35 in Italy and 25 in Germany.

Since the late 1960s, the number of manufacturers in Western Europe has been drastically cut from 34 to 12 major car companies: PSA Peugeot-Citroen (including Chrysler), Ford Europe, GM Europe, VW, Renault, Fiat, British Leyland, Daimler-Benz, BMW, Alfa Romeo, Volvo and Saab.[1] By 1990 the number of major companies should be even further reduced to no more than a handful. Western Europe still supports a number of smaller firms and, like North America, this is especially true of heavy CV manufacturers.

To illustrate the degree of concentration, Figure 7.3 shows the historical acquisition and merger strategy of Volvo, British Leyland, VW, Daimler-Benz and Fiat. It is worth recalling that whereas North America has three major manufacturers, a European market of similar size supports six or more major producers.

Ford

Ford has been particularly successful in its European operations, with production facilities in the UK, Belgium, West Germany and Spain offering an impressive model range. Ford was the first of the US multi-nationals to develop a more fully integrated operation based on a 'European' concept of manufacture and marketing. By using at least two and sometimes three separate sources for the supply of components and power train units, Ford has cushioned the disruptive effect of a halt in production at one plant. The arrangement has not been infallible: strikers at a Ford plant in the UK were successful in gaining a certain amount of trade union cooperation from Ford workers in Belgium, Spain and West Germany during a recent strike. Trade union solidarity of this sort could mean that production shortfalls in one area are not invariably compensated for by full production elsewhere. Since the introduction of 'multiple sourcing', Ford's ability to adapt to market requirements, and an element of financial pressure, have led to certain modifications in the policy, and Ford is now basing future development on a more flexible basis. In order to maximize its capacity utilization, Ford has instituted a 'rolling policy review' on a European scale. At least once every six months the company decides whether major changes are necessary, ie whether production should be switched from one plant to another, or whether several plants should all concentrate on

1. The recent merger between Volvo and Renault reflects this trend to greater concentration.

Table 7.6 Details of major manufacturers

Firm	European countries		Brand names	Majority ownership	Major links	Car capacity based on 5-day week (millions)	Cars segment	CV capacity (millions)	CVs segment
	Major	Minor							
Ford	UK West Germany Spain	Belgium Netherlands France	Ford	Ford (US)	—	1.8	Volume range	0.2	Entire range
GM	West Germany UK Spain	Belgium Austria	Opel Vauxhall Bedford	GM (US)	—	1.6	Volume range	0.1	Medium and small
Volkswagen	West Germany		Volkswagen Audi NSU	Private (40% owned by state of Lower Saxony)	MAN	1.8	Volume and luxury ranges	0.1	Small end of market
Renault*	France	Spain	Renault Berliet Saviem	State (99%)	(1) Peugeot-Citroen (2) Club Four (3) AMC	1.6	Volume range	0.2	Developing an entire range
Fiat	Italy Spain	West Germany France	Fiat Autobianca Iveco	Private (Libyan government has a 10% share)	Club Four	2.0	Volume and luxury ranges	0.2	Entire range
Peugeot-Citroen including Chrysler Europe	France	UK Spain	Peugeot-Citroen Talbot Commer	Private (but has had state loans)	Renault Volvo	2.5	Volume and luxury ranges	0.3	Entire range

| Firm | European countries | | Brand names | Majority ownership | Major links | Two shift capacity based on 5-day week (millions) | Cars segment | Capacity (millions) | CVs segment |
	Major	Minor							
British Leyland	UK	Belgium	Leyland, Austin Morris, Jaguar, Rover, Triumph and a host of CV names	State (95%)	Honda	1.0	Volume, specialist and luxury ranges	0.3	Entire range
Daimler-Benz	West Germany	–	Daimler Mercedes	Private (Kuwait government 15% share)	–	0.4	Top end of volume, luxury range and taxis	0.2	Entire range
BMW	West Germany	–	BMW	Private (but minority goverment interest)	–	0.4	Luxury		–
Alfa Romeo	Italy	–	Alfa Romeo	State (100%)	–	0.3	Some volume, and specialist range		–
Volvo	Sweden	Netherlands Belgium	Volvo Daf	Private	Club Four	0.3	Specialist range		Large
Saab	Sweden	Finland Netherlands	Saab Scania	Private		0.2	Specialist range		Large

Figure 7.3
Key mergers and acquisitions of selected
European motor vehicle manufacturers

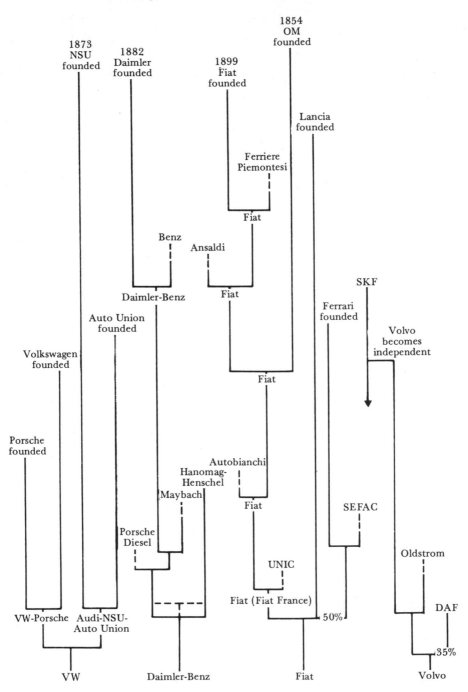

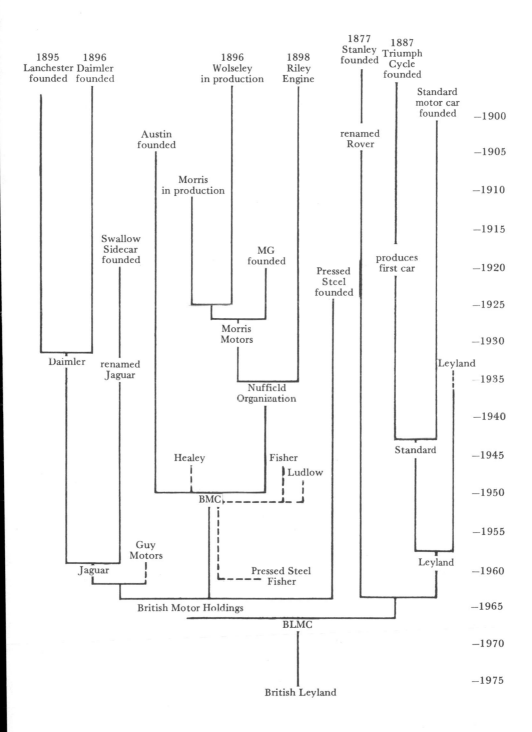

production of a single model.

The new Fiesta, which cost $1 billion to develop, and has been conceived on a truly 'global' basis, is produced in three countries. Spain produces most of the engine units, although some engine blocks may eventually be produced in the UK, and West Germany and the UK concentrate on the remainder of the manufacturing operations and, in the short term at least, all of the final assembly. Wisely, Ford have located automatic gearbox and power train production at their Bordeaux plant, thus providing a manufacturing presence in France.

Ford CV production is concentrated in the UK, with smaller plants in the Netherlands, manufacturing some of the larger heavy goods vehicles for long-distance motorway travel. Some of the Transit range of lighter trucks and vans are produced in West Germany, while plant in Belgium assembles components from both West Germany and the UK.

In general terms, Ford's success in Europe has been based on a deliberate attempt to manufacture a specifically 'European' car model range, taking the specific requirements and conditions of the market into consideration and capitalizing on Ford's reputation for reliable, if unadventurous, engineering. As a multinational, Ford enjoys one major advantage over its 'non-multinational' rivals such as Renault, Fiat and VW: with production capacity in the UK, West Germany, Belgium, Netherlands, Spain and, on a smaller scale, France, Ford is in a better position to adjust production and introduce minor variations in output to cater for 'national' variations in consumer taste and to accommodate any government regulations.

Ford, during 1978-82, plans to spend some $1.8 billion in the UK, and $0.7 billion in Germany on installing a new engine plant in Wales and expanding assembly plants elsewhere to gear up for its new front-wheel drive car codenamed Erika (Escort replacement). Ford received substantial aid from the UK government, amounting to over $400 million which is about 50 per cent of the capital investment cost and associated working capital of specific projects. This competition between European governments for industrial investment is a feature of the European industry.

Ford recently drew attention to the possibility of another assembly plant. With a major expansion already undertaken in the UK, some disillusionment with Spain (it has been difficult at the new greenfield site to get things right) the choices were limited. Germany was too high a cost base; France met with resistance from the French manufacturers and Austria was too close to the Iron Curtain. (No-one seriously considers Italy these days, since poor labour relations and a special commercial environment rule the country out.) Moreover, the profit budget that would have been needed to pay for the new plant was re-allocated to the troubled US parent. The new capacity that could be required to launch a new front-wheel drive Cortina (codenamed Toni) was deferred. Instead an interim plan of keeping up existing plants was proposed.

Ford became acutely embarrassed when GM announced a $2 billion expansion plan in Europe just after Ford's announcement cancelling the new assembly plant project. Now Ford are once again involved in talks with Spain, Portugal and Austria. The new Ford plant, should it be built, will cost $1 billion (including working capital) and provide 8000 jobs in the production of some 250,000 cars a year. Ford would expect some 50 per cent of the cost to be provided by the wooing government.

GM

The operational structure of Opel (West Germany) is similar to the Ford pattern, with assembly facilities in Belgium fed by West Germany. While Opel have been fairly successful with sales of conventional cars in the West German market, the performance of the Vauxhall GM division in the UK has been much weaker. Total Vauxhall production in 1975 and 1976 fell below 100,000 units, although maximum two-shift capacity is in excess of 300,000 cars per year.

Taking GM's European operation as a whole and as a profit earner the company is obviously running a rather poor second to Ford sales. Even Opel's future profitability is questionable for, although the company's performance to date has been satisfactory, Opel's strategy was until recently modelled on the potentially disastrous US approach, following an assumed upward trend to larger cars, and the company were badly wrong-footed by the effects of the oil crisis and the subsequent shift to smaller engined cars. The Opel problem, and unacceptably low output and profitability from Vauxhall, prompted a major policy reappraisal of the European operation, which in turn caused a sudden *volte-face* in policy objectives. The move bore the tell-tale marks of intervention by the US parent, for, if the European operation had been more successful, it would doubtless have been left to pursue a more independent course.

The same model duplication problems presently bedevilling the US parent company are in evidence, but GM (Europe) has moved towards a more fully integrated structure, particularly in the case of new 'global concept' cars (eg the 'T' car — the Chevette/Opel Kadett). GM has now centred its car production around Opel, and Vauxhall (under the Bedford brandname) has, for some time, been GM's only European CV producer. Both companies now report back to an integrated headquarters in the USA.

GM's plants in Germany and Belgium are run as one company, but GM's UK Vauxhall car plants are still not fully integrated with the other

European plants. GM has announced a major new assembly plant in Spain, with a capacity of 300,000 units a year and a new power train plant in Austria to supply the Spanish plant. Whilst this expansion is an obvious ploy to catch Ford, it is interesting to note that UK production is still way below capacity levels. The facilities are expected to come on stream by 1982. GM is also to build a components plant in Spain at Cadiz to supply the Zaragossa assembly plant. Existing facilities will also be expanded to meet the increased demand for components.

The total cost to GM of these developments is some $2 billion; to a company committed to spending up to $5 billion a year, such sums for European investment are relatively small. The rationale for investment was pride and the need to cut back Ford's high profitability and powerful position in Europe. Estes (president of GM) was reported as saying: 'I don't like the idea of GM being just another of the pack overseas . . . The aim . . . is to knock the hell out of the competition.' The Zarogossa and Cadiz plants will cost $1.6 billion alone. The Zarogossa plant will produce 300,000 cars using a labour force of 12,000. Ford's reaction to GM's aggressive tactics in Europe is summed up by Petersen, its vice-president: 'Ford is not in a state of shock because one more major competitor is making a run at world markets', and the attitudes of both sides indicate the probable ferocity of the struggle in the Western European battlefield.

After years of neglect, the GM parent company is now taking Europe seriously. In theory, Europe will be just as important as the US in future, though in practice it will take some time fully to integrate GM's European car operations. GM's Vauxhall (UK) plants are still operating substantially below capacity, although Vauxhall is currently producing the Opel range of cars. GM seem to have taken sensible steps in Europe and by the mid-1980s these actions should bear fruit.

Chrysler

Prior to the takeover of Chrysler (Europe) by PSA Peugeot-Citroen, Chrysler had been modestly pleased with its French subsidiary, which included Chrysler's Spanish plants. However, Chrysler's UK operation had been nothing short of disastrous, requiring successive loans from the UK government, which culminated in the 1975 package deal whereby the company received up to £165 million in government aid. With the Ford example and heavy losses as incentives, Chrysler tried, in a frantic scramble, to rationalize production on a European basis, but the decision came too late to save the company. Without European integration, even the French division had insufficient volume to achieve the necessary economies of scale to be fully competitive.

Peugeot-Citroen

In return for a $51 million loan, the French government in 1974 pro-
duced a rescue plan for Citroen providing for a Peugeot takeover
of Citroen and a Renault takeover of Berliet. In 1978, with some
encouragement from the French government, Peugeot-Citroen
purchased Chrysler's ailing European subsidiary at a cost of $430
million, with Chrysler US retaining a 15 per cent stake in the company.
These developments have produced several problems. First, there are
three distinct model ranges under a rather cumbersome merger
umbrella. As independent producers, all three companies had produced
volume cars with a marketing emphasis on quality, with Citroen
claiming greater sophistication in engineering, Peugeot emphasizing the
quality of manufacture and Talbot emphasizing a different set of
qualities. To rationalize production facilities and model ranges fully,
massive capital expenditures in excess of $15 billion over a 10-year
period may be necessary. Some model rationalization has already
occurred with the Citroen LN and Visa being based on Peugeot models,
but one can only speculate on the period required to complete the
process. Some observers feel that the new company will switch to the
production of three parallel model ranges with distinct brandnames,
based either on common body panels or at least common components.
On the other hand, the combine must continue to manufacture three
entirely separate model ranges until the model lives are exhausted.

In many respects, the original Peugeot-Citroen merger was an
unfortunate one as prior to the merger Peugeot had developed much
closer links with Renault. The family-owned Peugeot firm had already
reached agreement with Renault on a cooperative venture designed to
split the research, development and manufacturing costs of the Douvrin
(FSM) engine between two companies. Plans had been drawn up for
joint engine and automatic transmission plants with further cooperation
on a smaller scale in body production. Citroen had earlier been acquired
by the French tyre firm of Michelin, which had sold a minority holding
to the Italian Fiat company, which for a variety of reasons was unable
to proceed with a complete takeover. At the same time, Citroen could
do nothing to assist the troubled Maserati company in which it held a
75 per cent interest. And to further complicate the picture Citroen was
also associated with VW in a joint development programme to produce
a version of the Wankel engine. In simple terms, if the links that already
existed between the various companies at the time of the merger
proposals had been followed through, a Peugeot-Renault merger would
have been the logical outcome. As it is, the realignments have created
two companies — Renault and Peugeot-Citroen-Talbot — which are in
direct competition with each other and unlikely to achieve a spirit
of mutual cooperation in future. Peugeot, far smaller than Renault

initially, now towers over it.

The reasons for Peugeot-Citroen's decision to take over Chrysler Europe include:

1. Given rationalization and the greater commonality of body panels, power train and other parts, maximum economies of scale (about 2 million cars per year) should be available to the new group. This could give PSA Peugeot-Citroen a cost advantage of up to 5 per cent over its nearest competitors. However, it would take some time to reorganize production and models in order to reap the full advantage. However, maximum economies of scale could be achieved by just keeping Chrysler France and Chrysler Spain. There is no necessity to continue to prop up the UK plants to achieve full cost advantages.
2. Peugeot-Citroen had almost no interest in the CV field. By taking over Chrysler, Peugeot-Citroen inherited a fairly strong and well-organized CV operation. The UK produces the light and medium range trucks, while Spain produces the heavier range of CVs.
3. Chrysler remains a 15 per cent shareholder of the PSA Peugeot-Citroen group which may (at some future date) be allowed to use the Chrysler North American dealer network. In any case, the model programmes of the old Chrysler (Europe) will be very much linked in to the global programme of Chrysler.
4. Chrysler's European network of dealers will, after suitable rationalization, enable PSA Peugeot-Citroen to strengthen those areas where its dealer network is weak. It also provides the group with a ready-made CV dealer network throughout Europe.
5. Both Chrysler Europe and Peugeot have been very active in selling to the Middle East. Peugeot is due to start selling 305 kits to Iran in the near future. With the formation of the enlarged group, there will be a certain continuity, since Chrysler UK has been, and will continue to be, a major supplier to Iran.

Ultimately, the Peugeot-Citroen-Talbot manoeuvre will be a shrewd move for the company. It now has the scale to compete internationally and once production has been rationalized, the concern should be extremely viable. We return at the end of this chapter to a further consideration of the new company group.

Volkswagen

The eclipse of VW in the US market and the emergence of Opel as a strong contender in the West German market in 1973 were straws in the wind for VW. The recession and the burden of heavy financial losses prompted a radical reappraisal of policy and in record time VW had introduced a completely new range of cars to replace the Beetle. The luxury end of the VW range is marketed through Audi/NSU. At the bottom end of the market, VW has always produced two virtually parallel ranges, but there are now indications that in future the brand-names will be more conspicuously differentiated. VW's large share of the lucrative West German market (nearly one-third) has helped to dampen the fall in sales in the US.

VW have also revised their approach to non-car output, and are now concentrating on a more positive expansion of their CV facilities. The company also decided to go ahead with its plans for a US plant, a move which will, contrary to expectations, help to preserve jobs in West Germany, as the new facility depends on components imported from the latter. VW assembly in the US is expected to confer a slight price advantage, as labour costs are now significantly lower in the US than in West Germany, and assembly within the US would obviously avoid the transport costs of transatlantic shipping. The CV expansion, focusing on the medium weight truck market, in addition to the existing light-weight van range, has thus far involved an agreement with Perkins for the supply of diesel engines and VW has been increasingly cooperating with MAN.

VW also plans to expand, spending some $3 billion on an expansion programme in the US, Canada, Mexico and West Germany, and to increase US capacity to over 450,000 units a year. One of VW's weaknesses in the past has been the company's lack of representation in the heavy CV segment. VW and MAN seem to be getting closer together, and it is likely that they will eventually merge. At the moment, the two companies are cooperating on the production of trucks in the 6-9 tonne range, an area of the market not presently covered by either company. VW will make the cabs, rear axles and gear-boxes for the new truck range, while MAN will make the engines, frames, front axles and special bodies.

VW's own locational strategy of shifting assembly from Germany to the US, will ultimately have an impact on car production in Germany. The rationale for the move was to go into an area with a lower cost base. Labour (and social) costs in 1979 were DM 24.44 an hour at VW's German plant compared with DM 16.50 in the US, DM 5.83 in Mexico and DM 4.08 in Brazil. With sales in the US currently soaring (the US public switches to cheap, small cars in downswings), VW plan to eliminate the export of the power train from Germany to USA, and to build a new engine plant in Mexico and a second assembly plant in the US. The Mexican power train plant will feed VW's Mexican assembly plants as well as its two US plants. The cost of this expansion was announced as $820 million, but this figure is probably an underestimate, as a realistic cost would be in the region of $1.5 billion.

Renault

Renault has been one of the most successful of the European state owned firms. The car division has concentrated on reliable cars of fairly advanced design, with a particularly strong model range (centred on the ubiquitous R5) at the lower end of the market. With the acquisition of Berliet, Renault is also in a strong position as a CV producer. In its post-merger incarnation, Renault produces both cars and lightweight CVs under the Renault banner, with medium- and heavy-weight CV production from Saviem and heavy-duty highway trucks and 'off-road' commercial vehicles from Berliet.

Renault, although dwarfed in PR terms by Peugeot's antics, has not exactly been idle. Renault's link-up with AMC has been an adventurous ploy: it has bought a 22.5 per cent equity stake in the US company and will market US-built Renaults. AMC can obviously hope to sell Jeeps through Renault's European distribution networks; similarly Renault can sell its cars and heavy CVs through AMC's North American distribution chain. But a decision has to be taken as to whether Renault provides some cash for AMC to re-tool its US plants to assemble Renault-based products (eg R18). If Renault provides finance, it may become locked into AMC during future crises for the US company. Given VW's expansionist plans on the US front, Renault may not mind being dragged in to what must ultimately amount to a complete take-over of AMC. The French government will probably not object, as long as any such manoeuvre might create the possibility of more French jobs.[1]

Renault's CV industry has been troubled for some time, and comprises three separate operations, Renault, Saviem and Berliet. Berliet only became attached to Renault at the time of the Peugeot-Citroen merger. The CV division is making heavy losses and Renault plan to rationalize. The company is rationalizing and integrating its three operations and is introducing a new range of trucks. Originally Renault planned a $1 billion investment programme but the poor performance of its CV division has led to a certain reappraisal of these plans.

Renault has also recently announced plans to purchase a 20 per cent stake in the US independent heavy CV producer, Mack. In exchange for an equity injection into the company, Mack will market Renault trucks (for up to 10 years). Target volumes are in the region of 10,000 trucks a year. This underlines the importance that European manufacturers attach to establishing themselves in the stable US market, where some 300,000 medium-weight (9-15 tonnes) trucks are sold a year. For Mack, second to International Harvester, it provides an entry into the medium

1. The possibility of a new link-up between Renault and Volvo arose at the time the book went to press. This was a logical reaction to PSA Peugeot-Citroen's expansionary drive in the acquisition of Talbot. Although the link-up is purported to cover the car side only, the purchase by Renault of a 20 per cent equity stake in the Swedish company for $80 million inextricably ties the two companies together. This represents an interesting and entirely rational move for Renault and the European motor industry.

truck CV segment without a massive investment programme, which is important at a time when competition in this sector is increasing from Volvo, IVECO, MAN, etc.

Not content with these plans, Renault also wants 'to keep up with the Jones's' in European terms, which means following GM, Ford and Peugeot-Citroen south. Thus Renault plans to open a modest assembly plant and a major power train plant in Portugal. The company also opened a small components plant in Austria during 1978.

Fiat

Fiat, a large and fairly diversified company, is now divided into 10 divisions. The acquisition of Lancia supplied the missing link in an otherwise complete chain, and Fiat now markets a comprehensive range. The car divisions, however, have been threatened by the poor performance of the Italian economy and by persistent industrial disputes. The company was also subjected to external pressures to maintain high levels of car production during the 1974-75 depression. This has produced a massive build-up of stocks.

Fiat's CV division, IVECO, with headquarters in the Netherlands, is now very large by European standards, comprising UNIC in France, the West German Magirus Deutz, OM and Lancia CV. At the moment, the CV group is rather fragmented, but with further integration it could operate in much the same way as Ford, as a multinational producer with manufacturing facilities located in a number of different countries.

In 1979 Fiat decided to increase its stake in Seat (Spain) from 36 per cent to 51 per cent. Seat, which was 34 per cent state owned, has suffered from the influx of other European manufacturers into Spain. Fiat, with impeccable industrial logic, is to use Seat in a new integrated group; by linking Seat as a far-flung plant of the Italian firm, Seat would be able to rationalize and cut costs. Unlike GM, Fiat has plenty of experience of operating plants across nations and multi-sourcing, from its CV subsidiary IVECO. Fiat was toying with establishing a US assembly plant for CVs. Fiat plans to spend nearly $5 billion in modernizing and improving its car and CV plants over a five-year period.

British Leyland

British Leyland was rescued by the UK government in 1975, when it became apparent that the company would not be able to raise sufficient external finance to survive. Since then the company has spent over $3 billion but the rescue has not gone smoothly. With the stagnation of demand facing the company in the 1960s, the company had no competitive models on its drawing board. Outdated equipment and low productivity, due to bad work practices and chronic industrial relations, have created an even more difficult task for management. A new and more dynamic management in 1977, under the leadership of Michael Edwardes, now seems set to tackle these problems. One of the tragedies of British Leyland was its failure to rationalize production after the merger in 1968 of what was originally over 60 independent companies. After its rescue, models and plants were rationalized but this caught the company in a trap: by rationalizing models you lose market share. It will be interesting to see how Peugeot-Citroen-Talbot rationalize their production.

British Leyland also followed the classic cure for a company under pressure: retrenchment and withdrawal to its domestic base. Of its plants in Spain, Italy and Belgium, British Leyland has only retained the Belgium plant. These withdrawals and some closure of domestic plants, coupled with a declining market share, called for drastic action. With no models and, worse still, insufficient engineering staff to develop new models, British Leyland looked for a partner who would temporarily 'lend' a model. British Leyland found Honda, who have insufficient capacity to produce all the Accords they could sell. The link-up looks a shrewd move, though some commentators feel that British Leyland should have produced a medium car as their highest priority (rather than a new Mini), since the main profits are in the medium-car market.

British Leyland's association with Honda is a logical move for the company. British Leyland has been short of design engineers and technical staff, and whatever it has are fully stretched in producing a new Mini and a medium saloon. The latter will not appear until the mid-1980s, yet British Leyland is particularly vulnerable in the medium-car segments. The licensing agreement with Honda specifies that British Leyland will build a 1.5-2 litre saloon with a Honda engine, gear-box and transmission, and British Leyland built body pressings and other components. British Leyland will have exclusive sales rights in the European community and Honda will make the same model in Japan for sale in other parts of the world. The association with Honda is a sound one and in some ways is preferable to the previously rumoured association with Renault. Whereas Renault is far bigger than British Leyland, Honda is about the same size. Renault wanted to cooperate with British Leyland to plug into the quality ranges, fine for Renault but British Leyland did not find sales a particular problem in their quality range.

Current European thinking usually dismisses British Leyland as being irrelevant. But British Leyland is, in European terms, a major CV producer, and their specialist car division (Jaguar, Rover, Triumph) is far from dormant. The main problem centres around its 'volume' car division Austin Morris. (Austin Morris model runs are below the volumes for BMW and Mercedes quality cars!) If the Honda link-up is a success this could re-establish British Leyland's car image in Europe. However, British Leyland is neither a specialist nor a volume producer, and sitting on the fence simply will not be possible in the 1980s; British Leyland will either have to expand output (to achieve economies of scale), contract or enter into a more permanent partnership. It is, however, too early to write British Leyland off.

Alfa Romeo

Alfa Romeo is now controlled by the IRI (*Instituto di Ricostruzione Industriale*), an Italian government agency, which might explain in part the decision to locate the new Alfasud factory in the under-industrialized region near Naples, in the south of Italy. Unemployment in the area has always been high and in moving there Alfa Romeo announced their commitment to a policy of job creation. Both the new factory and the new model marked a radical departure from the familiar sporting image previously cultivated by the firm, but there have been serious problems in establishing the factory, and productivity has fallen far short of both acceptable levels and planned capacity. For some years, Alfa Romeo has been losing money. It has realized that it is too weak to survive by itself, and is currently searching for a partner for eventual joint ventures. Elsewhere, two smaller firms — de Tomaso and Mascrati — are under the control of another government agency, GEPI (*Gestione e Participazione Industriali*), which will eventually assume control, through de Tomaso, of the old British Leyland (Innocenti) plant.

Volvo and Saab

Although the two Swedish firms, Volvo and Saab, after agreeing to merge early in 1977, decided that such a move was too big a step for either company to take, the future of both companies must be linked together. Volvo have traditionally manufactured luxury (quality) cars, but with the takeover of DAF in 1974, Volvo extended their output to a two-model coverage, with the smaller 300 series and the larger 200 series. Broadly based and well-diversified, Volvo is Sweden's major turbojet engine producer, with a smaller car and assembly operation in Belgium and a limited assembly capacity of fewer than 20,000 vehicles per year in Canada. Volvo has had some state aid to keep its Dutch plant (ex-DAF) operational. The latest aid amounts to $115 million, which will be used to develop a successor to the 343. Volvo started construction of a US assembly plant but lack of funds forced a halt to this project.

Volvo, like Renault, has arranged a liaison with the US independent heavy CV manufacturer, Freightliner. Freightliner will market Volvo products in the US; the agreement is especially geared to the medium trucks in the 13-17 ton class (a market size of some 30,000 vehicles). As with Mack, Freightliner has no products in this area.

Volvo has, for some time, realized that as a motor manufacturer, the company is too small to be competitive. Volvo has made four attempts to solve the problem. The first was an abortive merger with Saab-Scania (it is rumoured that Saab thought that its CV operation, Scania, would be swamped by Volvo). Second, a complex but far-sighted, deal with the Norwegian government (the Norwegians wanted to gain too much from the deal and this led to a reappraisal). The third is to resort to the Swedish government for funds on the basis that without these Volvo is uncompetitive. The most recent is the link-up with Renault.

Saab, a much smaller Swedish firm, purchases many of its components from other manufacturers and production and marketing are geared to durability, reliability and safety for which the company has acquired a well-deserved reputation. Although Volvo collaborated with Peugeot and Renault in a joint engine project, Saab has even more substantial international links. Saab has reached agreement with Fiat on a collaboration programme for developing and manufacturing common components for the Saab and Lancia ranges. Saab also has extensive marketing agreements with VW and MAN. Volvo and Saab require some $1 billion for new model development. Without this money, both companies will be unable to maintain their position.

Porsche

Porsche is an independent company with close engineering and distributive ties to VW. As a relatively small scale manufacturer of luxury sports cars, however, it is of minor importance in the big league ranks, although it enjoys high prestige and status within the European market.

Daimler-Benz

The West German firm of Daimler-Benz restricts its activities to three sharply defined areas — the quality car market, custom-built taxi cabs and CV production. In recent years, the company has been particularly successful, expanding production even during the 1974 downswing. The CV operation was funded with a massive investment programme in the late 1960s and early 1970s, and Daimler-Benz has now begun to invest on a similar scale in its car production facilities, with planned expenditure of $2.5 billion in 1977-80.

Daimler-Benz has recently announced a $5 billion investment programme to produce a new small Mercedes car. Reports indicate that Daimler-Benz will try and make this small car a typical Mercedes and not comparable to volume producers. This marks a major change for the company in an attempt to produce a range of cars. Interestingly, both GM and Ford have been trying to imitate Daimler-Benz's commercial strategy to reap the level of profit made by the German group. This has led the US multinationals to move their products up-market. In response to this and/or the energy crisis, Daimler-Benz will be in danger of competing head on with the volume manufacturers. BMW has already succeeded in doing this. The next question to be asked is whether Daimler-Benz, with smaller economies of scale, can compete with the US multinationals? We return to this question in Chapter 8. Daimler-Benz is building an assembly plant for CVs in the US, with a capacity of some 6000 units by 1981.

BMW

BMW is a significant specialist West German producer, manufacturing high-quality, high-performance cars with the post oil crisis emphasis on luxury and economy. Although the *Land* of Bavaria has a minority interest in BMW, the company is effectively controlled by the Quandt group, whose other interests include Varta batteries, machinery, chemical and pharmaceutical products. BMW plans to spend some $1.5 billion over the next five years to improve and restructure production.

Spanish companies

The Spanish motor industry, although still in its infancy, has developed rapidly in recent years but is still, for the most part, dependent on foreign companies for design and development aid. Seat (*Sociedad Espanole de Automoviles de Turismo*) produces a Fiat-designed car. Fasa (*Fabrica de Automoviles SA*) manufactures Renaults and Citroen-Hispania produces Citroen cars and vans. The ex-Chrysler subsidiary (Chrysler-Espana) assembles Simca and Dodge cars and Barreiros diesel CVs.

In the CV sector, Authi was a BL licensee until 1978, but after liquidation the company was acquired by Seat. Alfa Romeo licence CV production at Fadisa and VW and Daimler-Benz jointly own the Mevosa subsidiary, producing lightweight Mercedes Benz vehicles and engines. Ford have now joined their other European manufacturing colleagues in opening the Valencia plant to produce Fiestas and Fiesta components for export to both the UK and West Germany. One of the few truly indigenous operations, the government controlled Enasa Corporation, manufacture light, medium and heavy CVs and Pegaso buses. Two smaller independent firms, Avia and Motor Iberica, also manufacture CVs.

Minor car producers

Table 7.7 lists most of the smaller European producers. A number of the smaller UK firms are in financial difficulty, but state aid has not been forthcoming. In Italy, several of the smaller companies are now dependent on government aid, and Ferrari have been bailed out by Fiat. Two of the smaller independents stand in splendid isolation as viable and successful concerns: the UK Rolls-Royce firm and the German Porsche company.

Table 7.7 *Minor car producers*

UK	AC, Aston Martin, Bristol, Ginetta, Lotus, Morgan, Reliant, Rolls-Royce/Bentley, TVR, Panther, Caterham Cars, Technical Exponents
France	Alpine, Ligier, Matra-Simca[1]
Italy	Innocenti,[2] Lamborghini, de Tomaso,[2] Maserati,[2] Ferrari[3]
West Germany	Porsche, Hanomog-Herschel
Switzerland	Monteverdi

1. Now 45 per cent owned by PSA Peugeot-Citroen
2. Publicly owned by the GEPI agency
3. Now supported by a larger manufacturer

Portuguese producers

Over 30 firms in Portugal are directly involved in the assembly of both cars and CVs, using parts supplied from the US, Japan and Western Europe. Fiat, British Leyland, Datsun, Toyota and Ford account for the largest share of the car assembly work, with Citroen-Peugeot, Renault, Toyota, Fiat and GM dominating the CV sector.

The CV industry

A distinctive feature of the Western European CV industry is a series of defensive mergers and cooperative ventures, which have now spread to North America. Figure 7.4 illustrates some (but by no means all) of the European CV relationships.

Ford, Chrysler, GM and British Leyland all have major CV facilities, giving Europe as a whole a substantial CV capacity. British Leyland, with government aid, is at present reorganizing and expanding its CV division, which should further strengthen the UK's position as one of the market leaders in the field. In an otherwise troubled motor industry, the strength of the CV market in the UK is partly the result of a flourishing and well-established components industry, and partly a reflection of high levels of demand within the UK. With the sole exception of 1974, the UK CV market accounted for more CV sales than any other in Western Europe.

In addition to British Leyland and the American subsidiaries, the Daimler-Benz operation is of equivalent size and standing in Western Europe. Owing to its premier position in CV sales and its highly priced cars, Daimler-Benz has one of the highest turnovers of all the motor manufacturers. Renault's position should be greatly strengthened by the acquisition of Berliet, a substantial addition to Renault's existing CV division, Saviem. Fiat's IVECO subsidiary, now incorporating Fiat, OM, Unic, Lancia and Magirus Deutz, must also rank as one of the larger producers. The shifting sands of merger, takeover and alliance have also produced the Club of Four, a joint project involving Daf, Magirus Deutz, Saviem (Renault) and Volvo. which are participating in a cooperative project to design, develop, manufacture and market a new medium-weight truck range, a new departure for all four of the participants. Fiat's ownership of Magirus Deutz has slightly complicated the arrangement, and Daf's position is even more difficult as the Daf CV division only survived the Volvo takeover of Daf's car interests by agreeing to a three-way split in the equity holdings of the CV division. One-third of the equity was retained by the original owners, the Van Doorne family, while one-third was sold to the State through the intermediary of the Dutch State Mines, and the remainder acquired by International Harvester, sole owners of the CV manufacturer, Seddon-Atkinson. International Harvester's multinational role raises a number of interesting questions on the nature of its involvement in the Club of Four project.

Of the remaining large independent manufacturers, MAN (West Germany) produces medium-weight vehicles and is associated to a limited extent with both Renault and Daimler-Benz, although it seems firmly set on a closer liaison with VW. In addition to British Leyland and Seddon-Atkinson, the UK also has two smaller, but nonetheless important, CV producers — ERF and Foden. Table 7.8 supplements the list of firms already mentioned with information on a number of smaller CV producers. Enasa is Spain's largest CV producer.

Links with a US manufacturer and/or assembly capacity in the US seem to be the current fad of the European CV industry. DAF are already partly owned and Seddon-Atkinson fully owned by International Harvester. Daimler-Benz is building a US assembly plant and Fiat might follow this lead. Volvo has an agreement with Freightliner, and MAN, in common with Renault, has a link with White. The rationale for this headlong rush into the North American market is that it offers a large stable market, and there has been a shift from petrol to diesel engines, and the US manufacturers are relatively inexperienced in the diesel field.

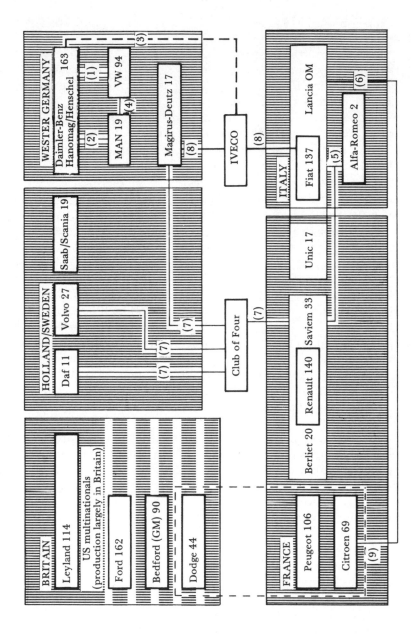

Figure 7.4 *European CV relationships*

(Figures show commercial vehicle production for 1977 in '000s excluding buses)

Key:

(1) VW and Daimler-Benz each own 50 per cent of a research and development organization (DAG).

(2) MAN and Daimler-Benz collaborate in truck manufacturing and marketing. There is a joint venture for the production of common components for heavy vehicles (MTU).

(3) Daimler-Benz and IVECO are principal partners in a joint venture to produce automatic transmissions (ATU). This group may eventually include Volvo and ZF.

(4) MAN and VW jointly manufacture 5-9 tonne trucks.

(5) Fiat, Alfa-Romeo and Saviem each own one-third of a light vehicle diesel engine plant in Sicily (SOFIM).

(6) Peugeot-Citroen and Fiat have joined forces to build a $280m plant for making 80,000 light vans a year in the south of Italy.

(7) Saviem, DAF, Volvo are all part of the 'Club of Four'. Each company uses its own chassis and components but share a common cab design.

(8) Eighty per cent of IVECO is owned by Fiat and 20 per cent by KHD, which formerly owned Magirus-Deutz. IVECO consists of Magirus-Deutz and Fiat's former subsidiaries UNIC, Lancia, OM and Fiat (CVs).

(9) Chrysler (Europe) and Peugeot-Citroen have merged.

Nb: Other link-ups include Audi-NSU's (VW) assembly of Porsche 924 and the manufacture of its power train; Fiat's 50 per cent ownership of Ferrari; the Renault/Peugeot/Volvo cooperation in the development of the Douvrin engine (FSM); and Audi-NSU's (VW) and Citroen 50—50 stake in Comotor.

Table 7.8 *Minor CV producers*

Austria	OAF, Steyr
Benelux	Ginat, FTF, Terberg
Finland	Sisu
France	Willeme, Sovam, Verney
Switzerland	FBW, Mowag, Saurer, Berna
UK	Dennis, Shelvoke and Drewey, ERF, Foden, Seddon-Atkinson, Bristol Commercial Vehicles
Italy	Sofim
West Germany	Carl Kaelble, Kassbohrer, Faun, MAN, Auwater
Spain	Enasa, Motor Iberica*, Ebro, Elva, Mevosa, Viasa (Jeep), Metalurgica de Santo Ana (Land Rover)
Sweden	Volvo, Saab-Scania
Netherlands	DAF
Portugal	Portaro, Unimag, Utic

* Now owned by Nissan (Japan)

Market segments

Cars

Table 7.9 outlines the market segments usually associated with the present European market. The largest of the market segments is the medium-car sector which has been dominated by the Ford Cortina/Taunus and GM's Ascona/Cavalier. It is also the most lucrative segment, which may explain why the two largest US multinationals are so strongly represented. The mini-car segments are especially strong in France, Italy and Spain. It is interesting to note that the Ford Fairmont, a medium-sized compact car on the North American market, is larger than Ford's European 'executive' class car, the Granada. (The US Ford Granada is even larger than the Ford Fairmont.) Some observers in Western Europe believe that the executive and luxury sections of the market are becoming less important as cars lose their emotive appeal and become simply another consumer durable.

As Table 7.10 shows, each market segment is covered by most manufacturers. Clearly, ample possibilities exist for the consumer to exercise a much greater degree of selectivity in any market segment than his North American counterpart. On the whole, the market is biased far more heavily than in the US towards the small luxury car. Daimler-Benz, BMW, part of the Peugeot-Citroen range, Alfa Romeo, the Lancia division of Fiat, Volvo and the Jaguar/Rover/Triumph divisions within British Leyland have all based their manufacturing and marketing

Table 7.9 Car manufacturers model policy
(main models only shown)

Manufacturer	Brandname	Extra-small	Small	Light	Segment Medium	Large	Executive	Luxury
PSA Peugeot-Citroen	Peugeot Citroen Talbot	2 CV	104 Visa 1100 Sunbeam	304	305 GS Alpine	504 CX C9	604 CX	
Ford	Ford	expected early 1980s	Fiesta	Escort	Cortina/Taunus		Granada	
GM	Vauxhall Opel		expected early 1980s	Chevette Kadett	Cavalier Ascona	Carlton Reckord	Royale Senator Monza	
VW	Volkswagen Audi		Polo 50	Golf Derby	Passat 80	Scirocco 100/Avant		
Fiat	Fiat/Seat Lancia Ferrari	126/Panda	127	Strada/Ritmo Delta	Mirafiori	132 Beta	Gamma	Ferrari
Renault	Renault	R2	R4, R5	R14	R18	R20	R30	
British Leyland	Austin Morris Jaguar, Rover, Triumph		Mini/Metro	Allegro	Marina Accord*	Princess MG, Triumph	Rover	Jaguar
Volvo	Volvo			343		244/5	264/5	
Alfa Romeo	Alfa Romeo			Alfasud	Giulietta	Alfetta		
Daimler-Benz	Mercedes					1981	200 series	3/4/600 series
BMW	BMW					300 series	500 series	700 series

* From Honda but assembled by British Leyland

strategy on the demand for what, in the US, has been a comparatively recent phenomenon, the luxury small (in US terms) car. Almost all of the producers mentioned have developed at least one car in their range which might be described as a thoroughgoing sports model, whereas of the US producers only GM, with the Chevrolet Corvette, produce anything which could be considered a reasonable comparison. In addition, the European market has shown a consistent strength in the demand for a 'heavyweight' luxury car of the sort produced either by the larger prestige firms such as Daimler-Benz, BMW, Fiat and BL, or by a number of smaller specialist producers such as Rolls-Royce, Porsche, de Tomaso, etc.

A real choice, rather than the apparent and largely illusory choice between one brandname or another in the US, is a conspicuous feature of the West European car market. A consumer could expect to choose not only from the ranges produced by the American and Japanese manufacturers, but also from an almost bewildering array of European firms, and the CV choice is equally wide.

But the Western European market has become integrated; most manufacturers are now marketing vehicles to most countries within Western Europe. The 1970s have witnessed a dramatic change in the fortunes of some companies. As shown in Table 7.10, British Leyland have experienced the most dramatic decline. Its global market share in cars fell from 8.6 per cent in 1972 to less than 5 per cent in 1978. Fiat (including Seat) and Chrysler have also suffered losses. GM and Ford suffered during the 1973 oil crisis. Until 1972 Ford (Europe) had shown a steady growth in sales and the company have been quick to react to the recent fall in car sales by launching a strong new model range. In the car market, the performance of Renault has been one of the notable successes in recent years. Volkswagen has also increased its market share with a dramatic change in model policy, and the creation of a new range of models that has set standards for every manufacturer to emulate. The other astonishing growth in market share is that of Japan.

CVs

Although the CV industry is often divided into three segments — car derived van (light), panel van (medium) and heavy — the latter segment covers a wide range. The shapes of each segment reflect the principle that you need different types of technology for the different segments. The car derived van and panel van segments are essentially volume operations with potentially large economies of scale. The heavy CV segment is less susceptible to scale economies. Table 7.11 shows the market shares by manufacturer in each of the principal CV segments. The most hotly contested segment is the heavy CV segment which is

Table 7.10 Car manufacturers market shares in Western Europe (%)

	1965	1970	1972	1973	1974	1975	1976	1977	1978	1980*	1985*	1990*
Peugeot-Citroen-Talbot	16	16	18.7	19.4	19.2	18.3	18.0	17.5	17.8	17.3	16.0	15.0
Renault	7	10	11.0	11.5	13.6	12.4	12.6	12.8	12.8	12.5	12.3	12.0
Ford	13	11	11.0	10.0	8.9	9.8	11.2	12.2	12.2	13.0	12.7	13.0
VW	13	10	9.8	10.0	9.9	11.0	10.7	11.8	11.5	11.2	11.0	11.0
Fiat	16	15	17.5	16.9	17.8	15.1	14.4	13.5	12.5	12.0	11.8	12.0
GM	12.0	11	10.5	9.6	8.2	8.9	10.3	10.0	10.3	10.5	11.0	11.0
Japanese imports	0.5	1.7	2.7	3.7	4.0	5.2	5.7	6.3	6.3	7.0	10.0	10.0
British Leyland	11	7	8.6	8.0	7.4	5.9	5.2	4.6	4.8	4.7	4.8	4.8
Daimler-Benz	2.1	2.5	2.6	2.6	3.0	3.2	3.0	3.0	2.8	2.8	2.8	2.8
BMW	1.0	1.6	1.7	1.6	1.8	2.5	2.3	2.3	2.4	2.3	2.2	2.2
Volvo	2.0	2.4	1.7	1.7	1.6	2.3	2.2	1.9	1.8	1.7	1.5	1.5

* Representative forecasts

Table 7.11 *CV market shares in Western Europe (1978)*

Car derived vans		Vans		Heavy CVs	
Manufacturer	Share (%)	Manufacturer	Share (%)	Manufacture	Share (%)
Renault	33.6	VW	20.2	Daimler-Benz	22.7
Peugeot Group	32.2	Ford	16.6	IVECO	16.7
British Leyland	10.1	Peugeot Group	11.7	Ford	8.4
Ford	9.4	Daimler-Benz	9.9	Renault	8.2
GM	7.6	Fiat	9.1	GM	6.1
Fiat	2.9	GM	6.6	Volvo	6.0
Japanese	2.5	Japanese	6.2	British Leyland	4.8
Ebro (Spain)	0.6	Renault	5.3	MAN	3.7
VW	0.3	British Leyland and Land Rover	6.9	Scania (Saab)	3.6

represented by all the major car manufacturers and a number of smaller
independent firms. Table 7.3 shows the tremendous range encompassed
by this segment — from light trucks to linehaul trucks.

Daimler-Benz established itself as a dominant CV producer in the
heavy segment. The creation of IVECO has challenged Daimler-Benz.
The struggle between these two CV giants can be seen in Figure 7.5.

Figure 7.5 *CV manufacturers market shares in Western Europe*

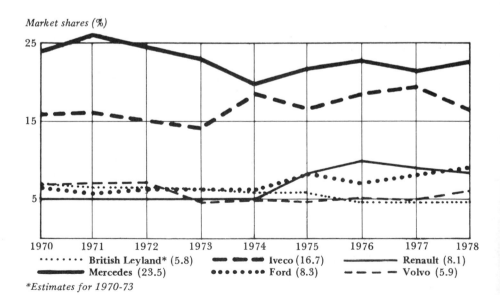

Market shares (%)

British Leyland* (5.8)   Iveco (16.7)   Renault (8.1)
Mercedes (23.5)   Ford (8.3)   Volvo (5.9)

*Estimates for 1970-73

Ford, Renault, Volvo and British Leyland are clearly in a different league. Almost every manufacturer made a loss in 1977 (see Table 7.12). International Harvester (which owns Seddon-Atkinson) also acquired a one-third share in the CV operations of DAF (the remainder being owned equally by the Dutch government and the original owners). Foden and ERF are two smaller UK producers, both from the same family (Foden).

Table 7.12 *Heavy CV manufacturers in Western Europe*

	Production locations		1977 Heavy Truck production[1] ('000s)	1977 Sales[2] $ millions	1977 Profit/loss[2] $ millions
	Main	Other			
IVECO (Fiat)	Italy	Germany France	109.0	2990	76
Renault group	France	—	39.3	3140	−51
Daimler-Benz	Germany	—	133.7	4446	N/A
Ford	Britain	Holland	40.5	1209	170
GM Bedford	Britain	—	33.9	558	N/A
MAN	Germany	—	16.4	1600	36
DAF)	Holland	—	13.0	400[5]	12
Seddon-) Atkinson) (International Harvester)	Britain	—	1.2	N/A	N/A
ERF	Britain	—	0.6	68	3
Foden	Britain	—	1.1	94	5
Volvo	Sweden	—	25.0	850	75
Scania (Saab)	Sweden	—	19.9	1150	40
British Leyland	British	—	22.5	884[4]	−58.8[3]
Peugeot-Citroen (Chrysler)	Britain	Spain	8.8	217[2]	Loss

1. Production over 3.5 tonnes GVW   4. 1978
2. Sales and profits for total commercial group   5. 1976
3. 1978 before tax

Production by manufacturer

Cars

Table 7.13 shows production by manufacturer since 1965. From this the decline of British Leyland and the rise of Ford and Renault become immediately apparent. Since the early 1970s, VW and Fiat (including Seat) have also suffered stagnation in production. The oil crisis in 1973-74 caught Ford at a bad time, with new models about to be launched, and until those models were launched, demand and therefore sales and production suffered. But Ford responded to these setbacks with energy and imagination. Apart from Ford, Renault's growth has been the most consistent and spectacular.

Table 7.13 European car production by manufacturer ('000s)

Year	Volkswagen Group	Fiat Group	Renault	British Leyland	Ford (Europe)	Peugeot-Citroen-Talbot	Daimler-Benz	BMW	Alfa Romeo	Volvo Group	Saab	GM (Europe)
1965	1268	1191	472	809	821	1093	174	93	61	138	49	841
1966	1296	1358	666	900	732	1305	192	98	60	140	37	813
1967	1089	1492	707	716	625	1276	200	100	77	188	45	737
1968	1256	1691	734	803	751	1310	216	109	97	226	53	895
1969	1570	1605	911	777	813	1453	257	140	104	244	62	958
1970	1582	1919	1056	770	1102	1653	280	159	108	277	74	990
1971	1642	1819	1069	887	1118	1933	284	164	123	290	73	1031
1972	1448	1918	1202	916	1229	2113	324	182	141	321	84	1055
1973	1774	1989	1293	876	1169	2255	332	196	205	347	89	1008
1974	1436	1782	1356	739	819	2015	340	185	208	303	93	715
1975	1255	1514	1235	605	937	1945	350	217	190	260	91	754
1976	1463	1624	1420	688	1187	2089	370	268	201	296	96	1028
1977	1596	1630	1483	651	1468	2193	401	285	201	212	76	1015
1978	1641	1688	1466	612	1418	2272	393	312	222	263	85	1043

CVs

Table 7.14 shows CV production by manufacturer. British Leyland's decline since the mid-1960s was mainly in the car-derived van and panel van segments. IVECO's new structure seems to have paid off in the 1970s. Daimler-Benz and Renault have had a steady growth, although Renault's production is concentrated at the lighter end of the market. VW and GM have had an indifferent record. Peugeot-Citroen, which has shown some growth, has only a small representation in the heavy CV segment and that was acquired from Chrysler.

The spectacular growth of Daimler-Benz in the late 1960s and the steadier and more sustained growth achieved by Renault both look impressive, although in the latter case growth may have been at the expense of profitability, which we discuss at greater length below.

When considering the European market (car and CV) in more general terms, the extent of government ownership and/or control of many of the major manufacturers is of central importance, as it suggests that in Europe at least, in sharp contrast to the motor industry elsewhere, making money may not be the sole or overriding objective. It has been rumoured that Renault, for example, was presented with a clutch of policy objectives by the French government, in pursuit of which the company is expected to maintain levels of employment, increase exports, and not *lose* money, though Renault is not under any pressure to generate profits. The poor performance of Chrysler UK and Vauxhall is explained in part by the generally lower growth throughout of the UK industry, a lack of investment, and the failure of the respective parent companies to take effective action in correcting the chronic weaknesses in both subsidiaries.

Financial position

Table 7.15 shows the actual profits generated by the principal motor manufacturers in Western Europe. The 1974 downswing meant that all of the major producers incurred losses in that year, with production levels well below capacity. Only BMW, Daimler-Benz and Volvo — for the most part specialist and up-market quality manufacturers — were at all profitable.

In the period preceding the 1974 depression, the Ford operation in West Germany and GM's Opel division had been two of the most profitable of the European concerns. At the other extreme, neither Chrysler UK nor Vauxhall had achieved even minimum profitability, despite a pre-1974 boom of unprecedented proportions. In 1970-73, of the major firms only VW had made any major technological change, moving from an air-cooled to a water-cooled engine technology. The switch required enormous capital expenditure, but even companies not

Table 7.14 European CV production by manufacturer ('000s)

Year	GM	Volkswagen	Peugeot-Citroen-Talbot	Daimler-Benz	Fiat IVECO	Renault Group	British Leyland	Ford (Europe)
1965	130	84	129	85	75	86	216	157
1966	115	84	133	90	85	96	200	151
1967	98	73	116	97	103	99	189	117
1968	107	99	124	112	118	101	200	200
1969	115	108	133	146	122	133	185	162
1970	111	103	134	171	138	140	173	164
1971	123	93	114	160	119	138	174	155
1972	97	104	159	168	114	149	140	170
1973	115	99	181	177	114	159	137	167
1974	117	70	196	161	119	171	125	175
1975	93	72	159	180	141	147	133	165
1976	89	94	187	193	144	212	120	181
1977	95	94	196	187	155	223	120	173
1978	121	93	195	173	175	208	131	148

Table 7.15 *European profitability profits before taxes*
($ millions)

	1971	1972	1973	1974	1975	1976	1977
GM (Europe)	114	230	214	−19	25	447	550
Ford (Europe)	20	190	252	−21	130	570	1093
Chrysler (Europe)	18	44	69	−53	−103	−16	−18
Renault	−28	23	23	8	−129	142	150
Peugeot-Citroen	54	101	119	−118	84	608	621
VW	62	158	134	−223	78	593	1139
Daimler-Benz	200	246	339	376	506	741	1070
British Leyland	78	81	125	5	−170	127[1]	−90
Fiat	64	73	67	60	5	153	140
BMW				26	65	133	340
Volvo				43	20	40	25
Saab				48	53	71	83

1. 15 months includes CV and special product divisions

Nb: British Leyland, Volvo-Saab and Fiat are diversified companies, and a major share of
   Daimler-Benz profits comes from CVs

involved in major capital investment programmes were unable to keep
capital expenditures low during the boom period although most of them
were able to provide the necessary finance for existing operations. The
greatest profits are achieved in the West German market: hence the high
profitability of the leading suppliers there (GM, Ford, VW, Daimler-
Benz and BMW). Of all the manufacturers, Daimler-Benz has been the
most consistently profitable.

Even in the peak period of demand in the 1970-73 boom, very few
of the West European companies could obtain acceptable rates of return
on capital. Even in 1976 77 only Daimler-Benz, Ford, GM and VW were
profitable in terms of the size of their overall operation. There seems to
be a razor's edge in the European motor industry: if you are profitable
you generate large profits, if not your company is little more than
marginal. Why is profitability so razor sharp?

Productivity and economies of scale

To answer the question posed above we must take a brief look at the
vexed question of productivity. Western European production has been
substantially below that of the Japanese, and also marginally below
North American levels. Comparisons of productivity levels are fraught
with difficulties. If we define an index starting from a base year of
1968, the evolution of productivity levels may provide an interesting

pointer. Figure 7.6 shows that whereas Nissan and Toyota have been consistently increasing their productivity, the major European producers have not: GM and Ford have only just held their productivity levels, although US multinational productivity is about 10 per cent higher in the US than their corporate average.

With a falling productivity level, there is inadequate output to achieve minimal scale economies. In Chapter 5 this was discussed at length. In order to compete in the world, a minimum of around 2 million cars per year, coupled with a certain level of automation, is required. Model runs in the central small-, light- and medium-car segments should be in excess of 400,000 per year, and certain common panels and components should be produced at the rate of 2 million cars per year.

Fiat, PSA Peugeot-Citroen and VW have the scale capacity to produce at these minimum economies of scale. Fiat's reorganization (integration with Seat) and Peugeot-Citroen's acquisition of Chrysler Europe have only occurred recently, and VW's production has not approached 2 million cars a year for some time. As we have already noted in Chapter 5, the same scale economies are not necessarily present in the heavy truck sectors; this allows the smaller CV producer to avoid cost penalties.

Has a potentially high cost structure (and the consequent possibility of low profits) led to any special developments in Europe that were not apparent in North America?

European trends

With only a brief descriptive summary of the sort possible here,[1] it is still apparent that, for the European motor industry, the 1970s have been a period of upheaval and dramatic change. Three developments deserve particular emphasis: a greater willingness on the part of manufacturers to establish formal or informal ties with each other; the gradual southward migration, as firms relocate in the few remaining low labour cost areas (set against a counter migration of labour from the lost cost areas in the south recruited by manufacturers to the north); and an increasing degree of government intervention and control in the motor industry.

Links within Europe

We have already noted the existence of complex inter-relationships as a characteristic of the European market, and Figure 7.7 is an attempt to summarize some of these convoluted associations. There are, however, one or two additional interconnections which should be discussed in

---

1. For a further analysis of the European marketplace see Bhaskar, K N *op cit*.

Figure 7.6 *Productivity in vehicle manufacture*
(unit output per man)

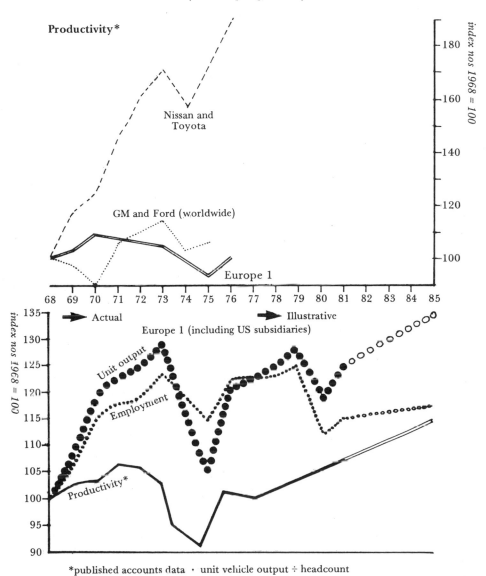

*published accounts data · unit vehicle output ÷ headcount

Europe 1 is defined as West Germany, France, Italy, UK, Spain, Netherlands, Sweden
and Finland

Europe 2 is defined as all the remaining countries in Western Europe not defined as
Europe 1

Source; *The European Car Industry Review 1978-82* Euroeconomics, Eurofinance

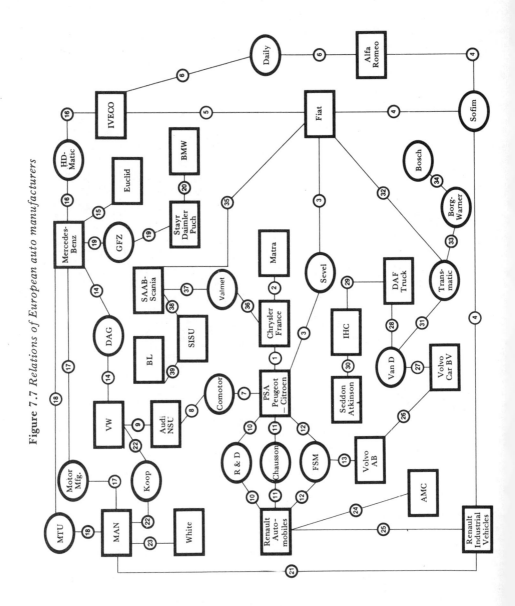

Figure 7.7 Relations of European auto manufacturers

Key to European relationships

1. PSA Peugeot-Citroen owns 100 per cent of Chrysler France, Chrysler UK and Chrysler Espana, while Chrysler Corporation in turn holds a 15 per cent interest in PSA Peugeot-Citroen.

2. Chrysler France and the automobile divisions of Engins Matra jointly produce two cars, the Matra-Simca Bagheera and the Matra-Simca Rancho. They are assembled in a Matra plant at Romorantin, and marketed through the Chrysler France dealer organization.

3. PSA Peugeot-Citroen and Fiat have a programme for joint development and production of a 1000 kg van. A joint subsidiary called SEVEL (*Societe Europeenne des Vehicules Legers*) has been formed and an assembly plant is under construction at Val di Sangro in the Abruzzi.

4. SOFIM (*Societe Franco-Italienne des Moteurs*) is jointly owned by Fiat (52.5 per cent), Alfa Romeo (14.5 per cent), and Renault Industrial Vehicles (33 per cent). SOFIM diesel engines are made at Foggia and used in the Fiat 131 and 132 cars, Daily van, Fiat tractors, Alfa Romeo AR8 van, and will power the 1980-model F-series Renault and Saviem vans.

5. IVECO (Industrial Vehicles Corporation) is an Amsterdam-based holding that comprises full ownership of Fiat's truck division including OM, Unic-Fiat in France, and Magirus-Deutz in West Germany. Fiat owns 80 per cent of IVECO, and Klockner-Humboldt-Deutz 20 per cent.

6. The Fiat Daily and AR8 vans are the same design, developed and produced jointly by IVECO and Alfa Romeo.

7/8. Comotor is a joint subsidiary of PSA Peugeot-Citroen and Audi-NSU Auto Union AG, created for the development and production of rotary engines. Comotor has a big facility at Gaarlouis, now used only for research. Production was suspended in 1975.

9. Audi-NSU Auto Union AG is a subsidiary of Volkswagenwerk AG.

10. PSA Peugeot-Citroen and Renault collaborate in research and development in certain areas (safety, emissions).

11. PSA Peugeot-Citroen and Renault are part owners of Usines Chausson, whose subsidiary, Chausson Carrosserie, assembles the Renault Estafette and Peugeot J-7 vans.

12. PSA Peugeot-Citroen and Renault are part owners of the Franco-Suedoise des Moteurs at Douvrin (all-aluminium four-cylinder and V-6 SOHC engines).

13. Volvo is a partner with PSA Peugeot-Citroen and Renault in the *Franco-Suedoise des Moteurs* (264 series engine).

14. DAG (*Deutsche Automobil Gesellschaft*) is a joint subsidiary held 50/50 by Daimler-Benz AG and Volkswagenwerk AG. DAG was created as a research organization but is not observed as being active.

15. Daimler-Benz AG owns 100 per cent of Euclid (Formerly a subsidiary of White Motor Co).

16. Daimler-Benz and IVECO have an agreement to collaborate on the development of automatic transmission for trucks and their possible future production.

17. Daimler-Benz AG and MAN (*Maschinenfabrik Augsburg-Nurnberg*) share diesel engine production facilities and components (a range of 4, 5, V-6, V-8 and V-10 engine blocks and crankshafts).

18. MU (*Motoren und Turbinen Union*) is a joint subsidiary owned 50/50 by MAN and Daimler-Benz AG, making diesel engines at Friedrichshafen and gas turbines at Munich.

19. GFZ (*Gelandefahrzeugbau*) is a joint subsidiary of Daimler-Benz AG and Steyr-Daimler-Puch AG for the production of the G-series 4x4 light vehicle.

20. Steyr-Daimler-Puch and BMW have established a joint subsidiary for the development and production of diesel engines for cars.

21. MAN and Renault Industrial Vehicles have an agreement for cooperation in production and marketing. It was signed in 1958 between Saviem and MAN and is expected to be cancelled when found redundant.

22. Volkswagenwerk and MAN have an agreement to collaborate on the development of a new truck range (Koop truck) and share component production for it. But MAN will assemble its own trucks at Salzgitter, VW at Hannover.

23. MAN acquired 12.6 per cent ownership of White Motor Co. in 1978 and is now seeking 51 per cent ownership.

24. American Motors and Renault have an agreement for mutual marketing of selected products in certain markets, and Renault currently has a 22.5 per cent equity stake in AMC.

25. Renault merged its two truck subsidiaries, Saviem and Berliet, as Renault Industrial Vehicles in 1978.

26/27. Volvo Var BV (ex-DAF) is a Dutch-based subsidiary of AB Volvo which produces the 66 and 343 models. Volvo has majority control but shares ownership with De Staats Mijnen (a state owned mining corporation) and the Van Doorne family (founders of DAF).

28/29. DAF Truck is controlled by the Van Doorne family, but International Harvester Co has a 33 per cent stake in the company.

30. International Harvester Co owns 100 per cent of Seddon-Atkinson, makers of diesel trucks at Preston in Lancashire.

31. Transmatic is a continuously variable transmission developed by the Van Doorne family outside of its former DAF activity.

32. Fiat and Borg-Warner share a 40 per cent interest in Van Doorne Transmissie (Transmatic).

33. Renault has a 20 per cent interest in the Borg-Warner Corporation.

34. Robert Bosch AG has a 20 per cent interest in the new Lancia small car (Delta? Epsilon?) and will distribute it in Scandinavia with a Saab label.

35. Saab took part in the development of the new Lancia small car (Delta? Epsilon?) and will distribute it in Scandinavia with a Saab label.

36. Valmet has an agreement with Chrysler France to assemble the Simca 1100 and Horizon in Finland.

37. Saab-Scania has a 50 per cent interest in Valmet.

38/39. Saab-Scania and BL Vehicles are part owners of Finland's diesel truck builders, Sisu.

Nb. The link-up between Volvo and Renault occurred too late to be incorporated into this diagram.

Source: *Automotive News* market survey

the European context.

We have already outlined the Club of Four agreement, but it is not an isolated instance of cooperation. The research, design, development and manufacture of the Douvrin engine is a further example of the way in which producers have adopted a joint approach. In this case, Peugeot, Renault and Volvo agreed to undertake the Douvrin (FSM) project on a collective basis, as all three participants were anxious to develop a larger engine. The success of the undertaking was by no means assured, as all three firms produced conflicting performance specifications and the end product of their deliberations is considered something of a compromise. The cars now fitted with the new engine — the Renault R30, Volvo 264 and Peugeot 604 — compare unfavourably in performance tests with the larger-engined Ford models, but if the engine itself is less than totally impressive, the mutual benefits of this sort of joint financing have established a useful precedent, and should encourage further experiments in joint projects in the future.

Labour costs and southward migration

In the 1960s and early 1970s, attempts were made to ease the high labour cost pressures in West Germany and elsewhere, by recruiting cheap labour from Yugoslavia, Turkey, Greece, Southern Italy and Northern Africa. The existence of communities of 'guest workers' on this scale solved existing manpower difficulties but created new social and political problems, especially when a period of depressed demand made swingeing redundancies and lay-offs necessary.

The solution to the problem was found in a reversal of the traffic. If the presence of guest workers acted as a social and even industrial irritant in Northern communities, the mountain would have to go to Mohammed — the work would be taken to the workers. Relocation promised other advantages: constructing plant in low-cost areas would be mutually beneficial to host countries (for obvious reasons) and to producers, who could gain substantial price advantages from utilizing low-cost labour reserves in less developed areas, and who had hopes of employing a more amenable workforce.

Not all of the established European producers have shown the same enthusiasm for southward migration: most of the German manufacturers have decided against such a move, and it is certainly clear that transfer south is by no means a straightforward undertaking. A suitable physical infrastructure — roads, houses, schools, drainage and irrigation systems, etc — has to be created where it does not already exist, which is often the case, and a components and supply industry must be established to avoid an otherwise costly traffic in the thousands of small components required. Similarly, training programmes are necessary to acquaint a locally recruited workforce with the unfamiliar disciplines of assembly line working, and to train a smaller group of workers in more specialist skills. Alfa Romeo encountered all of these difficulties when establishing their Alfasud factory in Southern Italy, compounded by the problem of poor-quality and sub-standard work at the outset. Elsewhere, the promise of a docile workforce has proved to be illusory. Spanish workers are rapidly acquiring a more sophisticated approach to labour/ management relations as they discover the advantages of worker solidarity. The ritual of strategically timed pay demands is already well-established, and Spain may not prove to be a particularly low labour cost area for very much longer. Political problems could also erode the economic advantages of a migration strategy in the future, and the possibility of increasing government intervention is a further deterrent. Ford, in return for permission from the Spanish government to establish new plant in Spain, were obliged to offer a guarantee to export two-thirds of their Spanish output, an undertaking that could cause problems if Ford were ever burdened with a production surplus elsewhere. The advantages of moving to lost-cost areas within Europe are by no means clearly established.

The late 1970s has seen an increase in the southward migration phenomenon. Ford are contemplating increasing the capacity of their Spanish plant, GM have announced a 300,000 car plant in Spain, Peugeot-Citroen-Talbot is expanding its ex-Citroen and ex-Chrysler plants, and Renault is planning a $400 million engine and assembly plant in Portugal (although assembly capacity will be small and the bulk of the engines will be exported). It is surprising that there is this rush to Spain and Portugal at a time when domestic demand is not strong and Ford has experienced great problems which have severely reduced the profitability of the Fiesta project. The reasons for this headlong rush are partly government money (up to 50 per cent of the investment) and cooperation, and partly that there are very few other countries left. When Ford thought of placing a new plant in France, Renault and PSA Peugeot Citroen rushed to the government with their own schemes and effectively eclipsed France from Ford's list of possible places for plant development.

Government control

We have already noted the number of companies now under direct or indirect government control in Europe. In nearly every case, government intervention has been justified as a legitimate response to the importance of the motor industry, particularly in those countries where the industry is regarded as a quasi-utility, providing jobs and essential services and under an obligation to function at acceptable levels of efficiency. In this context, a government chooses to intervene in order to exercise control over the industry's activities. Alternatively, a government might be approached by the industry itself, or might offer assistance to it as the lender of the last resort. The French government's role in the Peugeot-Citroen merger could be described as intervention of the first sort: in the 'public' interest, a hesitant (in contrast to the Chrysler takeover) Peugeot was persuaded to complete an unlikely merger with Citroen and to abandon existing ties with Renault. The sum of $50 million offered by the government may have sweetened the bitter pill momentarily, but Peugeot, which could lose several times that amount as a result of the deal, might have found that small consolation in the long run. This takeover in practice simply served to whet Peugeot's appetite, and they went on to take over Chrysler Europe with very little encouragement.

The British government, on the other hand, acted as lender of the last resort in British Leyland's transition from private to public ownership, although, at the time, intervention was also mooted as a means of salvaging an essential industry (the quasi-utility argument). Chrysler UK secured a $325 million package in 1975 funded by the British government without relinquishing ownership, whereas VW sold a further 4 per cent of its equity to the West German government in 1974 to restore the company's flagging fortunes. Bavaria owns a minority shareholding in BMW, and the Italian government have now assumed total control, through GEPI, of de Tomaso, Maserati and less directly of Innocenti. Even Volvo has not emerged unscathed: in 1974 the Swedish government employees pension fund acquired a 4.7 per cent interest in Volvo, for the sum of $50 million, which made the Swedish government the largest single shareholder in the company, and the company has also received direct state aid.

Table 7.6 shows some of the principal goverment links with the major European motor companies. Even without a majority or minority government share of ownership, it seems that many European governments operate on the assumption that the ultimate responsibility for the control of the industry is theirs of right, judging from the incidence of state 'interference' in the French, Italian and UK motor industries. This chapter has examined the present position in Western Europe, and Chapter 8 attempts to anticipate future developments. One observer has pointed to the industry's central dilemma in Europe:

> There is a spectrum of possibilities facing the Europeans. At one end of this spectrum is the view that the Europeans should group themselves more closely. Cynics label this the 'King Canute' strategy. At the other end of the spectrum is the view that Europe should allow competitors into its markets, provided that this adds to the development of the European manufacturing industry base. This latter view has tended to be less than fully explored because it is regarded as political heresy. In the case of cars, the argument that the only acceptable basis for trading is that close to a 'one-for-one', finished product balance has always been nonsense in theory, logic and practice.

At almost every turn in the debate about the strategic development of the West European car industry, political factors are involved. This is true to the extent that the solutions derived from rational, dispassionate analysis seemed condemned never to be applied. But there is a not-too-difficult to identify group of European car makers whose growth and viability prospects are seriously threatened. To the extent that they face pressure at an early stage in the period between now and 1985, the chances of them accepting some rational analysis are that much greater. The longer they wait, the greater the loss of potential.[1]

1. Hinks-Edwards, Michael (1977) of Eurofinance in a paper presented to the European Motor Industry Conference at Frankfurt.

Chapter 8

Western Europe
in the Future

The market and manufacturers found in Western Europe have evolved in a very different environment to that of North America. At the same time Western Europe's maturity is less well established and it is reasonable that some of the market characteristics found in North America will eventually be reproduced in Western Europe. The combination of Western Europe's unique development and lessons from the more mature North American market provide a daunting future for the Western European producers. European manufacturers will experience some of the same problems found by their US counterparts, some of which are listed below.

1. *Increased import penetration and reduced exports.* As the European market matures, so other non-European producers will compete for a share in a market second in size only to North America. Imports from Japan and the Communist Bloc producers may in the longer term compete with imports from Korea, Iran and Turkey. As import penetration rises, the European producers will face even stronger competitive pressure in existing export markets from countries with low labour costs.
2. *Increased competitive pressure.* A stronger import challenge in the domestic market, and the threat of growing competition in export markets could link in with slower growth and a more cyclical fluctuation in the pattern of demand to increase competition between European producers.
3. *Labour problems.* Following the US model, Europe too will have to adjust to the consequences of a shorter working week (except perhaps in the UK, Spain and Italy) and more widespread dissatisfaction with assembly line work. But whereas the United Automobile Workers Union in the US has accepted the inevitability of automation, European unions may be less agreeable to the introduction of automation on a wider scale, and renew their demands for worker participation in management decisions and a greater commitment to industrial democracy. Two countries, Italy and the UK, are already troubled by poor industrial relations and conditions elsewhere could deteriorate in the future.

Although labour costs in Europe show considerable variation from country to country, from an extreme high in Sweden to a low in Spain, labour costs in the area as a whole will eventually become more uniform. Lower cost areas will catch up and Europe generally will become a high labour cost region.

4. *Possible economies of scale.* The annual production totals among some of the major European manufacturers are very small compared to the totals of the US or Japanese producers, making it difficult for effective economies of scale to be applied.

5. *Government controls.* Although the extent of government control within Europe will probably fall short of the restrictions and controls enforced by governments in Japan and the US, they will nevertheless have some impact on costs and production.

6. *Automation.* Despite union resistance, greater automation will be more or less inevitable as a means of controlling costs and maintaining effective competition in pricing. European productivity already falls far behind productivity in Japan and North America. Should the US and Japanese manufacturers increase their lead in this respect, an outcome which many observers feel is almost a foregone conclusion, European producers cannot ignore the challenge and lag even further behind. Automation will require heavy capital investment.

7. *Technological problems.* Conventional engineering has thus far been the hallmark of cars produced by the US and Japanese manufacturers, whereas European firms have adopted a more adventurous approach to new developments in technology and engineering. Although intra-European competition should continue to stimulate innovation along these lines the Japanese and North American producers, most of whom will be investing in massive research and development programmes, will in future present a much greater technological challenge. This too will necessitate heavy research, design and development expenditure.

8. *North American down-sizing.* North American manufacturers are producing a more 'European' product which may be exported to Europe. With enormous potential economies of scale, the North American product may be cheaper than the European product. This advantage may lead to large imports from North America, but it is unlikely that either GM or Ford would wish to import cars into Europe when they have their own highly profitable subsidiaries in Europe and are extremely eager to expand their European capacity. Moreover it is doubtful whether Ford or GM have sufficient spare capacity in North America (except during slumps) to undertake such an exercise.

European imports and exports

Table 8.1 shows net imports into Western Europe and the exports from European producers to non-European markets. Imports have been steadily rising and exports falling. In the late 1960s, when Europe exported around one million cars to the North American market, Europe had a positive balance of trade of over 1.5 million cars. As the European marketplace matured during the 1970s, so it inherited one of the North American symptoms: the import of cheap basic cars. Although the imports have been mainly Japanese (see Figure 8.1), there is a steadily growing import penetration from the Communist Bloc. The remaining imports are mainly from North America with a smaller number from South Korea and South America.

Table 8.1 *Western European balance of trade in cars ('000s)*

	Imports			Exports	
	Total imports	Japanese imports	Communist Bloc imports	Total exports	North American exports
1968	96	57	25	1740	1062
1969	119	71	35	1783	989
1970	175	113	50	1737	973
1971	254	193	50	1901	1154
1972	408	330	66	1716	997
1973	460	362	82	1758	967
1974	428	344	63	2019	982
1975	629	487	120	1463	687
1976	815	633	140	1406	632
1977	865	661	160	1527	708
1978	940	750	140	1450	661
1979	940	750	140	1600	700
1980*	1000	800	160	1500	600
1985*	1000–1700	800–1500	150–300	1300	550
1990*	1250–2250	1000–1500	200–500	1200	500

* Representative forecasts

Will the Japanese share of the European market continue to increase? If left to market forces the answer must be yes. The North American model illustrates that the Japanese can and will gain a significant slice of a mature market — say 20 per cent. However, political arguments and pressures are likely to be more intense in Europe than North America, and evidence of this is provided by the example of the Japanese/UK government agreement (dubbed 'orderly marketing') to limit imports into the UK. This establishes a precedent for the rest of Europe's car manufacturing nations.

If one takes the periphery of Western Europe, Japanese import penetration has already reached levels of 15-20 per cent. In the main

Figure 8.1 *Market shares of Japanese produced cars in Western Europe*

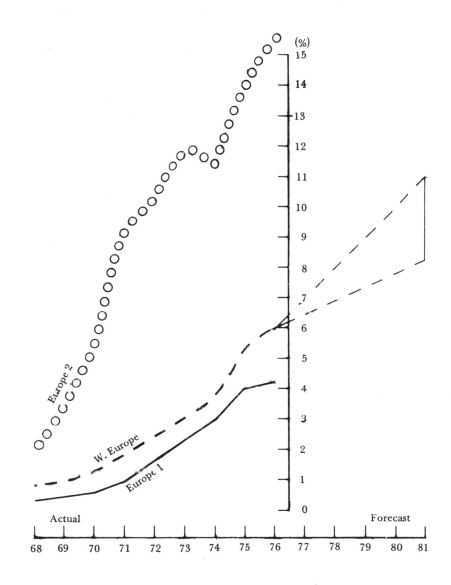

Europe 1 is defined as West Germany, France, Italy, UK, Spain, Sweden, Netherlands and Finland.

Europe 2 is defined as all the remaining countries in Western Europe.

Source: The European Car Industry Review 1978-82 Euroeconomics, Eurofinance

European countries, where European manufacturers are located, the market has been less open and the manufacturers have trodden more gingerly (see Figure 8.1). The signs are, however, that import penetration is rising: 1979 saw a significant improvement in the Japanese share of the West German market. Japanese import penetration will, by 1990, have reached 1-1.5 million cars, which puts the Japanese share of the market significantly lower than their current North American share. With increasing imports from the Communist Bloc and other newer producers, total imports by 1990 will cover a broad range. A protectionist Western Europe might limit imports to around 1.5 million but, if Western Europe follows the US pattern, import penetration should have exceeded 20 per cent by 1990.

The major export markets, excluding exports to the Communist Bloc and some of the Mediterranean countries, are given in Table 8.2, showing that by far the largest market is North America, followed at a considerable distance by markets in Africa, the Near East and Central and South America. Within the various markets, West Germany has captured the lion's share of the North American export market, while France is strongly represented in Eastern Europe, Africa, the Pacific zone and the Near East. The UK, meanwhile, has done particularly well in the Near East.

The fall in Western European exports can be directly traced to a decay in North American demand. This decay resulted from the European product becoming more mature and the Japanese product being cheaper and more suitable as the basic, low-cost car. The Japanese product also established a reputation for reliability which was never quite matched by the Europeans.

The prospects for Western European exports look bleak. First the long-run trend has been for European currencies to gain against the dollar making the European product more expensive. Second, major European exporters are now following the US pattern of establishing plants in the major markets; such locational change switches production away from Europe to the export market. Third, in newer and developing markets the possibilities of an open market for built-up cars are diminishing and sales are gained only through fierce competition; instead local manufacture and/or assembly is the most common trend. Fourth, export markets might attempt to contain imports. We must examine these points in greater detail.

Export prospects in North America

As the largest single car market in the world, the US offers important export opportunities for West European firms. Of total European exports, nearly half are to the United States, and any change in that volume would have an immediate effect on the industry in Europe

Table 8.2 Major car exports of Western Europe

	1977 Exports from Europe ('000s)									1977 Exports to other Western European countries ('000s)	1977 Total imports from all countries[1] ('000s)
	Eastern Europe	Africa	Far East	Near East	Pacific	North America	Caribbean	Central and South America	Total		
West Germany	19	38	34	21	15	504	2	23	656	1282	891
France	39	125	6	72	9	38	10	45	344	1258	431
UK	3	34	24	106	38	59	0	0	307	168	718
Italy	8	41	7	10	5	57	3	8	139	504	457
Sweden	2	4	2	3	6	47	0	1	60	66	145
Belgium	1	0	0	1	0	4	0	0	6	953	420
Spain	1	3	1	1	0	0	0	2	7	290	65
Total	73	245	74	214	73	709	15	79	1519	4521	Total European imports 3127

1. Excludes Communist Bloc, South America and other newer producers

Nb. 0 indicates less than 500 cars

Source: Automobile International

(see Tables 8.1 and 8.2).

As we have already noted, the US market followed the familiar pattern of an early 1970s boom, followed by a post oil crisis recession-led slump in demand, with some recovery recently. The growth rate in the immediate future is not expected to be particularly rapid. Imports have accounted for a growing share of the US market over the last decade and this and the CAFE programme have encouraged the domestic producers to launch a direct counter-offensive, spearheaded by a new range of down-sized European-type models which could, if successful, reduce the import share of the market considerably. Increased competition from US manufacturers would certainly have some effect on the imports of volume cars, although sales of specialist and luxury models, such as British Leyland's MG, would be less affected than, say, the VW range. Both VW and Volvo have announced plans to establish manufacturing and assembly facilities in the US in a move to retain their current market shares, and this could also severely depress demand for a more expensive import.[1] VW's plans have come to fruition but Volvo's have not, mainly because the company has insufficient cash. Renault may assemble the R5 and R18 in an AMC plant. But these moves ignore the most important fact: a cheaper Japanese product has almost eclipsed the Western European producers in the North American market. Only VW through aggressive marketing and the installation of assembly capacity in North America, has been able to hang on to a significant, albeit reduced, market share.

Prospects for European exports to Japan

Imports account for only a fraction of total sales (1.1 per cent) in the Japanese market. Traditionally, German firms have supplied most of the cars imported into Japan, but in recent years sales of US cars have risen substantially and now represent roughly one-third of the total import share, with the balance divided between a number of European firms.

Why is the import share of the Japanese market so low? Import tariffs are in fact lower than those imposed by the EEC, and imported cars are not liable to any discriminatory tax. Foreign capital investment in the Japanese motor industry is no longer restricted, so that in theory 100 per cent foreign ownership and control would be possible. The introduction of rigorous emission control standards for foreign cars, already mandatory for Japanese manufacturers, has been deferred for two years, by which time they may be no more stringent than requirements elsewhere. And the Japanese have forcibly demonstrated that the remoteness of a market is no bar to a successful export performance.

The apparent accessibility of the Japanese market is a little misleading, however, as these relatively favourable conditions have only applied in

1. The link-up with Renault makes this possibility more remote.

recent years. For some time the Japanese market was highly protected, making it virtually impossible for a foreign manufacturer to establish even a skeleton distribution network. A recent survey revealed that there were just over 50 dealerships with some 110 sales outlets between them handling all import sales. In contrast, Toyota alone works through a network of 250 principal dealers responsible for a total of 2600 sales outlets. Purely commercial considerations make it almost impossible for foreign manufacturers to entice existing dealerships away from an entrenched allegiance to Japanese manufacturers. The only possible alternative — to invest in the creation of an entirely new dealer network — would face the almost insuperable problems of acquiring suitable sites, staff and providing the necessary credit at competitive rates. Poor distribution and poor coverage have inevitably produced poor sales.

Ford and GM, in effect, both have subsidiaries (or the equivalent) in Japan and it is unlikely that either will export to Japan except as a tied import (ie in exchange for exports). British Leyland and Honda may also make some sort of reciprocal arrangement, with Honda selling British Leyland's quality models in Japan. The likelihood of reaching similar franchise agreements with other Japanese car firms is remote, and European manufacturers cannot expect to achieve more than modest growth in market share in those areas where their product is in direct competition with the Japanese. Only where this is not the case, at the luxury end of the market, for example, is there any real potential for increased sales.

Access to remaining world markets

Access to many of the developing countries is by no means straight-forward, as many of them are interested in developing car industries of their own and have imposed import bans or quotas to protect local industry. Table 8.3 summarizes the incidence of protection in outline, and shows very clearly the limited opportunities for greater access to some of these potentially large and prosperous new markets. The European manufacturer hoping to sell a fully assembled car can expect to run the gauntlet of import tariffs, quotas and licensing restrictions. Even where cars are exported in knock-down form a local government will usually insist on a gradual increase in local content, ie in parts and components manufactured locally. This has been so with Talbot (Chrysler UK) exports of unassembled cars to Iran, and it is certainly the case that a steady growth in export sales can not be guaranteed in those markets which are determined to establish a motor industry of their own.

One final factor militates against any substantial growth in export sales to developing countries. The Japanese, forever the bugbear, have already acquired a formidable market share in many of the adjoining

Table 8.3 *Import restrictions in major Third World markets*

Market	Limitation on imports		
	Restrictions on BU Imports[1]	Discriminatory Tariff on BU Imports[2]	Local Content Rules for Assembly[3]
Brazil	Yes	Yes	Yes
Australia	Yes	Yes	Yes
Mexico	Yes	Yes	Yes
South Africa	Yes	Yes	Yes
Argentina	Yes	Yes	Yes
New Zealand	No	Yes	No
Iran	Yes	Yes	No
Nigeria	Yes	Yes	Yes
Philippines	Yes	Yes	Yes
Indonesia	Yes	Yes	Yes

1. Bans, quotas, licences making BU imports difficult, etc
2. Significantly higher tariffs on BU vehicles than on parts or CKD units
3. Either legal minimum or *de facto* minimums to avoid tax penalty

Source: The Future of The British Car Industry CRRS

Pacific or Far East markets, and within the next few years their market share in the area could increase significantly. As production facilities are established in developing countries, the need to import either assembled cars or components will necessarily diminish, taking with it any prospect for future export growth in other than highly specialized models.

In sum, where export sales exist, they are unlikely to increase greatly, as in nearly every case European manufacturers must now compete not only with a local industry, but with the fiercely competitive Japanese. In developing markets, exports of cars or even of components or kits will be subject to increasingly punitive restrictions. Attempts to circumvent tariffs, quotas, etc by establishing local subsidiaries may in future be difficult if not impossible. Fiat have had some success in exporting a complete manufacturing package to Communist Bloc countries, but a limited success of this nature does not alter an otherwise pessimistic export future.

It seems likely that exports will face a steady decline. At best this decline might be arrested by 1990; at worst Western European exports could approach those of North America (ie almost negligible levels). A plausible, if conservative, hypothesis is that Western European exports will decline to around 1.2 million cars by 1990.

These predictions amount to a dramatic change in the fortunes of the Western European producer. In the 1960s these producers had the whole of the Western European market to themselves and enjoyed additional exports of 1.5 million cars. This is a classic characteristic of a newly maturing market, and a position currently enjoyed by the Japanese. By the 1990s however, Western European producers at best face a market only equal to the Western European market (exports are exactly balanced by imports at around 1.2 million cars); at worst Western European producers will supply a market up to 15-20 per cent less than the Western European market (ie imports of around 2 million cars with no exports).

We define two alternative assumptions to be used in our analysis of the future of the Western European market. The first hypothesis — the low import scenario — assumes that exports will fall to 1.2 million in 1990 with imports of about the same level. This is the most plausible optimistic assessment and there is good reason to believe that firms such as Renault, Fiat, VW, Daimler-Benz and Peugeot-Citroen will endeavour to achieve this situation. The second hypothesis — the high import scenario — assumes that imports in 1990 will rise to 2.2 million and exports will remain at 1.2 million implying a negative balance of trade of some one million cars. Even this is by no means the most pessimistic of possible outcomes.

Table 8.4 *Forecasts of Western European demand in 1990*

Population in 1990: 376 m		
	Cars	CVs
Vehicle life in 1990 (years)	12	13
Vehicle parc in 1977 (m)	89.9	10.3
New demand in 1990 (m)	0-1.5	0-0.2
Low demand scenario		
Number of vehicles per 1000 people	300	33
Persons per vehicle	3.33	30.3
Vehicle parc (m)	110.1	12.11
Replacement demand (m)	9.2	0.93
Demand range (m)	8-12	0.8-1.23
Central demand scenario		
Number of vehicles per 1000 people	350	37
Persons per vehicle	2.86	27.0
Vehicle parc (m)	128.5	13.6
Replacement demand (m)	10.7	1.05
Demand range (m)	9-13.5	0.9-1.35
High demand scenario		
Number of vehicles per 1000 people	400	40
Persons per vehicle	2.5	25.0
Vehicle parc (m)	146.8	14.7
Replacement demand (m)	12.23	1.13
Demand range (m)	10.5-14.0	0.95-1.45

The trends in cars tend to be repeated in the CV industry but with a delay of several years. Import penetration in the European CV market will follow the pattern set by cars for the same reasons, except in the heaviest segments of the CV market where transport costs are significant. In 1977, Western European CV exports were 325,000 and imports were around 110,000 (mainly from Japan) — a positive trade balance of 215,000 CVs (from 206,000 in 1973). Exports are mainly to less developed or developing countries. It seems plausible to argue that a low import scenario in 1990 would produce a positive trade balance of some 100,000 CVs whilst a high import scenario would balance imports and exports.

Having established two plausible scenarios for trade balance, future Western European demand is now considered.

Future projections of demand

The European market will experience much more volatile demand in future. Patterns of demand in Europe are similar to those forecast for North America, with cyclical fluctuations adjusted for three sets of assumptions concerning saturation levels in the European market.

Assuming a 3 per cent growth in *per capita* GNP, the European average of $4903 will increase to $7416 in 1990 (at constant prices) which is higher than the current North American *per capita* GNP. Given the same standard of living, Western European vehicle density levels are likely to be lower for structural and institutional reasons (lack of space, alternative transport media, etc). If the growth rate in population is 0.5 per cent, the population in 1990 will be some 367 million. We further assume that the vehicle life will be 12 and 13 years for a car and CV respectively. In the low demand scenario (see Table 8.4) vehicle ownership is forecast at a lower level (300 cars and 33 CVs per 1000 people); this yields a replacement demand of 9.2 million cars and 930,000 CVs. Actual replacement demand will be slightly lower, being a function of purchases previously made, but the replacement demand calculated serves as a basis to allow for the progress of some of the less developed regions in Europe. New demand is predicted to be up to 1.5 million cars and 0.25 million CVs. Combining the replacement demand with new demand and making an allowance for cyclical fluctuations, in which replacement demand in effect can be deferred (ie stored for future years), provides a demand range in the low demand scenario of 8-12 million cars and 0.8-1.3 million CVs.

The central demand scenario is less pessimistic about vehicle ownership with 350 cars and 37 CVs per 1000 people. These assumptions predict demand at 9-13.5 million cars and 0.9-1.45 million CVs. The high demand scenario is more optimistic about car demand with vehicle ownership at 400 cars and 40 CVs per 1000 people. These figures,

though less plausible, are significantly below current and predicted
North American ownership levels. Under these assumptions demand is
forecast at 10.5-14.0 million cars and 0.95-1.45 million CVs.

Of the three hypotheses, the central demand scenario is the most
plausible, though any is possible. Table 8.5 summarizes a variety of
other forecasts for European demand.

Table 8.5 *Selected future forecasts of Western European demand
(millions)*

	1980	1985	1990
Ryder Report (UK)	10.6	11.7	
Euroeconomics (1975)	9.9	11.3-12.3	
Euroeconomics (1979)	10.4	12.4	
CPRS Report (UK)	8.8-10.1	11.3-12.6	
Manufacturer A	10.4	11.5	
Manufacturer B	11.1	13.0	
Manufacturer C	10.0	—	
Manufacturer D	9.6	—	
Manufacturer E	10.7	12.5	
Predicasts	13.0	14.7	
Economic Forecasters Publications		13.0[1]	
Business International[2]			
— standard case (assuming current economic conditions)	7.56	9.1	12.39
— preferred case (lower growth/ higher inflation)	7.49	7.89	8.51

1. 1984
2. Includes only Austria, Belgium, Denmark, France, West Germany, Italy, Netherlands,
   Spain, Sweden, Switzerland and the UK

Market for Western European producers

The predictions as to the size of the Western European market in 1990
are now added to import and export assumptions to yield a net market
size for Western European producers. Table 8.6 shows for both cars and
CVs, the range estimates for the market open to European producers. A
central projection has been made using the 'equilibrium' replacement
demand prediction. With the central demand assumption and a low
import scenario, new vehicle registrations should be 10.7 million cars
and 1.15 million CVs per year by 1990. With a high import scenario,
new vehicle registrations may be 9.7 million cars and 1.05 million CVs.
In effect this means that overall Western European production will not
increase beyond the peak of the late 1970s.

Western European capacity is currently over 13 million cars and CV
capacity is in the region of 1.7 million (see Table 8.7). Both capacity
figures are to expand. By 1990 Ford and GM will both have added new

Table 8.6 Market size for Western European producers in 1990 (millions)

Demand	Low		Central		High	
	Low import scenario	High import scenario	Low import scenario	High import scenario	Low import scenario	High import scenario
Cars						
New registrations	8-12	8-12	9-13.5	9-13.5	10.5-14.0	10.5-14.0
Trade balance	0	−1	0	−1	0	−1
Market faced by Western European producers						
– range	8-12	7-11	9-13.5	8-13.5	10.5-14.0	9.5-13.0
– central projection	9.2	8.2	10.7	9.7	12.2	9.2
CVs						
New registrations	0.8-1.23	0.8-1.23	0.9-1.35	0.9-1.35	0.95-1.45	0.95-1.45
Trade balance	0.1	0	0.1	0	0.1	0
Market faced by Western European producers						
– range	0.9-1.33	0.8-1.23	1.0-1.45	0.9-1.35	1.05-1.55	0.95-1.45
– central projection	1.03	0.93	1.15	1.05	1.23	1.13

Table 8.7 *European car manufacturing capacity (millions)*

	1980	Early 1980s capacity as publicized	1990 predicted capacity
Major manufacturers			
Ford	1.8	2.1	2.1
GM	1.3	1.6	1.9
PSA Peugeot-Citroen	2.4	2.5	2.2
Fiat	2.0	2.0	1.8
Renault*	1.4	1.6	1.5
VW	1.8	1.8	1.5
	10.7	11.6	11.0
Small manufacturers			
British Leyland	1.0	1.0	
Alfa Romeo	0.3	0.3	
BMW	0.3	0.4	2.5
Daimler-Benz	0.4	0.7	
Volvo	0.4	0.4	
Saab	0.2	0.2	
	2.6	3.0	2.5
Total of all European manufacturers	13.3	14.9	13.5

* Excluding Volvo

assembly capacity (if their plans come to fruition). Both the French manufacturers plan a modest expansion of car capacity, and Daimler-Benz and BMW are also planning to expand. On the CV front, Renault, Iveco, PSA Peugeot-Citroen and VW-MAN are all planning to increase capacity (albeit marginally).

Western Europe as a whole appears to have excess capacity. However, this is unimportant as some companies will be unable to use spare capacity while others will be operating at full capacity. Both Fiat and VW have had to shed capacity since 1970 when both firms could produce up to two million cars a year. Similarly during the mid-1970s, the UK had spare capacity of over one million units yet many European manufacturers were unable to fulfil all potential orders. Even GM, with unused capacity in the UK, chose not to use it. The shedding of capacity is only undertaken if the sales potential is chronically below capacity levels.

The significance of the over-capacity is that this excess supply will mean increased competitive pressure. If a firm's marketing strategy is incorrect, or the models are not fully competitive, that firm will have spare capacity, which in turn implies reduced profits or even losses. Failure to generate sufficient cash to plough back into the business to correct marketing/model mistakes will cause a worsening financial situation, ultimately leading to collapse, so each firm will be trying harder to produce a marketing strategy/model line-up which is better, or at least not worse, than its competitors.

Manufacturers' strategies

So far we have calculated the potential demand for vehicles in the European market and the likely trade balance in vehicles between Europe and the rest of the world. As a whole Europe will have a degree of excess capacity but, on the basis of past experience, this surplus capacity will not be concentrated evenly throughout the manufacturers, and will affect a few firms worst. Those firms that have a chronic surplus capacity will have to take one of four possible actions: retrench by shedding capacity, collapse, be taken over or forge some partnership with a stronger company, or require government assistance. Of these, collapse is unlikely and government aid will usually be forthcoming in an emergency to defend national manufacturing interests and protect jobs.

In order to predict which companies may have surplus capacity, an analysis of the strategies of the major manufacturers must be made. An assessment of whether each company will succeed in its projected strategy provides some indication of the future structure of the industry.

Cars

The lion's share of European car capacity is in the hands of six manufacturers. Table 8.8 gives a summary of the market share by location and manufacturer.

Ford make most of their money selling the Cortina/Taunus in Germany and in the UK. Their new front-wheel drive Cortina replacement (codenamed Toni) and their Golf rival (codenamed Erika) will establish the meat of their model line-up in the 1980s. Ford will probably produce a model in the 'extra-small' segment too. By seeking to maintain or increase share in their most profitable markets (Germany and the UK) Ford will be in a good position to improve share and profitability in the southern European markets. Overall Ford will endeavour to expand production.

Ford's immediate problem is GM who are committed to vigorous competition in Europe and whose expansion plans rival those of Ford. GM has already beaten Ford in producing their equivalent of the Erika project (ie the new front-wheel drive Kadett/Chevette). GM will also introduce their Cortina equivalent before Ford, though a Fiesta rival will not be introduced until the new Spanish plant comes on stream in 1982-83. GM will emulate Ford's policy of increasing market share in Germany, the UK and Southern Europe. Part of GM's strategy must be

Table 8.8 *European manufacturers' market share of car market by country (1978)*

	Britain (%)	Germany (%)	France (%)	Italy (%)	Spain (%)	Other (%)	Total (%)	Average return on sales 1975-77[1] (%)
Peugeot/Citroen/Chrysler	11.0	6.1	44.6	11.2	25.2	14.7	17.9	1.9
Renault	4.4	4.7	34.2	8.4	28.7	7.0	12.8	0.6
Fiat/Seat	5.3	3.5	3.6	53.4	34.9	7.3	12.6	1.1[2]
Ford (Europe)	24.6	13.9	4.4	5.6	10.6	12.4	12.2	4.5
VW/Audi	4.0	29.8	2.9	3.6	0.1	9.7	11.5	2.8
GM (Europe)	9.7	20.0	2.3	4.2	0.1	12.6	10.3	3.5
Japanese	11.0	3.7	1.8	0.1	0	16.4	6.3	4.6[3]
British Leyland	23.5	0	1.3	0.4	0	3.8	4.8	Loss
Others	6.5	18.3	4.9	13.1	0.4	16.1	11.6	N/A

0 = negligible
1. After deduction of taxes
2. Excludes Seat
3. Nissan and Toyota only

to improve its marketing image and distribution networks; the former will be achieved by high marketing expenditure prior to and during the launch of new models.

Ford has discovered that it will take five to seven years to achieve full European integration of its model policy and production facilities. GM too, will not achieve its integration objectives overnight. The result of the Ford/GM battle will only become apparent in the late 1980s. For the other European manufacturers the presence of two sparring US multinationals, both of whom will be aggressively expanding their production, is not encouraging.

Apart from the Japanese importers there will be no other company committed to expansion. British Leyland, producing the equivalent of the Honda Accord, will increase market share but this can be classified as increased utilization of British Leyland's spare capacity. It is conceivable that another Japanese manufacturer will install a major European assembly plant, but this new capacity can merely be substituted for projected Japanese imports to Western Europe. A Japanese assembly plant in Europe will simply serve to facilitate the predicted increase in their market share.

It follows from Ford's and GM's onslaught on the German market that VW will increasingly feel under pressure. VW's response will be to increase penetration in the executive/luxury segments and seek to maintain its position in Germany. VW might try to increase share in France and the UK. The company's main problem is that it operates from West Germany which is a high cost base. With the loss of all its North American exports, VW is almost bound to shed capacity.

Renault is following GM's and Ford's move into the southern European market and must feel under some threat from the now much larger PSA Peugeot-Citroen group.[1] Although Renault may seek to improve market share elsewhere, the main objective will be to maintain its current position within Europe.

One of Fiat's major markets is Spain. With GM, Ford, Renault and PSA Peugeot-Citroen all attacking this market, Fiat will find it difficult if not impossible to maintain market share. Similarly, Fiat's traditional domination of the Italian market (traditionally over 50 per cent) may also come under increasing pressure. Any increase in market share obtained in the UK or France will be balanced by a loss elsewhere. Fiat, however, has announced plans to install additional capacity in the Communist Bloc; this new capacity will be integrated into a common European production policy. Such action may help to achieve economies of scale but it will not necessarily improve sales. One worrying feature for Fiat is the lack of profitability in what was hoped would be a major money spinner, the Ritmo/Strada. Fiat have also used some new robotic technology (see Chapter 5) which is experimental and seems at the moment a high cost/low output alternative to the type

1. This explains its recent link-up with Volvo's car operations.

of automation the other manufacturers are adopting. Given these difficulties, Fiat will probably shed Western European capacity.

This leaves the problematic PSA Peugeot-Citroen. The group's future is problematic because its financial resources are fully stretched; it is doubtful whether the company has sufficient managerial resources to run the enlarged operations; there is a mammoth rationalization and integration task ahead of the company; and the Talbot (Chrysler) operations are continuing to generate losses. Ford and GM plan to manufacture their small, light and medium cars in Europe with production runs in excess of 400,000 units annually. Peugeot-Citroen on the other hand want to split such volumes among three distinctive brandnames, but to maintain the three brandnames of Peugeot, Citroen and Talbot, something more than badge engineering is expected (eg Citroen LN and Vita models based on Peugeot products). Although many of the scale benefits can be tapped by introducing many common components into the three brandnames, there will still be some unique components requiring unique investment. The unit cost of the Peugeot/Citroen/Talbot product will therefore be some 1 or 2 per cent higher than an equivalent company operating under one brandname. PSA Peugeot-Citroen would argue that this cost penalty would be worth incurring if the increased cost could be more than offset by increased unit profits on a larger volume. The company might also argue that three brandnames allow a marketing advantage through distinctiveness. Ford US also have three brandnames for equivalent volumes to PSA Peugeot-Citroen, but the current strategy of the companies are very different: Ford US produced their Ford/Mercury series with the smallest of differences, whereas PSA Peugeot-Citroen wish to go much further.

The choice for PSA Peugeot-Citroen is complicated. British Leyland, following state ownership in 1975, attempted to integrate its model range and distribution network. The immediate response to these moves was a dramatic (and some believe permanent) loss in market share. To follow the Ford US or GM Europe technique of marginal stylistic differentiation between brandnames will be playing the Americans at their own game. As Karcher[1] (General Director of Citroen) said: 'Consolidating an enormous industrial strength around a standardized range, the US manufacturers are going to be in a position to wage a price war in the mid-1980s.'

The European response will be multi-sided: lengthening a product run, implying a large number of body styles, engines and transmissions arising from a single model, with an accent on flexibility to adapt to new circumstances. Karcher sees this trend continuing:

1. Xavier Karcher, General Director Automobiles Citroen in a paper entitled *The Automobile Industry in 1985 — A New American Challenge.*

> From a given basic model, the versions and variants will multiply to better
> match the local regulations and technical restraints and customer wishes by
> means of an elaborate mechanic combining the various elements produced
> throughout the world.
>   The products will then be more defined by the manner to combine the
> basic elements than by the personality or origin of the components themselves
> . . . This accounts for the importance of the marketing teams, styling depart-
> ments . . .
>   It is also the manufacturers who will be most able to better control their
> 'product styling' and meet the customer requirements through most appro-
> priate combinations of standardized elements who will have better chances to
> survive. Imagination is more than ever a prerequisite.

Chrysler UK will also prove something of a thorn in PSA Peugeot-
Citroen's flesh. Not only is the company unprofitable, but poor
industrial relations and a difficult political situation are going to reduce
the parent company's freedom of action. Ultimately the car plants in
the UK will either become pure assembly or be substantially reduced.[1]

PSA Peugeot-Citroen's basic industrial logic in taking over Chrysler
Europe is faultless. The additional economies of scale will ultimately
reap rewards. However, the financial problem of Chrysler Europe and
the enormous reorganization task will probably mean that the best the
group can hope for is to maintain its position. Realistically, the group
will also probably shed capacity (probably in the UK).

Although British Leyland is strictly speaking not a major producer,
the company is worth mentioning. By using a Honda product to attack
the light- and medium-car segment and filling the smaller and larger car
products with reasonable (though not outstanding) Austin Morris
products, and continuing to increase output of its successful Jaguar/
Rover/Triumph products, British Leyland could substantially increase
its market share, especially in the highly profitable German market.
Regardless of whether British Leyland will still be assembling Honda
products or producing its own medium cars (codenamed LC10 and
MC10) in 1990 the company's capacity in the UK may not decrease.

As for the remaining smaller companies, their overall capacity will not
significantly change, though Daimler-Benz's expansion will be matched
by a contraction elsewhere (eg one of the Swedish manufacturers).

These strategies are combined together and shown in Table 8.9. The
higher than average number of dealers and advertising expense for PSA
Peugeot-Citroen illustrates the type of additional expense incurred in
maintaining three distinct brandnames. By combining all the marketing
strategies and their probable degree of success, the capacity estimates
(previously shown for comparative purposes in Table 8.6) can be
deduced (see Table 8.9). The net effect on capacity by 1990 will be a
marginal increase over the 1979-80 level of installed capacity, although

---

1. This is the conclusion reached in Bhasker, K N *op cit.*

Table 8.9 *European car strategy*

	Market coverage (%)	1978 Advertising expense $ (millions)	1977 Number of dealers	Cost base	Market share strategy 1988 versus 1978	Product strategy	Resulting European capacity forecast description	capacity (millions)
Peugeot/Citroen/Talbot	93	82.8	7096	medium	maintain	maintain/retrench	slight reduction	2.2
Renault	89	46.8	2961	medium	maintain	maintain	slight increase[2]	1.5
Fiat/Seat	93	51.8	3045	low	retrench	maintain	reduction	1.8
VW/Audi	89	50.6	3222	high	maintain	expand in executive/luxury segments	reduction	1.5
GM	73	56.6	3335	high	expand	increase market coverage and expand in all segments by 1985	increase	1.9
Japanese	69	42.2	7904[1]	medium	expand	maintain/expand in more expensive segments	—	
Ford	89	36.9	2340	medium	expand	expand in all segments (including extra-small) to defend/meet GM challenge	increase	2.1

1. Includes multi-franchise
2. This may take the form of increased use of Volvo's capacity

some firms will increase capacity and others will shed it. The UK and Italy will probably lose capacity to Southern Europe, and Germany is bound to suffer a loss in capacity switched to the US. In France a marginal reduction will probably occur though it may just preserve its capacity.

There is sufficient European capacity to produce around 13.5 million cars per year. Of course since manufacturers are not going to produce equally successful models, it would be difficult to achieve a production volume approaching the limit. With a low import/central demand scenario, the annual European market will be in the range of 9 to 13.5 million cars and imports will be exactly balanced by exports. Car production by the European producers should exactly match demand.

Table 8.10 shows the historical picture for total car demand and production. The projection to 1985 and 1990 is illustrative only; a boom in 1985 takes demand to above average levels which is followed by a slump with a recovery in 1990.

Table 8.10 *European car production and new registrations ('000s)*

	Car production	New car registrations
1960	5090	3545
1961	4828	3979
1962	5768	4610
1963	6896	5473
1964	7244	5831
1965	7469	6209
1966	8057	6287
1967	7686	6460
1968	8754	6675
1969	9552	7385
1970	10,352	7934
1971	10,893	8494
1972	11,138	9314
1973	11,471	9430
1974	9943	8159
1975	9326	8398
1976	10,760	9542
1977	11,213	10,067
1978	11,353	10,432
1979	11,455	9830
1980	11,320	10,215
1985*	12,600	12,150
1990*	11,275	11,425
1990 range*	9-13.5 million	9-13.5 million
Central projection	10.7 million	10.7 million

* Representative forecasts

The assumptions which would produce a greater installed capacity than our prediction is the low import/high demand scenario. The high import/central demand, low import/low demand and high import/low demand scenarios produce progressively severe regimes for European manufacturers. The most severe (high import/low demand) would reduce average production to levels achieved in the 1960s (a range of 8-11 million cars a year) and maximum production would leave a surplus of some 2.5 million cars.

CVs

The situation is more complicated in the CV industry as the market and the producers are divided up into a number of segments. In Table 7.17 we predicted that the most significant segment of the market would be in the heavy CV area. The car-derived van segment share of the market would fall and panel vans would marginally increase. The largest increase in the market would be for the linehaul truck (over 15 tonnes and over 250 hp and designed for motorways). This segment of the market will be around 100,000 units in 1990. The 12 tonnes plus segment of the CV market will exceed 200,000 units but installed European capacity exceeds 250,000 units per year. This partly explains the desire of the heavy CV manufacturers to plug in to the US market.

Table 8.11 is a reminder of how the pattern of manufacturing varies at the heavy end of the CV industry. Daimler-Benz and IVECO clearly dominate the most rapidly growing segment and this is likely to cause the remainder of the producers to re-assess their position. We return to this in the next section as any one move might trigger a series of moves in the European heavy CV industry, which Eurofinance has called a 'structural chess-board'.

The following predictions are largely informed speculation. Daimler-Benz will simply attempt to maintain its position. IVECO has now completed its highly successful reorganization and expansion, and its task will be to maintain its position. Although VW and MAN are increasingly cooperating, their coverage of the market is not good: VW are strong in vans and MAN are strong in the heaviest truck segment, and the result must be either expansion or a further partner. Renault is now reorganizing its three CV divisions (Renault, Berliet and Saviem) under one umbrella and badge (Renault Industrial Vehicles). Renault has good market coverage and two potential sales outlets in the US (AMC and Mack), and it may be a candidate for modest expansion.

Ford and GM will not be content idly to watch while others carve out a lucrative market for themselves. Ford is committed to spending $1 million in the next few years; this will involve an increase in market coverage with a modern medium and heavy truck range and new CV production facilities, probably in Spain, Portugal or Austria. Ford

Table 8.11 *European truck production by market segment in 1977 ('000s)*

Gross vehicle weight		4-6 tonnes	6-12 tonnes	12+ tonnes	Total
Daimler-Benz		34.4	40.7	55.2	130.3
IVECO		12.2	26.6	46.2	85.1
	□ Fiat	11.1	12.8	27.1	51.0
	□ Magirus Deutz	–	5.8	11.2	16.9
	□ Unic	1.1	8.1	7.9	17.1
Renault		9.9	5.8	23.7	39.4
	□ Saviem	9.2	2.2	8.2	19.6
	□ Berliet	0.7	3.6	15.5	19.8
Ford (UK)		2.5	17.7	21.3	41.5
British Leyland		2.9	9.8	12.0	24.7
PSA Peugeot-Citroen		1.9	3.3	9.0	14.2
	□ UK	1.9	3.0	4.2	9.1
	□ Spain	–	0.3	4.8	5.1
Volvo		–	2.5	22.8	25.3
Scania		–	–	19.9	19.9
DAF		–	1.0	13.0	14.0
Enasa (Spain)		0.4	0.6	8.7	9.7
Steyr-Daimler-Puch		–	0.8	3.6	4.4
MAN		–	1.2	17.5	18.6

Source: Chambre Syndicale des Constructeurs d'Automobiles

however have major problems — including low productivity, absenteeism and poor quality — at their Amsterdam plant, which produces Ford's heaviest CV model. GM will still concentrate production in the UK although some sourcing from the Communist Bloc may occur. GM will also try and improve market share in the 12 tonnes plus segments; it will expand capacity in the UK and may invest in another European CV plant.

Volvo, Scania (Saab) and Enasa (Spain) may maintain their positions or retrench. International Harvester through DAF and Seddon-Atkinson are likely to expand in Europe as a *quid pro quo* for the European invasion in the US. British Leyland will seek to establish itself in the heavy CV segment. In the panel van field, British Leyland is looking for a licensing agreement and who better to supply such an agreement than their car partner, Honda. PSA Peugeot-Citroen will attempt to maintain its panel van position and has yet to decide what to do with the ex-Chrysler heavy CV operations.

The situation is confused. A significant number of CV manufacturers will attempt to expand in the heavy CV segment and some must fail.

In the panel van field, there will be no new entrants (apart from the possibility of British Leyland's 'licensed' van) and all manufacturers will be seeking to maintain their share in the face of rising imports.

Again assuming a low import/central demand scenario, CV production in 1990 should in total be some 100,000 vehicles higher than new CV registrations. This implies a production range of some 1.0-1.35 million CVs. This is similar to levels for 1976-78. Table 8.12 shows the historical development of total European CV production and demand. The outlook in the future is for production either to remain static at current levels or decline. Under the more unfavourable assumptions, production could revert to levels experienced in the early 1960s (ie less than one million units). The two segments within the CV market which will experience some growth are vans and heavy linehaul trucks, and these areas will be hotly contested.

Table 8.12 *European CV production and new registrations ('000s)*

	New CV registrations	CV production
1960	683	974
1961	745	1003
1962	740	995
1963	792	1024
1964	844	1101
1965	847	1093
1966	858	1100
1967	842	1114
1968	884	1014
1969	1006	1270
1970	1014	1304
1971	1073	1267
1972	1133	1213
1973	1002	1330
1974	903	1319
1975	804	1224
1976	932	1370
1977	989	1409
1978	1161	1395
1979	1109	1370
1980*	1038	1250
1985*	1150	1300
1990 range*	900-1350	1000-1450
Central projection	1150	1250

* Representative forecasts

Given the low import/central demand forecast, there is sufficient capacity to meet European demand. However the total market, because of a switch in segments, will see a reduction in car-derived vans, a small increase in van capacity, and a more substantial increase in linehaul capacity, but this assumes that at least one of the independent CV manufacturers disappears.

We now analyse the implications of these predictions in the industrial structure of the Western European motor industry.

Implications for industrial structure

We have already seen that the US multinationals face difficulties in the years ahead, despite their enormous financial resources. For most of the European producers, times will be even harder. Although import penetration is lower in the European market than in North America, this relative advantage is more than offset by excess capacity and high cost structures. In simple terms, the European motor industry will have to undergo even more radical changes than those already predicted for the North American industry, and even then the future is bleak.

Cars

On a 'European' scale, the car industry would operate more sensibly at a much reduced level, with four or five major manufacturers producing at least two million cars each, supplemented by perhaps two or three firms operating on a smaller scale as specialist producers.

There are two ways in which this sort of rationalization might be achieved. First, a neo-Darwinian process of survival of the fittest (the 'shake-out') would constrain governments to withhold support from weaker firms, accepting their eventual collapse and encouraging the consolidation of the industry on the basis of the stronger surviving manufacturers. Or, second, companies seeking to remedy particular deficiencies could negotiate defensive mergers with suitable firms, although such mergers could only succeed if both parties existed as viable units prior to the merger and could agree on the need for radical restructuring and a fully integrated operation.

Until recently, mergers have taken place more or less *within* national boundaries and with the active cooperation (some might say connivance) of governments. The formation of British Leyland, the Peugeot-Citroen merger, the Fiat takeover of Lancia and VW's acquisition of Audi can all be placed in this category. In contrast, the proposed Fiat-Citroen merger failed to materialize in part because of the cross-national character of the alliance. The Volvo-Daf merger, the creation of IVECO, PSA Peugeot-Citroen's takeover of Chrysler Europe, Fiat's increased stake in Seat, and the British Leyland/Honda and Renault/Volvo link-ups have transcended national frontiers. Before these mergers, it was felt that market forces would not operate and that integration on this scale would demand not just passive concurrence on the part of the countries involved but active encouragement of a dynamic European strategy for the car industry. This may be true in the more difficult environment in 1990, when European governments may be less willing to see control and ownership of indigenous plant pass elsewhere.

In the case of both merger and shake-out, survival would be assured only if certain preconditions were met, and we will therefore examine both possibilities in greater detail.

The shake-out

A 'natural' compression of the industry would involve technical economies, strong marketing, diversification, availability of finance and managerial expertise. In an emergency, the availability of government aid might also be necessary. With the exception of managerial talent, which is not a particularly constant or quantifiable factor, the other requirements are tabulated firm-by-firm in Table 8.13 on a best and worst case analysis of actual and potential strengths and weaknesses. Viewed in this way, it seems that the weakest manufacturers are Volvo, Saab, Alfa Romeo, British Leyland, BMW and Daimler-Benz (car division only). The latter two are included despite an excellent financial record; their inclusion is simply on the basis of the constructed indices in Table 8.13. This is a surprising outcome as BMW and Daimler-Benz were the ones to weather the storms of the 1974-75 recession most successfully. Past financial success, however, is no guarantee of a certain future. Volvo is particularly weak because its new medium saloon (the 343) built in the DAF factories has not been a financial success. Moreover the traditional products of all the specialist producers are under attack as the so-called volume manufacturers attempt to gain a foothold in the highly lucrative executive/luxury market. Ford's Granada and GM's Senator models are examples of such moves.

Another key factor is the degree of financial resilience a company may have. For example, it would only take one unsuccessful major model by BMW for its financial reserves to be severely strained. As the energy problem begins to affect the Western world more severely, the acceptability of the traditional specialist producer may be in doubt. Daimler-Benz and BMW might then try to move down-market. (BMW has already achieved this with its Series 3 and Daimler-Benz plans to introduce a new 'small' car.) If the specialist producers react in this way, they will then be competing directly with the major car manufacturers but without the economies of scale. The specialist producers survived and prospered because they exploited gaps in the market. The erosion of these gaps places serious question marks over the long-run future of the specialist manufacturer.

Table 8.13 *Relative strengths of Western European manufacturers*

	Technical economies		Actual marketing strength	Diversification (risk-bearing economies)	Financial strength	Likelihood of government aid in an emergency	Current model strength
	Actual	Potential					
Fiat group	3	4	Lancia, Ferrari and IVECO	4	2	5	2
Ford (Europe)	4	5		1	1	2	4
GM (Europe)	3	5		1	4	1	3
Renault*	2	3	Jeep	3	1	5	3
VW	3	3	Audi, NSU, weak in CVs	1	3	4	4
British Leyland	1	3	Complete range	2	1	3	1
Citroen-Peugeot-Talbot	2	5	Weak in CVs	1	1	4	4
BMW	1	1		1	3	1	3
Daimler-Benz	2	2	Taxis and CVs	3	4	2	3
Saab-Scania	1	1		4	1	3	1
Volvo†	1	1			1	3	1
Alfa Romeo	1	1		1	1	2	1

Indices 5 = best
       1 = worst

* Excludes Volvo's car operations
† Includes DAF car operations

Merger

In the aftermath of the Peugeot-Citroen-Talbot merger, and excluding any involvement on the part of Ford or GM, very few merger possibilities remain. Fiat, spurred on by an approach from Nissan, may merge with Alfa Romeo (the latter is known to be seeking partnerships); Peugeot-Citroen-Talbot could merge with Renault (unlikely at the moment); in Germany possibilities exist between VW, BMW and Daimler-Benz.

Beyond national boundaries there are greater opportunities for achieving economies of scale and increased efficiency. Saab's existing links with Fiat seem to be strengthening, which in part explains Volvo's formal link-up with Renault. The two state owned companies of Renault and Alfa Romeo could usefully merge as the models of each company do not significantly overlap, although Fiat (or a Japanese manufacturer) remains a more likely contender. Similarly Renault and British Leyland could conceivably move closer together after their initial abortive negotiations on a technical partnership. However, British Leyland's current partner, Honda, looks a more promising relationship at the moment.

Being slightly more adventurous, merger possibilities might exist between VW, Fiat and either Renault or PSA Peugeot-Citroen. Fiat's current miscalculation with its Ritmo-Strada model underlines the severity of erring in model policy: one mistake can throw a company into a difficult financial vicious circle. Fiat might just be willing to attempt such a merger, and a grouping of any two of these three would create a company whose capacity would be third in the world after GM and Ford.

As well as inter-regional mergers there are possibilities of mergers with companies in other mature markets. For example, the Renault-AMC, British Leyland-Honda and Chrysler-Mitsubishi relationships. Rumours suggest that both VW and Peugeot-Citroen-Talbot may be negotiating for the purchase of Chrysler US. These examples only illustrate the range of merger possibilities, and later we discuss which mergers are most likely.

Non-merger solutions

In theory, mergers represent an attractive and practical means of achieving economies of scale otherwise beyond the scope of individual firms, but a merger on orthodox lines may not be the only means of achieving the desired end. An alternative 'non-merger' solution to the fragmented nature of the car industry would not match the efficiency of a fully integrated structure, but this might be offset by marketing advantages. Economies of scale could be obtained either through *ad hoc* agreements on a joint approach to particular problems or by agreement on a less vertically integrated structure, within which large component manufacturers could pass on savings achieved through their economies of scale to manufacturers operating on an almost exclusively assembly basis.

The first alternative — a functional merger with specific objectives — is already much in evidence in Europe. The joint Peugeot-Citroen/Volvo/Renault undertaking to develop and manufacture a complete engine range is a recent and striking example of a functional alliance with obvious financial benefits for all concerned, although participants in the equivalent Club of Four project (organized along similar lines and involving DAF, Saviem, Magirus Deutz and Volvo), have had difficulty in reconciling their conflicting interests, and a successful outcome to the project is in some doubt.

Less vertical integration

If vertical integration within the car industry was reduced, components, for example, could be produced in sufficient quantity by one component manufacturer to supply a number of firms, all of whom would benefit from the economies of scale achieved without the entanglements and complications of an actual merger. This is already a feature of the UK CV industry, where a number of the smaller CV firms have survived by concentrating on assembly work only. Even the giant multinationals have adopted the assembly only approach, with Ford (Europe) assembling their new Transcontinental highway range of lorries using Cummins engines, Rockwell axles and Fuller gearboxes. Similarly, GM (Bedford) fit either Spicer or Fuller gearboxes and Eaton or Soma rear axles, while British Leyland use Cummins engines in some of their larger vehicles, with Fuller gearboxes and Eaton axles. At present, the use of common components bought in from elsewhere for assembly is restricted to the CV sector, where maximum benefits can be gained by buying in engines, gearboxes, braking systems, axles, chassis, some body pressings, electrical components, etc.

Predicted solutions

Reducing vertical integration is the possibility that appears least likely. Manufacturers with a wary eye on their highly profitable component suppliers are increasingly entering the component manufacturing business thus increasing vertical integration in the industry. Technical and function mergers, joint ventures, and other types of collaboration between suppliers are now part and parcel of the European motor industry, and evidence suggests that it will increase, especially among the indigenous Western European manufacturers.

Despite the success and growing frequency of these semi-formal arrangements, full mergers and takeovers, resulting in an increased concentration of the European motor industry, are inevitable. We now analyse which mergers are most likely in the period up to 1990.

GM, Ford and PSA Peugeot-Citroen have all reached a production volume of two million cars per year which is sufficient to gain most economies of scale. PSA Peugeot-Citroen may decide to go for the next level of scale economies which occurs at around the one million cars per model per year. To support the necessary sales to achieve this, PSA Peugeot-Citroen would have to take over Chrysler US (possible), Honda (less likely) or Mitsubishi (unlikely). One further possibility is to merge with Fiat creating three major production centres in France, Spain and Italy. Such a possibility, though feasible, seems remote. PSA Peugeot-Citroen is unlikely to relish the thought of taking over one of the other major European manufacturers (or even British Leyland) since it would produce a group with too large a market share in Western Europe which might prove difficult to maintain.

The three other European producers, VW, Renault and Fiat, could reach the two million car level by 'mopping up' some of the smaller manufacturers (eg Volvo, Saab, Alfa Romeo and even BMW). Alternatively, one of them could go for broke and risk absorbing British Leyland. A less likely, though again not impossible, scenario is for two of these three major companies to merge.

A Volvo-Saab merger is still a possibility (by means of a Renault-Volvo-Saab merger), although it makes better sense for Saab to join Fiat. Alfa Romeo may still merge with Fiat and VW and a Japanese manufacturer are also possible partners. British Leyland and Honda appear to be well matched and it would be difficult to improve upon it in Europe (where all available partners are bigger or smaller than British Leyland).

Further state involvement in the European motor industry is more likely to come about during a crisis. If Fiat was in difficulty, for example, the Italian government could combine it with Alfa Romeo to produce a nationalized car industry. The French government, if PSA Peugeot-Citroen failed to make a success of its enlarged operations, could form a new state owned grouping round Renault-Peugeot-Citroen-Talbot. The West German government might engineer possibilities involving VW and Daimler-Benz (or BMW). With its CV operations Daimler-Benz is too large to be taken over by any company except PSA Peugeot-Citroen or perhaps VW.

Smaller car producers

The plethora of smaller, independent car producers is a characteristic of the European market, but one which could vanish in the near future.

Because of the small scale of their operations the smaller producers are more vulnerable to the effects of recession and less likely to attract aid or subsidy in the event of a financial crisis. The situation has been resolved for some of the smaller companies: Ferrari are now part of Fiat; Porsche have all but joined VW; De Tomaso, Maserati and Innocenti are state controlled; Matra-Simca will probably be drawn into PSA Peugeot-Citroen, as will Alpine into Renault.

As a group, the smaller independent producers can be divided into four main categories. First, the prestige producer Rolls-Royce (others such as Porsche are no longer independent). Second, sports/luxury car producers such as TVR, Lamborghini, Lotus and most recently De Lorean. Given the persistent rumours of Lamborghini's imminent collapse it is surprising to find the US-sponsored De Lorean sports car being built in Northern Ireland with some engineering expertise being provided by Lotus. Lotus itself has weathered a number of stormy periods and is now supported by the financial strength of American Express. Third are those spcialist producers who have diversified, if only on a small scale. Reliant, for example, has successfully exported low-scale production techniques to Indonesia, Greece and Israel, and has been able to attract and sustain a small but steady demand for the sporting Scimitar and the Robin three-wheeler. Fourth, are the 'coach builders' — Bristol and Panther — both of whom restrict production to limited numbers, only produce on the strength of an order and never increase production to meet demand, which as a result always outstrips supply. If these companies were to integrate with larger firms or seek greater economies of scale by buying in components from elsewhere, the quality and reliability of their product would in all probability be adversely affected. Assuming that in most cases such a change would be unacceptable, it would seem that only those firms determined to remain independent and confident of a continued demand for their specialist product can hope to survive.

Before looking at the major CV manufacturers we may examine the future of the small CV manufacturer.

Small CV producers

Although the motor industry and large-scale output appears to be synonymous it would be wrong to suppose that all the small-scale CV specialists are at risk in competing with larger firms in the relatively small market for heavy vehicles. In fact, the large-scale European makers often produce engines and cabs at lower output levels and with higher costs than British specialists such as Perkins or Motor Panels. By concentrating on the small-scale assembly of premium products utilizing bought-out components made in large numbers, ERF, Seddon-Atkinson and others have found themselves in a prosperous position.

As long as sufficient external economies are obtained for cost-plus pricing to be viable in a competitive environment, the break-even output levels are normally a very small proportion of total capacity, fixed costs being so low.

Some rationalization of the smaller CV producers is however inevitable: DAF and Seddon-Atkinson may be forced closer together. ERF and Foden may become a single family entity again, MAN may take over some of the specialist West German CV producers; and some restructuring of the Spanish CV industry is bound to occur.

CVs

The dominance of Daimler-Benz and IVECO in the heavy CV segment has created a real problem for the remainder of the CV producers. Even these two producers thought it necessary to collaborate on the manufacture of a new heavy automatic gearbox for urban buses, though the deal was eventually killed by West German anti-trust regulations. (This places a doubt on whether market forces will be allowed to bring about the rationalization of the European motor industry in such a way as to compete with the US and Japanese producers.)

For the remaining European CV producers, joint ventures and the possibility of mergers seem to be the order of the day. The volume gap between the industry leaders and the rest is extremely wide. Renault and PSA Peugeot-Citroen lead in the car-derived van segment, VW and Ford lead in the van (medium) segment, though here the gap is less wide, and Daimler-Benz and IVECO lead in the truck segment.

The alternatives for restructuring the CV industry are broadly the same as in car production. But the present *status quo* in the European CV industry cannot be maintained since it is essentially unstable. The reasons for this are given below:

1. Ford wishes to obtain a significant share of all sectors in the CV industry. GM will follow Ford's lead. An unstable equilibrium will be created in the European CV industry with these two US multi-nationals determined to expand.
2. If British Leyland does market a 'Honda' van (or equivalent) in Western Europe, British Leyland's future in Europe looks promising. This would cause some concern to VW which is the current market leader in this field.
3. Volvo and Scania (with or without its Saab parent) would create a major heavy CV grouping with equivalent capacity to IVECO.
4. Although PSA Peugeot-Citroen is strong in the smallest CV segments, Chrysler Europe's truck facilities provide an entrance into the expanding heavy truck segment. PSA Peugeot-Citroen must decide what to do; it is inconceivable that the company would wish to

continue the operation on its current scale. Options include expansion, merger, closure or sale.

5. The Spanish truck industry is in a state of flux. Enesa and Motor Iberica (Ebro) are the largest producers. Massey Ferguson plans to sell its 36 per cent stake in Motor Iberica. The Spanish state holding company, INI, has the opportunity of merging Motor Iberica with Enasa thereby creating an indigenous Spanish CV manufacturer which with careful development would be capable of becoming competitive in European terms.

6. IVECO still seems to be searching for international partners despite its strong position within Europe (eg talks with Rockwell concerning a joint venture in heavy vehicle components).

These factors may or may not trigger various set-piece moves on the European CV industry chessboard. If Saab-Scania forge closer links with Fiat, Volvo's CV operations may move closer to Renault's. If Renault and PSA Peugeot-Citroen merge, VW/MAN will woo the Swedish and Spanish manufacturers. If Volvo and Saab merge, VW/ MAN will look for a partner, British Leyland, Enasa or Motor Iberica perhaps. If VW/MAN and Daimler-Benz move closer together, IVECO will make overtures to the Scania part of Saab and perhaps Volvo's CV (but not car) operations. A merger of British Leyland and Renault would cause PSA Peugeot-Citroen to think of Volvo and Saab or alternatively VW/MAN as a potential partner. A British Leyland/Honda link up in CVs would lead VW/MAN to seek a partner, perhaps a Swedish or Spanish producer.

There are only three constants: Renault will remain in French hands, IVECO will not be allowed to merge with Daimler-Benz and GM and Ford will stay out of the European merger business. Again the above only illustrates what *may* happen, and how one move will determine others; it does not predict what *will* occur.

Strategic implications

Whichever mergers occur in the future, there will be three other strategic considerations for European manufacturers. First, the European phenomena of joint ventures will continue as a response to the greater scale of the US and Japanese producers and the 'Europeanization' of the North American product. Second, production in Europe will become progressively more complicated as companies try to gain the last ounce of scale economies. The production of motor vehicles in a particular European country or indeed even in Europe itself will become meaningless. Components produced on highly specialized machines will be shipped across Western Europe and indeed the world. Third, the commercial strategy of those European companies which survive in

Europe will spread their international operations. VW, Renault and PSA Peugeot-Citroen have already relocated parts of their production in other areas of the world. This tendency to spread internationally will continue since protectionist policies will close these markets without local assembly/production facilities. In any case, to achieve maximum economies of scale or to utilize low labour cost production, European companies are finding that there are a growing number of instances in which it is commercially more attractive to import components into Western Europe from their plants abroad (eg Brazilian-made 1050 engines for the Fiat 127). Figure 8.2 shows how Fiat's interests have grown faster outside its domestic market, and the same is true for the other three big Europeans, especially VW. In fact many of the Western European car and CV manufacturers will continue to establish assembly plants in both mature markets (ie North America) and less developed markets.

Finally, two questions might be resolved. Who will win in the Ford versus GM battle fought in Europe? And will PSA Peugeot-Citroen's gamble in taking over Chrysler Europe succeed? The answer to the former is Ford by a narrow margin and only if it adopts a more rational financing policy in the US. The process of integrating production across national boundaries is not easily learned and the ability to run such a complex operation efficiently requires special managerial expertise; these abilities are precious assets which Ford has acquired. This expertise has taken some 10 years to develop to its current perfection. Adding to Ford's advantage, GM, in choosing Austria to build an engine plant of 300,000 units a year, has revealed a fundamental weakness in an area that should be its greatest advantage. There are enormous economies of scale to be gained in power train production (see Chapters 4 and 5), but a plant geared to produce only a maximum of 300,000 engines a year suffers a cost penalty. Ford's equivalent new engine plant in South Wales has a capacity in excess of 500,000 units a year and could be geared up to produce even more. GM's smaller production will result in higher unit costs of 5-10 per cent. Moreover, Ford are used to building new plants in Europe and expanding production and GM are not, and Ford appear to be adept at planning flexible production facilities. New plants will be built with both long production runs and flexible multiple sourcing in mind. GM will still be a major force in Europe but the company will not overtake Ford.

The main battle will be between Ford and PSA Peugeot-Citroen. Will PSA Peugeot-Citroen make it? Yes and no. PSA Peugeot-Citroen has a very high proportion of its capacity in France. Domestic economic events will play an increasingly significant role for PSA, and herein lies the problem. PSA Peugeot-Citroen may become a tool for implementing economic policy by the government (for example to reduce unemployment in certain areas) which can threaten PSA in many different ways.

Figure 8.2 *Commercial strategy (Fiat car production worldwide)*

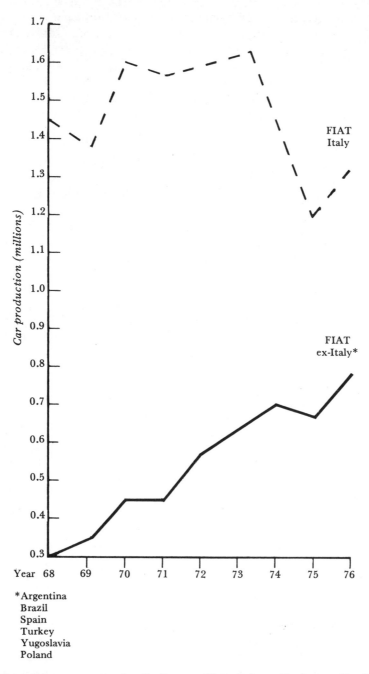

*Argentina
Brazil
Spain
Turkey
Yugoslavia
Poland

Source: A paper presented to the European Motor Industry Conference, Frankfurt 1977, Euroeconomics, Eurofinance

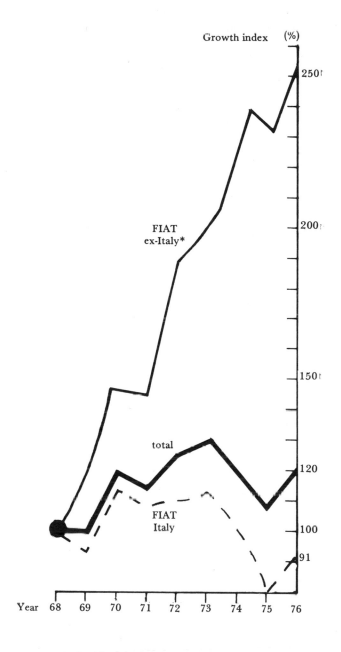

Growth index (%)

FIAT
ex-Italy*

250

200

150

total

120

FIAT
Italy

100

91

Year 68 69 70 71 72 73 74 75 76

This could prevent PSA from achieving the level of efficiency it would have desired. On the other hand it could be an advantage and, if PSA was in danger of collapse, the French government would have no hesitation in providing state aid.

In 1990, PSA Peugeot-Citroen will probably still lead Ford in production, but Ford will be generating high profits while PSA Peugeot-Citroen may be less concerned with sheer profitability, and pursue other objectives such as generating employment opportunities in France.

Conclusion

The motor industry in Europe will continue to occupy a central position on the European industrial stage closely identified with the economic prosperity of the region as a whole. A decline in the industry would cause far greater government concern in Europe than elsewhere, making government intervention to preserve that industry (almost irrespective of cost) likely.

Although we have discussed future possibilities in some detail it is impossible to predict with any certainty just what specific actions will be taken to resolve the structural weaknesses inherent in the industry. Some of the plausible alternatives are long term, costly and may create widespread unemployment. Although in theory it would be possible to implement radical (but effective) measures on a 'continental' scale, the possibility of joint agreements of a truly international character among the larger European manufacturers is remote. Economies of scale could be achieved without resorting to a fundamental restructuring of the industry, but with or without an international solution, further concentration (or retraction) is almost certainly inevitable.

Chapter 9

Japan

Japan is the youngest of the three major producers. Although it has a much smaller population than either North America or Western Europe, it is one of the richest countries in the world, with a *per capita* GNP only just below the strongest of the Western European economies, and above those of the UK, Italy and Spain (see Table 9.1).

Table 9.1 *Comparative economic statistics*

	Japan	North America	Western Europe
Population in 1976 (millions)	113	233	344
GNP *per capita* in 1976 US $	4465	7029	4903
	1960-73 (%)	1965-73 (%)	1966-76 (%)
Growth rates for Japan			
Population	1.1	1.2	1.3
Per capita GNP	9.4	9.6	6.8
Comparative *per capita* GNP growth rates:			
US	3.1	2.5	1.9
West Germany	3.7	4.0	3.2
France	4.7	5.0	4.1
UK	2.4	2.3	1.5

Unlike Western Europe, Japan is a single compact market with one set of national loyalties. With a land mass about two-thirds the size of France, Japan has a population more than double that of the French. Because of the mountainous terrain, only one-third of the country is suitable for habitation, and most of the population live in the crowded urban areas.

We have discussed some of the problems confronting the motor industry in North America as it adjusts to changes in patterns of demand and increased competition from producers in developing countries. We have suggested that developments there foreshadowed developments in the less mature West European market, and predicted a fundamental restructuring of the motor industry in Western Europe as the market further matures. In comparison, the Japanese industry is still at a development stage. Its role is currently defined in terms of the production of cheap, basic cars, but it is an industry on the verge of change, moving towards greater maturity and producing a more sophisticated product as it becomes a much higher labour cost area.

In 1978 Japan produced just under 6 million cars. If this figure is compared to the US total output of 6.7 million in 1975, it is possible to gauge the size and importance of the Japanese industry. In 1975 Japan's labour force numbered some 47 million workers, of whom one in ten were directly employed in the motor industry. Other industries depended heavily on the motor industry which consumed 67.3 per cent of all indigenous light metals and alloys, 67.6 per cent of aluminium die cast production, 12.2 per cent of regular steels, 13.5 per cent of special steels, 41.3 per cent of rubber products, 19 per cent of paint products and 26 per cent of glass products. The motor industry accounted for 9.2 per cent of the value of all production in 1978; if the other sectors of the economy involved in the supply of goods or services to the motor industry are taken into account, the total value of that industry would be about 20 per cent, which gives some indication of the central importance of the industry to the Japanese economy.

One of the most significant factors in explaining the rise of Japan as a motor producer is that the country's main motor manufacturers are independent, and locally owned and controlled in Japan. This provides the companies with enormous incentives to grow, thereby achieving greater economies of scale, through exports. If the Japanese industry had been built up by GM and Ford, it would probably do little more than supply the domestic market. Tables 9.2 and 9.3 show that production is usually double the level required to support the Japanese market, and the residual (ie 50 per cent of production) is exported.

Evolution of the Japanese market

The Japanese market has shown a clearly evolutionary pattern of growth along more or less classic lines, although the rapid pace of development has compressed the sequence of events into a very short period of time. In the early stages of development, bicycles, mopeds and motor bikes were the most widely used means of private transport. Table 9.2 shows that it was not until the 1970s that car production outstripped the production of two wheel vehicles. Car sales were initially restricted to more affluent members of the community, top-level executives and government officials, foreign diplomats, taxi fleet sales in urban areas (often three-wheelers rather than more orthodox saloons) and a growing market for utility vehicles in rural areas. Until the 1960s over 40 per cent of car sales were classified as non-private,

Table 9.2 *Japanese automotive production ('000s)*

	Cars	Trucks* and Buses	Three-wheelers	Motorcycles	Motor scooters
1966	878·	1409	33	2413	34
1967	1376	1771	26	2209	32
1968	2056	2030	22	2244	8
1969	2611	2063	17	2577	0
1970	3179	2110	14	2948	0
1971	3718	2093	12	3401	0
1972	4022	2272	3	3565	0
1973	4471	2612	3	3763	0
1974	3932	2620	1	4509	0
1975	4568	2373	0	3803	0
1976	5028	2813	0	4235	0
1977	5431	3083	0	5577	0
1978	5976	3293	0	5700	0
1980†	5900	3000	0	6000	0
1985†	6500	2700	0	5500	0
1990†	6000	2600	0	5000	0

* Includes utility vehicles
† Representative forecasts

Source: Japan Automobile Manufacturers Association and author's estimates

Table 9.3 *New registrations ('000s)*

	Cars	CVs	Three-wheelers
1966	741	1306	32
1967	1129	1574	22
1968	1562	1732	14
1969	2032	1803	10
1970	2974	1726	6
1971	2395	1625	5
1972	2618	1749	2
1973	2941	2012	1
1974	2280	1573	0
1975	2731	1581	0
1976	2450	1656	0
1977	2501	1656	0
1978	2858	1695	0
1980*	2600	1500	0
1985*	3000	1750	0
1990*	3000	1500	0

* Representative forecasts

Source: Japan Automobile Manufacturers Association

purchased mainly to equip taxi fleets or as official transport vehicles for Japanese firms.

With increasing affluence came the development of a relatively inexpensive, basic car and a growing demand for a more comprehensive range of commercial vehicles to meet the transport requirements of a developing industrial nation. A proliferation of model ranges and larger engine sizes (within which the consumer can be persuaded to trade up) and the tendency to add optional extras are both signs of a maturing market. More sophisticated cars become commonplace and eventually supplant their cruder forebears as the norm, and trucks are gradually replaced by larger commercial vehicles with a greater carrying capacity.

Table 9.4 illustrates the gradual shift away from the production of very small cars, which peaked in 1970 and then went into a steady decline, matched by a corresponding growth in production of cars in the 1500-2000 cc class (ultra small by US but large by Japanese standards). Although the oil crisis had a marginally negative effect on production of medium-size cars in this category, production of cars in excess of 2000 cc was unaffected and growth in production is apparently accelerating.

Table 9.4 *Car production by engine size (%)*

	360 cc[1] and less	361 cc[2] −1500 cc	1501 cc −2000 cc	Over 2000 cc
1957	—	100	—	—
1958	2	98	—	—
1959	6.3	92.4	1.3	—
1960	21.8	77.0	1.2	—
1961	21.6	58.8	19.2	—
1962	21.6	52.8	25.7	—
1963	19.1	48.5	31.6	1.5
1964	11.8	60.9	23.8	1.0
1965	13.5	68.5	17.5	0.4
1966	13.7	68.6	17.1	0.5
1967	20.6	64.0	14.5	0.9
1968	23.4	56.1	19.3	1.2
1969	21.4	55.0	22.6	1.0
1970	23.6	44.8	30.0	1.6
1971	17.1	44.0	37.0	1.9
1972	12.1	48.3	37.2	2.4
1973	8.4	50.1	39.2	2.3
1974	6.3	52.0	38.0	3.7
1975	3.5	53.8	38.1	4.6
1976	3.3	41.6	48.9	6.2
1977	3.3	37.4	51.2	8.1

1. 550 cc and less from 1976
2. 551-1500 cc from 1976

Source: Japan Automobile Manufacturers Association

Similarly, CV production was originally geared to an output of light- and medium-weight trucks, but by the 1970s this middle range was in decline as manufacturers concentrated instead on models at the light-weight and heavy duty extremes of the market.

This sort of evolutionary pattern is important not only for an under-standing of the Japanese industry in its present form, but as a model for developing countries throughout the world. For the moment, however, we are concerned only with Japan, and with what might be described as the final stages in this evolution, during which the Japanese market will probably follow the European and eventually the North American pattern, with greater product diversification and a significant level of import penetration. The CV sector would, if such an analysis is correct, show a marked tendency towards more specialized 'utility' vehicles and ever larger 'highway' trucks.

Japan's rapid growth through exports strategy has led to a very high growth rate for the Japanese manufacturers. Most manufacturers achieved annual growth rates of 20 per cent or more in 1954-73. Even during the period 1969-73, car production grew by 10 to 17 per cent per annum for the manufacturers, though CV growth had slowed to 4 to 6 per cent. This super-growth phenomenon is unlikely to be repeated ever again — we return to this point in Chapter 16.

The Japanese market

The changing pattern in the use of automotive products is illustrated in Table 9.5.

Table 9.5 *Japanese registrations and vehicle densities*

	Vehicle parc (millions)	Vehicle Densities	
		Number of persons per vehicle	Number of vehicles per 1000 people
1966			
Cars	2.8	36	28
CVs	5.1	20	51
3-wheelers	0.6	167	6
2-wheelers	8.2	12	82
1973			
Cars	14.5	7.4	134
CVs	10.5	10.3	97
3-wheelers	0.14	771	1
2-wheelers	8.5	13	79
1977			
Cars	19.8	6	175
CVs	12.2	9.3	108
2-wheelers	9.3	12	82

In the mid-1960s, Japan was still developing: demand for personal transport was satisfied by 2- and 3-wheelers, and the CV parc was greater than the car parc. By 1973 car ownership was more common than 2- or 3-wheeler transport. The car parc exceeded the CV parc for the first time in 1970, and car ownership approached current Spanish levels, and since then ownership levels have continued to rise. But, because most of the CVs are in the car-derived van segment, CV density levels are far higher than in Western Europe and approach those of the much more mature North American market with its finely tuned RV demand. This is illustrated in Table 9.6 where CV production by weight class is shown. The panel van segment increased production by nearly 300 per cent in 1975-77, showing that even this modest segment is a relatively new development for the Japanese. Production of light, medium and heavy trucks is small. The bulk of the goods transported in the congested urban areas of Japan are by means of vans with small carrying loads, which explains the large CV parc and high CV demand.

Table 9.6 *CV production by weight class ('000s)*

	1975	1976	1977
Weight class			
< 2 tonnes[1]	2049	2323	2423
3-4 tonnes[2]	187	355	500
5-6 tonnes[2]	30	30	39
7-8 tonnes[3]	20	18	19
9+ tonnes[4]	44	38	44
Tractor	4	5	7
Crane truck	3	2	2
Special purpose vehicle	1	1	1
	2337	2772	3035

1. Car-derived van segment
2. Panel van segment
3. Light truck segment
4. Light, medium and heavy truck segments

Source: Japan Automobile Manufacturers Association

Therefore, although the Japanese and West European CV parcs are similar in size, the composition of the parc is entirely different. There is some evidence to suppose that the limit for CV demand may be approached soon: over 98 per cent of all goods carried in the 1-100 kilometre range in Japan are transported by CVs and the equivalent figure for greater distances is over 80 per cent. CVs are still increasing their share of the freight transport market, at the expense of railways and marine transportation. Once these alternatives have been eclipsed in all feasible circumstances, growth of the CV parc must be related to the demand for freight transport, which is dependent on the level of activity in the Japanese economy.

Tables 9.2 and 9.3 also provide useful information on the evolution of the Japanese market by providing car, CV and 3-wheeler production and new registrations. Car demand continued on an upward trend, completely unaffected by a Japanese recession in 1971, until the worldwide downswing in 1974; 3-wheeler demand fell rapidly in the same period, and disappeared in 1974. Unlike North America and Western Europe, the late 1970s saw a depressed level of new registrations with no recovery to the peak of 1973. Slower growth in demand for CVs is a clear indication of a mature economy, reflecting the transition from capital goods to consumption goods. This picture of a maturing market is supplemented by the figures for 2-wheeler registrations also shown in Table 9.3, where falling demand received a (temporary?) boost in the period immediately following the 1973-74 oil crisis.

Several reasons, such as volatile commodity prices and Japan's toughened engine emission controls, have been put forward for the prolonged halt in the growth of new car registrations. However, the real reason must surely be that Japan's increase in ownership up to 1973 more than satisfied Japan's appetite for new car purchases, and that everyone who required motor transport and had sufficient means had achieved their objective. One factor which may explain the sluggishness of demand is the level of car and CV ownership, which is currently at 3.5 people per vehicle. This combined density figure is higher than Western European levels in 1973. There may therefore be an element of substitutability between cars and car-derived vans.

Import penetration

In the wake of the 1965 Japanese trade liberalization measures, there are now no restrictions, in theory, on the levels of imports into Japan from overseas manufacturers. In fact, however, access is restricted in practice by a barrage of troublesome administrative problems, and a tightening of safety and anti-pollution measures. Although obstacles of this sort are not insuperable, they make access to the Japanese market far from straightforward and could eventually isolate the Japanese market. The Japanese have, in any case, adopted a more or less protectionist stance in their unwillingness to overcome an entrenched resistance to the purchase of foreign goods. As yet, the import share has not exceeded 1.8 per cent in a period of reduced demand and even this represents a significant demand for specialist and luxury cars. As the market matures and the demand for specialist models grows, importers may benefit. The Japanese will also be producing suitable top-end vehicles, but at least the importers will fight from a stronger position. Table 9.7 and Figure 9.1, giving import shares for various foreign

Table 9.7 *Car imports into Japan by country ('000s)*

	1969	1973	1974	1975	1976	1977	1978
West Germany							
VW	5	13	16	16	16	16	19
Opel	1	1	1	2	2	1	1
Daimler-Benz	1	2	3	3	3	3	4
Other	1	4.5	0.5	1	1	1	2
BMW	0	1	1	1	2	2	2
	9	18	22	22	22	22	29
US							
GM	2	4	6	7	7	7	7
Ford	2	5	6	8	7	7	7
Chrysler and AMC	1	1	1	2	2	2	2
	5	10	13	18	16	16	15
UK	2	1	1	2	2	1	2
Others	1	11	4	3	3	3	4
Total	17	40	40	45	43	42	50

Figure 9.1 *Imports by country and company of origin (1978)*

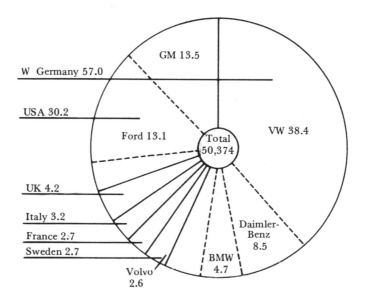

manufacturers, show that the bulk of Japanese demand for foreign cars is met by West German and US producers. Despite an intensive marketing campaign in 1975, importers were only able to improve their share by 7.7 per cent at a time when the market expanded by 8.9 per cent.

In response to pressure, some concessions have been made to importers (eg granting a three year delay in the application of emission standards to importers). This resulted in a dramatic increase in imports (albeit from a miniscule base) in 1978: UK and French imports doubled, and other European manufacturers achieved a 30 per cent improvement in a total market that only grew by 11.6 per cent. Nevertheless, there are hidden obstacles and importers will always find the Japanese environment a difficult one.

The structure of the industry

In Japan, unlike either Europe or the US, each car manufacturer has a CV division and there are no independent truck and bus manufacturers. The Toyota and Nissan groups between them exercise a near monopoly in the car sector, and are only marginally less dominant in the CV sector. The Toyota group consists of the Toyota, Daihatsu and Hino manufacturers, while the Nissan group incorporates Nissan Motors (brandname Datsun), Nissan Diesel and Fuji Heavy Industries (brandname Subaru). Three of the smaller Japanese firms have reached trading agreements with US multinationals: Mitsubishi (tradename Colt) with Chrysler, Isuzu with GM and Toyo Kogyo (Mazda) with Ford. Suzuki, the smallest of the car manufacturers, remains independent. Honda has recently established a trading link with British Leyland.

Both Honda and Suzuki were attracted into motor vehicle production when the small engine was the most significant segment. In the smallest segments there were certain common components (eg engines) between small cars and motorcycles, in which both companies were already established. As the Japanese motorist demanded a more mature product, Honda and Suzuki had to follow the trend and in so doing lost some of the commonality with their motorcycle business.

The Japanese motor industry has always been highly concentrated, because of the comparatively late development of the industry, the existence of independent indigenous manufacturers and the high levels of vertical integration achieved at the outset to cope with the demands of CV production to which the industry was initially geared. Before the 1962-70 period, the industry was already dominated by two firms — Nissan and Toyota. In the mid-1960s the MITI, the Japanese Ministry of International Trade and Industry, drew up proposals for the reorganization of the Japanese motor industry to strengthen the existing combines and to ensure that the industry, as a whole, could resist the pressures of increased competition from manufacturers abroad.

Toyota acquired Hino Motors (in 1966) and Daihatsu (in 1967), and undertook to provide its partners with assistance in technical, financial and personnel matters. Nissan made a similar agreement with Fuji (in 1968) and the Nissan Diesel Company, and purchased the Prince Motor Company. Neither Toyota nor Nissan like to publicize that these subsidiaries are part of the parent company. One advantage of this policy is that, when an export market begins to protest about Toyota and Nissan imports, the parent company can freeze sales of their major brandname and switch to introducing one of their minor brandnames. Examples of a successful implementation of this strategy can be found in the US and Europe. The UK countered by its 'orderly marketing' agreement with the Japanese: Toyota and Nissan could not escape from this as total Japanese imports was the control criterion.

Figure 9.2 shows the clear dominance achieved by Toyota and Nissan. Although Toyota had traditionally led Nissan in production, it seemed possible that Nissan would catch and overtake Toyota in 1976-77. Toyota responded strongly, retaining their lead in the domestic market and establishing superiority in exports.

Figure 9.2 *Japanese car production*

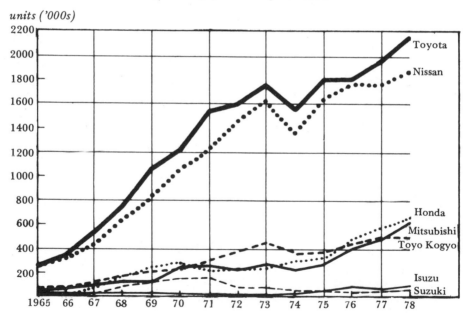

The 1974 recession, the first in which production actually declined, hit Toyo Kogyo (Mazda) badly, partly because of the company's commitments to the high-consumption rotary engine, which with increased oil prices, seemed a less economic system (though recent engineering developments by Toyo Kogyo have counteracted this criticism of Wankel engines), and made it appear that the company had based its massive US export drive on an apparently unsaleable engine. Only Honda has been able systematically to increase output regardless of the 1973-74 oil crisis. Suzuki's dramatic fall in production was due to a switch to larger cars; its products had been traditionally in the smallest of segments.

The dominance of the two larger producers in CV production has been established but by a smaller margin than with cars (see Figure 9.3). Toyo Kogyo's production has stagnated, whilst Isuzu has leapt ahead of both Mitsubishi and Toyo Kogyo. Honda is less well established in the CV field and only offers a limited range of products in the light van segment of the market. Its products were so positioned at the bottom of the market that, as the Japanese CV consumer demanded larger vans, the company was ill-equipped to adjust to the change in the type of CV demanded.

Figure 9.3 *Japanese truck and bus production*

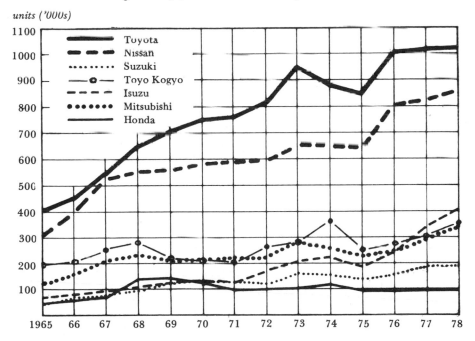

Figure 9.4 *Japanese links*

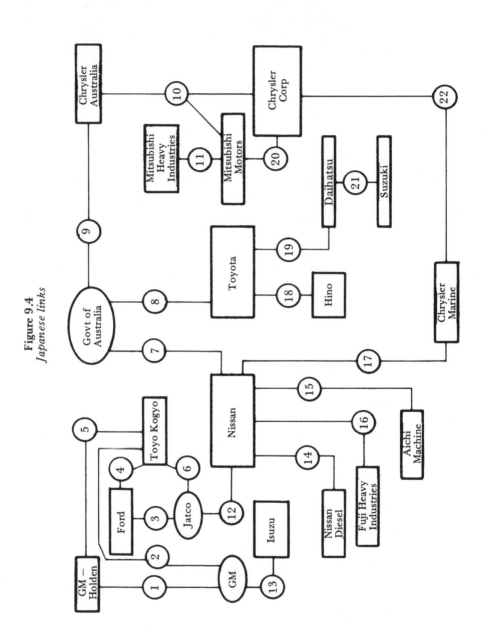

Figure 9.4
Japanese links

1. GM-Holden's is a fully owned subsidiary of General Motors.

2. General Motors has a technology-sharing agreement concerning rotary engines with Toyo Kogyo.

3. Ford Motor Company is a majority partner in Jatco-Japan Automatic Transmission Company.

4. Ford Motor Company has purchased a 24 per cent stake in Toyo Kogyo and will probably extend its holding.

5. Toyo Kogyo buys body shells and chassis for its largest car from GM-Holden's.

6. Toyo Kogyo is a minority partner in Jatco.

7. The government of Australia's Australian Industry Development Corporation is the principal sponsor of a four-way scheme to manufacture four-cylinder car engines. Nissan Motor Company is one of the partners.

8. Toyota is a partner with the AIDC in the four-cylinder engine project.

9. Chrysler-Australia is a partner with AIDC in the four-cylinder engine project and would contribute its Lonsdale plant.

10. An equity stake of 30 per cent in Chrysler-Australia was purchased from Chrysler Corporation by Mitsubishi. There is an option in which Mitsubishi may take up a controlling interest.

11. Mitsubishi Heavy Industries owns 85 per cent of Mitsubishi Motors.

12. Nissan Motor Company is a partner in Jatco.

13. General Motors owns a 34.2 per cent share of Isuzu Motors.

14. Nissan Diesel is a subsidiary of Nissan Motor Company.

15. Aichi Machine Company is a subsidiary of Nissan Motor Company.

16. Fuji Heavy Industries (makers of Subaru) is a subsidiary of Nissan Motor Company.

17. Chrysler Corporation, Marine Engine Division, is US distributor for Nissan light-duty diesel engines.*

18. Hino Motors is a subsidiary of Toyota Motor Company.

19. Daihatsu is a subsidiary of Toyota Motor Company.

20. Chrysler Corporation has a 15 per cent share in Mitsubishi Motors.

21. Suzuki has a contract for emission control technology-sharing with Toyota and Daihatsu.

22. Chrysler Marine Engine Division is a division of Chrysler Corporation.

* The agreement ran out in 1976

Source: Adapted from *Automotive News*

Ownership, control and links with US multinationals

Through strong protection and government encouragement, Japan bred a number of manufacturers. Eventually Nissan and Toyota came to the fore and took over a number of smaller manufacturers. If it had not been for restrictions on the activities of foreign manufacturers, the Japanese motor industry would be mostly in foreign hands, and Mitsubishi, Isuzu and Toyo Kogyo are all partly foreign owned.

Links between Japanese firms and the US multinationals are still in their infancy, but an outline of the agreements in force is given in Figure 9.4. The Mitsubishi-Chrysler association (Chrysler have a 15 per cent share in Mitsubishi) was established in 1971 as a result of the Japanese company's failure to establish links with another domestic manufacturer. In the same year, GM acquired a 34.2 per cent holding in Isuzu Motors. After a series of fruitless negotiations, Toyota abandoned attempts to gain control of Toyo Kogyo or the two smaller Japanese firms and has remained resolutely non-aligned, although in 1974 Suzuki concluded an agreement with Toyota on a joint contract for research into emission control technology. Isuzu has locked into GM's worldwide model policy to produce a version of the GM T car (Chevette).

Ford had been trying to take over Toyo Kogyo since the early 1970s, but concern over foreign ownership and other considerations hampered negotiations. The oil crisis of 1973-74, however, hit Toyo Kogyo badly, seriously affecting both car and CV sales to a greater extent than its rivals. A mistake or bad luck with model policy can be one mistake too many. A major equity holder, the Sumitomo bank, got cold feet and finally agreed to let Ford buy a 25 per cent stake with an implicit understanding that Toyo Kogyo should be integrated into a unified Ford corporate model policy and production programme — a technique which Ford pioneered in Europe.

Chrysler's financial problems in the US have led to the indefinite postponement of their merger programme with Mitsubishi, whereby Chrysler were to increase their holding in Mitsubishi by investing 35 per cent of the capital required to undertake a joint research and development project, culminating in the creation of an independent motor company assembling Chrysler vehicles in Japan or importing Chrysler engine and gearbox units for assembly in Mitsubishi bodies.

Chrysler's original 15 per cent stake in Mitsubishi was to have worked like this: Chrysler would use Mitsubishi-produced vehicles to supply the sub-compact and compact segments, while Mitsubishi markets Chrysler's products in Japan. It has not been successful. Chrysler's sales of Mitsubishi's products have lagged behind all the other Japanese imports, and Chrysler sales in Japan have been insignificant. Meanwhile Chrysler developed its own range of small cars. Moreover, Mitsubishi is an enormously diversified company, and it is causing Mitsubishi some embarrassment to be partly owned by a weaker company. Mitsubishi even came to Chrysler's aid by buying Chrysler's ailing Australian subsidiary. The relationship is clearly unsatisfactory at the moment. Mitsubishi wants to achieve 300,000 plus sales of cars in the US, and it cannot rely on Chrysler US to help. Mitsubishi itself is short of cash because of the continuing slump in shipbuilding and other heavy machinery sales. It is rumoured an offer has been made by Mitsubishi to Chrysler US (alongside rumours that VW and PSA Peugeot-Citroen are also interested) for extensive aid in exchange for a more satisfactory and permanent solution. At the moment the situation is in flux.

Honda and British Leyland have no formal ownership links but a successful conclusion to their trading links could result in a more formal association. Meanwhile the smallest manufacturer, Suzuki, has no association with any foreign manufacturer and, despite its large 2-wheeler business, Suzuki's future independence must be in doubt.

Share of domestic market

Table 9.8 shows how the Japanese producers have fared in their own marketplace. Traditionally, Toyota, with roughly 40 per cent of the total car market, has always had a slight lead over Nissan in both car and CV output but, with a new marketing impetus in both domestic

Table 9.8 *Manufacturers sales share of Japanese market (%)*

Cars						
	1973	1974	1975	1976	1977	1978
Toyota Group	40.1	42.3	42.4	39.5	38.4	41.3
Nissan Group	34.3	32.0	34.2	34.6	34.0	32.0
Honda	6.8	8.3	5.9	6.8	6.6	6.0
Toyo Kogyo (Mazda)	7.3	6.4	6.5	6.7	7.0	6.0
Mitsubishi	6.9	5.7	6.2	7.6	8.7	9.1
Suzuki	2.8	2.6	1.7	2.1	2.0	2.1
Isuzu	0.5	0.8	1.5	1.2	1.5	1.7

CVs						
	1973	1974	1975	1976	1977	1978
Toyota Group	36.9	36.5	35.2	36.6	37.0	35.4
Nissan Group	22.8	22.9	24.1	24.8	22.8	22.1
Toyo Kogyo	9.1	9.0	9.0	7.9	7.3	9.4
Isuzu	6.7	6.4	6.2	7.1	7.5	7.4
Mitsubishi	12.0	11.4	11.0	11.4	12.4	12.8
Honda	4.9	5.9	5.5	5.0	4.7	4.5
Suzuki	7.6	7.9	7.9	7.5	8.3	8.3

and export markets, Nissan's production may overtake Toyota. Honda's fortunes in the car market have been on the decline in recent years, but its new model, the Accord, has revitalized flagging sales. If the fuel consumption disadvantage of the rotary engine can be overcome, Toyo Kogyo's sales should similarly recover. Of the two other principal producers, Suzuki's performance has been adversely affected by the lack of a comprehensive model range; while Isuzu's market share has increased slightly. Mitsubishi's share of the domestic market in cars and CVs has increased.

Exports

The Japanese motor industry is heavily dependent on exports which in the late 1970s accounted for about 50 per cent of total production. Japan's success story is in part due to its export policy. By growing faster than the domestic market would allow, Nissan and Toyota created, in the early to mid-1970s, the volumes necessary to achieve equivalent economies of scale to Ford, Chrysler and most European producers. Apart from GM, no producer was getting the benefit of more economies of scale than Toyota and Nissan. The existence of scale economies meant that the two large Japanese companies could be fully competitive. Expanding to twice what the domestic market would normally take also allowed the component firms supplying the motor industry to grow and benefit from the economies of scale.

Table 9.9 shows the growth of total exports and exports to the principal markets.

UNITS.

Table 9.9 *Total Japanese exports ('000s)*

	Total exports of motor vehicles	Exports to US	Exports of KD units*	Exports to North America	Exports to Western Europe	Middle East	Far East
1965	194	34	39				
1966	256	65	58				
1967	362	82	79				
1968	612	183	122				
1969	858	281	177				
1970	1087	422	177				
1971	1779	814	264				
1972	1965	840	295				
1973	2068	823	381	914	401	208	195
1974	2618	1000	512	1138	387	139	269
1975	2678	920	535	1004	526	242	264
1976	3710	1370	631	1498	704	395	320
1977	4353	1715	712	1855	707	441	424
1978	4601	1893	859	2030	760	370	400

* Included in all export statistics

Exports have grown phenomenally in the last 15 years. Exports of motor vehicles from Japan for 1978 were 4.6 million units, of which cars accounted for 3 million units. Apart from a period in the mid-1960s, North America has been Japan's largest market, receiving some 45 per cent of total exports. Table 9.10 shows the regional split separately for cars and CVs. In cars, Europe was the second most important market. Although North America is still Japan's largest CV market, other (especially the less developed) areas are only slightly less important.

Table 9.10 *Japanese exports by manufacturer (1978)*

	Cars ('000s)	CVs ('000s)	Total ('000s)	Cars exported to US ('000s)
Nissan Group				
Nissan	855	364	1219	338
Nissan diesel	–	10	10	–
Fuji	61	90	151	103
	916	464	1380	441
Toyota Group				
Toyota	900	482	1382	442
Daihatsu	20	47	67	–
Hino	–	20	20	–
	920	549	1469	442
Toyo Kogyo	341	195	536	75
Honda	488	7	495	275
Mitsubishi	321	135	456	104
Isuzu	55	168	223	19
Suzuki	1	40	41	–
	3042	1558	4601	1356

	Cars	CVs
Total exports 1977 (millions)	2.96	1.39
Proportion (%)		
North America	49.5	28.0
Europe	22.4	6.9
South-east Asia	6.0	21.1
Middle East	6.0	18.6
Oceania	7.2	5.8
Central and South America	4.8	9.3
Africa	4.0	10.3

Exports of KD (knock-down) vehicles are increasing to the less developed countries. Usually these countries are not open markets and require some local assembly in order for a sale to be made. By region, KD exports among all motor vehicle exports were 76 per cent to

South-east Asia, 52 per cent to Oceania and 47 per cent to Africa. North America and, for the most part, Europe, only import built-up cars.

The relative export strengths of the Japanese producers can be gauged from the figures given in Table 9.10. Even the smallest manufacturers are clearly export-oriented: Isuzu's and Mitsubishi's marketing agreements (with GM and Chrysler respectively) should enable them to increase their export sales to the US.

Marketing policy

Product ranges for all of the major Japanese producers are given in Table 9.11. Both Toyota and Nissan, through their various subsidiaries, cover the entire range but are poorly represented at the lower end of the scale (vehicles with an engine capacity of less than 360cc). Honda has now developed a second model, the Accord, to complement the existing Civic range. Isuzu's product is essentially a smaller version of the global concept T car (Chevette). Toyo Kogyo's commitment to the Wankel (rotary) engine caused marketing problems in the aftermath of

Table 9.11 *Marketing policy*

	<360cc	360-1000cc	1001-1500cc	1500-2000cc	>2000cc	Sporting	2-wheelers	Vans	Light trucks	Medium-duty trucks	Heavy-duty trucks	Specialized trucks	Four-wheel drive	Buses	Other
Toyota Group															
Toyota			x	x	x	x		x	x	x	x	x	x	x	Tractors
Daihatsu	x	x						x	x	x	x	x	x		
Hino											x	x	x	x	Tractors
Nissan Group															
Nissan		x	x	x	x	x		x	x	x	x		x	x	
Nissan Diesel											x	x	x	x	
Fuji	x		x					x	x				x		
Honda		x	x				x		x						
Isuzu			x	x	x						x	x	x	x	Tractors
Mitsubishi		x	x	x	x	x		x	x	x	x	x	x	x	Tractors
Toyo Kogyo		x	x	x	x	x		x	x	x	x	x			
Suzuki	x	x					x		x				x		
Kawasaki							x								
Yamaha							x								

the oil crisis as the engine had an unacceptably high rate of fuel consumption, but this setback has been overcome and the company has proved that with further development a rotary engine could consume *less* fuel than a conventional internal combustion unit. Suzuki, like Honda, began as a producer of 2-wheelers and subsequently diversified into cars, but has suffered from a limited range too heavily biased towards small cars.

Integration

After Fiat and GM, the Japanese firms of Toyota and Nissan are two of the most vertically integrated motor manufacturers in the world, Toyota having a marginal lead over Nissan in this respect. In fact, vertical integration is a conspicuous feature of the Japanese motor industry as a whole, with suppliers either wholly owned by manufacturers or totally dependent on particular producers through exclusive supply contracts.

Finance

In normal accounting terms, the Japanese companies are very profitable: typical performance ratios include returns on sales of between 5-7 per cent, returns on equity of 15-20 per cent and returns on assets of 10-17 per cent. Table 9.12 shows the net income (profits after tax) figure for some of the Japanese companies. Honda's and Toyo Kogyo's figures are straightforward; Nissan's and Toyota's are not. Both Toyota and Nissan are large conglomerates with the total process of vehicle production and sales fragmented across many companies. No consolidated accounts are produced. Toyota Motor Company, which is the heart of the group, employs some 45,000 people and generated about $570 million in both 1977 and 1978, but though normally identified as the total company, it is but a small part of the group. The entire Toyota Group employs some 150,000 people and generated a total estimated net profit in both 1977 and 1978 of some $1.3-1.7 billion.

This discrepancy highlights what is immediately obvious in Table 9.12. Taking the figure for the profit of Toyota Motor Company, the profits generated are significantly below those of the American counterparts. However, with the profits from all the other firms in the group, the profit compares favourably with the US multinationals. Nissan is organized in a similar manner but even less information is available: it probably employs about 140,000 people and makes a total profit of some $1 billion (1977-78).

Contrasting these larger figures with Honda and Toyo Kogyo clearly demonstrates the importance of scale in the motor industry. Even in the peak years of 1972-74, profits were not great for these smaller

Table 9.12 Comparative profit after tax figures ($ millions)

	1972-73	1973-74	1974-75	1975-76	1976-77	1977-78
Honda	60	66	28	18[1]	118	69
Nissan	234	202	92	255	416	394
Toyo Kogyo	41	26	−8	5	6	13
Toyota (Toyota Motor Company)	47	60	175	486	570	567
Toyota Group[2]	860	650	700	1100	1350	1300
Ford (worldwide)	870	361	323	983	1673	1589
GM (worldwide)	2163	950	1253	2903	3338	3508

1. Six months
2. Estimate

companies. Profitability was severely reduced during the recession following the 1973 oil crisis. However, the real problem is still to come: if Honda is to compete internationally with the major companies, they must be prepared to spend up to $500 million a year. Honda raised $50 billion in 1977 and is currently trying to raise $130 million internationally, but this is only the beginning.

Honda's management is astute and recognized the company's financial problem. Only two basic car models are produced (Civic and Accord) and one tiny van. Annual production runs exceed 300,000 for the car models and 80,000 for the CV model. At one point, the company was almost a one-product company producing around 500,000 Civics a year. Concentrating on a few models and spreading scale economies over parts for the motorcycles (which use four- and six-cylinder engines) helps to make Honda profitable. Honda's willingness to collaborate with British Leyland is further evidence of a rational policy by a management which fully understands the motor industry and acted with great foresight and from a position of strength.

Toyo Kogyo's management certainly has courage. Having led a marginal existence in the years 1975-78 and with its shareholders and bankers breathing down its neck, the company managed to introduce five new models and the President (Yoshiki Yamasaki) announced his intention of exceeding one million vehicle sales a year. It is hardly surprising that Ford wants to take over Toyo Kogyo whose energy and enthusiasm must be a major attraction. But herein lies the problem: a company producing substantially less than one million vehicles cannot compete internationally from a medium cost base, the cost penalties through insufficient volume exceed 10 per cent, other things being equal. Even Toyo Kogyo's single integrated ultra-efficient factory cannot overcome these disadvantages.

There can be no doubt that the financial performance of the industry to date has been encouraging and in worldwide terms, the Japanese motor industry ranks as one of the most profitable. However, despite the increased volume of production, profitability has declined. In real terms, Toyota made far more money in 1973 on a volume of 2.4 million vehicles than it did in 1978 on a volume of 3.4 million vehicles. We return to discuss this decline later.

Competitive strengths of the Japanese manufacturers

The Japanese producers have been successful in penetrating most overseas markets. Why? One reason was its low cost base and the availability of cheap labour, but other factors contributed to its success.

Labour and productivity

Japan's labour force is apparently more amenable than most and is certainly one of the most productive in the world. This may be explained by the traditional and culturally reinforced loyalties of the Japanese worker to his employer, and by the fact that the industry has benefited from massive capital investment in sophisticated and highly efficient plant which, in itself, would enhance productivity in virtually any industry anywhere in the world. The diligence of Japanese workers and the freedom from industrial stoppages have been major contributing factors in Japan's competitiveness. Striking illustrations of Japanese productivity are readily available, although for a variety of reasons they should not invite direct comparison with figures from other developed industrial countries. In 1974 Toyota produced as many cars as VW, but with only one-third of the total workforce, 55,000 employees compared with VW's 148,000! These figures, although compelling, may be misleading, as they do not indicate how many of the employees are directly engaged in car production, nor the extent to which groups of workers are engaged in work of a comparable nature.

We touched upon this statistical problem earlier. The Toyota Group comprises 16 companies employing some 150,000 people. The Toyota Auto Body Company makes bodies, the Toyota Motor Sales Company sells vehicles, the Nippondenso Company makes electrical components, and so on. Normally the productivity of Toyota looks impossible: Toyota Motor Company made just under 3 million vehicles in 1978 with only 45,000 employees, a productivity level of 63 vehicles per employee per year. This should be contrasted with European and American norms of 10 to 20 vehicles per employee per year. Including the full 150,000 employees of the Toyota Group brings the productivity level down to 20 to 25. Honda's consolidated figures show a productivity for cars in excess of 30, and this is probably a genuine figure. Figure 9.5 suggests that, applying the criterion of value per employee, the Japanese and other major manufacturers are roughly equal, but there is little doubt that the Japanese motor manufacturers have achieved remarkable levels of productivity. Whereas the Fiat worker contributes 2.8 times more than the 'average' Italian worker to his country's GNP, the Toyota car worker contributes an astonishing 15.25 more than an 'average' Japanese employee to his country's GNP. Moreover, Fiat employs over one per cent of the total Italian workforce, whilst Toyota employs less than 0.1 per cent of the total Japanese labour force.

In Chapter 8 evidence was provided which demonstrated that the Japanese manufacturers are constantly improving labour productivity. The current Japanese technology is to pass a car down an assembly line with multi-arm robotic machines capable of being computer controlled.

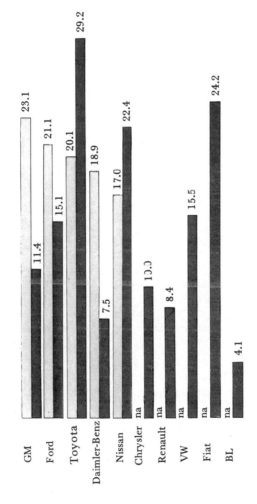

Figure 9.5 *Productivity comparisons 1974 ($ '000s)*

GM 23.1 / 11.4
Ford 21.1 / 15.1
Toyota 20.1 / 29.2
Daimler-Benz 18.9 / 7.5
Nissan 17.0 / 22.4
Chrysler na / 10.0
Renault na / 8.4
VW na / 15.5
Fiat na / 24.2
BL na / 4.1

▨ Productivity of labour (gross value added divided by average number of employees)
▨ Fixed assets *per capita*

Source: The Motor Industry of Japan 1977 published by Toyota

Thus, from the available evidence and an examination of current trends, it appears that differences in productivity will increase.

Economies of scale

By plotting production against price, the considerable savings achieved by the Japanese from economies of scale can be impressively demonstrated (see Figure 9.6) which, to some extent, explains the Japanese export emphasis, for the domestic market alone could not support the production volumes at which these economies are achieved. Both Nissan and Toyota are now in a position to benefit from most of the economies of scale available to volume producers (ie total production in excess of 2 million units a year). To achieve any further economies of scale, they would have to produce model runs of around one million. In fact, in 1977 Toyota achieved the largest production run for a single identical model, with 817,000 Corolla vehicles.

The smaller producers must either restrict their range and settle for limited competition in specific market sectors, or they must expand. Toyo Kogyo and Mitsubishi both experienced faster rates of growth in the 1969-73 period than their two larger rivals; further growth for either Nissan or Toyota will most probably reflect an increase in relative shares of existing markets (achieved by scoring points off each other), as well as some modest growth in total sales.

Other strengths

Two other strengths should be briefly mentioned. First, the Japanese have a very high standard of academic and professional management. The industry is also able to attract and retain first-class engineers. Second, in the formative years of the industry, a considerable part was played by the banks, under the aegis of the Minister of Finance, in providing loan capital. There is some evidence that the banks still play a useful role, but do the other competitive strengths still exist?

Japan's future economic prosperity

Earlier we noted that the financial performance of the Japanese manufacturers had begun to deteriorate in the late 1970s. An analysis of the reasons for this decline spans the wider question of Japan's economic prosperity in the future. Although there seemed to be no limit to Japan's post-war economic growth, purely physical constraints will eventually apply. Until now, neither lack of natural resources nor scarce availability of land have affected growth, but by the early 1980s Japan could be almost completely urbanized, the pool of reserve labour (ie convertible rural labour) will have run dry and land for new industrial sites will be virtually non-existent. The Japanese have already

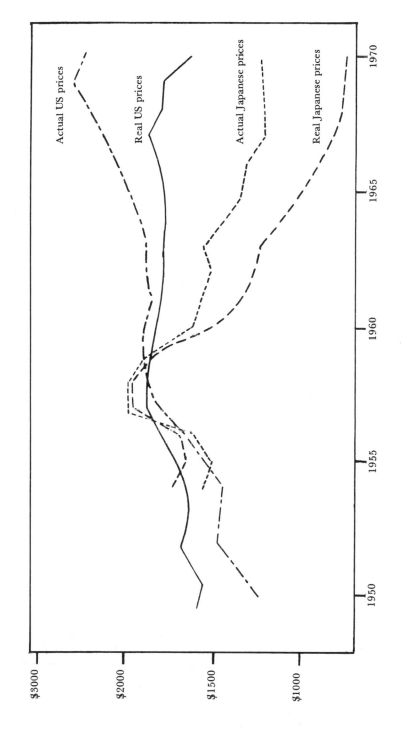

Figure 9.6 *Average wholesale prices of automobiles against time (1950-70)*

Actual US prices

Real US prices

Actual Japanese prices

Real Japanese prices

$3000

$2000

$1500

$1000

1950   1955   1960   1965   1970

Source: The World Automotive Industry to 1995 Business International

begun to invest in plant and facilities elsewhere and this process will continue at a faster pace, partly to ensure continued growth and partly to secure access to the vital raw materials and other resources with which Japan is singularly poorly endowed. Japanese capital is already at work in Korea, Taiwan, Singapore, the Philippines, Indonesia, Australia, Hawaii, Alaska, Mexico and Brazil, either as a straightforward investment in real estate, or to fund the establishment of large-scale sub-contracted manufacture of components and materials for export to Japan.

Growth in the expansion of Japanese business interests abroad will not be unimpeded, however, for as Japanese firms move into unfamiliar industrial terrain they will encounter problems already commonplace elsewhere but alien to the Japanese experience. A less disciplined workforce would be an obvious example, but they could also meet more resolute political resistance to further expansion. The US, for example, can eventually be expected to insist on a limit on Japanese imports, in order to achieve a state of rough equilibrium in US-Japanese trade, and other nations will probably seek ways of avoiding a gross imbalance of trade in favour of Japan. The upper limit to further Japanese growth must, therefore, be determined by restrictions on growth in its major export markets abroad, rather than a loss of momentum.

Japan faces two other major problems: first, Japan is no longer a cheap cost base relative to other major world producers; second, as in the US, state interference is now having a detrimental effect on cost structure.

Cost base

Japan's traditional position as a relatively low labour cost area — which has given Japanese producers an edge in pricing in world markets — has been eroded. Japanese wage rates have been rising faster than anywhere else. A second factor is the continual and relentless rise of the Japanese exchange rate against other major currencies. Japan is now a medium or high cost base for labour: Toyota's average wage in 1978 was $19,030, compared with $7550 for British Leyland and $17,863 for VW.

State interference

The development of Japanese industry was fostered to a considerable degree by the protectionist policies of MITI. The level of state intervention in industry is surprisingly high for a newly developed industrial economy, although it would be considered unexceptional in the more fully developed economies of Western Europe and North America. But this state involvement in Japanese industry is a natural extension of a protectionist attitude: it is a short step from protecting an industry in its infancy to encouraging stronger industrial groupings within that industry through merger or other means of affiliation.

Intervention by the Japanese state closely mirrors the American experience in the enforcement of stringent regulations governing acceptable levels of exhaust emission, which naturally concerns a heavily polluted country such as Japan. Japan has the strictest emission control standards in the world, and regulations have posed serious difficulties for the producers. One should not underestimate the Japanese, however, as even this could be turned to their advantage: imagine the impact of a 'clean', pollution-free Japanese car on the maturer world markets!

Location strategies

The erosion of Japan's traditional position as a relatively low labour cost area has made domestic manufacture a less attractive strategy than heretofore. Recent expansionist moves by both Nissan and Toyota (the former now operating in Chile, Peru and Mexico, the latter in Peru, Thailand, Brazil and other parts of South America) suggest that both firms are adopting the 'federal' approach of Ford and GM in exploiting the cost advantages of underdeveloped regions, and by doing so overcoming resistance to Japanese exports abroad. Table 9.13 gives a more complete picture of existing plant location overseas. In Toyota's case, expansion of production facilities overseas has been a relatively recent development, possibly promoted by monetary developments in the last few years. In the late 1970s the company produced around 3 million vehicles, over 90 per cent of which were still manufactured in Japan.

As far as locational strategies are concerned, Mitsubishi is in a rather different position. The company began as a shipbuilding operation, later merging with an aircraft manufacturer (1934), a machine-tool producer (1945) and a locomotive works (1950). The company's activities are highly diversified, and in 1973 over 65 per cent of Mitsubishi's business was generated by the non-automotive divisions (which account for 66 per cent of Mitsubishi's sales). With a greatly reduced dependence on turnover in the motor divisions, the company has resisted the temptation to relocate plant elsewhere, in strong contrast to the policies currently pursued by Toyota and the other major motor manufacturers.

Future demand

Demand in the domestic market is far less crucial for the Japanese than it is for the US, or even for producers in Western Europe (still a net exporting region). Nearly 40 per cent of total Japanese production is

Table 9.13 *Overseas plants of Japanese vehicle manufacturers*

Toyota (assembly only) Thailand, Philippines, Malaysia, Indonesia, Burma, Taiwan, Pakistan, Iran, Saudi Arabia, Guatemala, Honduras, El Salvador, Nicaragua, Costa Rica, Jamaica, Dominican Republic, Bolivia, Paraguay, Canada, Brazil, Ecuador, Australia, New Zealand, Ivory Coast, Ghana, Nigeria, Sierra Leone, Liberia, Togo, Dahomey, Cameroon, South Africa, Ireland, France, Portugal, Switzerland, Greece, Cyprus, Trinidad and Tobago
Honda Thailand, Belgium, Korea, Taiwan, Philippines, Malaysia, Indonesia, Pakistan, Bangladesh, Iran, Turkey, Syria, New Zealand, Mozambique, Nigeria, Angola, Morocco, Mexico, Peru, Uruguay, Nicaragua, Guatemala, Jamaica, Brazil, Portugal, Italy, Ireland, Yugoslavia
Nissan Thailand, Taiwan, Philippines, India, Indonesia, Malaysia, Singapore, Iran, Australia, New Zealand, South Africa, Ghana, Nicaragua, Portugal, Ireland, Mexico, Peru, Chile, Venezuela, Costa Rica, Trinidad and Tobago, Angola
Toyo Kogyo Korea, Malaysia, Philippines, Indonesia, Burma, Pakistan, Iran, South Africa, Kenya, Ghana, Greece, Portugal, New Zealand, Costa Rica, Trinidad and Tobago, Ireland, Thailand

exported, compared with less than 15 per cent of the total European output. We now analyse domestic demand.

Domestic demand

The Japanese government is quite prepared to take a tough stance on issues such as emission standards, and is equally likely to take an uncompromising stand on energy conservation. This, together with increasing congestion in urban areas, will affect consumer choice. There can be little doubt that saturation levels in Japan will be lower than in North America and could be lower than in Europe. One of the peculiarities of the Japanese market is the large ownership of vans, which, if necessary, could double up as personal transport. In total vehicle ownership, Japan has already exceeded the UK and average Western European levels. Forecasting future indigenous demand is difficult. Japan may move away from small CVs to larger trucks, and, if this occurs, personal transport needs that were previously satisfied by vans would switch to cars. The assumption made in this demand projection is that there is some switch to larger CVs but that there will still be a very substantial demand for small CVs, and therefore a CV parc of vans in 1990 which can satisfy an element of the personal transport demand.

Assuming a population growth rate of 1.2 per cent, Japan will have a population of 135 million by 1990. A vehicle life of 12 years is taken for both cars and CVs. Two alternative scenarios are outlined in Table 9.14. In the first, we specify vehicle densities of five people per car and ten people per CV. These provide a wide range for cars and CVs, although CV demand never exceeds the 1973 peak. The second, an optimistic high demand scenario, assumes a vehicle density of four people per car (above current European norms) and a CV density equivalent to North America's. The total CV parc by 1990 will have reached 40 and 50 million vehicles for the medium and high demand projections respectively.

A low demand scenario would envisage a vehicle parc of about 35 million vehicles and would require a total collapse of demand between now and 1990. New registrations would run at 1-2 million cars and less than one million CVs. Assuming that exports could not fill the demand vacuum, production would fall by 25-30 per cent, perhaps leading to unemployment for 250,000 direct workers and one million indirect workers. With an ailing shipbuilding industry, the Japanese government will take steps to see that this does not happen, and domestic demand for motor vehicles will be promoted. The low demand scenario can, therefore, be ignored.

The range estimates given in Table 9.14 cover a wide span and some explanation is necessary. When a developing country expands its vehicle parc rapidly, and catches up to a Western level of vehicle ownership, a larger element of new registrations will be for replacement vehicles. If a

Table 9.14 *Forecast of Japanese demand in 1990*

Population: 135 m	Cars	CVs
Vehicle life in 1990 (years)	12.0	12.0
Vehicle parc in 1977 (m)	19.8	19.2
New demand in 1990 (m)	0.25-1.25	0.1-0.6
Medium demand scenario		
Number of persons per vehicle	5.0	10.0
Vehicle parc (m)	27.0	13.5
Replacement demand (m)	2.25	1.13
Demand range (m)	2.0-3.75	1.0-2.0
Central projection (m)	3.0	1.5
High demand scenario		
Number of persons per vehicle	4.0	8.0
Vehicle parc (m)	33.8	16.9
Replacement demand (m)	2.75	1.41
Demand range (m)	2.5-4.25	1.4-2.5
Central projection (m)	3.5	2.0

significant proportion of the vehicle parc is new, as in Japan's case, replacement demand will be substantially below equilibrium levels until the vehicle parc has aged and thus leads to a healthy replacement demand.

In both scenarios growth in new CV registrations will either be non-existent or will decline (although the CV parc will expand slightly). Future demand should follow the tendency in the other mature markets of increased growth in demand for larger trucks, assuming that the Japanese highway network is improved to cope with the demands of heavier road usage. However, this trend will not be present to as great a degree as in the other mature markets.

Export demand

The major export markets are discussed separately below. There are, however, a number of common factors which must be discussed. Japanese, European and American cars will become much more standardized. The Japanese car will no longer be marketed as a cheap basic product, but durable, sophisticated and extremely reliable (though much more expensive). The Japanese export product of the 1990s will be more similar to the European product of today. Pressure in export markets will, therefore, come from two sources: first, the European and American producers whose products will be indistinguishable and, second, the new producers discussed in Part 3 which will take over the role of supplying a cheap and more basic product.

Exports, in the analysis below, are defined to include KD kits for assembly in an export market, since current Japanese kits still have some 70-80 per cent of the value of the assembled car manufactured in Japan.

NORTH AMERICA

Once a manufacturer has established a major distribution network in an export market, it is extremely difficult to dislodge its market share. The Japanese marketing machine is also a highly sophisticated and adept machine, which can be finely tuned and has been shown to be responsive to the needs of the public. Thoughts that Japanese exports to North America could be rolled back by US and European producers are unrealistic. Only political pressure and/or trade barriers could achieve a major reduction in exports to North America. Japan should, therefore, be wary of overselling itself in North America, but competition between the individual manufacturers will obstruct a more rational and politically astute export policy. The range of Japanese exports to North America in 1990 will not be less than one million cars and 0.3 million CVs; the highest likely sales would be 2.5 million cars and one million CVs. Table 9.15 gives an illustrative projection.

Table 9.15 Japanese export performance ('000s)

Cars	1973	1974	1975	1976	1977	1978	1980*	1985*	1990*
North America	659	796	735	1162	1464	1528	1500	1700	1500
Western Europe	360	341	483	634	663	649	700	1000	1250
Africa	78	105	106	117	119	146	100	150	100
Far East	98	100	87	115	152	185	200	150	100
Middle East	36	63	78	143	181	165	150	125	75
Oceania	151	239	212	266	239	250	200	300	310
Caribbean	27	33	31	49	59	43	50	50	50
Central and South America	44	51	45	54	83	75	50	50	25
Total	1355	1728	1827	2540	2960	3041	2950	3525	3410

CVs	1973	1974	1975	1976	1977	1978	1980*	1985*	1990*
North America	255	342	219	336	390	501	450	550	600
Western Europe	44	47	44	71	94	96	125	140	150
Africa	69	109	108	119	144	163	150	125	100
Far East	110	168	177	206	272	320	300	250	250
Middle East	43	76	164	252	260	250	200	100	100
Oceania	45	76	67	102	103	110	100	100	100
Caribbean	6	9	10	10	12	10	10	10	10
Central and South America	45	62	58	72	118	107	100	125	150
Communist Bloc	0	0	2	1	1	1	10	20	50
Total	617	889	849	1169	1394	1558	1445	1400	1460

* Representative forecasts

WESTERN EUROPE

There is still room for further growth in the European marketplace which will suffer from increasing import penetration as the region becomes increasingly mature. Table 9.16 shows that Japan has, until now, acquired only a relatively modest market share in a number of West European countries, principally West Germany, France and Italy. Japan will take a larger share of the German market, though the Spanish, French and Italian markets will be more difficult to penetrate (partly due to government support of the indigenous motor industry). It is unlikely that Japanese exports to Western Europe will fall much below 700,000 cars and 100,000 CVs, and they may be significantly higher.

Table 9.16 *Japanese exports to Western Europe*

	Japanese share of market 1977		
	Units sold ('000s)	Market ('000s)	(% of registrations)
Norway	35	145	24.1
Finland	17	90	18.9
Portugal	8	76	10.5
Belgium	87	423	20.6
Denmark	23	141	16.3
Netherlands	113	552	20.5
United Kingdom	151	1324	11.4
Switzerland	33	234	14.1
Ireland	18	82	22.0
Sweden	26	241	10.8
Austria	16	296	5.4
Germany	69	2561	2.7
France	42	1907	2.2
Greece	23	98	23.5
Italy and Spain	3	1891	6.6
	664	10,061	

OTHER AREAS

As will be seen in Part 3, more and more markets are being closed, usually through the introduction of local assembly coupled with heavy protection of the local market. The Japanese will have a hard time retaining their existing markets; some markets will gradually but steadily be lost. The internal upheavals in Iran, bringing a new government which has banned car imports, is an example of what the Japanese have to face. Total exports will remain substantial (see Table 9.17), and CV demand will remain strong, since it will be impossible for all developing markets to establish a full range of CV production.

Production

Table 9.17 tabulates growth prospects given plausible high and low estimates for the year 1990. Import penetration is assumed to rise to a realistic figure of 10 per cent for cars and 5 per cent for CVs. The total production figure is derived by adding the domestic and export sales and deducting imports. This sum is not a realistic figure since not all export markets will simultaneously do well (or poorly). A range estimate has to take this into account as well as adjusting for domestic cycles in demand. Of the two, the low scenario is the most likely to occur. A central estimate for production is 6 million cars and 2.6 million CVs. In 1978 production reached almost 6 million cars and exceeded 3 million CVs, and there is a good chance that in the mid-1980s demand for Japanese vehicles will peak at 6-7 million cars and at 3-3.5 million CVs. The Japanese will gear up capacity to meet this peak, but by 1990, Japan will have excess capacity. This creates difficulties for the future for the Japanese manufacturer.

Table 9.17 *Projections of Japanese production in 1990 (millions)*

	Cars		CVs	
Scenario	Low	High	Low	High
Home market sales	3.0	3.5	1.5	2.0
Export sales				
North America	1.35	2.0	0.3	0.6
Western Europe	0.75	1.5	0.1	0.2
Other	1.0	1.5	0.6	0.8
Total Japanese sales	6.0	8.5	2.5	3.6
Less imports	0.3	0.35	0.08	0.1
Total Japanese production	5.7	8.15	2.42	3.5
Production range estimate	5-6.5	6-7.5	2-3	3-4
Central production estimate	6		2.6	

Industrial strategy

How will the Japanese manufacturer react to over-capacity? Before this problem will become apparent in the late 1980s, there will be a number of more pressing needs requiring action. First, as the Japanese product becomes more sophisticated and competes directly with the American and European producers, the Japanese firm will have to get used to spending US-style sums (around $1 billion annually) on capital investment. Toyota and Nissan can both afford this, but expenditure of this order is out of the question for the smaller firm. Second, with an increasing tendency for the domestic market to face cyclical fluctuation, the Japanese manufacturer will suffer reduced profitability. With the exception of 1974, the Japanese producer has always been at or near capacity, so profitability was assured. In the future, a Japanese firm will have to get used to operating at a range of capacity utilizations and be able to at least break even at output levels of only 40-50 per cent of capacity. During 1974 Toyota's break-even point was 66 per cent. In future, Toyota must be able to make sufficient profits at 70-80 per cent capacity utilization not only to declare a dividend (to keep its equity owning bankers happy) but also to plough enough into the company for new technology and new model development.

There is no doubt that both Nissan and Toyota will survive and will be major manufacturers in 1990; their profitability, along with all other motor manufacturers, will, however, have suffered. There may even be a requirement for some discreet government aid, if a number of circumstances conspire against one of the firms (eg a model mistake and energy crisis). In this event, aid will probably be forthcoming. What of the smaller firms?

Toyo Kogyo is now locked into Ford and will therefore reflect Ford's performance. Suzuki must either pull out of cars, merge with a Japanese manufacturer (Nissan is most likely), or merge with a foreign firm (VW is the most probable). Isuzu's fortunes are linked in with GM's.

Honda's association with British Leyland should logically lead to a merger between the two companies. However, British Leyland does not see it this way; they are still developing models similar to Honda's for separate launch in the 1980s. A rational policy would see both companies in an extremely strong position, with a comprehensive worldwide range[1] and just sufficient volume to benefit from scale economies (combined capacities are around 1.8 million cars). Production would have to be integrated and the Japanese consumer might find the British product unacceptable in terms of workmanship, which could be overcome by testing and correcting faults on the factory-ships[2] that carry cars from Japan to the UK.

If British Leyland and Honda part company in the mid-1980s (perhaps sooner if Honda's current poor profitability continues), Honda will look for other suitors. Another Japanese manufacturer is unlikely (Honda is too large) and a European producer (for example, VW) would be a more logical partner.

This leaves Mitsubishi, whose fortunes are only dependent on the motor industry to a smaller extent. Logically, the ideal solution for the company would be to take over Chrysler US and integrate the worldwide production of the two companies but to retain the two brandnames.

1. This assumes that Honda will develop a new range of large panel vans.
2. Japanese manufacturers carry out a certain amount of final assembly, finishing and testing on these ships, which are fully fitted to allow such work to be carried out.

Some design, engineering and production capacity may be shed in North America in a moderate retrenchment proposal by Mitsubishi. If this worked, Mitsubishi's next move might be a foray into Europe and possible targets include Volvo, Saab, Motor Iberica, Italy's state-owned Innocenti and BMW. It is possible that Mitsubishi may buy some under-utilized plant from a European manufacturer (eg UK plants owned by PSA Peugeot-Citroen) and a greenfield site cannot be ruled out entirely. Mitsubishi would then become a multinational, with a total capacity of some 4 million vehicles a year.

Basic Japanese manufacturing technology and management expertise are highly developed and should be able to keep abreast of new developments. Toyota and Nissan will be a major force in the world motor industry. The rest of the motor industry in Japan will follow the European pattern, which will involve a further concentration of the industry. One new development that must be considered is collaboration between Toyota or Nissan and European manufacturers. The president of Nissan Motor Company, T Ishihara, has said that the Japanese motor manufacturers cannot afford to remain isolated while manufacturers elsewhere are entering into tie-ups of various kinds. He has offered emission control know-how to European producers, presumably in exchange for front-wheel drive know-how, which is probably Nissan's weakest and most vulnerable point. (The problem is not technical expertise but simply the time and money spent in perfecting a new system.)

The possibilities for future links are not good. Mr Ishihara has asked Ford to part with half of its 50 per cent stake in JATCO (see Figure 9.4) which supplies automatic transmissions. This is not the best way to encourage partners.

Following the US pattern of locating plant overseas, Toyota and Nissan will continue to adopt a more federal approach to their operations overseas, although they could reserve the right wherever possible to supply at least some (if not all) of the components from Japan. The Japanese are well placed to utilize even lower cost labour by locating plant in adjoining Asian countries.

By the 1990s, Japan, already densely populated, could have become almost completely urbanized. This would create a much greater domestic demand for rapid urban transport systems rather than private cars, or other means of individual transport. With the growth in demand for rapid transit systems, the Japanese motor vehicle producers could be expected quickly to diversify their operations into this area, developing transit systems to meet the demand. It is possible to predict the same outcome in the rapid development of new technologies required to produce electric cars, should the need (and the demand) arise in future.

Conclusion

The Japanese motor industry will ultimately experience the problems and difficulties which confront the mature motor industries in North America and particularly Western Europe. Until then, Japanese producers can expect to enjoy a modestly healthy period of further growth and continuing profitability, although they will face the continuing danger of either possible import controls in their major export markets, or greater obstacles to domestic production in the shape of further extensions to existing government controls and regulations. The Japanese motor industry is more certain of survival than that of Western Europe, though as a mature market the industry can expect to play a very different role. We must now ask who could replace the Japanese as producers of low-cost, basic vehicles? To do so, we turn to the newer and fast developing motor industries elsewhere. But it is unlikely that the speed and success of the Japanese motor industry's development will be repeated elsewhere.

Part 3:
Minor Markets and Producers

Chapter 10

The Minor Markets:
An Overview

In Part 2, the three major producers and markets were analysed. It was postulated that the Western European and Japanese markets would follow some of the US trends. In Part 3 we ask who will succeed Japan as a major producer and exporter in this dynamic cycle? The answer to this question lies in one of the areas discussed in the next four chapters. These areas (the Communist Bloc, South America and the Middle East) are experiencing rapidly growing demand and have established the basis of a viable motor industry. There are, however, many contrasts in these markets: the Communist Bloc growth is largely dictated by central planners, the Middle East growth critically depends on petrodollar revenue and South America has had a less spectacular but steadier growth record.

Japan's rate of growth distinguishes it from these newer producers. Both the Communist Bloc and South America had a larger motor industry than Japan in 1950, but Japan's growth far outstripped them. The following chapters argue that both the Communist Bloc and South America may have established motor industries equivalent to Japan's present level towards the end of the century. The development of these two potentially mature markets has been relatively slow and steady. South America has been dominated by US and European producers, while the Communist Bloc has remained independent, albeit sometimes using Western technology. Both regions have now reached a critical take-off stage; either the industry must grow to reap the benefits of scale economies and thereby become competitive, or the industry must remain smaller, uneconomic, perhaps protected by trade barriers and certainly reliant in some way on the other mature markets. We believe that both the Communist Bloc and South America will become mature markets, though the energy shortage makes their development precarious.

Unlike the other two regions, the Middle East's development as a motor market and producer began in the 1970s. With Japanese-type growth rates, the Middle East would become a mature market by the 1990s, but this is unlikely. Not every emergent motor producer will be able to make the critical take-off stage and recent internal upheavals in Iran (the major producing country) reinforce our scepticism. The

Middle East will be an important minor market and an important producer, but it is doubtful whether it will ever become a mature producer.

Other markets and producers

Other important minor markets unlikely to become mature producers, are Australia, New Zealand and South Africa. Although demand is well established, the areas are too small to support a viable motor industry. Without the necessary scale economies, their indigenous manufacturing/ assembly facilities must be tied into the mature markets. Local content regulations only serve to make production more difficult for the established assemblers, which provides an opportunity for penetration by the newer mature producers (ie Japan at present). Local content rules also force the price up of locally produced components and it is the consumer who ultimately suffers. The 'Old Colonials' will always be an important minor market, but perhaps not as significant as the Middle East. In terms of worldwide importance to the motor industry, they reached their apogee in the late 1950s and early 1960s, when production and demand outstripped Japan for a short period.

The Old Colonials currently look to all three mature producers for their local production facilities. The Middle East, however, could develop links with the Communist Bloc as well. Since the South American manufacturing firms are subsidiaries of the existing manufacturing firms in the mature markets, South America is never likely to develop close links with other countries. The Communist Bloc, attached ideologically to parts of the world which also look to Eastern Europe for technology and aid, may develop such links and is, therefore, potentially the most significant of the less mature developments.

The last chapter of Part 3 deals with a number of infant producers. Too small to be classified as significant minor markets, and nowhere near the take-off point, the infant producers show a remarkable degree of heterogeneity. India, for example, has been an established producer for some time, though exhibiting no growth. South Korea has established its own motor industry independent of the mature producers. There are other areas approaching an interesting stage, and it is conceivable that the next region to become a mature producer may be a current 'infant' producer.

Dispersion

Whatever the development pattern of the motor industry, demand for motor vehicles will continue to spread throughout the world. Differences in vehicle ownership will tend to be reduced, although will not become equalized throughout the world: industrialized and urban societies will always depend on motor vehicles. The growth of new markets will be entirely consistent with increasing real income *per capita*: those countries and regions which cannot control population growth will probably be least susceptible to an increase in the demand for motor vehicles.

The manufacture of motor vehicles will follow demand and become more dispersed throughout the world. The dispersion of production will not however keep pace with the dispersion of demand. There are several reasons for this, and we must examine the main ways in which a motor industry has been developed in new areas. The usual method is development by one of the major multinational manufacturing firms, with the encouragement and involvement of national governments. The other is autonomous development (as in South Korea), with fewer connections with outside manufacturers. The latter approach can either be under state auspices (eg in Eastern Europe) or by local private companies with the active support and approval of state bodies. The outside manufacturers in both types of development were mainly GM and Ford before World War II; and GM, Ford and Chrysler in the post-war period. The European manufacturers have been increasingly involved since the 1950s. Japan began to develop foreign subsidiaries in the 1970s and is expected to become increasingly involved in the 1980s.

Development phases

The reader will have obtained an insight to the development of a motor industry from following the progress of Japan in Chapter 9. There are a number of distinct phases in the development of a motor industry and we now turn our attention to these before examining the newer producers separately.

Bloomfield[1] defines four stages in the growth of a motor vehicle industry:

1. Import of completely built-up (CBU) vehicles by local retailers. This involves the setting up of branch offices by the major manufacturing companies. Parallel with the import of the complete motor vehicles is the import of spare parts and other equipment necessary to build up the motor industry infrastructure. There may develop a small body building facility for some trucks and buses.
2. Assembly of completely knock-down (CKD) vehicles imported from the home plants of world manufacturers. The process of CKD assembly is a logical extension of the setting up of branch offices. The impetus is either government insistence on local assembly

1. Bloomfield, Gerald (1978) *op cit*

coupled with financial threats or economic factors. The latter include local modifications to suit local market conditions and the imposition of high import duties on CBU vehicles. The rationale for government is to encourage employment and manufacturing development. Much of the finance for the assembly plants is local (private and/or state) with three common organizations: local motor agents assembling imported vehicles, distribution organization formed to build and run assembly plants, and new enterprises created to assemble vehicles on contract.

3. Assembly of CKD vehicles with increasing locally made content. Again this phase arises from a mixture of government action by selective tariff charges on parts in CKD kits and the growth of an indigenous component industry. The latter begins by making replacement parts for such typical items as tyres, batteries, silencers, axles, and other parts especially where cheap labour costs may offset scale economies. This phase gradually sees the increased substitution of locally made components for imported items. This will increase to the point where the CKD kits only comprise principal body pressings and the power train. Finally local pressing will be undertaken and the only imported item will be the power train. Figure 10.1 illustrates the way in which costs increase with higher local content for differing production levels.

4. Full manufacture of motor vehicles. For some countries full manufacture includes everything except the power train, but others may manufacture this too. It is the production of the power train which will lead to the establishment of an industry at such a level that it must achieve the necessary economies of scale to compete with the other mature producers. Full manufacture of a model by a major manufacturer still requires substantial economies of scale both in motor vehicle manufacturing and component supply.

Linking into an internationally produced car requires annual volumes of the following orders of magnitude to be competitive (assuming that at least two companies are involved):

- [ ] Power train output   200,000 +
- [ ] Assembly plant output   100,000 +
- [ ] Company output   500,000 +
- [ ] Industry volume   1,000,000 +

These figures assume that cheaper labour offsets the greater economies of production elsewhere. Import duties make little difference since the increase in costs below these volumes quickly outweighs any import duty penalties. The volumes for CV truck manufacture are substantially lower. For example linking in to an internationally produced model would only require annual volumes of:

Figure 10.1 *Cost increase as a function of local content*

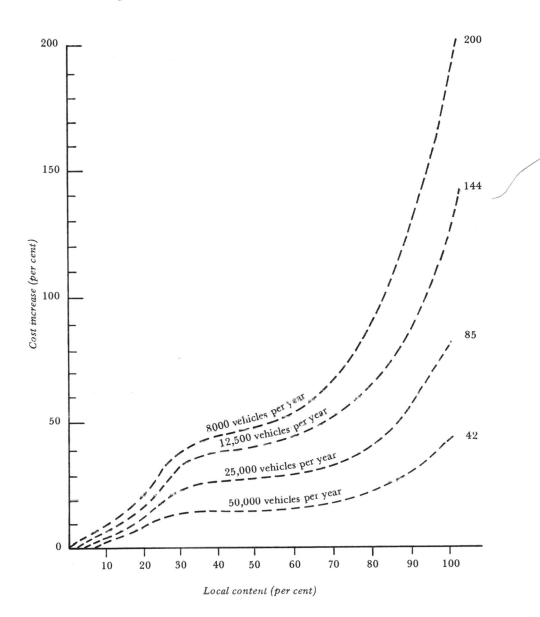

Source: Asociación de Fabricas de Automotres (1969) *Informe Economico 1969* Buenos Aires

☐ Power train output   20,000 +
☐ Assembly plant output   10,000 +
☐ Company output   20,000 +
☐ Industry volume   40,000 +

These volumes would progressively increase as one approached the volume end of the CV market.

The question of economies of scale has tended to modify both the attitudes of some governments and multinationals. It is accepted that some countries can never develop a viable autonomous motor industry without that industry being spread across an entire region with regional manufacture as the ultimate goal. Where the major world motor corporations are not involved, a number of alternatives have been developed. First, smaller companies (ie not GM, Ford, Chrysler, etc) in the major producing areas have been used to establish emergent industries. Second, licensing arrangements with the larger firms have been used to resist complete foreign control of new enterprises. Third, specialist engineering expertise has been used to develop a purpose made product. In general the opportunities and scope for the large multinationals to develop further is limited as they face growing international resistance by new developing governments anxious to retain their control and autonomy, and avoid being dictated to by companies whose wealth may be far greater than the country's total GNP.

Government involvement

One difference that has been put forward to differentiate a mature from a developing motor industry is the degree of government involvement. However it could be argued that this is no longer valid. Governments are involved in propping up and controlling the motor industry in Western Europe and now even in the USA. However, during the development of an emergent producer, tariff structures and import duties, local content regulations, direct encouragement, the provision of state aid (including finance), and the parallel planning of the necessary components/supply industry (eg steel, rubber, glass and plastics) are necessary conditions for growth. An indigenous government must use both carrot and stick if it is to overcome the scale economies of the mature producers. Even with government support, an emergent producer faces enormous cost penalties, and we may wonder how motor industries develop at all. The US is spending nearly $100 billion in the next decade; no developing nation could afford such expenditure. How then do new developments occur?

Product differentiation

As in Japan the precondition of a motor vehicle industry is the development of more basic forms of transport — bicycles, motor-assisted bicycles, tricycles, motor-assisted tricycles, etc. Since the major motor vehicle manufacturers have regarded such products with disdain, local manufacture/assembly of these simpler automotive products may lead to the development of a motor industry.

The motor industry product of a developing country is very different to that demanded and produced in mature markets. There is a requirement for cheap and unsophisticated vehicles such as the VW Beetle. Inadequate road networks often mean that a four-wheel drive utility vehicle (eg Jeep or Land Rover) provides the necessary degree of flexibility. The light multi-purpose pick-up or van is also a feature of a modern developing society and, therefore, of its motor industry.

The major manufacturers are beginning to respond to their neglect for a product suited to the needs of these developing nations. An example is the GM Basic Transportation Vehicle which is sold and/or assembled in a number of different markets such as Malaysia (the Harimon), Philippines (the Harobos), Thailand (the Plai Noi) and Ecuador (the Audino). VW has a similar vehicle called the Mule. Chrysler and Mitsubishi together developed the AUV (Asian Utility Vehicle). International Harvester developed the WUT (World Utility Transporter).

Implication of diffusion

The diffusion of the motor industry implies that there will be more local assembly and manufacture, and that no one mature market will dominate these regions. As developing markets mature, the opportunities to provide CBUs will be reduced. However, in order to maximize scale economies the manufacturing process may become more complex. Bloomfield[1] cites the Ford Fiesta as an example: it is assembled in the Philippines, with engines from Taiwan, transmissions from Australia, axles from Mexico and steering gear and brakes from Britain.

Economics of scale and the pressure on governments to export are leading the emergent producers to export more vehicles and components to the mature markets. VW's Beetle production is confined to South America. Fiat uses a South American engine in some of its European products (eg Fiat 127). The Volvo Laplander is now only made in Hungary.

Conclusion

The degree of geographical concentration in the world motor industry will decline, though, with established producers financing many

1. *The World Automotive Industry op cit.*

operations in developing countries, ownership and control may be less dispersed. There will be new mature producers, new emerging producers and a greater diffusion of demand. The role of the established producer is no longer certain.

Chapter 11

The Communist Bloc

For the purposes of our discussion, the term 'Communist Bloc' includes the USSR, Poland, Romania, East Germany, Czechoslovakia, Hungary, Bulgaria and Yugoslavia. We have excluded Albania (whose motor industry is not significant) and China (which is dealt with later). The motor industry, in the region as a whole, has developed in a fairly uniform manner and now ranks just behind Japan in terms of productive capacity.[1] With a total output in the late 1970s of over 2 million cars and one million CVs, its 20 per cent growth rate compares favourably with the rate of expansion in Japan. Although slower rates of growth are now expected in the Japanese economy, the growth of the Communist Bloc's motor industry could continue at higher rates for some time.

The Communist Bloc area has some similarity with both Western Europe and Japan. Like Japan, it has developed its industry independently but, like Europe, has a rather fragmented industry. The area as a whole is likely to become a mature producer in the next decade and oust Japan from its position as the major motor vehicle exporter.

Economic policy

In Chapter 3 we noted that vehicle density levels in Communist Bloc countries were very low compared with areas where more or less unrestrained market forces were allowed to determine the supply and demand of goods. Although an improvement in living standards is an objective to which all Communist countries are committed, the methods employed to achieve that end are very different to those of the West. The economy is centrally planned, and the demand for cars – non-essential commodities – can be artificially dampened by banning imports and not channelling resources into domestic production. Such measures would not usually be enforced to curb CV demand which must keep pace with the requirements of an industrial economy. In Western Europe, CV sales are over 1.5 million per annum (compared

---

1. Available statistics relating to the Communist motor industry in Eastern Europe are notoriously unreliable and should be treated with a degree of circumspection. Figures quoted in this chapter have been compiled from a number of different sources and do not necessarily tally in all respects.

with sales of over 10 million cars per year); annual CV demand in the Communist Bloc is over one million, ie similar to Western Europe whose level of car production is far higher.

If levels of car demand have until now been stringently controlled, what are the future prospects for growth in Eastern Europe's car industry? There is no compelling reason for Communist Bloc countries to emulate the Western pattern of growth and further development. If car production was to be geared solely to meet domestic requirements, further developments would certainly be unnecessary. Noncommunist societies depend to a far greater extent on personal mobility, and there is no evidence to suggest that Communist countries have reached the stage where they are obliged to rely on private transport or that they would find such a state of affairs desirable. If, however, we examine future prospects in terms of export potential, there are good reasons for assuming that the Communist Bloc motor industry will expand along Western lines, or that it will at least find the Japanese example an attractive one and follow their lead in exporting a substantial proportion of total car production to overseas markets.

Before we consider these alternatives in greater detail, we will look more closely at the present character of the market to understand more fully the macro-economic framework within which the motor industry operates. Table 11.1 shows that though the USSR has a much larger population than any of the other Communist Bloc countries, East Germany and Czechoslovakia have a much higher *per capita* GNP, roughly equivalent to the UK figure. At the other extreme, Bulgaria, Romania and Yugoslavia are the poorest of the Bloc countries.

Table 11.1 *Comparative economic statistics*

		Population		Economy GNP per capita*	
		1976 (millions)	Growth rates 1970-76 (%)	Market prices in 1976 ($)	Growth rates 1970-76 (%)
USSR		257	0.9	2600	5.5
Poland		35	0.9	2500	6.7
Romania		21	1.0	1600	10.0
East Germany		17	—0.3	4000	5.2
Czechoslovakia		15	0.7	3500	5.0
Hungary		11	0.4	2100	5.6
Bulgaria		9	0.5	2100	7.7
Yugoslavia		22	1.0	1540	5.5
	Total	387			

* Estimates

The USSR holds most of the military, political, ideological and even economic trump cards, and can exert a formidable influence on developments in countries within Eastern Europe. Any future developments in the motor industry will proceed at a pace and in a direction dictated by the Soviet planners, but this does not imply that future Soviet economic strategies will differ in any significant respect from the strategies employed elsewhere. Soviet politicians and economic planners share with their Western colleagues an interest in the allegedly 'capitalist' concern for economies of scale, industrial organization and management responsibility. The 1965 Russian factory reforms, for example, introduced the concept of profit as a proportion of capital employed as a guideline for industrial management, and in most other matters of economic and industrial strategy there is a remarkable degree of consensus between Western and Communist economic theorists and planners. This is particularly so in matters of energy policy and pricing. Until recently the USSR fixed prices for its oil for a five-year period, but it now intends to keep energy and other raw material prices roughly in line with world trends, and to this end an annual price review has been introduced. As oil exported from the USSR to other countries within the Bloc accounts for 90 per cent of their total energy requirements, a quinquennial price review effectively protected them from the inflationary shock of the steep increase in the price of oil which had such a disastrous effect on Western economies between 1973 and 1975. The introduction of an annual upward adjustment in energy prices, which reached world levels by 1978-79, destroyed the stable economic character of the area and necessitated the post oil crisis adjustments already familiar in Western industrialized economies. Such a radical change in pricing policies had some effect. Potential for growth in East/ West trade was checked, albeit temporarily, and there was evidence of a much firmer resolve to integrate Communist Bloc economies. Efforts have been made to reduce trade deficits with the West either through restrictions on imports or a concerted attempt to increase exports, or a combination of the two. Western trading partners, increasingly aware of the importance of maintaining trade with Eastern European countries, have responded by offering ever more attractive credit terms in an absurd race to go even faster simply to stay where they are. However, the change in energy prices was gradual and led to a halt in the growth of the motor industry rather than a decline in production.

Import cutbacks and reliance on oil supplies from the USSR have greatly strengthened the Soviet grip on industrial policy within the Bloc, as evidenced by the renewed advocacy of the intra-Bloc trade and development projects. Higher prices within the Bloc depressed growth in domestic demand, which was only partially offset by increasing exports. A period of economic recession was averted by the gradual adjustment to energy prices and the postponement of some of the expansion plans.

In the long term, recovery and further growth for the area are closely linked to the future growth of the Russian economy. The USSR possesses some 10 per cent of the world's recoverable oil resources and produces more oil than the USA; it is currently in the favourable position of being a net exporter of crude oil. The Russians also have large reserves of natural gas and substantial mineral deposits. Two factors will influence future economic growth in the USSR: her ability to exploit energy reserves and mineral deposits (for which they will have to import technology, plant and equipment from the West), and plans for further industrial development in Siberia and the under-exploited areas to the East. As a major oil producer upon which most of the Communist Bloc countries are dependent, the USSR is in a virtually unassailable position *vis à vis* her satellites and can be expected to intervene whenever possible in determining the industrial and economic policies of the Bloc countries within its sphere of influence. The USSR will wish to encourage an expansion of trade to fill three crucial gaps in her economic armour — the need for grain, technology and credit.

Grain

The USSR is evidently unable to produce enough grain to meet its requirements and will be obliged to rely on regular and substantial imports of grain from the West. These requirements increase the USSR's balance of payments deficit with the West, but the existence of such a deficit creates the opportunity for more durable trading agreements which will have a far greater impact on East/West detente than the 'push-pull' politicking of generations of statesmen on both sides.

Technology and credit

If the USSR and the Communist Bloc hope to develop their economies as planned, they have no other option than to buy both credit and technology from the West. To those who would argue that with a shortage of hard currency and a persistent trade deficit the Communist Bloc countries cannot afford to expand their trade with the West, one can only say that they cannot afford not to. International trade in the twentieth century is surprisingly adept at overcoming trade finance difficulties: barter, buy-back agreements, government-to-government or banking consortium credits are all commonly employed as alternatives to cash on the counter.

On balance, the future prospects for East/West trade suggest a continuing expansion, with the gradual removal of tariff barriers and other restrictions on access to markets as the level of trade increases.

The motor industry

In the context of the major world motor vehicle producers, two things are immediately apparent: the CV industry is much more important than the car industry; and the figure for total imports expressed as a percentage of apparent consumption shows, perhaps surprisingly, that the Communist Bloc market is no more 'protected' than the EEC.

In the case of the CV market, further substantial growth in this sector is highly likely. Rapid urbanization (already a feature of the Communist Bloc), has stimulated demand for light- and medium-weight CVs to meet the short haul requirements of the construction, distribution and service industries which tend to flourish in an urban environment. Further growth in demand for public transport motor vehicles can be expected, while in the long haul freight market, demand for heavy-weight CVs should be encouraged by the industrial development programmes which are now a prominent part of a more integrated approach to development within the Bloc.

It is often argued that the inadequacy of existing road networks in the Bloc is an important factor in explaining the slow growth in car ownership and low car density levels. But which comes first: roads to drive on or cars to drive? Even if a straightforward relationship between the two could be established, would it explain slow growth in the car sector? In other markets, the absence of a fully, or even partially, developed road network has done little to restrain growth in demand where all other possible restraints have been discounted. In the Communist Bloc, the road network is certainly poor but it is only one of many more potent disincentives to car ownership in an economy where availability of private vehicles is a matter of economic planning rather than consumer demand. There are relatively few private vehicles in the Communist Bloc countries as a matter of deliberate policy: very few cars are available for sale and very few people are in a position to afford them. Once acquired, there is very little in the way of a servicing and repair infrastructure; where facilities exist at all, shortages in petrol and spare parts have encouraged a flourishing black market, further reinforcing the notion that car ownership is a luxury open only to the privileged (or influential) minority.

There is greater emphasis in Eastern Europe on the development of CV production and the provision of public transport facilities at the expense of private car ownership and production. Table 11.2 illustrates the difference in emphasis between the CV and car sectors within the Bloc compared with markets elsewhere. With one or two exceptions CV vehicle ownership levels are nearly up to Western European standards. Car ownership levels on the other hand are much below European levels, although East Germany, Czechoslovakia, Poland and Hungary have the densest car ownership (equivalent to European conditions in

Table 11.2 *Vehicle ownership in the Communist Bloc (1977)*

	Car parc (millions)	Persons per car	Households owning a car* (%)	CV parc (millions)	Persons per CV
USSR	5.66	46	4.2	5.70	45
East Germany	2.05	8	21.4	0.55	31
Czechoslovakia	1.56	10	20.9	0.30	50
Poland	1.2	29	7.7	0.52	66
Bulgaria	0.45	19	7.0	0.11	80
Yugoslavia	1.74	13	na	0.17	125
Romania	0.24	107	3.8	0.10	215
Hungary	0.65	16	11.9	0.21	50
	13.55	29		7.66	51
UK	14.4	4	53	1.82	30
France	16.3	3	63	2.41	25
West Germany	19.2	3	60	1.45	42
Italy	15.9	4	55	1.25	45
US	109.7	2	80	27.6	8

* 1973 figures

the early 1950s). The growth of passenger miles by road and cargo miles by road is nearly 10 per cent a year. At this rate the road traffic is nearly trebling every decade. There are signs that the road network is being developed to support an increased dependence on the motor vehicle.

The motor industry has grown rapidly and is exploiting to the full infusions of expertise and technology it has been obliged to import from the West. But it remains a relatively unsophisticated, under-developed industry with severe organizational weaknesses and major loopholes in marketing and export strategy, and this may inhibit or prevent the emergence of a fully-fledged, highly integrated motor industry in future.

The structure of the motor industry and the market

Table 11.3 provides a statistical outline of the motor industry in the Communist Bloc. In 1977 the region as a whole had a vehicle parc of 21 million, producing over one million CVs and 2 million cars. Exports were estimated at 200,000 cars and 45,000 CVs, with imports of approximately 8000 CVs and 75,000 cars. Apparent consumption (production less exports plus imports) almost matches current production. Trade between Bloc countries accounted for between 330,000 and 380,000 cars and over 50,000 CVs. Both car and CV production have grown rapidly since the mid-1960s before which

Table 11.3 *Vehicle production in the Communist Bloc ('000s)*

	Cars	CVs
1960	297	457
1961	317	478
1962	332	495
1963	353	498
1964	369	505
1965	444	502
1966	494	558
1967	544	602
1968	609	664
1970	653	684
1971	758	749
1972	979	749
1973	1214	868
1974	1490	903
1975	1598	952
1976	1956	1004
1977	2051	1024
1978	2212	1065
1980	2700	1202
1985	3500-4500	1400-1800
1990	5000-7000	1800-2500

CV production had remained more or less static and growth in car production had been minimal. A change of policy encouraged rapid growth in both sectors: car production has more than quadrupled and CV production has more than doubled. CV production is relatively more sophisticated, although most of the refinements to the basic technology (and much of the plant and equipment) have been imported from the West. Production in 1976 and 1977 was only a marginal improvement on 1975, reflecting the delayed impact of the oil crisis. It is significant that car production suffered more than CV production.

Country-by-country analysis

We now analyse the constituent countries of the Communist Bloc. Figure 11.1 and Table 11.4 show car and CV production by country.

The USSR has by far the largest car industry within the Bloc, followed by East Germany, Poland and Yugoslavia, all of which have smaller car industries roughly similar in size. Romania has the smallest and newest car production facility. Production of commercial vehicles follows much the same pattern: the USSR leading the field, followed by Poland, East Germany, Czechoslovakia and Romania. Yugoslavia has a modest CV industry, and Bulgaria and Hungary are the least developed.

Figure 11.1 *Car production*

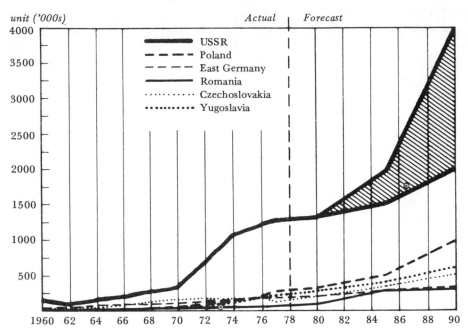

In the 1950s and early 1960s Hungary was a producer of heavy trucks and buses, and East Germany and Czechoslovakia concentrated on cars and light CVs. Since the mid-1960s there has been far more competition between the countries, although the USSR has been allowed to dominate both car and CV production. Economies of scale have forced concentration of car production, but not of CV production, and most of the countries in the Communist Bloc have some domestic CV capacity. This raises interesting questions on intra-bloc exports, imports and consumption. Table 11.5 shows car and CV exports for 1975. The figures quoted have been drawn from estimates compiled by Euroeconomics and do not wholly correspond with figures given earlier.

Hungary and Bulgaria import their entire requirement of cars. Poland, East Germany, Czechoslovakia and the USSR export some cars outside the Bloc, and Poland, Romania, East Germany and Czechoslovakia depend to a large extent on their ability to export a substantial proportion of their production. With CVs the proportion exported for all countries is lower: East Germany, Czechoslovakia and Poland are the main exporters, and the USSR exports surprisingly few CVs.

Table 11.4 CV production ('000s)

	USSR	East Germany	Poland	Czechoslovakia	Romania	Yugoslavia	Bulgaria	Hungary
1960	385	13	22	18	9	5	—	5
1961	406	12	20	18	11	6	—	5
1962	412	13	25	17	13	9	—	6
1963	414	10	30	14	14	10	—	6
1964	418	12	28	13	16	12	.|	6
1965	415	15	30	13	17	12	—	6
1966	445	20	34	21	19	12	—	7
1967	477	23	37	22	23	12	—	8
1968	521	25	40	25	28	14	2	9
1969	551	27	46	26	33	14	4	9
1970	572	27	53	27	38	17	3	10
1971	614	29	60	28	38	18	4	10
1972	649	30	67	28	39	19	4	13
1973	686	35	75	32	41	19	4	11
1974	727	35	80	32	43	18	5	12
1975	763	37	85	36	40	23	5	15
1976	786	40	83	37	37	23	5	13
1977	808	45	80	40	39	27	5	13
1980*	900	50	120	45	48	35	6	20
1985*	1300	75	200	60	55	50	10	35
1990*	1600	100	250	80	75	70	25	50

* Representative forecasts

Table 11.5 *Vehicle statistics in the Communist Bloc (1975)*

(a) Cars ('000s)	Parc	Production	Apparent consumption*	Exports	Imports
USSR	3040	1210	951	260	1
Poland	830	147	127	55	35
Romania	240	75	45	35	5
East Germany	1770	160	160	80	80
Czechoslovakia	1320	173	135	120	82
Hungary	560	—	90	—	90
Bulgaria	330	—	65	—	65
Yugoslavia	1350	103	153	10	60
(b) CVs ('000s)					
USSR	5650	775	755	35	15
Poland	430	77	67	20	10
Romania	100	40	38	3	1
East Germany	300	37	20	24	7
Czechoslovakia	260	37	31	10	4
Hungary	130	15	24	5	14
Bulgaria	110	5	10	0	5
Yugoslavia	160	21	23	2	4

* Apparent consumption = production minus recorded exports plus recorded imports

Source: Euroeconomics, Eurofinance

USSR

CARS

The first serious attempt at producing a rational development programme for the USSR motor industry was undertaken in the 1966-70 five-year plan. Attention had previously been focused on the development of CV production, and in 1966 the car industry was neglected, under-capitalized and dominated by large, self-contained production units. Virtually no work had been done on product development or specialization, and the vital components industry was fragmented and insufficient. Since 1970, the Fiat-Togliatti project has been underway, centred on a fully integrated plant which in the long term involves component supply contracts with other Bloc countries (furthering the move to a more closely integrated industrial structure within the Bloc). Renault participation in the reorganization of the Moskvitch plant has been planned with domestic component supply and market demand requirements in mind, although component supply contracts could be placed elsewhere in the Bloc.

Table 11.6 gives current USSR capacity and details of existing plans for expansion and projected capacity levels.

Table 11.6 *Projections of USSR car capacity*
based on existing plans

	1975	1980-85 ('000s)	1985-90*
Zhilgulf/Lada	660	1000	1750+
(Fiat 124 + 125 types and Niva)			
Moskvitch	420	700	1000+
Volga	50	100	250+
Zaporozhet + GAZ	150	200	500+
	1280	2000	3500+**

* Medium-term plans are inevitably more tentative
** Perhaps plus capacity from new plants

Nb: Volga is the luxury/specialist car, GAZ is a 4-wheel drive/Jeep type car,
    Zaporozhet is a people's car

The USSR currently produces the up-market cars manufactured by ZIL and the Volga and Chaika produced by GAZ; the Moskvitch (similar to Poland's Wartburg); slightly more sophisticated products developed by VAZ from the Fiat products (called Zhilgulf in the Bloc and Lada outside the Bloc); and, at the bottom of the range, the ZAZ organization has unsuccessfully tried to develop the 'people's car' (the Zaporozhet). GAZ and VAZ have developed four-wheel drive utility vehicles. Lada production is to be increased from 660,000 to one million units per year (original plans were to achieve this by 1980 but the oil crisis has caused delays). The Moskvitch plant is also to be increased from 420,000 to 700,000 units per year with a new product, and perhaps a replacement for the outdated Moskvitch. This may be a European model in the same range, and Renault and Citroen have shown interest in the project. There is still some doubt whether production of the Zaporozhet, with a totally new small car, will be increased from 150,000 to 500,000 units per year.

CVs

Although the Russian CV industry is still a higher industrial priority than car production, performance levels have been generally poor, bedevilled by low product quality, unreliability, lack of spares and irregular servicing. Although strenuous efforts have been made to remedy the situation, it has been estimated that at any one time 30 or 40 per cent of all registered CVs in the USSR are off the road, because of breakdown or unavailability of necessary parts. Despite the fact that production is currently running at high levels, matched by a corresponding rise in the number of new CV registrations, the USSR CV parc has not increased greatly. Soviet producers are now concentrating on reducing the technology gap between East and West and strengthening a network of component and part suppliers in Eastern Europe, in an attempt to establish the Russian CV industry as the pivot for a more fully integrated CV industry throughout the Bloc.

Table 11.7 shows existing and projected capacity levels. Plans for the revitalization of the industry have now got under way and have to some extent corrected earlier problems. Previous production centred around GAZ and ZIL products. CV production was much more dispersed with a number of plants throughout the USSR. The new Kama River production complex is the largest of the new CV development projects. Costing over $5 billion and using Western technology (including Renault and GM) the complex, spread over six integrated production plants, will produce 120,000 trucks in the 8-11 tonne class, 50,000 trucks in the 15 ton class and 250,000 diesel engines per year, providing employment for 80,000 people. Only marginally less spectacular is the USSR/International Harvester deal proposing an additional capacity of 150,000 medium to heavy trucks and diesel engines. Capacity will be further extended by the IVECO licence purchased by the USSR for the production of 50,000 air-cooled diesel engines annually.

Table 11.7 *Projections of USSR CV capacity*
based on existing plans

	1975	1980-85 ('000s)	1985-90
Existing plants	820	1000	1250+
International Harvester project	—	150	300+
Kama River project	—	125	250+
		1275	1800+

East Germany

CARS

The East German car industry is small and in technological terms rather primitive, with a very low development priority. The industry has capacity at present for some 120,000 Trabant models per year, with a further 20,000-30,000 unit capacity for Wartburg models. This constitutes the entire car industry, though plans for a joint venture with Czechoslovakia suggest a slightly more promising future. Long standing East German plans for the introduction of a new (and much needed) Wartburg model, which began life as a proposed East/West cooperative venture, have now been redrawn on the basis of cooperation with other manufacturers within the Communist Bloc. A four-cylinder water-cooled engine for the new car is to be supplied by the Czechs who in turn will receive East German components for use in a similar Skoda model. Some components may be supplied by Hungary. Renault is to supply a stop-gap engine until the new Czech engine is available. Any other deals involving expansion of existing capacity (around 165,000 units per annum) are impossible in the present economic climate, and significant growth is unlikely in the immediate future.

CVs

Although East Germany is one of the richest and most heavily industrialized of the Communist Bloc countries, it has a small, highly fragmented and rather neglected CV industry, which has suffered from a lack of investment in new plant and technology. About 65 per cent of total CV output is exported to other countries within the Communist Bloc (most of it to the USSR), but information in this area is sketchy and unreliable: one can only conjecture that the East German CV industry will remain a satellite producer, very much in the shadow of its more powerful Soviet colleague. Future plans for development of the East German CV industry are uncertain. Despite pressure (generally from the Russians) to restrict cooperation to industrial concerns within the Communist Bloc, the East Germans might prefer to ignore such a 'recommendation', and continue the search for an alliance with a suitable Western producer. Although Daimler-Benz would be an obvious candidate the West German firm has shown little interest in joint participation and IVECO, another suitable partner, would probably be more interested in developing existing projects within the Bloc than entering into new agreements. Future developments, therefore, probably depend on joint developments with the Czechs. Citroen have been reported to have had talks about the modernization of East Germany's CV industry.

Poland

CARS

In recent years the Polish car industry has been virtually transformed with the installation of plant to produce a complete Fiat-based range. The development of the Polski-Fiat has now reached such a stage that the Polish engineers are capable of redesigning and modernizing the original Fiat product, as the Polski Polonez illustrates. Expansion plans include increasing the Polski-Fiat capacity from 130,000 to 150,000 units per year and the replacement of all indigenous Syrena production by a Fiat 126. The Polski-Fiat 127 output is to be increased from the present 5000 to 50,000 units per year. Assembly of the Zastava 101, a Yugoslav version of the Fiat 128, is now under way. Polish car capacity was to be doubled by 1980, growing to some 400,000 units per year; the recession has caused a slight setback but this figure should be surpassed during the early 1980s.

CVs

The Polish CV industry is one of the most highly developed in the Communist Bloc, although its supremacy has been established primarily through the investment or assistance of Western producers, principally Saviem, Fiat, BL, Volvo, GM, Steyr-Daimler-Puch, and Massey Ferguson. The CV sector concentrates on production of lightweight vans and trucks (currently 30,000 to 35,000 units per year), marketed under the brandnames of Zuk and Nysa, with a flourishing 12,000 unit bus production facility and a middle-weight, 8-10 tonne production plant manufacturing 2500 Jelcz trucks a year, for which diesel engines are produced under licence from BL.

Poland has been particularly successful in arranging 'industrial cooperation' agreements and both of the major expansion projects involve developments along these lines. GM are participating in the construction of new plant for production of 100,000 lightweight vans and trucks by 1980, using GM Bedford design and technology in a deal involving cheap credit, buy-back agreements and parts interchange and dual marketing. Similarly Steyr-Daimler-Puch have agreed to sell assembled CVs, components and production licences to the Poles and are involved in the construction of a diesel engine plant in Poland with a target capacity of 50,000 units annually by 1980. On a smaller scale, a Saviem-Berliet bus production agreement with the Poles is to be expanded to 5000 units per year and Massey Ferguson have agreed on plans for the construction of a diesel engine plant with a planned capacity of 40,000 six-cylinder engine units per year by 1980.

FIAT

Recent announcements seem to indicate that Fiat is to bring Polish production into Fiat's global production plans. Fiat will sell to Poland CKD kits for a new small car. In turn, Poland is to supply Fiat 126s on a one-for-one basis. Fiat will phase out its own 126 production and concentrate on the new 'Panda' model. There will be a similar barter arrangement with a new pick-up truck.

Czechoslovakia

CARS

The Western-equipped Skoda factory gives Czechoslovakia potentially the strongest manufacturing base in the Communist Bloc, although the components supply industry is at the moment ill-equipped to meet production targets. This could prevent the Czechs from reaching the optimum annual capacity of 240,000 units from their Skoda plant, although the Czech car production target for 1980 is 300,000 units per annum. In Eastern Europe, Czechoslovakia comes nearest to official approval of car ownership (although the endorsement is couched in suitably restrained terms), and Czech planners consider a car density of one vehicle per five people an acceptable level. This would give a car parc of some 3 million vehicles by 1985, more than double the estimated current level. The Czechs originally planned a joint venture with the East Germans (announced in 1971) to construct a new plant at the Mlada Boleslav complex for production of a new 1500 cc Skoda model, supplementing the planned expansion of existing capacity to 240,000 units, but it would appear that the Czechs have assumed responsibility for development of the new 1500cc car, as the joint venture now centres on a longer term plan for development of a new 1200-1300cc model. Plans for the original 1500cc car have been seriously delayed, and the Czechs may seek an infusion of capital and expertise from a Western manufacturer to complete the project.

CVs

As with car production, the Czech CV industry is one of the most sophisticated in the Communist Bloc, emphasizing heavy-weight 12 to 16 tonne trucks and specialist CVs (Tatra). Plans have also been announced for the expansion of light-weight truck and van production (the Avia range, which makes French Saviem trucks under licence). Czechoslovakia's strategy is thus to develop its medium to heavy CV industry. The Tatra plant (producing medium-weight trucks) is to be expanded to a 15,000 unit capacity, and the Avia factory, which currently concentrates on licensed assembly of Saviem models, is to increase annual output from 5000 to 15,000 units. On a smaller scale, production of the Liaz/Skoda medium-weight truck range is also to be increased. Czechoslovakia has the most developed component manufacturing unit in Eastern Europe and the country will supply components to the rest of the Communist Bloc.

Romania

CARS

Romania has the newest of all the Communist Bloc motor industries, and has achieved much independence from the group through cooperation with Western European manufacturers. The industry was created as the result of an agreement with Renault, whereby the Romanians have begun assembly of the Renault 8 and 12 models, reaching an agreed production target of 50,000 by 1973. Production is now based entirely on assembly of the Renault 12 and marketing under the brandname Dacia. Future expansion plans will take the Renault based Dacia product and a Citroen based product to a total combined capacity of about 300,000 cars per year. The ARO type Jeep production has been successful and production is in excess of 10,000 units.

CVs

The Romanian CV industry is as independent in character as its car industry, comprising Bucegi and Carpati lightweight trucks (about 30,000 units per annum), road tractors and buses. Further development is based on swopping existing outdated capacity for modern MAN products. Further development is expected in the mid-1980s.

Hungary

CARS

Hungary occupies a marginal position within the Communist Bloc motor industry, supplying components for the Russian Fiat operation but with no assembly or manufacturing plant of its own. Honda's 1971 attempt to establish a car assembly plant in Hungary was unsuccessful, partly, it is thought, because of the intervention of the Russian authorities. No plans have yet been announced for any development activity, although assembly and manufacturing facilities could be established on a small scale in the 1980s. Until then, Hungary's role in car production will be limited to that of a component supplier.

CVs

Hungary's truck industry is one of the smallest in the Communist Bloc, centring on production of the Csepel model which uses Steyr-Daimler-Puch cabs, Saurer engines and components from Czechoslovakia and the USSR. In 1974 Volvo negotiated an agreement with Csepel for the production of Volvo Laplander multi-purpose CVs in Hungary, with an initial production target of 1000 units per year. Volvo has now concentrated all Laplander production in Hungary. Bus manufacture is of far greater importance in the Hungarian CV industry. Output is already in excess of 30,000 and plans are under way for expansion of existing facilities, with a target of 66,000 units at the end of the current five-year period in 1980. Most of the total output is exported, principally to the USSR and East Germany, with some exports elsewhere within the Communist Bloc and to non-Comecon markets abroad. Bus production which forms the basis of the Hungarian CV industry, has already been stretched to full capacity by existing demand although further expansion is unlikely. The Volvo Laplander facility could grow further, but total CV output is unlikely to exceed 70,000 units per year by 1990.

Bulgaria

CARS

No cars are produced in Bulgaria, although some 1300 Russian Moskvitch models are assembled annually, supplemented by imports of built-up models. The Bulgarian authorities are apparently now planning to phase out the Moskvitch assembly operation and meet all domestic requirements with fully assembled import models mainly from the USSR, Poland and Czechoslovakia. The indications are that this would be only a temporary solution and that a manufacturing base would eventually be established. However, no plans for further expansion have been announced, although the components industry, one of the major suppliers for the USSR Moskvitch plant, has grown steadily.

CVs

The same conditions apply in the CV sector: the industry is at present equipped for assembly operations only. Facilities could be expanded to accommodate full manufacture in future, though there are no existing plans for development.

Yugoslavia

Yugoslavia is the odd man out in the Communist Bloc: its foreign and economic policies differ, it is more independent of the USSR, and its statistics are relatively reliable.

CARS

Yugoslavia both manufactures and assembles cars: production operations centre on the licensed manufacture of Fiat models — the Zastava 750, 1300, 1500 and 101 — by the Polish firm of Zastava. Zastava also assemble the Fiat 132, the Polski Fiat 125P and the Russian Lada. It has been estimated that Zastava assemble approximately 30,000 units per year and produce 150,000 units. 'Cimos', a joint venture between Yugoslavia and Citroen, involves the assembly of some 9000 units per year. IMV assembles 30,000 Renaults and TAS (in which VW have a 49 per cent holding) assembles some 10,000 Volkswagens. With four assembly plants and one producer operating in a market with an annual demand for only 250,000 vehicles, the Yugoslav car industry is in need of rationalization, despite the fact that annual sales are expected to rise to 500,000 vehicles by the mid-1980s. Both Renault and VW, currently involved in assembly-only operations, could be pressured to switch to full manufacture: the Yugoslavs are as eager as anyone else to build up a fully integrated domestic car industry. Future plans for the Yugoslavian Zastava concern are uncertain but further expansion is indicated.

CVs

The international character of car production and assembly work in Yugoslavia is mirrored in the CV sector, with active cooperation and involvement from Daimler-Benz (which has been instrumental in the creation of a Yugoslav CV facility) and IVECO (Magirus). The latter originally licensed production in Yugoslavia but the arrangement has been subsequently transformed into one involving more active participation as a result of a 1971 agreement on industrial cooperation. In addition, the Yugoslav firm of UMI produces 5000 buses and utility vehicles annually and Zastava's CV division manufactures some 8000 lightweight commercial vehicles and minibuses per year. The poor performance of the Yugoslav economy in recent years, however, indicates that most of the CV producers are operating below capacity.

Expansion of the Fap-Famos and Tam CV facilities are already under way with targets of 10,000 and 12,000 units respectively. Plans for increased output from the Zastava lightweight CV division (which is to be undertaken in conjunction with IVECO) should boost production levels to 25,000 vehicles by the early 1980s.

Future developments

Despite overall central control, the motor industry in Eastern Europe has experienced many of the difficulties of a highly fragmented industrial structure familiar from our discussion of the industry in Western Europe. Only the USSR has a relatively integrated industry. Vehicle manufacture in any one country within the Bloc has developed on the basis of a single producer or complex of smaller producers functioning as part of one operation. Demand is not a reflection of the market forces encountered in the other regions we have discussed so far, but is determined by centrally planned decisions. But, despite centralized planning, integration of production has not been achieved.

As the nature of both supply and demand within the Communist Bloc differs in so many fundamental respects to markets elsewhere, forecasts and predictions on future developments will necessarily be of an even more tentative nature, as so many of the criteria we have used elsewhere simply do not apply in the special conditions of the Communist Bloc.

Demand

The potential size of the market is difficult to estimate. Despite some degree of anti-consumerism and an emphasis on public transport systems, the size of the market for new cars must be roughly equivalent to Western Europe or North America, though its development is several decades behind them. Demand may reach 8-10 million cars and 1.5-2 million CVs a year, assuming a relatively modest growth in demand during the early 1980s (as the Communist countries adjust to higher fuel costs) and an acceleration in demand to produce fairly rapid growth after the mid-1980s; estimates for *new* car registrations by 1990 vary from 4-7 million. Total demand of 5 or 6 million new cars would seem to be realistic. In the CV sector, growth in demand has already outstripped most projections, but future consumption could be much less spectacular and is certainly not expected to follow the explosion in car demand. The CV parc (8 million units) is already quite large, and it is unlikely that the planners would permit further expansion of the sort experienced in the US. Future planning decisions on haulage provision will possibly show a preference for development of alternatives to road haulage for cargo transport.

Supply

Two theories project different types of development for Eastern Europe's motor industry: the first argues that the supply of motor vehicles will simply expand to keep pace with the growth in demand, with no attempt to produce a supply of vehicles in excess of domestic requirements; the second suggests that producers may expand capacity and seek economies of scale, joining the band of mature producers and becoming a major net exporter. Before deciding which outcome is more plausible we must summarize plans for future development (see Table 11.8). By the early 1980s capacity should be greater than 3 million cars and about 1.7 million CVs, though the achievement of these targets could be affected by possible delays in the installation of new plant. The type of car produced follows the Japanese pattern of a cheap and basic model, with only a minimum of concession to styling and comfort. CV production will concentrate on truck models in the medium-weight range.

Table 11.8 *Production capacity estimates ('000s)*

| | Cars | | CVs | |
	1980-85	1985-90 Range	1980-85	1985-90 Range
USSR	1950	2150-2950	1280	1400-2000
East Germany	200	250- 350	65	80- 150
Poland	400	450- 600	210	230- 290
Czechoslovakia	345	396- 496	55	78- 125
Romania	145	160- 270	75	90- 150
Yugoslavia	250	350- 520	65	70- 100
Bulgaria	—	25- 50	12	15- 25
Hungary	—	10- 50	35	40- 70
	3290	3791-5286	1797	2003-2900

Nb: The date at which the 1980 plans are to be achieved has been modified to 1980-85 to allow for the effects of the oil crises; the price adjustment was gradually introduced during the late 1970s.

Source: Euroeconomics, Eurofinance

Longer-term developments

If existing economies of scale are to be maintained it is likely that the established producers would try to stop either Hungary or Bulgaria building up indigenous car manufacturing industries. The USSR will almost certainly expand the Kama River project, which could effectively prevent developments of other large-scale ventures elsewhere. Three scenarios for the car industry, therefore, can be suggested:

1. The USSR could emerge as the dominant producer, emasculating the motor industry in Poland, Romania, East Germany and Czechoslovakia.
2. The USSR could restrict its activities to volume car production, leaving specialist and/or CV production to the rest of the Eastern European producers.
3. All of the producing countries in Eastern Europe could ignore economies of scale through expansion of capacity to around one million units. The USSR would restrict its activities to similar expansion of existing facilities.

Table 11.9 outlines these scenarios in terms of their medium-term impact on productive capacity. Given the lack of more detailed information, and the nature of the decision-making process within the Communist Bloc, it would be pointless to suggest which outcome is the most likely. The future development of the CV sector is even more obscure, although the fact that economies of scale are generally less accessible in CV production could imply a further distribution of manufacturing facilities rather than an attempt to concentrate plant in any one sector.

Table 11.9 *Capacity projections (1990)*

Scenario	Cars (millions)			CVs ('000s)
	1	2	3	1-3 (range)
USSR	2.5-5	2.25-4.5	2.0-4.0	1300-2000
Poland	0.4	0.5	0.8-1.3	200- 300
Romania	0.2	0.3	0.4-0.5	70- 150
East Germany	0.2	0.4	0.8-1.0	60- 150
Czechoslovakia	0.4	0.5	0.8-1.0	50- 150
Hungary	—	—	—	50
Bulgaria	—	—	—	25
Yugoslavia	0.3	0.4	0.5	60- 150
Total	4.0-6.3	4.35-6.6	5.3-8.3	1815-2975
Probable range		5.0-6.0		1900-2500

Although the picture is rather confused, we can attempt some further classification by returning to the question of demand strategy, and the alternative outcomes proposed earlier: that production be permitted to follow demand, or that domestic demand could be depressed and production geared to the supply of cars and possibly CVs for export. However, there is a third strategy: domestic car demand might be checked during periods of excessive deficits in the balance of payments, creating an excess capacity from which export sales could be made to improve the trade position. Although CV demand is less susceptible to artificial controls of this sort, decisions and strategies are required: GM's presence in Poland might encourage otherwise hesitant planners to exploit the possibilities for earning much-needed foreign exchange with a CV export drive, as one way of recouping at least some of the capital used to purchase Western technology and expertise.

Assuming that the appropriate central planning decisions are made, a substantial growth in the export of cars and to a lesser extent CVs (particularly to sympathetic developing countries in the Far East and Africa) would seem likely.

It is more difficult to evaluate the likely level of imports from Western producers, although a substantial import penetration of the Communist Bloc market is unlikely. Western manufacturers already involved in cooperative industrial projects will presumably continue to have access to the market, albeit limited, but further participation by companies not yet active in the Bloc could be severely restricted. In any event, if demand continues to be artificially controlled, the potential for import sales would be only marginal.

Trade

The expansion of full-scale domestic production, particularly in Poland, Czechoslovakia, Romania and East Germany, would reduce the scope for intra-Bloc trade and increase the number of Communist Bloc producers seeking export opportunities elsewhere. With a contraction of trade between Communist Bloc countries, export markets, particularly in Western Europe, would be an obvious method of dealing with excess capacity and persistent balance of trade deficits. Success in export markets might be adversely affected by the inability (or reluctance) of Communist Bloc producers to invest in the sales and servicing infrastructures needed to support an export drive. They could handle distribution through an independent dealer network, establish a centralized trading organization handling sales of all export models irrespective of national origin, or negotiate a joint distribution agreement with a Western producer, providing reciprocal sales and service facilities. At present exports are distributed through an independent dealer network and rely for sales solely on the basis of their price competitiveness (export models consistently undercut equivalent European models by as much as 30 per cent). Although this price advantage will probably be maintained, it cannot guarantee a major export success for the Communist Bloc producers. Most of the export markets within which a price advantage can be usefully exploited (ie the hard currency markets) will be experiencing more sluggish and uncertain growth in demand in future, and more producers will be competing for a shrinking market. However, a strong and effectively organized export drive could have a considerable impact on the West European, African and Asian markets where demand exists for the type of cheap basic car pioneered by the Japanese.

If one accepts the possibility of general expansion of the motor industry in Eastern Europe, and if the decision is made to repress domestic demand to create an exportable surplus, total exports may reach 2 million cars a year during the 1980s. Conversely, if the USSR expands production, stifling the motor industry elsewhere in the Bloc and gearing supply to meet Bloc demand only, exports would be negligible. With so many intangibles, no firm conclusions are possible, but there are reasonable grounds for assuming that in the 1980s the Communist Bloc will be looking for net exports of 0.5-1 million cars with a rather smaller volume of CV exports (50,000-200,000). The time-scale for growth in export sales is open to question.

In summary, the Communist Bloc may exploit export opportunities for cars and to a lesser extent CVs, particularly in Western Europe. Although the Bloc offers few opportunities for imports of assembled cars from Western Europe or elsewhere, scope exists for a limited participation by non-Communist producers in industrial cooperation projects involving sales of systems and technology, profitable for the vendors and much needed by the Communist Bloc producers if they hope to expand their motor industry and become fully competitive in a larger world market.

Chapter 12

South America

The second major developing market, South America (including Central America), has not experienced growth rates as high as those in the Communist Bloc, though growth has been remarkably sustained since World War II. Table 12.1 summarizes the economic statistics of the region.

Argentina, Brazil and Mexico, the most densely populated of the South American countries, have well-established motor industries of some importance. Chile, Columbia, Peru, Uruguay and Venezuela have facilities for car and CV assembly only, and Ecuador, Bolivia and Paraguay — the poorest and most sparsely populated South American countries — have no motor industry. Although Brazil is the largest country geographically, Venezuela is the wealthiest, with substantial oil deposits providing revenue. Most of the other South American countries have modest reserves of oil, and the 1973 and 1979 oil price rises will be of some benefit to the region, but it cannot expect to profit from oil sales to the same extent as the Middle East or the USSR (once the latter has brought its oil prices into line with world prices).

The market

Table 12.2 gives the peak market size up to 1978 for cars and CVs in 1973 77. The high CV to car ratio (almost 1 : 3) suggests that the area is still at the development stage, with the major markets in Brazil, Argentina and Mexico, and a smaller but not insignificant market in Venezuela. As with most of the developing markets discussed so far, it is difficult to establish whether the growth in South American demand encouraged the development of an indigenous motor industry or the existence of a motor industry fostered a growth in demand. The debate continues and may never be satisfactorily resolved.

Although growth in new car registrations over the last 15 years has been disappointingly slow, it has been faster, in relative terms, than growth in the CV sector, a sign of a maturing market. But although the South American *per capita* GNP has reached a level which corresponds to the point at which the Japanese market expanded rapidly, recurring economic difficulties have curbed any similar expansionist trends.

Table 12.1 *South American statistics*

	Population 1976 (millions)	Population growth rate 1970-76 (%)	GNP per capita 1976 (US $)	GNP per capita growth rates 1960-73 (%)	Car parc 1977 ('000s)	CV parc 1977 ('000s)	Number of people per car	Number of people per CV
Argentina	25.7	1.3	1840	2.7	2588	1101	10	23
Brazil	109.2	2.8	1100	3.6	6349	1750	17	62
Mexico	62.3	3.5	1130	3.3	2641	1033	24	60
Chile	10.5	1.8	960	1.7	263	172	40	61
Colombia	24.4	2.9	540	2.4	408	98	60	248
Peru	16.1	3.0	700	2.1	300	156	53	103
Uruguay	2.8	0.6	1240	−0.2	165	90	17	31
Venezuela	12.4	2.9	2070	2.0	1083	350	11	35
Ecuador	7.3	3.4	621	1.9	55	100	132	73
Bolivia	5.8	2.7	350	2.5	31	41	187	141
Paraguay	2.7	2.8	574	1.9	26	15	104	183
Others	20.9				405	230	21	58
Total	300.0				14,314	5136		

Table 12.2 *Peak market size for individual countries during the period 1972-78*

	Cars ('000s)	CVs ('000s)
Argentina	220	75
Brazil	822	170
Chile	53	16
Colombia	48	20
Mexico	260	135
Peru	30	17
Uruguay	4	2
Venezuela	201	110
Ecuador	7	29
Others	43	75
Total	1688	649

Table 12.3 shows that the growth of car and CV demand has also been adversely affected by the 1973 oil crisis.

Table 12.3 *South American car and CV registrations*

	New car registrations ('000s)	New CV registrations ('000s)
1960	331	220
1961	371	229
1962	378	198
1963	368	194
1964	456	255
1965	510	251
1966	595	248
1967	570	242
1968	660	293
1969	788	339
1970	804	315
1971	990	345
1972	1143	406
1973	1260	440
1974	1450	464
1975	1523	490
1976	1514	492
1977	1509	515
1980*	1750	625
1985*	2000-2500	750-1000
1990*	2500-4000	1000-1500

* Representative forecasts

Only Brazil enjoys a reasonable rate of growth in *per capita* GNP, although Venezuela with its substantial oil reserves may prove to be an exception in the future. Elsewhere hyper-inflation and political instability have severely shaken economic confidence. Increased energy costs have taken their toll, and recent crop failures (notably the loss of most of the Brazilian coffee crops after unseasonal frosts) have underlined the vulnerability of most of the South American economies.

The manufacturers

Total production figures for all motor vehicles are given in Figure 12.1. Brazil has more than doubled production output since 1970, but Argentina has achieved only 9 per cent growth in vehicle production over the same period. Mexico, the third of the major producers, has achieved 50 per cent growth. The 1973 oil crisis seriously affected production: motor vehicle production in Argentina fell by more than one-third and the country has been experiencing economic mismanagement and hyper-inflation. Conversely, Brazil and Mexico have continued their growth throughout this period. Those countries with assembly capacity only have suffered a mixed fate: Chile's assembly has fallen by 76 per cent, which is consistent with the hyper-inflation experienced

Figure 12.1 *The motor vehicle industry in Central and South America*

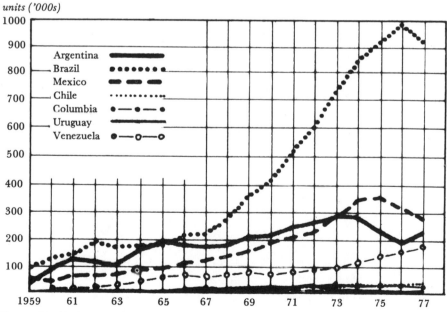

Source: World Motor Vehicle Date (1978) MVMA

Table 12.4 South American motor vehicle production and assembly by country 1977 ('000s)

	Argentina	Brazil	Colombia	Mexico	Peru	Venezuela
Ford	56	130	—	51	—	62
GM	21	154	—	35	—	32
Chrysler	23[1]	22[1]	14[2]	58	7	32[2]
Nissan	—	—	—	37	5	5
Toyota	—	3	—	—	6	7
VW	—	472	—	52	6	5
Fiat	47	74	5	—	—	5
Renault and AMC	35	—	18	46	—	11
PSA Peugeot-Citroen	34	—	—	—	—	—
Daimler-Benz	7	53	—	—	—	1
Volvo	—	—	—	—	1	—
IME	9	—	—	—	—	—
Saab-Scania	—	5	—	—	—	—
International Harvester	—	—	—	1	—	1
Mack	—	—	—	—	—	2

1. VW has recently bought a share in these companies with an understanding that it will eventually acquire complete control
2. Bought by GM

since 1973 (the 1970 = 100 index is now greater than 100,000!); Venezuela with its petrodollar currency has thrived on its extra wealth derived from oil earnings.

South America's motor industry development seems to have run on classic lines — import, assembly, assembly with local content and finally production. South America seems to have duplicated the European fragmentation of the market with both the US and some European companies established. Not content with manufacturers from both of the most mature markets, Japan (Nissan and Toyota) has also established a presence. The largest companies are represented by VW, GM, Ford and Fiat. Chrysler has sold most of its subsidiaries and the other companies are in trouble. We return to the financial problems of the region later.

Table 12.4 shows the relative strengths of the various manufacturers in 1977 (a good year), and Table 12.5 gives the major manufacturers' level of activity. Chrysler's production facilities were more or less evenly distributed throughout the region, but the company has now sold off some of its concerns. VW dominates the area, with substantial interests in Mexico, Brazil and Argentina (formerly Chrysler Argentina). GM and Ford have both established major manufacturing operations in Brazil, with additional capacity in Argentina, Mexico and Venezuela. Fiat is well represented in Argentina and is establishing a major base in Brazil, and Renault plants are operating in Argentina, Mexico and Venezuela. AMC are prominent in Mexico, and Daimler-Benz plants are operational in Argentina, Brazil and Venezuela. The Japanese have established a modest presence in the area. There are a number of CV producers such as Mack, White, International Harvester, Volvo and Saab-Scania with plant in South America.

Detailed model-by-model production figures for the main producers are shown in Table 12.6, which indicates the proliferation of companies attempting to buy their way into the expanding South American market by establishing local assembly (and eventually production) facilities. The carrot to the manufacturers was a share of a lucrative and growing market; the stick was high tariff walls (eg 200 per cent for Brazil). The result of individual action by manufacturers and governments in an artificially created economic environment is a fragmented, uneconomic and non-viable industry with 10 major multinationals and some minor manufacturers, few of which can hope to be profitable at current capacity levels.

Indeed the South American motor industry has experienced many problems; GM has ceased its vehicle operations in Argentina (after a 53 year presence) and Chrysler is in the process of selling all its South American companies. South American governments have adopted a protectionist attitude towards the motor industry, but there seems to be a growing awareness that protection and heavy subsidies have not made the sector more efficient.

Table 12.5 South American production and assembly by manufacturer ('000s)

	1970	1971	1972	1973	1974	1975	1976	1977	1980*	1985*	1990*
GM	145	165	180	226	280	259	266	243	500	750	1000
Ford	160	202	238	284	327	299	305	300	400	700	1000
Chrysler	85	94	114	155	176	174	176	156	70	0	0
Nissan	18	22	28	33	34	41	45	47	100	200	250
Toyota	4	5	8	10	10	14	16	15	25	100	250
VW	281	354	405	467	549	624	636	543	750	1000	1200
Volvo	0.1	0.3	0.6	0.9	1.1	1.5	1.6	1.2	5	10	15
Renault and AMC	80	90	95	106	107	121	121	111	125	200	250
Fiat	51	62	64	74	86	64	68	134	200	250	300
Daimler-Benz	25	28	35	43	47	53	58	62	70	75	85
PSA Peugeot-Citroen	44	45	52	46	46	40	32	34	50	100	250

* Representative forecasts

Table 12.6 *South American production 1977*

Manufacturer's name make and model	Total	Cars	Trucks and buses
Argentina			
Citroen	14,044	11,750	2294
Chrysler Fevre	23,434	—	—
Diesel	—	—	6994
Dodge	—	16,440	—
Deutz	80	—	80
Fiat Concord	47,837	40,409	7428
Ford Motor	56,795	—	—
Diesel	—	—	20,036
Falcon	—	18,094	—
Fairlane	—	1680	—
Taunus	—	16,985	—
General Motors	20,897	—	—
Chevrolet	—	9968	10,929
IME	9036	221	8815
Mercedes Benz	7845	—	7845
Renault	34,744	—	—
Jeep	—	—	1181
Renault	—	27,237	—
Torino	—	6326	—
Safrar (Peugeot)	20,170	19,016	1154
Total	234,882	168,126	66,756
Brazil			
Chrysler	21,970	15,303	6667
Cummins Nordeste S/A Indl.	—	—	—
Fabrica Nacional de Motores SA	4271	4271	—
Fiat Automoveis SA	73,692	65,052	8640
Ford	130,197	97,593	32,604
General Motors	153,836	126,244	27,592
Mercedes Benz	52,957	—	52,957
Puma	2898	2898	—
Saab-Scania	4534	—	4534
Toyota	2695	—	2695
Volkswagen	472,192	460,248	11,944
Total	919,242	771,609	147,633
Mexico			
Chrysler de Mexico SA	57,956	—	—
Valiant	—	11,239	—
Dart	—	23,401	—
Le Baron	—	3168	—
Monaco	—	928	—
Dodge	—	—	19,220
Diesel Nacional SA	27,559	—	—
Renault	—	20,602	28
Dina 500/600	—	—	6929

Table 12.6 *continued*

Manufacturer's name make and model	Total	Cars	Trucks and buses
Mexico *(continued)*			
Fabricas Autocar Mexicana SA	203	—	203
Ford Motor Co SA	50,503	—	—
Maverick/Fairmont	—	14,911	—
Ford Galaxie/Ltd	—	8716	—
Mustang	—	2503	—
Ford	—	—	24,373
General Motors de Mexico SA de CV	34,638	—	—
Chevy Nova	—	13,826	—
Impala/Caprice	—	4063	—
Chevrolet	—	—	16,749
International Harvester Mexico SA	772	—	772
Kenworth Mexicana	428	—	428
Mexicana de Autobuses	916	—	916
Nissan Mexicana SA	37,066	—	—
Datsun	—	24,984	12,082
Trailers de Monterrey SA	65	—	65
Trailers del Norte SA	—	—	—
Vehiculos Automotores Mexicanos SA	18,564	—	—
Gremlin	—	5682	—
American	—	9535	—
Classic	—	—	—
Pacer	—	1245	—
Jeep	—	—	2102
Volkswagen de Mexico	52,143	42,834	9309
White	—	—	—
Total	280,813	187,637	93,176
Peru			
Chrysler Peru SA	7169	—	—
Hillman	—	3457	—
Dodge Coronet	—	246	—
Dodge D-100	—	—	765
Dodge D-300	—	—	1283
Dodge P-300	—	—	84
Dodge D-500	—	—	49
Dodge P-500	—	—	24
Dodge PP-500	—	—	188
Dodge DP-500	—	—	583
Dodge D-800	—	—	7
Dodge DN-800	—	—	470
Dodge W-100	—	—	13
Motor Peru SA	6075	—	—
Volkswagen 1300	—	6075	—
Volkswagen 211	—	—	—
Volkswagen 231	—	—	—
Volkswagen EA-489	—	—	—

Table 12.6 *continued*

Manufacturer's name make and model	Total	Cars	Trucks and buses
Peru *(continued)*			
Nissan Motor Del Peru	5270	—	—
Datsun JNL-710	—	2280	—
Datsun NL-620 PU	—	—	2990
Toyota Del Peru SA	5502	—	—
Corona RT-102 Sed	—	—	—
Corona RT-117 S/W	—	—	—
Corona RT-104 Sed	—	4462	—
Corona RT-118 S/W	—	1040	—
Volvo Del Peru SA	1208	—	—
Volvo N-7	—	—	102
Volvo N-10	—	—	567
Volvo N-12	—	—	170
Volvo BB-57-OB	—	—	169
Volvo B-58-OC-OD	—	—	200
Total	25,224	17,560	7664
Venezuela			
Chrysler	32,430	22,094	10,336
Fiat	4889	4056	833
Ford	61,665	37,832	23,833
General Motors	32,281	23,994	8287
Hillman	102	102	—
International Harvester	878	—	878
Mack and Land Rover	1538	422	1116
Mercedes Benz	564	107	457
Nissan	5223	5223	—
Renault	5153	5153	—
Toyota	7172	7140	32
Volkswagen	5340	5340	—
Willys/Jeep	5801	5801	—
Other	261	—	261
Total	163,297	117,264	46,033

Source: Automobile International

Country-by-country analysis

Brazil is the leading South American producer and six major companies operated in the country: VW, which dominates the market, GM, Chrysler, Ford, Fiat and Daimler-Benz. But Chrysler found the competition too great and, needing funds in the USA, sold a 67 per cent stake in its Brazilian offshoot to VW. Fiat has developed new production facilities and may catch up with the US manufacturers. Alfa Romeo (FNM) and an indigenous sports car (the Puma) are produced on a small scale. Daimler-Benz and Saab-Scania are independent CV producers.

In Argentina, Fiat-Concord have already acquired a majority market share in the car sector, although Fiat plants are currently running well below capacity levels. With the success of their smaller models, Renault now have a substantial share of the Argentinian market. PSA Peugeot-Citroen have two separate production facilities. Of the three American firms, Ford is the largest and most successful. There is a government owned CV plant (IME). Profitability has been poor (see Table 12.7); Chrysler is in the process of selling its Argentinian subsidiary to VW. GM ceased its operations in Argentina in 1978.

Table 12.7 *Financial results of motor companies in Argentina (millions of pesos)*

Company	1974		1973	
	Sales	Profits	Sales	Profits
Fiat	4903	(71)	4031	(6)
Ford	3300	(231)	2798	46
Renault	2222	(114)	2401	(28)
Chrysler	1916	(110)	1478	(40)
GM	1896	(270)	1397	(153)
Peugeot	1673	(32)	1253	(58)
Mercedes	1054	(50)	899	(26)
Citroen	686	(79)	489	(84)
Massey Ferguson	608	39	298	30
John Deere	606	43	370	83
Perkins	456	3	261	7

The Argentinian government is aware of the poor state of its motor vehicle industry, and has reduced protection in an attempt to increase efficiency. Car tariffs were reduced and new local content rules introduced. Until 1977 manufacturers were not allowed to import components if a local source was available, irrespective of the cash penalty. Manufacturers are now allowed to import more components (about 15 per cent of total content) and establish their own component manufacturing plants. Components can be imported if the price of the local product is 200 per cent more than the imported component.

In Mexico, VW is again the principal producer, followed by Chrysler, Ford and GM and, on a smaller scale, Nissan, which has been increasing output slowly but steadily since 1966.

Since there are too many producers sharing too small a market in South America, rationalization is bound to occur, and has already begun. Chrysler, in difficulty in the USA, could not afford to subsidize its South American subsidiaries. GM bought Chrysler's Colombian and Venezuelan companies; VW is purchasing the Brazilian and Argentinian subsidiaries. But the principal competitors will not accept the economic realities of the market: following Fiat's expansion to 100,000+ cars a year, GM announced in 1979 a major expansion programme in Brazil and Mexico, and Ford retaliated by announcing an expansion programme in Argentina. With the exception of VW, the Europeans are still too small to compete with the American manufacturers.

Where do these conflicting moves leave the South American industry? As a world producer there can be no doubt that tariff barriers and the multiplicity of foreign-owned manufacturers will ensure that supply only keeps pace with domestic demand; supply will not exceed domestic demand. The Japanese model requires exceedingly cheap costs based on gaining the maximum economies of scale. South America, with its fragmented industry, does not enjoy the same economies of scale or the same degree of automation. There are, therefore, compelling reasons why South America will not follow the export policy of the Japanese industry.

Brazil will probably remain the principal vehicle producer in South America, although rapid growth could be greatly inhibited by the low purchasing power of most of its population and by the problems of creating an efficient road network in such a large and geographically diverse country. The Brazilian product is years behind the more sophisticated and refined European and North American product, particularly in safety and exhaust requirements, and is suited to specifically South American conditions. Several factors will, therefore, tend to inhibit the growth of Brazil's motor industry and its export potential.

In Brazil the effects of the oil crisis were not really felt until 1976 when there was a 16 per cent fall in the sale of cars and light CVs. Although this fall is expected to be temporary, the car lobby has reacted strongly and put pressure on the Brazilian Government to relax controls. During this difficult period, Fiat successfully made its entry into this new and important market. VW with a cheaper and more basic product managed to increase its market share. Ford and GM, however, were badly hit, both falling from 20 to 13 per cent of market share, and thus making losses on their operations in Brazil.

Venezuela has begun to press local assemblers to change to full-scale production and establish a 90 per cent local content by 1985. Talks with Fiat came to nothing and it looks as if GM (including Chrysler) and Ford will be left to provide the increased capacity to service the current 250,000 vehicles per year production target.

Imports

Imports by region to the whole of the Central and South American continent are shown in Table 12.8, although it must be remembered that these figures include knock-down units for local assembly as well as wholly assembled vehicles. France, Japan, North America and

Table 12.8 *Exports to South America* by country of origin*

	Cars ('000s)	Trucks ('000s)
Belgium	0	0
Canada	62	36
France	45	1
Italy	8	10
Japan	83	118
Sweden	1	1
UK	6	3
US	27	42
West Germany	23	4
Total	255	215

* South America is taken to include Belize, Costa Rica, Cuba, Gruiona, Guatemala, Guyana, Honduras, Nicaragua, Panama, El Salavador, Surinam and others

Source: Automobile International

West Germany are the major sources of imports. As Table 12.9 shows, Mexico and Venezuela, which account for the largest number of imported units also have large motor industries. By contrast, Brazil, with the largest motor industry, is virtually self-sufficient. Bolivia, Chile, Colombia, Ecuador, Paraguay, Peru and Uruguay are all dependent on imports of either fully assembled vehicles or knock-down kits for assembly, though imports are not exclusively European in origin and are often purchased from other South American countries. The figures for this intra-continental import and export traffic are not always included in official statistics, which makes it virtually impossible to gauge the volume of trade.

Table 12.9 *Imports to selected countries (1977)*

	Cars ('000s)	Trucks ('000s)
Argentina	1	1
Bolivia	1	3
Brazil	1	7
Chile	33	10
Colombia	20	11
Ecuador	7	29
Mexico	63	19
Paraguay	2	3
Peru	7	5
Uruguay	1	1
Venezuela	83	62

Source: Automobile International

Table 12.10 gives imports on a country-by-country basis. It shows that the importance of the French motor industry in South America corresponds fairly closely to the extent of its commitment to local assembly and production facilities (spread throughout Argentina, Mexico, Colombia and Venezuela). Canada has a substantial export trade with Venezuela in both built-up and knock-down units, and Japan, with virtually no manufacturing capacity located in the area, has built up an extensive export trade to Mexico.

Exports

Until recently there have been no exports from South America to markets elsewhere, but the area has now started to export a significant number of vehicles. Brazil produces the VW Beetle for a world market, and Fiat exports a modified 127 engine (the 147) to Europe for assembly in the Italian version of the Fiat 127. Fiat have announced plans to export up to 20,000 147s to Europe annually. Similarly, Mexico exports a sizeable proportion of total output to neighbouring countries and to the USA. The US market is an attractive one for South American producers (excluding subsidiaries of US companies), and they can be expected to seek export sales in the USA.

Some of the US firms operating in South America might rationalize production and manufacture smaller models only in their South American plants, switching production of larger models back to the USA. Of the European producers, Fiat and VW have already moved in this direction and other European firms may follow their example.

The future market

In the long term car densities may approach European levels and CV densities exceed European levels (as distances to be covered are greater and alternative transport systems less developed). Some observers believe that the oil crises of the 1970s spell the end to future growth in demand, but the vehicle density in South America has been rising consistently: one car to 59 people in 1965, increasing to 1/26 in 1975 and 1/21 in 1977. We may expect South America to reach a standard of living consistent with car densities in the poorest European countries ie 6-10 persons per car. CV densities should increase to current European levels of 30 persons per vehicle.

Assuming an annual 2 per cent growth in population, South America will have 350 million people by the 1990s. Living standards cannot be expected to rise uniformly: Bolivia and Paraguay could remain relatively poor, while Venezuela and perhaps Ecuador could benefit substantially from oil revenue. Brazil will continue to be the largest market.

Table 12.10 *Imports of cars and CVs to South America 1977 ('000s)*

Exporter	Mexico		Chile		Colombia		Peru		Venezuela	
	Cars	CVs	Cars	CVs	Cars	CVs	Cars	CVs	Cars	CVs
France	18	0	0	0	18	1	0	0	6	0
Italy	0	0	0	0	0	0	0	0	5	3
Japan	25	13	26	6	1	10	7	4	0	15
Sweden	0	0	0	0	0	0	0	2	0	0
North America	3	3	5	4	1	1	0	0	72	44
West Germany	17	3	0	0	0	0	0	0	0	0

Nb: 0 means less than 500 units

Source: Automobile International

We assume the life of a vehicle to be longer than that in a mature market, say 15 years for both cars and CVs. The projected equilibrium replacement demand for motor vehicles is some 2.3-3.3 million cars and just under one million CVs. (See Table 12.11), but replacement demand in 1990 will be somewhat lower, being based on purchases made during the 1970s and 1980s. New demand for vehicles can cover a wide range. Total demand for cars in 1990 can therefore span a range of 2.5-5 million. To produce estimates of supply, car demand can be taken at low and high levels of 2.5 and 4 million. CV demand is assumed to be one million and 1.5 million in the respective scenarios. These sets of assumptions give annual new car registrations in South America of 2.5 and 4.8 million, and new CV registrations of one and 1.5 million respectively.

Table 12.11 *Projections for vehicle demand in South America in 1990*

Population = 350 million	Car	CV
Vehicle densities in number of people per vehicle	6-10	30
Vehicle life (yrs)	15	15
Projected car parc (m)	35-50	11-12
Replacement demand in equilibrium (m)	2.3-3.3	0.7-0.8
Replacement demand at 1990 (m)	2.0	0.6
New demand at 1990 (m)	0.5-2	0.3-0.9
Total demand at 1990 (m)	2.5-5	0.9-1.5
Low scenario (m)	2.5	1.0
High scenario (m)	4.0	1.5

Can South America afford to develop its motor industry in the face of rising energy costs? There is some oil in the group of countries (Venezuela, Mexico and Chile), and Brazil's plans to use alternative fuels are the most advanced of any nation's, and Brazilian cars already run on a mixture of 84 per cent petrol and 16 per cent ethyl alcohol.

Although the South American market is relatively basic by North American or European standards, one can expect to see a close parallel with the development of the Japanese market. Average income is low, and a small, basic, inexpensive car is the most that middle income earners can afford. The VW Beetle is a fairly expensive product in South American terms. Low average earnings are offset in part by high rates of inflation which encourage consumer spending and keep demand buoyant. This partly explains the survival of the Argentinian vehicle market in a period of grave economic difficulty and hyper-inflation. Paradoxically, hyper-inflation also accounts for the relatively slow long-term growth in demand for vehicles. Periodically, governments intervene to reduce inflation by deflating the economy; without such deflationary spasms growth in the 1970s might have been much faster.

The inadequate road infrastructure will mean that CV demand will continue to concentrate on smaller trucks and four-wheel drive and 'utility' vehicles suitable for rough terrain. Buses will remain important as a means of public transport, with no serious competition from the rail and water networks, which are not sufficiently developed to serve large, sparsely populated areas.

The major companies and various government agencies will no longer account for most of the vehicle sales in poorer regions. As elsewhere, 'fleet' sales of this nature will give way to an increasingly large volume of private car sales as *per capita* GNP and income levels rise. But these predictions only hold if *laisser faire* policies are pursued, ie if governments do not adopt rigorous central planning and demand regulation.

The future for the producers

In the Communist Bloc and Japan, growth in the motor industry was indigenous, despite the partially successful efforts of US producers to buy into the Japanese industry. In South America, however, there are very few indigenous manufacturers and the industry is dominated by US and European producers. Although VW's stranglehold is now threatened by Fiat's activities in Brazil, the Italian firm has considerable ground to cover before it can match the scale of VW's operation. Fiat and Alfa Romeo have already embarked on a number of cooperative ventures, and there are signs of similar cooperation between the French firms operating in the area. None of the French producers has so far made any significant impact on the large Brazilian market, but this may change. PSA Peugeot-Citroen will probably attempt to integrate their operations, and there are strong arguments in favour of a joint Peugeot-Citroen and Renault undertaking, despite the fact that the two companies are in direct competition in Argentina and Chile.

The Japanese producers will probably seek to establish local assembly facilities in the region, but the future role of the major US producers is less certain. For political reasons, it is unlikely that any of the US firms will be allowed to achieve a dominant position in the South American motor industry, and US manufacturers may prefer to adopt a low profile in their operations in the region, contenting themselves with relatively minor production and/or assembly facilities. US firms may concentrate on the use of existing plant and attempt to integrate South American production with production in the US in a complementary rather than a competitive strategy. Larger and relatively luxurious models would be imported from the US, with a reverse flow of smaller, cheaper models produced in South America for sale in the US.

In reality, GM, having lost ground to Ford in Europe, has taken an aggressive and expansionist stance in South America. This will lead to a three-cornered fight involving Ford, VW and GM. GM's purchase of parts of the Chrysler operation has left Ford the smallest of these major operators in South America. In order to achieve minimum economies of scale, these companies will have two options: establish production facilities of around 2 million cars per year and thus be large enough for the South American company to survive without being integrated into another market; or build up production to a level exceeding one million units in the area and integrate production with their US and European facilities, implying specialization of models and power train. The market does not justify all the companies having capacity of around 2 million cars; increased integration with other areas is therefore probable.

Of the smaller manufacturers, Nissan and Toyota are likely to establish assembly plants with some sourcing from Japan. Renault/ AMC, Fiat and PSA Peugeot-Citroen may form some residual grouping whose combined production would approach one million, though their independence would require continual subsidy in terms of profits foregone elsewhere. All the car manufacturers will establish a light CV presence and the independent CV manufacturing firms (eg Daimler-Benz and Volvo, International Harvester) will continue to expand their operations in the medium to heavy truck segments.

Brazil is almost certain to increase its lead and establish an unassailable position as the major producer in South America. Oil wealth will tempt Venezuela to develop production facilities to augment the existing assembly capacity, but such expansion would be unwise, for the home market is too small to support a viable motor industry. It is likely, therefore, that the Venezuelan industry will be integrated with the larger Brazilian industry. Brazil's productive capacity will expand to give VW, GM and Ford a substantial manufacturing presence of one million plus units each. Argentinian plant and production, which are further south, may not be as closely integrated with Brazil as the Venezuelan industry. The desire to achieve scale economies will, however, ensure a non-autonomous future in Argentina for Ford and GM. Any major expansion of the motor industry may depend on a combined Renault/PSA/Fiat group.

Mexico is the odd man out. The Mexican industry will be less integrated with the rest of South America and more oriented towards the US. VW may succeed in disposing of its Mexican subsidiary to Ford or GM; Chrysler is almost compelled to sell its subsidiary. Mexican production will thus be dominated by GM and Ford and integrated with North American production. Some links with South America may be continued on the basis of product differentiation: the South American product differs from that of North America, and Mexico should be tied to South American productive facilities to maximize volume and scale economies on the South American product.

A high demand scenario gives a domestic market for cars of some 4 million in 1990, and one would expect the region's motor industry (with some exceptions such as Cuba) to be largely self-sufficient. This suggests a production capacity of some 3 million units in Brazil, 0.5 to one million in Mexico and 0.5 to one million in Argentina. The area would not be a net exporter, though some models would be supplied on a *quid pro quo* basis to both the European and North American markets, and South America, because of its reliance on established mature producers, would not emulate the Japanese. There may, however, be periods when the area is a small net exporter. The region could, with some rationalization, support all the manufacturers — Ford, GM, VW, a European grouping and some Japanese assembly operations — though further rationalization may occur in the long term.

A low scenario forecasts car production at 2.5 million by 1990, in which case the local market could only support all the manufacturers by becoming a major exporter of vehicles. More likely there would be forced rationalization. High levels of exports are unlikely for 'political' as well as economic reasons, and most of the producers would be reluctant to compete with their own models produced elsewhere. VW Brasil, for example, could not be expected to usurp VW's domestic European market nor the US export market. Vehicles would be exported from South America to markets elsewhere to complement sales of other models as part of an overall marketing and production strategy, rather than in direct competition with them. Exports to Japan, where US and European producers are not established, may be possible. The South American motor industry has some way to go before it has sufficient spare capacity and a suitably refined product to launch a successful attack on the Japanese market, but the omens are strongly in favour of such an outcome in the longer term. US producers who already have links, albeit tenuous, with Japanese firms would be less interested in such a counter-attack.

South American motor manufacturers, while retaining strong links with their respective parent companies, may, however, pursue a much more independent line. Indigenous governments will monitor their activities very closely and be anxious to preserve national interests. VW Brasil, for example, has signed an important contract for construction of a turnkey car plant in Iran, a prestigious (and lucrative) order in which the parent company did not intervene. It would seem that company loyalties elsewhere will be similarly discarded as other South American firms seek to assert their independence and their right to self-determination, particularly if the Middle East emerges as another potentially valuable export market.

Unlike the erratic growth of the market in the Middle East, which has made projections hazardous, the slow, steady growth of the South

American market makes a forecast of continued growth plausible. The fragmented state of the industry and the reliance on major multi-national companies means that South America's progress to the status of mature producer will be slow. The price of using Western technology appears to be subservience to Western goals. The South American region will ultimately be established as a mature producer, but the path to maturity will not be similar to the Japanese route and South America will never become a large net exporter.

Chapter 13

The Middle East

South America's motor industry has developed steadily and has relied heavily on Western manufacturers. The development of the Middle East[1] has been much more rapid, and has both indigenous producers (set up with the aid of Western firms) and foreign-owned projects.

Since 1973 the price of oil has more than quintupled, and this has greatly enhanced both the political status and potential buying power of the Arab states, but the region is still a high risk area in terms of industrial investment. The threat of a renewed outbreak of the Arab-Israeli conflict and the Palestinian problem create uncertainty. Moreover, increased wealth and the process of modernization have increased internal tensions and instabilities, and the Iranian revolution has made Western manufacturers and governments more wary of investing in the Middle East. There is considerable disagreement in the Arab community on a variety of issues: the Iraqi-Kurdish problem, territorial claims on Kuwait, the ramifications of superpower diplomacy in the area, and Libya's maverick line on foreign policy. The situation in Iran is still fluid, and the full implications of Egypt's isolation within the Arab world are yet to be seen.[2]

Continuing political uncertainty does not, however, wholly invalidate the area's enormous potential for industrial and economic development. The area as a whole is grossly underdeveloped in industrial terms: GNP is low, the manufacturing base small and agriculture still the principal employment (except in Kuwait). Moreover, the area's oil reserves are extensive but *not* limitless. Using current estimates of full-capacity working, Iraq and Kuwait have sufficient reserves for over 50 years, Saudi Arabia for 40 years, and Iran for 25. Oil revenue is not an absolute guarantee of perpetual wealth, nor are its benefits evenly distributed throughout the Middle East. Three distinct groupings can

1. We have limited the analysis to Iran, Iraq, Israel, Saudi Arabia, Syria, Kuwait and Egypt, though other countries will be referred to briefly.
2. The forecasts and predictions in this chapter are based on a certain level of stability (not exhibited towards the end of 1979). If the region continues to lurch from crisis to crisis, then the estimates in this chapter will be optimistic and should be scaled down appropriately. With this caveat in mind, we continue on the implicit assumption that political and economic uncertainty is constrained to acceptable levels. (Predictions that might have been appropriate for 1980 have been delayed by spreading the forecast over the period 1980-85.)

be discerned: Iran[1] , Syria and Iraq are pursuing a policy of diversified industrial development; Saudi Arabia and Kuwait, the chronic surplus countries, enjoy oil revenues far in excess of domestic requirements, and overseas investment is a more realistic (and more profitable) strategy than industrialization; Egypt and Israel have been economically devastated by the Arab-Israeli conflict and are engaged in economic reconstruction and recovery.

Table 13.1 gives population, GNP statistics, vehicle parcs and vehicle densities for the region. The figures show rapid growth in GNP in 1965-73, but only Saudi Arabia recorded a higher growth rate (10.1 per cent) than Japan (9.6 per cent).

The market

With only 2.4 million cars and 1.4 million CVs, the market is the smallest encountered so far, but in 1977 there were over 700,000 new vehicle registrations. To illustrate the rapid growth, these figures should be contrasted with the 1975 vehicle parcs of 1.5 million cars and 0.6 million CVs, and the figure of 550,000 new vehicle registrations. Tables 13.2 and 13.3 provide figures[2] on the structure of the Middle Eastern car and CV markets.

The Middle East is an attractive market for established manufacturers. The car import sector is dominated by the Japanese and US firms, which together account for almost 75 per cent of the total car and CV market (0.75 million units). Iran is the principal market: its population equals that of Iraq, Israel, Syria, Saudi Arabia and Kuwait combined, and has a standard of living which can support widespread vehicle ownership.

Table 13.4 traces the rapid growth in car and CV demand in Iran which we predict will continue.

Imports of built-up units have also increased but are expected to fall in the future. The substantial number of second-hand car imports — a curious feature of the Iranian market which, in part, explains the disparity in figures for apparent consumption (or new registrations) compared with figures for the growth in the total car parc — is not given. In recent years more than 30,000 second-hand cars have been imported annually, and although tax exemptions on used cars have now been abolished, the second-hand import trade will not diminish in importance until domestic producers are equipped to meet local demand, which should be within the next three to five years.

More than three-quarters of the Iranian car market centres on the

1. The Iranian revolution interrupted industrial development and may have a more profound, long-term effect on the process of modernization to which the previous regime was committed.
2. Statistics from 1975 — this lag in the availability of statistical information is often encountered in analysing current trends in the Middle East.

Table 13.1 Economic and vehicle statistics for the Middle East

	Population 1976 ('000s)	growth rate (%)	GNP per capita 1976 ($)	growth rate 1965-73 (%)	Vehicle parc 1977 ('000s) Cars	CVs	Vehicle density Number of persons per vehicle Cars	CVs
Major countries								
Iran	33,590	2.7	1700	7.4	582	475	58	71
Iraq	11,510	3.4	1280	2.9	94	73	122	158
Israel	3530	2.9	3288	6.7	297	104	12	34
Syria	7600	3.3	750	3.6	55	38	140	200
Saudi Arabia	9240	3.0	4990	10.1	276	350	33	26
Kuwait	1060	6.1	11,300	−2.9	237	84	4	13
Egypt	38,070	2.2	310	0.8	236	51	161	746
	104,600		1520		1777	1175	59	89
Minor countries								
Lebanon	2960	3.1	700		225	26	13	114
Jordan	2720	3.2	780		40	15	70	181
Libya	2510	4.0	5000		263	131	9	19
Oman	791	3.1	2400		23	20	34	40
United Arab Emirates	700	15.2	11,000		61	41	4	17
Bahrain	259	3.2	2030		26	8	10	32
Qatar	210	11.4	9000		20	10	5	21
	115,750		1622		2435	1426	47	81

Table 13.2 *Middle East car market structure 1975 ('000s)*

	New registrations	Local assembly	Built-up imports	Local manufacture
Iran	141	111[1]	30	0
Iraq	14	0	14	0
Israel	20	5[2]	15	0
Syria	7	0	7	0
Saudi Arabia	50	0	50	0
Kuwait	40	0	40	0
Egypt	15	10[3]	5	0
	287	126	161	0

1. Chrysler UK, Citroen, GM
2. Ford UK
3. Fiat/Polski Fiat

Table 13.3 *Middle East CVs vehicle market structure 1975 ('000s)*

	Imports of built-up and complete knock-down kits of all CVs	New registrations	Local assembly	Built-up imports	Local manufacture
Iran	67	65	34[1]	51	0
Iraq	35	25	6[2]	10	0
Israel	6	5	1[3]	4	0
Syria	14	14	0	14	0
Saudi Arabia	112	50	0	50	0
Kuwait	27	20	0	20	0
Egypt	9	9	0	5	4
	269	188	41	143	4

1. Daimler-Benz, Chrysler UK, Nissan, Mazda, GM
2. Saviem
3. Ford UK

Source: Some of the information in this table can be found in *The Middle Eastern Automotive Markets*, Euroeconomics, Eurofinance

wealthy and highly developed Teheran region. The contrast between the capital and the rest of the country is marked: in Teheran there is one car to every six people; elsewhere it is 1 : 150. Teheran has higher income levels, and a superior infrastructure and services and distribution network to that found elsewhere. Outside the capital, family incomes are too low for car ownership. This has created a marketing paradox in Iran: Teheran, with an acute traffic congestion problem and high car density levels, is approaching the status of a mature car market, marooned in an underdeveloped and singularly immature market. If the

3333

33333333333

THE MIDDLE EAST 303

Table 13.4 Iranian motor vehicle production and demand ('000s)

	Car output	Car demand	Built-up car imports	CV output	CV demand	Built-up CV imports
1966	2.5	9.2	6.7	7	12	5
1967	5	12.2	7.2	8	14	5
1968	8	21.4	13.4	10	14	4
1969	20	25.3	5.3	11	14	3
1970	29	35.5	7.5	11	13	2
1971	31	35	5	13	14	1
1972	45.6	43	2.4	17	19	2
1973	51.5	53	6.5	19	21	2
1974	72	93	26	29	36	7
1975	111.4	141	29.6	39	72	33
1976	125	163	38	45	98	53
1977	100	172	72	60	100	45
1980*	200	210	35	100	130	40
1985*	300	300	40	170	200	50
1990*	500	400	45	250	300	75

Source: Data from 1966-76 from *The Middle Eastern Automotive Markets* Euroeconomics, Eurofinance

* Representative forecasts

market in Teheran has reached near saturation level, market growth in the country as a whole will inevitably slow down.

Three hypotheses on the future of Iranian car demand, and two hypotheses for CV demand, are shown in Table 13.5. Current trends indicate that the lower projections are more plausible.

Table 13.5 *Forecasts of Iranian motor vehicle demand ('000s)*

	1975	1980	1985
Cars			
Plausible		212	294
Optimistic	141	263	415
Very optimistic		535	1023
Goods vehicles			
Central		126	179
Optimistic	65	224	423

Source: *The Middle Eastern Automotive Markets* Euroeconomics, Eurofinance

The manufacturers

With the exception of Iran, none of the Middle East countries can yet be classed as a motor vehicle manufacturer, although Saudi Arabia, Iraq and perhaps Egypt could achieve full or partial manufacturing status in the next 10 years. GM, Daimler-Benz and Honda are committed to various joint development projects in Iraq, and Iraq has also embarked on the first intra-Middle East development project in cooperation with Egypt.

Egypt has assembly capacity for the production of about 10,000 Fiat cars annually, and it hopes to increase annual production to 25,000 medium-size saloons. In the CV sector, Magirus and the Romanian ARO are both active; British Leyland has developed production facilities for 10,000 Land Rovers a year. This project was a triangular deal involving British Leyland technology and equipment and Kuwaiti finance. The Arab Industrial Investment Company, jointly owned by Egypt, Iraq and Kuwait, is promoting some truck and component production which may be complementary to the Iraqi development programme. GM are developing small facilities. Iraq is dependent on imports of fully assembled (built-up) cars, but car plant installed by VW Brasil (with a target capacity of 50,000 units per year) had planned to commence operations in late 1970s. Renault, Scania, Toyota, Ikarus (Hungary) and Daimler-Benz have all signed contracts for local CV assembly. The Saudi Arabian motor industry, wholly dependent on North America up to the late 1960s, is now dominated by the Japanese. Hino have a small-scale truck assembly plant (some 1200 trucks a year) and Nissan in association with the Saudi Zahran company has modest car facilities. Honda, Daimler-Benz and GM have small assembly facilities. Israel has very small-scale assembly facilities (owned by Ford, British Leyland and Mack).

Libya plans to introduce some small-scale assembly of cars and CVs, and the logical choice as manufacturer was Fiat as Libya is the second largest shareholder in the company. Fiat has invested some $50 million in setting up a 4000 units a year truck plant. Syria, Kuwait and the 'minor' group of countries (excluding Libya) have no manufacturing or assembly facilities, although Peugeot-Citroen and VW have been in active negotiations with several countries. Lebanon, Jordan, Oman, United Arab Emirates, Bahrain and Qatar will always import built-up (or mainly built-up) units; Libya may succeed in developing assembly plant. Saudi Arabia and joint ventures may achieve some progress, but the development of the motor industry depends crucially on Iran, the largest and most wealthy market.

Iran

Before 1974, the Iranian car industry consisted of assembly operations only. Iran National, assembling five versions of the Chrysler UK Hillman Hunter (marketed under the brandname Peykan) accounted for over two-thirds of the total car output; Iran Citroen, assembling the Citroen 2CV 600cc car and pick-up models, the Mehari utility vehicles and Iran Jeep with the GM Opel Rekord model, accounted for the rest. Iran National is currently looking for an alternative supplier to Chrysler UK ('l'albot). Table 13.4 shows annual totals for Iranian car output (ie cars assembled in Iran from knock-down sets imported from manufacturers elsewhere) and statistics for total car demand. Car output in Iran fell in 1977 and this indicates the problems involved in setting up a new motor industry. Iran National blamed Chrysler UK, but Chrysler felt they were not to blame. The real reason, it is argued, is the difficulty of industrializing a country quickly: during 1974-76, port congestion and freight transport problems prevented a smooth flow of CKD kits to Iran National, and though these problems were overcome, 1978-79 saw the onset of Iran's internal political problems. Whether Iran can actually cope with production in excess of 100,000 units is now a critical question.

The 1974 revisions to the Fifth Development Plan involved a major expansion programme for Iranian passenger car production in the period up to 1982, increasing output from the 1975 level of 114,000 units per year to a target of 1,045,000 units annually by the end of the period, with plans for a dramatic increase in the local content of assembled units, rising to over 80 per cent by 1982. The intention was to increase output ninefold and to acquire full manufacturing status for the Iran motor industry in just over six years. Thus far, expectations have not been fully realized, for the most part because targets were wildly optimistic. The current political upheavals in Iran are interrupting development: production in most sectors of the economy ceased for a period of time. Although production has resumed, it is questionable whether the new regime will wish to continue with these development plans for the motor industry. Even if plans had proceeded without hitch, it is doubtful whether domestic market demand could have supported production at such levels by the mid-1980s. Iran National was also to have produced a Peugeot 504 derivative car; the takeover by Peugeot-Citroen of Chrysler Europe (Talbot) was a stroke of good fortune for the Iranian company, as they will only have one supplier to deal with. Renault are involved in a project for the assembly of their R5. GM's Chevrolet car assembly plant will probably remain small scale despite ambitious targets.

CAR PRODUCTION

During the early 1980s, annual car production is likely to exceed 200,000 and should reach 300,000 by 1985. The composition of this output is uncertain, as negotiations and developments are in progress. However, the major car producer is likely to be Iran National with other companies taking second place. By 1990, output could be as high as 500,000 cars if Iran has started to export; otherwise, car production will match car supply, with small volumes of imports and exports.

THE CV INDUSTRY

The Iranian CV industry is currently dominated by the Japanese (in the lightweight CV sector), and Daimler-Benz (in the medium- and heavy-weight bus and truck sector), although if the objectives of the revised development plan are achieved (in whole or in part), GM would emerge as the dominant CV producer. Small-scale assemblers also include Volvo, British Leyland and Mack. Table 13.4 gives available figures for output and demand in recent years. The classificatory problems already encountered in analysing figures for the car sector are even more pronounced in the CV market, as local content in many of the KD units assembled in Iran already exceeds 50 per cent. Should these be considered as imports or as Iranian CV output? Available figures are virtually unverifiable and the totals given here must be read as reasonable approximations. Iranian CV output is further broken down into various market categories in Table 13.6.

The key to future development in the Iranian CV sector lies in the success or failure of the GM project. A GM plant, with a 20,000 unit truck output, should be operational in the early 1980s, with a projected annual target of 160,000 units by mid-1980s, which would represent roughly 70 per cent of total CV output. Given the shortfalls and

Table 13.6 *Output in the Iranian commercial vehicle industry*
1974-75 ('000s)

Producer	Production
Vehicles < 4 tonnes	
Iran GM–Jeep	3.2
Moratab (Land Rover)	2.2
Iran National (Peykan)	8.0
Iran Citroen	3.6
Zamiad (Nissan)	4.5
Iran Mazda	4.9
Other	0.1
	26.5
Vehicles > 4 tonnes	
Leyland	1.0
Kaveh (Mack)	1.3
Khawar (Daimler-Benz)	5.6
Zamiad (Volvo)	0.4
	8.3
Buses	
Pars Lux (Magirus)	0.3
Iran National (Daimler-Benz)	4.0
	4.3
	39.1

Source: Iran Statistics Centre

inadequacies of the Iranian components industry, output on this scale would seem to be excessively high if the local content target of 80 per cent is to be met. If this figure were scaled down to a more realistic level (ie to a level commensurate with domestic production capabilities) there would still be a substantial increase in output. Table 13.7 gives a range of scenarios for the CV sector. In the best scenario, domestic demand is met from domestic output (ie locally assembled vehicles with a fairly low local content). Assuming appropriate levels of production, a small surplus to domestic requirements would remain and could be exported. For these assumptions to be realized, the GM project is of crucial importance, and without it potential demand would have to be met through imports of assembled CVs. This occurs in the 'worst case' hypothesis outlined, in which the market share of imported CVs rises to 50 per cent of the total market. Assuming import restrictions, on the grounds that a high volume of imports would be unacceptable for any length of time, potential demand in such conditions could not be met. In practice, Iran could find it difficult to manufacture all its own requirements for CVs, owing to the diverse nature of the product. We can, therefore, expect Iran to build up exports, while importing its specialized needs. Even so, the success of the GM project is vital.

Table 13.7 *Iranian goods vehicle potential demand and output*
1980-85 ('000s)

Range estimates	1980-85	1985-90
CV parc	356-496	660-1129
CV demand	126-244	179-423
Assumed output	150	210
Imports (built-up range)	2-74	2-213
Exports (implied)	25-0	30-0
Central projection	**1980-85**	**1985-90**
CV demand	175	300
Imports (built-up)	50	75
Exports (implied)	25	30

Source: The Middle Eastern Automotive Markets Euroeconomics, Eurofinance

Motor vehicle production potential

In summary it seems that by the late 1980s only Iran, Saudi Arabia, Iraq and Egypt will be producing (or assembling with a local content of greater than 50 per cent) motor vehicles. Before the region can establish itself as a major producer of motor vehicles, a number of problems must be successfully overcome, and the failure of some key projects would critically weaken the motor industry and its potential for growth in the Middle East. Success will depend upon:

1. The development of Iran National, including a replacement model for the Peykan and the full development of power train production capacity.
2. The implementation of some of Iran's other car plants involving Renault and GM.
3. Some success with GM's various projects in the region, and substantial progress in GM's Iranian CV operations.
4. Some success with the VW Brasil's project in Iraq.
5. The successful implementation of the various Japanese ventures in Saudi Arabia.
6. The successful operation of the Egyptian/Iraqi vehicle manufacturing joint venture.

Future markets

As we have seen, forecasts for the Iranian car and CV industry have been wildly optimistic. It is more useful to consider prospects for the motor industry in the region as a whole. Assuming 3 per cent growth in population annually, total population would reach 151 million by 1985, rising to 175 million in 1990. Oil revenue will have peaked and may have begun to decline. By 2000, Iran's oil reserves will be virtually exhausted as the stocks of other producers will be depleted and their prestige and status threatened. Vehicles are not well maintained and vehicle life should be less than that for the mature markets, say 10 years.

Table 13.8 suggests a range of car ownership levels.

Table 13.8 *Alternative car density levels for the Middle East*

Scenario	1	2	3	4
Population (m)	150	150	150	150
Persons per car	5	10	15	25
Resulting car parc (m)	30	15	10	5
Replacement demand (m)	3	1.5	1	0.5

These projections have been made in the belief that car densities will not approach the US or European levels. Several arguments support this assumption: a much smaller percentage of the population is urbanized, the distribution of wealth is extremely uneven, and large tracts of land in the region are virtually uninhabitable. Car densities of 15-25 people per car by 1990 would seem realistic. The unequal distribution of wealth suggests a continuing demand for imports of fully assembled luxury cars, and the geographical factors indicate a continuing demand for four-wheel drive, utility and special purpose vehicles, at least until an adequate road network has been evolved. Table 13.9 summarizes car and CV demand for the next decade (although political upheaval could radically alter these demand projections).

Table 13.9 *Future supply and demand of motor vehicles in the Middle East ('000s)*

Cars	1975	1980	1985	1990
New car registrations	287	500	750-1000	1250+ substantial growth still possible
Built-up imports	161	150-250	250-500	Increasing
Local assembly	126	150-250	100-150	tendency to
Local manufacture	0	50-150	250-500	become self-suffient
CVs				
New CV registrations	260	300-400	500-700	600-700+ but fairly slow growth
Built-up imports	196	50-150	50-150	Increasing tendency
Local assembly	60	100-200	100-300	to become self-
Local manufacture	4	100-200	250-450	sufficient in the most popular variety of CVs

Vehicle ownership and densities will be below European levels, and demand may stabilize at 1.5-2.5 million cars and 600,000 CVs. Substantial growth in car demand may be possible in the long term, but a conservative interim forecast would be 750,000 cars and 500,000 CVs.

Future supply

Figures for local assembly and manufacture were given in Table 13.9; planned targets for domestic manufacturers and increased local content are unrealistic. Imports of assembled (built-up) vehicles will probably remain a permanent feature of the Middle East market, particularly in the luxury and specialist sectors.

Neither Kuwait nor Israel are likely to develop any indigenous manufacturing base and, apart from small-scale assembly of CKD kits, will remain open markets for assembled vehicles from abroad. Conversely, Iran and Saudi Arabia may develop motor industries capable of meeting most domestic demand. If the Middle East motor industry is to benefit from economies of scale as a viable volume car producer, however, it would have to be developed on a regional basis, and there is little prospect of a cohesive regional strategy. The Land Rover deal — a cooperative venture between Iraq, Egypt and Kuwait — is a small beginning, and the possibility of a more fully integrated regional approach is remote. Cheap labour costs may partially offset the diseconomies inherent in fragmentation, but to be competitive internationally a company must exceed annual production of one million cars. Iran National could just reach these figures, though political and commercial obstacles will be considerable.

A realistic, if cautious, estimate suggests that the Middle East could not expect to *manufacture* more than about 300,000 cars per year by 1985-90, which would meet only 40 per cent of the total demand. Imports of assembled vehicles may account for 45 per cent, leaving 15 per cent to be met from local assembly. In the CV sector, a manufacturing capacity of just under 300,000 units by 1985-90 would meet some 60 per cent of total Middle East demand. A further 25 per cent could be filled from locally assembled CVs, leaving a market share of 15 per cent for imports of assembled CVs.

Longer-term supply considerations will be influenced by two factors. First the depletion of oil reserves will force the oil producing countries to diversify, and motor vehicles are an obvious revenue-earning substitute. By the late 1980s the area may develop a self-sufficient manufacturing base for certain vehicles; it may concentrate on the development of a basic car designed primarily for export markets. To do so, however, the industry would have to be restructured to achieve the necessary economies of scale. It is unlikely to develop on a fully integrated regional basis, and the most likely candidates for full manufacturing status, Iran and Saudi Arabia, would have to expand productive capacity to levels far in excess of domestic demand to achieve even the minimal economies of scale necessary for volume car production.

Pattern of trade

All of the Middle Eastern markets discussed are involved in imports of either assembled or KD motor vehicles. North America has increased its share of exports to the Middle East; Western Europe, the major supplier to the Middle East until 1976, has been overtaken by the Japanese, and Western Europe's absolute sales have fallen. The bulk of Western European exports come from the Chrysler UK-Iran link. With the takeover of Chrysler Europe by PSA Peugeot-Citroen, and Peugeot's own Iranian plant (whose output was to have risen to 100,000 units per year by 1982) PSA Peugeot-Citroen dominate the car field. As manufacturing is established in Iran, so the export of CKD kits will decline. This will leave the Japanese in an even stronger position, though imports of Communist Bloc vehicles will slowly increase. Table 13.10 summarizes the volume and pattern of supply to the various Middle Eastern markets.

Table 13.10 *Pattern of exports of motor vehicles to Middle East ('000s)*

	North America	Western Europe	Japan	USSR	Total
1970	8.7	89.7	19.5	15.6	133.5
1971	12.2	93.1	21.8	17	144.1
1972	15.3	130.4	44.3	14.9	204.9
1973	20.3	128.8	51.7	10.9	211.7
1974	33.4	215.3	102.4	15.9	367
1975	88	244.4	202.6	17.8	552.8
1976	97.7	220.2	395	20	740.9
1977	93	218.6	440.8	25	777.4
1980*	90	150	475	25	750
1985*	70	100	405	50	625
1990*	60	75	290	75	500

* Representative forecasts

Most exporting countries export to a range of countries in the Middle East, but the UK, with the highest total of car exports to the region exports almost all of them to Iran. The Japanese have spread their exports more evenly. The US producers, already strongly represented in Iran and Saudi Arabia, are certain to increase their market share. The involvement of the German motor industry focuses on the performance of Daimler-Benz in Iran and Iraq (with possibilities for market expansion if the VW Brasil project in Iraq is successful).

The export/consumption pattern illustrated here raises a number of interesting points. In 1973-75 the car market doubled in size, and the CV market nearly quadrupled; even the newly rich oil nations of the Middle East cannot sustain such phenomenal rates of growth. CV markets in Iran, Iraq and Saudi Arabia have shown particularly rapid growth, and in Saudi Arabia, the market may have been brought very close to saturation level in the CV sector, at least in the short term. The growth of Japanese CV exports to this area has leapt ahead of the other major producers, although the bulk of the Japanese CV trade is accounted for by sales to Saudi Arabia. The character of the German export package has changed radically and is now dominated by CV sales, principally to Iran, Saudi Arabia and Iraq. Only one CV supplier, Italy, failed to increase exports to the Middle East in 1975, although in future other producers can expect a fall in export sales to the area. In the car sector, only three producers — the UK, Japan and North America — increased their exports to the Middle East in the 1975 boom. Israel's car and CV imports fell sharply in the same year, giving a clear indication of the economic difficulties facing the country.

Policy considerations

The Iranian market by 1990 will not be large enough to support an industry with sufficient economies of scale to be competitive. This implies that Iran, to achieve economies of scale, will have to grow through exports. Will Iran National have sufficient competitive spirit to go out and export? It is too early to say. The company faces a further problem: many local export markets will be closed through the development of indigenous assembly and/or production facilities. This implies that the automotive policy of the area should be conducted on a regional basis. If this could be achieved, the region may by the early 1990s have an annual car demand of 2 million cars and one million CVs, which would support two car companies and several truck manufacturers.

Conclusion

The prosperity of the Middle East has launched this area into the consumption and production of motor vehicles with almost unprecedented growth. The uneven distribution of wealth may prevent continued rapid growth, and the decline in real earnings from oil will reinforce this tendency for the rate of growth to slow down. But the Middle East is now an established growth market and, like the Communist Bloc, is trying to create its own productive capacity (in contrast to South America where manufacturers are exclusively US, European or Japanese subsidiaries). Continuing political uncertainties could reduce the importance of this developing region, and this factor places a severe question mark over the predictions and projections made in this chapter.

Chapter 14

South Africa, Australia and New Zealand

This chapter attempts to characterize the old colonial markets of the UK — South Africa, Australia and New Zealand. Because of the small total population of these areas, the market is relatively unimportant (see Table 14.1). Both South Africa and Australia used to suffer from a proliferation of models and manufacturers. The Australian market has now been at least partially rationalized, and a similar process will occur in South Africa. This chapter argues that, though of some current significance, these markets will not be important in global terms in future. Aggregate vehicle densities are higher than those in Europe, but the same characteristics found in South America are present in these markets: there are too many producers with too low volumes to be efficient chasing too few domestic customers, and the lack of indigenous producers reduces motivation to export.

Table 14.1 *Economic statistics*

	Estimated population in 1976 (millions)	Population growth rate 1970-76 (%)	GNP per capita 1976 (US $ market prices)	GNP per capita growth rate 1965-73 (%)
Australia	14	1.8	6288	3.0
New Zealand	3	1.8	3663	2.0
South Africa	26	2.5	1070	2.0

	Car parc in millions 1977	CV parc in millions 1977	Persons per car	Persons per CV
Australia	5.3	1.3	2.6	11
New Zealand	1.2	0.2	2.6	14
South Africa	2.2	0.9	12	29

South Africa

South Africa has two subeconomies, black and white, with entirely different consumption characteristics. This makes it impossible to discuss it as a single market; it must be seen in terms of one small and rather 'refined' market (similar to the Canadian market) and a much larger, underdeveloped market. Government regulations have forced most of the major producers to concentrate on local manufacture rather than the import of built-up units. This has created an unusually broad representation of foreign firms, with 15 major car manufacturers and many more CV producers operating in the country.

The market

South Africa has a population of 26 million, of whom 4 million are white. Car ownership density among the white population was 470 cars per 1000 people in 1973, compared with 11.5 cars per 1000 people among non-whites. Car density figures for the latter have more than doubled in the last 10 years and are still growing.

Until recently, cars were one of the few consumer durables which whites in South Africa could buy, but in 1976 cars had to contend not only with the effects of the oil crisis, but also with an entirely new commodity — a television service. Car sales in 1976 were 19 per cent down on sales for the previous year. Table 14.2 shows the pattern of growth of new registrations: South Africa has shown signs of maturity for some time, experiencing fluctuations in demand in a somewhat unimpressive growth record for cars, though not in CVs.

Table 14.2 *South African new registrations ('000s)*

	Cars	CVs
1960	91	19
1961	71	18
1962	36	10
1963	92	24
1964	123	38
1965	136	43
1966	125	37
1967	140	41
1968	135	45
1969	158	56
1970	187	72
1971	183	92
1972	183	109
1973	220	110
1974	215	112
1975	216	130
1976	173	110
1977	155	86
1978	183	101
1980*	200	110
1985*	150	100
1990*	100-300	50-200

* Representative forecasts

Ford dominates the South African market, though the Japanese firm of Nissan is a strong contender. VW, GM, Toyota and Sigma (Mazda/Mitsubishi) are also important. European manufacturers account for over 40 per cent of the market (though this proportion is falling); the US manufacturers have over 30 per cent (and rising) and the Japanese 25 per cent (and rising). Table 14.3 gives sales by manufacturer for both cars and CVs.

Table 14.3 *South African motor vehicle sales*

Car sales	1975	1976	1977
Alfa Romeo	6807	5371	3916
BMW	5310	6040	6218
British Leyland	13,188	9846	7490
Nissan	29,563	24,187	19,298
Fiat	7278	4972	6767
Ford	31,162	28,117	27,739
GM	28,475	21,254	17,836
Mercedes	10,749	9158	7628
Sigma (Mazda/Mitsubishi/Chrysler)	21,773	15,921	18,549
Sigma (Peugeot-Citroen only)	17,946	12,620	12,075
Toyota and Renault	16,803	17,484	14,134
VW	35,943	28,912	24,960
Volvo	2231	508	5
Others	1802	112	129
Total	229,030	184,502	166,744

Truck and bus sales	1975	1976	1977
British Leyland	8292	7952	5376
Nissan	19,273	20,852	18,807
ERF	—	177	163
Fiat	244	266	341
Fodens	—	146	155
Ford	19,967	15,536	11,519
GM	19,148	16,763	9676
International Harvester	1624	1469	759
Mack	299	—	—
Magirus-Deutz	257	292	137
MAN	347	253	282
Mercedes	5392	4098	2727
Oshkosh	275	214	197
Scania	104	67	104
Toyota	27,003	22,060	18,943
Sigma (Peugeot-Citroen, Mazda, Mitsubishi and Chrysler)	17,311	13,292	13,463
Volvo	140	43	23
VW	14,459	11,475	7294
Others	439	161	71
Total	134,574	115,116	90,037

Source: Automobile International

The most popular car in the market used to be the 105 inch (2.67m) wheelbase Chevrolet (based on the Opel Rekord), but this has now been overtaken by the Datsun Sunny. The sudden switch could have been a late reaction to calls for greater economy at a time of escalating car prices. In 1976 Datsun sold 13,500 Sunnys (14,400 in 1975), while GM sold 12,800 Chevrolets (18,600 in 1975). The VW Beetle ranked third with sales of 11,775 (12,250 in 1975).

The market is a surprisingly sophisticated one: the market shares of Mercedes-Benz, Audi (VW), Peugeot-Citroen, Volvo and the quality divisions of British Leyland (Jaguar, Rover, Triumph, MG) provide a combined quality market share of 20-25 per cent, indicating that the white, urban sector of the market at least is a fully mature one. The growing non-white market is for a far more basic car (eg the Datsun Sunny or used quality car). In the CV sector, about 65 per cent of the market is for lightweight CVs (below 2250 kg) and another 20 per cent for a light- to medium-weight truck (2250-10,000 kg). GM, Ford, Toyota, Nissan and VW dominate the market, and the two Japanese firms have 40 per cent of total sales.

The manufacturers

The structure of the assembly industry in South Africa is probably the most complex, fragmented and potentially uneconomic in the world. In 1978 there were over 20 companies representing nearly all the manufacturing companies, including some, like Alfa Romeo, BMW, ERF, Fodens and Oshkosh (the specialized CV producer based in the USA), which have little productive capacity outside their domestic market. Once companies started to establish their presence, this acted as a magnet; the other companies felt compelled to compete. Why were the companies willing to fight so hard for this minor market? Why should the Europeans and more recently the Japanese have been attracted to this area in the face of severe difficulties? The manufacturers must have hoped that South Africa would serve as a motor vehicle production centre for the whole of Africa, but its political isolation has made this impossible. Moreover, domestic pressures and internal political problems affect corporate planning and locational strategy: cars must be manufactured in accordance with the South African government's programme, which requires a local content of 66 per cent in cars (predicted to increase to 70 per cent). The sales figures in Table 14.3 closely mirror the production/assembly figures in South Africa; not only are there too many manufacturers chasing too small a market, but, with 40 basic models available, manufacturers have manifestly failed to rationalize their output. This proliferation of companies and models is an effective bar to any one company in South Africa achieving much needed economies of scale. Despite these difficulties, there is no suggestion that they withdraw from the field. The non-white South African market and its potential spending capacity is apparently 'too juicy a carrot for any motor mogul to abandon' (*Financial Times*). Moreover, many smaller firms have invested heavily in plant, and are prepared to undertake sub-assembly work and body pressing on a contract basis, enabling car manufacturers to meet the local content requirements through sub-contracting and without a major commitment to plant and facilities of their own.

However, the desire to stay in the market for low or negative returns in anticipation of a future boom in non-white sales has created an interesting and extreme extension of the 'incremental volume' marketing strategy. Based on the premise that with high fixed costs, profitability is peculiarly sensitive to sales revenue, manufacturers cover every gap in the market in an attempt to achieve a higher volume of sales. Real or imaginary gaps are filled in the search for fractions of a percentage point in extra penetration of the market. Furthermore, companies operating in South Africa show little sign of receiving clear direction from parent companies. Model proliferation is the apparent result of this autonomous development, but recent falls in total sales figures must surely prompt a firmer approach by the parent companies and the possibility of rationalization and withdrawals from the South African market. The growing strength of the Japanese is a further argument that the *status quo* is doomed.

There are three possibilities for any company contemplating a change: withdrawal and actual or functional merger, and each will emerge over the next decade.

Pattern of trade

Trade patterns for South Africa are greatly obscured by the requirements of the assembly and local content programme. The leading importers are Japan, the UK, West Germany, France, Italy and Canada.

Conclusions

South Africa's racial policies are generally condemned, and no economic forecast can afford to ignore this political reality. In the longer term, it must be assumed that the 'white' South African market will disappear, absorbed into the larger, non-white market. The market may retract and, in these circumstances, many of the manufacturers may have to write off their investment. Alternatively, sole ownership may be replaced by some form of co-ownership, especially as the political climate deteriorates. Higher defence spending and emigration could create a stagnant or declining white market, with compensating growth in non-white market sales (encouraged by a government anxious to show the non-white population that they can also enjoy the benefits of consumer durables under the existing regime. These market changes would involve a shift away from the prestige, quality market towards a more basic car, which the Japanese are well placed to exploit. Any short- or medium-term growth in demand, therefore, must favour the Japanese, though European subsidiaries in South America (eg VW Brasil) may benefit. Ultimately, the market will shift towards one that is wholly characteristic of a less developed country, at which point many producers would either leave or switch to a more basic product.

Australia and New Zealand

Unlike South Africa, the Australian and New Zealand market is much more homogeneous, with a population of some 17 million people (see Table 14.1). In common with South Africa, there are too many manufacturers and a proliferation of models. With the withdrawal of British Leyland and VW from manufacturing (both now assemble from CKD kits only) the industry has been at least partly rationalized, although there is ample scope for further improvement. Table 14.4 shows the growth in new car registrations and production. Like South Africa, the cyclical fluctuations seen in the new registrations are typical of a mature market.

The market

In 1978 Australia and New Zealand had a vehicle parc of almost 7 million cars and over 1.5 million CVs, roughly 350 cars per 1000 people. With no limitation on space and greater distances to travel, one might expect saturation to occur at levels close to those of the US, but growth since the mid-1960s has been sluggish (see Table 14.4). The oil crises and high prices (with 45 per cent import duty and uneconomic local content programmes) have created periods of total stagnation in recent years, punctuated by an acceleration in the Japanese sales drive. The Australian offshore oil fields could encourage a small growth in sales, by alleviating anxieties over the supply of oil. The market has been declining steadily since 1974, though there was no great drop in demand following the 1973 oil crisis. Confidence in the recovery of demand to 1973-74 levels is waning. If Australia has reached saturation level, this poses an interesting problem for the manufacturers: production must be geared to a replacement level (with no element of new demand).

Until recently, large cars dominated the Australian market. In the early 1970s, some 50 per cent of the market consisted of sales of eight-cylinder engines, and six-cylinder cars took another 20 per cent. Their market share is now only 20-25 per cent and the market is

Table 14.4 *Vehicle production in Australia and New Zealand*

	Australia				New Zealand	
	New car registrations ('000s)	New CV registrations ('000s)	Production and assembly cars ('000s)	Production CVs ('000s)	New registrations Cars ('000s)	CVs ('000s)
1958	175	62	110	na	30	9
1959	197	71	130	na	26	7
1960	245	66	157	na	32	8
1961	188	49	133	na	35	9
1962	267	56	209	na	39	8
1963	307	67	230	na	55	10
1964	333	75	274	na	63	10
1965	332	75	307	na	64	10
1966	307	72	261	na	59	12
1967	336	78	292	na	52	9
1968	369	81	316	na	46	8
1969	401	87	337	na	53	12
1970	413	89	392	82	70	17
1971	417	87	391	79	71	20
1972	406	94	367	81	86	17
1973	460	112	376	86	102	18
1974	475	113	394	101	99	16
1975	472	121	351	87	84	18
1976	468	138	386	90	74	18
1977	430	131	316	73	72	18
1978	450	126	330	80		
1980*	450	130	325	100	70	20
1985*	500	150	400	120	100	20
1990*	500	150	400	120	100	20

* Representative forecasts

dominated by four-cylinder models. Emphasis on a larger car reflects the dominance of the US producers, with over 50 per cent of the market (see Table 14.5). The rapid growth of the Japanese share (over 30 per cent and rising) suggests, however, that a market for smaller cars does exist, and this shift to smaller cars is probably now established as a long-term trend. This increase of popularity of small cars can be contrasted with North America, where down-sizing is being *imposed* on the consumer. The switch to smaller cars has also affected New Zealand where the Japanese share of the market now exceeds 50 per cent.

New car registrations in New Zealand are 18-22 per cent of Australian levels. Again, there is a considerable model proliferation. Unlike Australia where manufacturers compete for primacy, British Leyland is the established market leader. GM, Ford and Toyota dominate the CV sector in both Australia and New Zealand, with the major emphasis on sales of lightweight trucks. In the heavier CV segment, International Harvester, Ford, Volvo, Mercedes-Benz, MAN and Kenworth are the principal producers.

Table 14.5 *Australian motor vehicle production ('000s)*

	1972	1973	1974	1975	1976	1977
Australian Motor Industry (Toyota)	24	28	30	34	40	39
British Leyland	32	34	29	7	10	9
Chrysler/Mitsubishi	44	51	49	36	34	24
Ford	131	124	121	120	123	123
GM	186	201	190	134	132	116
International Harvester	6	7	6	5	6	5
VW	—	—	17	15	17	7

Manufacturers

Most of the manufacturing capacity in the region is concentrated in Australia, and New Zealand is largely assembly only. In Australia import quotas of 90,000 units a year were imposed to protect local industry; though lifted temporarily, they were reintroduced when the import share rose above 20 per cent. Further encouragement was supplied by various incentive schemes, offering greatest protection to those manufacturers achieving high levels (about 85 per cent) of local content. Some commentators feel that this incentive backfired, because the Japanese were quick to exploit various loopholes and benefited from the scheme.

The industry in Australia has four main manufacturers — GM, Ford, Chrysler/Mitsubishi and Toyota — which manufacture over 80 per cent of domestically-produced vehicles. There are several assemblers with varying degrees of local content. Table 14.5 shows the recent total production of some of the major producers. GM-Holden is the major manufacturer and engages in little assembly work. Ford is the second largest manufacturer. British Leyland has reduced its operation to some CV production and assembly. Ford's production has remained constant, while GM's production has fallen steeply. Ford has been willing to introduce its European model into Australia, and is increasingly looking to Toyo Kogyo to supply models and components to Australia. Ford Australia's 'Falcon' is the last bespoke model for the Australian market.

Chrysler's policy of retrenchment has allowed Mitsubishi to obtain 30 per cent of its Australian subsidiary, with the option to purchase a controlling interest. Chrysler's Australian subsidiary must, therefore, now be regarded as a Mitsubishi subsidiary. Australian Motor Industries (50 per cent Toyota) and Nissan (the most recent company to have established assembly operations) plan to establish 85 per cent local content by 1980 (partly in response to government pressure). VW, which used to assemble Nissan products, has now become a small-scale assembler. There are several small CV assembly operations, although International Harvester consistently produces/assembles about 5-6000 CVs.

The Australian government's attitude is firmly protectionist, arguing that since Australian manufacturers' production runs are shorter than those of the major international producing centres, their costs are higher and protection thus necessary. Protection takes the form of government persuasion and tariff concessions on imported components, which are extended to manufacturers whose entire model range has an average local content of at least 85 per cent. Much higher import tariffs are imposed on CKD units. Import tariffs on built-up units were scrapped in favour of import quotas (currently 20 per cent of the market). This hit the Japanese hardest, and partly explains the actions of Toyota, Nissan and Mitsubishi.

No manufacturer can afford to set up bespoke engine plants to support the Australian market, and this has led to some interesting manoeuvres. The collapse of the proposed four-party consortium of four-cylinder engine production (involving Nissan, Toyota, Chrysler and the Australian Industry Development Agency) left Chrysler and Nissan to collaborate on a joint project, while Toyota has decided to buy four-cylinder engines from GM. All of the US-owned companies have suffered from an over-reliance on large cars. To correct the imbalance, GM-Holden is planning to spend $200 million on new model development, modernization, etc, and an additional $210 million budgeted for a new four-cylinder engine plant. Toyota and Nissan are also planning to spend up to $100 million on new engine plants. GM, before going ahead with its new engine plants, is trying to persuade the Australian government to relax its current local content rules as a *quid pro quo*.

Herein lies the dilemma: the Australian subsidiaries can only be economic either if substantial exports can be achieved, or if the Australian plants are integrated into the production operations of larger plants elsewhere. The Australian government's current policy is achieving neither and simply causing high-priced vehicles to be produced by companies whose financial viability is marginal (nearly all the Australian manufacturing companies made substantial losses in 1978). Since Australia has no indigenous manufacturers, a more realistic course of action is to integrate the motor industry with other worldwide plants.

The future

Unlike the South African motor industry, the Australian industry has already undergone some degree of rationalization, leaving Ford, GM and the three Japanese firms to share the market between them. The failure of the four-cylinder engine project suggests that further mergers are unlikely, although functional mergers on a smaller scale should not be ruled out.

With an annual demand in 1990 of some 650,000 cars and 170,000

CVs, the market is not very large and further growth is unlikely. The market is safe but uninspiring, with little growth potential in the future.

Australia's proximity to Japan and the success of Japanese imports will lead to the closer integration of Australian plants with their Japanese counterparts. GM will move closer to Isuzu, its Japanese associate; Ford, already committed to worldwide integration, will link Australia into assembly operations in Europe and Japan (Toyo Kogyo). There may be some casualties before full rationalization can occur. The Australian government must be persuaded to allow increased imports of components in exchange for some exports (ie import an engine and export a gearbox, thereby allowing both components to be manufactured at a suitable volume). On this basis Australia will probably be able to produce or assemble the equivalent of some 80 per cent of its market requirements.

In global terms Australasia is no longer a major market or key production centre. The industry has no major market to sustain a viable, independent motor industry, and adjacent markets are too close to Japan for Australia to gain an entrée.

Chapter 15

The Infant Markets

In this chapter we consider less developed countries. As well as providing a brief overview, we examine the process whereby infant markets gain some degree of maturity — as South America, the USSR and the Middle East have.

Infant markets are diverse but, as the development of the Japanese market tends to suggest, the demand for small trucks is of paramount importance. A secondary demand begins with industrialization. The often indifferent state of the roads does not allow larger trucks, but does promote demand for four-wheel drive cars. Demand for cars is initially related solely to government and official agencies and embassies and a wealthy élite.

Economic background

Earlier we postulated that urbanization and industrialization promoted the establishment of healthy market demand for cars and CVs respectively. Less developed countries are predominantly rural and agrarian; farming is not commercially oriented; geographical mobility is low; the service infrastructure is poor, and demand for vehicles is very low. This is reinforced in countries (eg India) where other transport media are (or were) relatively good, or in areas (such as Eastern Europe) where emphasis is placed on the development of public transport systems.

Urbanization and industrialization are proceeding, and demand for motor vehicles will increase substantially in the longer term. It is unlikely that the mature markets will continue to supply the less developed countries, for political as well as commercial reasons, some of the latter will probably attempt to establish their own industries. In fact, it seems to be the rule that where there is an infant market with some growth potential, local assembly and/or manufacture usually follow closely. Investment in the motor industry tends to move to areas of low-density vehicle ownership. This movement of productive resources away from developed countries will benefit the less developed countries with good natural resources. This partial relocation of the motor industry in less developed countries will gradually gather momentum, but only some less developed countries with special characteristics will benefit.

Production of cheap, basic passenger cars and utility vehicles in the developed economies is unlikely, and the established producers may find that their opportunities for participating in the development of the motor industry in less developed countries are very limited. The lower labour costs in less developed countries offer obvious cost advantages, but organized labour in the mature markets will oppose the movement of investment capital abroad, and the developing countries can be expected to resist the spread of foreign ownership and control. The experiences of South America and the 'Old Colonials' have reinforced the notion that foreign control of the motor industry is not necessarily beneficial to the developing country. Although some new developments will attract the major multinationals, which will ensure that supply will only match the demand for the product, other new developments will seek different solutions and the development of a truly indigenous industry. It is therefore likely that the major producers will increasingly limit their activities to the supply of technology or of complete turnkey systems, providing a source of high-technology components and acting as contract managers in constructing and supervizing new plant.

How does a less developed country 'create' a motor industry? Chapter 10 analysed this question in the context of minor rather than infant producers. Russia and the Middle East imported more or less complete systems, whereas South America's industry developed more gradually. Using the development of these markets as a model, and adjusting the analysis to existing conditions, one can detect an underlying and consistent pattern. Most of the less developed countries begin with imports of assembled vehicles, establishing some local content with the manufacture of tyres, batteries, paint, gaskets, upholstery, shock absorbers and flat glass. This is followed by an increasing 'local content' programme which widens the local production of items such as minor body pressings, axles, radiators, etc. At this stage 'local content' is more of an exercise in public relations than a means of cutting costs, as savings are generally minimal. As a long-term marketing ploy, however, it offers many advantages: the company establishes a presence and an identity, and is therefore in a position to exploit growth in the market. Local assembly is increased and facilities for local manufacture are developed, initially on a small scale. In the final stages, local manufacture expands to accommodate all of the machining and production requirements, including the production of power train, of a self-sufficient motor industry. To be viable, this stage requires large volumes: if production is fragmented and the domestic market small, it is almost impossible to be competitive. The industry must have some protection, but protection without the motivation to grow through exports leads to a small, unprofitable and over-priced product.

Different areas proceed at a very different pace and arrive at different solutions to the problems of establishing a motor industry. India, for example, has moved rapidly towards full self-sufficiency, despite low production volumes (less than 50,000 units per year). Conversely, despite a much higher output, Iran is still at the stage of mixed manufacture and assembly. When Iran eventually becomes self-sufficient it will be equipped for manufacture at much higher volumes than India, and will be in a much more competitive position as a result.

As we examine specific areas in which this process is under way, two points should be kept in mind: first, an assembly plant may 'work' for a number of manufacturers, and, second, there is almost always a government stake, if not a controlling state interest, in the motor industry. South Korea is virtually the only exception to this rule.

Preconditions for the growth of a motor vehicle industry

Cars

Healthy domestic demand is the essential prerequisite for the establishment of a local motor industry, and demand is a function of *per capita* disposable income. It has been suggested that take-off occurs when *per capita* income is about twice the price of acceptable cars; this may be the case in Communist Bloc countries, but it does not apply in South America or the Middle East. The explosion in Japanese demand in the 1960s occurred when *per capita* GNP passed $500. Inflation has probably doubled this figure, but South America (where Brazil, one of the wealthiest South American nations, had a *per capita* GNP of only $760 in 1973) supports a flourishing motor industry.

At this stage we must recognize a number of secondary factors, which can inhibit or encourage the growth of a viable domestic motor industry. A number of key variables affect local supply:

1. Local demand which must be high enough to make production a viable proposition.
2. Close proximity to existing or potential export markets.
3. A sizeable and adequately trained labour force.
4. A well developed and reasonably sophisticated industrial infra-structure.
5. Available finance for the capital expenditures involved.
6. Military or defence requirements which may encourage the growth of local industry.
7. Political considerations.

CVs

CV demand will initially outstrip car demand. Although alternatives to road haulage affect the growth in demand for CVs, there is a more direct relationship between growth in CV demand and growth of total GNP.

The infant markets

Table 15.1 gives statistics relevant to the development of a motor industry during the next decade. These statistics can be considered as proxy variables for the list of attributes given above.

Population is the key determinant of the growth of a motor industry: few countries with a population of less than 10 million could support domestic capacity. The second critical statistic, and perhaps the most sensitive to new developments, is the standard of living (expressed as *per capita* GNP). Third, the energy consumption of a country indicates the degree of industrialization, and the level of crude oil production serves as a measure of whether a country is, or may be, able to develop a motor industry in a period of high-priced energy.

The following countries already have established infant industries: China, India, Indonesia, Nigeria, the Philippines, Thailand, Turkey, South Korea, Morocco, Algeria, Taiwan and Kenya. The following countries can be ruled out because they are too small and/or too poor: Zambia, Libya, Tunisia, Ghana, Uganda, Zaire, Nepal, Tanzania, Afghanistan, Ethiopia, Burma and Bangladesh. Population can be traded off against poverty: India, for example, despite its poverty has a sufficiently large population and a suitably sized middle class, urban population to support a domestic motor industry.

This leaves 16 countries (shown in Table 15.2 ranked by *per capita* GNP) which may experience significant demand for motor vehicles and have the possibility of further developing their motor industry.

According to the demand relationships postulated in Chapter 3, a certain level of *per capita* GNP can be expected to provide given motor vehicle densities. Most of these countries have relatively high levels of *per capita* GNP and can thus be expected to support indigenous motor manufacture.

Area studies

An examination of each geographical area produces some interesting observations on the likely development of 'infant' industries. There is little· uniformity, and we limit the discussion to countries where conditions seem to favour the establishment of a motor industry.

Table 15.1 Critical statistics for development of an infant market

	Population 1976 (millions)	GNP per capita 1976	Energy consumption 1975 (kg)	Crude oil production 1976 ('000 tonnes)	Cars per 1000 people 1976	CVs per 1000 people 1976
China	852	380	660	85,000	0.1	1
India	610	132	221	8623	1	1
Indonesia	140	242	178	74,029	3	2
Bangladesh	79	85	28	341	0.3	0.3
Pakistan	72	180	183	0	3	1
Nigeria	65	350	90	102,655	1	3
Vietnam	47	160	200	0	2	4
Philippines	44	360	326	0	9	6
Thailand	43	358	284	0	8	7
Turkey	41	980	630	2568	12	6
South Korea	36	641	1038	0	3	4
Burma	31	110	51	1160	1	0.1
Ethiopia	29	108	29	0	2	0.4
Zaire	26	124	78	96	3	3
Afghanistan	20	110	52	0	1	1
Sudan	19	230	140	0	2	2
Morocco	18	360	274	0	18	7
Algeria	17	840	754	50,090	12	6
Taiwan	16	970	600	247	16	3
Tanzania	16	150	69	0	3	3
Kenya	14	220	220	0	6	6
Sri Lanka	14	214	127	0	7	4
Nepal	13	120	10	0	0.5	0.3
Malaysia	12	840	588	8024	36	12
Uganda	12	240	55	0	2	1
Ghana	10	230	182	0	6	5

Table 15.2 *Projected and actual motor vehicle parcs*

	GNP per capita 1976	Motor vehicle parc in 1977 (millions)	Vehicles per 1000 people 1977	GNP per capita growth rate 1965-73 (%)
Turkey	980	0.8	19	4.4
Taiwan	970	0.3	20	7.3
Algeria	840	0.4	20	4.3
Malaysia	840	0.6	45	3.7
South Korea	641	0.3	8	8.7
China	380	0.7	1	4.6
Philippines	360	0.7	16	2.6
Morocco	360	0.5	26	2.5
Thailand	358	0.7	15	4.5
Nigeria	350	0.5	7	8.3
Indonesia	242	0.7	5	4.5
Sudan	230	0.1	5	−0.6
Kenya	220	0.1	12	3.3
Pakistan	180	0.3	4	2.5
Vietnam	160	0.3	6	−0.7
India	132	1.5	3	1.5

Definition of area

We first examine areas where an infant motor industry has already developed (see Table 15.3). Although many countries with infant motor industries have not been specifically referred to in this chapter, those discussed are broadly representative.

North Africa

Morocco and Algeria have relatively large populations and are geographically near to the West European market, but both have large tracts of desert which may obstruct growth. If Algeria develops an infant motor industry, it may be tempted to follow through its historical connections with France. Renault are certainly well equipped to supply complete systems, but both Fiat and VW could submit highly competitive tenders. Morocco has no detailed plans for expansion, but this does not exclude the possibility of a joint industrial development programme with Algeria, which would be of mutual benefit. Although Morocco has, at present, a much larger vehicle parc than its Algerian neighbour, it has no proven oil reserves, which would certainly make Algeria the stronger partner. One large establishment assembles Renault, Fiat, Opel and Chrysler products in Morocco (see Table 15.6 p 340). Algeria has announced plans for the development of a manufacturing and assembly complex capable of producing 150,000 cars per year by

Table 15.3 *Regional vehicle parcs, ownership and production*

	Vehicle parc 1977 ('000s)		Production/ assembly 1976 ('000s)		Vehicles per 1000 people (1976)	
	Car	CV	Car	CV	Car	CV
North Africa						
Algeria	220	130	0	6	12	6
Morocco	323	131	23	11	18	7
Tunisia	105	72	2	2	18	12
Turkey	471	308	63	46	12	6
West Africa						
Nigeria	281	194	1	12	1	3
Ivory Coast	89	58	5	0	15	10
Ghana	64	46	1	3*	6	5
Central and East Africa						
Kenya	98	69	0	1	6	6
Zaire	95	85	2*	2*	3	3
Angola	147	39	1	1*	21	4
Zambia	104	61	4	1	18	13
Madagascar	72	52	2*	2*	7	6
Mozambique	108	24	0	1*	10	3
East Asia						
China	42	685	5	100	0.1	1
South Korea	126	150	27	23	3	4
Taiwan	260	55	20*	20*	16	3
South-east Asia						
Indonesia	421	255	40*	13*	3	2
Malaysia	447	111	43	10	36	12
Philippines	402	291	31	22	9	6
Singapore	142	54	6*	3*	66	23
Thailand	363	294	16	9	8	7
South Asia						
India	822	711	32	54	1	1
Pakistan	190	89	2*	2*	3	1

* Estimate

the mid-1980s. Algeria currently produces 6000 CVs annually. Tunisia only has some small-scale assembly.

Turkey

Turkey is fairly wealthy and has already established a motor industry of modest proportions. It has a population of 41 millions, a comparatively high *per capita* GNP, and is close to the West European market and the expanding Middle Eastern market. These factors suggest that the industry has substantial growth potential. Turkey assembled some

60,000 cars and 4000 CVs in 1977. Details of production figures by manufacturer are shown in Table 15.6. There are numerous CV assemblers but only three car manufacturers: Fiat, Renault and Otosan-Ford. The latter is interesting, since it is an independent indigenous manufacturer. In 1960 Otosan, a subsidiary of the Koc Company in Istanbul, began to assemble Fords. Reliant (small car specialists in the UK) designed a lightweight plastic-bodied car for Otosan, which went into production in 1966, using a Ford power train. Otosan provides Turkey with a measure of independence. Turkey may become a centre for the assembly of Japanese vehicles for export to Western Europe and the Middle East. Toyota has proposed plans for a 100-200,000 capacity integrated assembly and production plant, and Nissan have toyed with the idea of a light truck plant. Renault is to double the capacity of its plant (currently 35,000 cars a year). Otoyol and Tofas (Fiat) also plan to expand. GM, British Leyland, Chrysler, MAN, Magirus, Mercedes and International Harvester are represented by CV assembly operations.

West Africa

This region currently supports motor industries in Nigeria, the Ivory Coast and Ghana. Oil-rich Nigeria has a large population (65 million) and is an important and rapidly expanding market, with a high growth rate for its *per capita* GNP. The country is sharply divided: while many Nigerians are close to subsistence-level farming, others are involved in lucrative industrial activity and have been quick to adapt to a more affluent life-style which may encourage car ownership and foster growth in demand. Annual car sales could reach 100,000 by the mid-1980s, with CV demand running at 30,000 units per year; these figures make Nigeria an infant market of sizeable proportions. The Nigerian motor industry is expected to move rapidly from the transitional assembly-only stage to full manufacturing status.

Nigeria's development programme is most advanced in its CV operations. The country has gone to the multinationals to develop its industry: Fiat, Daimler-Benz and Steyr will each have CV plants of some 7000 units a year, and British Leyland will install capacity of around 12,000 units a year to cover CV and Land Rover assembly. Car assembly plants have been in existence for some time, operated by Peugeot-Citroen and VW and with a capacity of 18,000 cars a year. Nigeria's plans seem to centre on satisfying domestic demand, and the industry is highly protected by tariff barriers and licensing restrictions. Nigeria's development follows the classic lines of foreign ownership and development: protection, the involvement of several foreign companies and a programme of increasing 'local content'. British Leyland planned to begin pressing panels and fabricating Land Rover sub-assemblies and CV cabs in 1979. Local content is planned to increase by about 10 per cent a year, so that by 1990 Nigeria will have a fully-fledged production industry. The country has sensibly limited the number of Western manufacturers, and developments are not wholly financed by foreign manufacturers: the British Leyland investment in Nigeria was only some $10 million, and the rest of the money was provided locally.

The Ivory Coast and Ghana have relatively small-scale production. Renault is involved in the Ivory Coast, and Ghana has a number of local assemblers building several different makes.

Central and East Africa

Most of the countries in this region are not yet in a position to support a viable motor industry, though Angola[1], Kenya, Zambia, Madagascar and Mozambique have experienced some development.

Although Kenya is a tiny market in absolute terms, the market there is similar to South Africa's, with a small but affluent minority (in this case Asian) and an unexpectedly broad range of car and truck models. Both factors account for the disproportionately large Kenyan car and CV parc. The CV market is particularly important: road networks are good and the road haulage industry is well-developed, and is important economically and politically. CV sales were expected to reach 7000-8000 units by 1980. Kenya hopes to establish a viable CV manufacturing industry by supplying not only its expanding domestic market, but the neighbouring markets of Southern Sudan and Ethiopia. Construction of three new CV assembly plants, which will have a total capacity output of 10,000 vehicles per year and should employ almost 1000 workers, is under way.

Kenya's decision to concentrate on CV production is wise: the country could not hope to support a volume car industry, where economies of scale are vital to the profitability of the venture and low-volume production carries heavy cost penalties; CV production can be small-scale and more specialized, and demand is more stable, particularly in less developed countries.

Zambia's small population belies its significance as a motor producer, since it currently has the largest output of vehicles in this area. Although Kenya may overtake Zambia in total motor vehicle production, it has no plans to assemble cars.

Zaire has a number of small-scale assembly plants. A number of companies (eg Renault, Peugeot, GM, British Leyland) had high expectations of Zaire which, in retrospect, were misplaced. Madagascar and Mozambique have extremely small-scale assembly facilities.

Potential capacity in this region is high, although current capacity is

1. Angola has experienced decolonization, civil war and foreign intervention in recent years. It is still in a state of flux, statistics are not readily available, and Angola is therefore excluded from this discussion.

low. Total capacity in the area, including Kenya's planned expansion, is 35,000 cars and 40,000 CVs a year. A detailed breakdown is shown in Table 15.4. If Kenya's plans come to fruition, the country will dominate the motor industry in Central and Southern Africa.

Table 15.4 *Capacity in Southern and Eastern Africa**

| Country | Manufacturers | Annual capacity | |
		Cars	CVs
Zambia	Fiat	5000	2000
Zaire	British Leyland, Fiat, Magirus, GM, Sonofar (Renault and Peugeot)	10,000	3000
Madagascar	Peugeot-Citroen, Renault	1000	1000
Mozambique	Honda, Mercedes-Benz British Leyland, Fiat, Daimler-Benz, Steyr, Peugeot-Citroen, VW and Fiat	18,500	33,500

* Angola has a CV capacity of some 1500 vehicles but future production is uncertain

East Asia

Mainland China has a vast population, a relatively high *per capita* GNP, a reasonable growth rate and some oil production. China is an enormous and untapped market; insularity and ideological isolation have constrained the supply of motor vehicles, but the political climate is changing and foreign companies and ventures are now being encouraged. Harpers International, a Hong Kong company, encouraged by the availability of cheaper land and labour and the possibility of building a bridgehead for trade, is planning small-scale assembly of buses in China. GM, Ford, Mitsubishi and other Japanese manufacturers have been negotiating for a much larger project. AMC has started detailed planning to begin Jeep production. Although China offers amazing opportunities, it will never become a leading exporting nation (unless it chooses to place export above all else) as production will be fully consumed by domestic demand.

One of the problems in attempting to establish a motor industry in China is its peculiar contractual arrangements. In some cases the foreign company supplies raw materials and components, which are processed by the Chinese for a fee. Another method is compensation trade where the foreign partner supplies capital equipment, the cost of which is repaid by products made with the equipment.

With a population of 36 million, a relatively high and growing *per capita* GNP, South Korea seems to have monopolized the industrial headlines. The country is usually described as a major growth market for the development of manufacturing capacity, but the South Korean case may have been overstated. Annual car demand is currently around

30,000 units (1977). Production (see Table 15.6) is dominated by four firms, three of which are still assembly only. The fourth, Hyundai Motors, is of far greater importance. Hyundai Motors, a subsidiary of the largest industrial corporation in South Korea, began by assembling mainly Ford products, before starting to produce its own indigenous product. KIA Industrial builds Toyo Kogyo products (and presumably Ford products in the future following the Ford-Toyo Kogyo link up). Shinjin Motors builds Jeeps and Asian Motors assemble Fiat cars and Unic trucks. GM set up a joint company with local interests (Saehan Motors) and recently increased its stake in this company.

With a former BL director, George Turnbull, in charge until recently and government support, Hyundai manufactures a small CV range (with locally produced Perkins diesel engines) and the Pony compact four-cylinder car. The latter shows a strong European influence in conception and design; it is manufactured in a fully integrated plant with over 90 per cent local content, though the original Hyundai Pony used a Mitsubishi power train, a body designed in Italy, and pressings, mechanical and electrical components from France and the UK. A replacement for the Pony will be designed in Korea and will buy in certain engine components, it is rumoured from Renault. Hyundai, however, faces several problems: local demand is not large enough to make car production at the existing plants viable; exports are essential, but to be successful in export markets necessitates capital expenditure in overseas dealer networks and replacement stocks.

The South Koreans plan to double car output every year to 2 million in 1991, of which 900,000 would be for export. These plans are ambitious, implying a domestic market of over one million cars per year. Predictions made at the end of this chapter suggest that this forecast is slightly optimistic but not inconceivable. Hyundai's initial capacity was doubled from 50,000 to 100,000 cars in 1979, and plans to increase output to 300,000 cars a year in the mid-1980s are well advanced. Hyundai's export performance has been good: exports in 1977 were 9100 cars and 33,000 cars in 1978, with targets of 60,000 in 1979, 110,000 in 1980 and 160,000 in 1981. Saudi Arabia is Hyundai's principal market, but the Pony sells in 46 countries, largely in developing areas.

The Korean industry is unlikely to let production grow only in line with demand. The government and the manufacturers are ambitious and believe in their capacity to rival Japan's car production. Government action has been designed to encourage exports. One scheme allows the import of CKD kits of Ford Granadas (to meet a growing demand for six-cylinder cars) only in exchange for exports (one imported Granada for five exported Ponies). Another scheme links the financing of domestic car sales to export performance. Direct export subsidies may be introduced, although some observers feel that the government should first remove (or reduce) the punitive Korean car and petrol taxes to encourage domestic demand.

The South Korean labour force is far cheaper than its Japanese counterpart. This gives Korea a competitive advantage over Japan, which may outweigh the lack of economies of scale and enable Korea to undercut Japan's product. Direct competition with the Japanese is obviously not feasible at present, though low labour costs and some scale economies, may confer a price advantage in the long run. (Hyundai, by producing only one model, has achieved the maximum scale economies from their limited production runs; contrast this with the South African and Australian development model.)

Although Taiwan's population is small (16 million), it has a *per capita* GNP equivalent to that of Turkey. Taiwan is becoming highly industrialized and is more advanced in this respect than South Korea. A government forecast projected a vehicle parc in 1991 of 3.8 million, with domestic demand increasing from 75,000 in 1977 to 760,000 units per annum in 1991. Current capacity is about 82,000 vehicles, and the proposed mid-1980s output is planned to be around 200,000 units a year. Of the five car assemblers, four have foreign partners: Nissan, Ford, Honda and Mitsubishi. Nissan is the largest and its projected annual output is over 100,000 units. This foreign owned industry is heavily protected, and production will do little more than meet the projected increase in demand. The components industry is, however, becoming increasingly aware of export potential. Ford have built an engine plant which may source the Philippines and Australia. GM and Ford are discussing plans to build heavy duty trucks with a potential output of 10,000 a year by 1985.

South-east Asia

Indonesia and Malaysia both have substantial levels of oil production *per capita*, and this makes South-east Asia especially important for motor industry development. Indonesia's large population (140 million) places the country in an extremely advantageous position. All the countries in this area have followed the same development path, using manufacturers from the mature markets. In consequence, none of the manufacturers can expect to become major exporters.

The growth of Indonesia's industry has occurred comparatively recently (since 1969), and now comprises some 14 firms assembling a variety of different makes, although there is a predominance of Japanese manufacturers. The Gaya Motor Company (Toyota) is the largest, followed by Nissan. One firm assembles both Mercedes-Benz and VW vehicles. VW's basic transportation vehicle (the 'Mule') is assembled here.

Malaysia, with only 12 million people and a lower *per capita* GNP than Brazil, has the highest car density level in Asia (excluding Japan). Although the Malaysian government hopes to increase local assembly and the local content of existing assembly, the country seems to be too small to support a large manufacturing presence. However, Malaysia is on a par in its motor industry development with Indonesia because of its additional wealth. Most of the companies engaged in the assembly of vehicles are Malaysian-owned and assemble various makes. GM used Malaysia as a base for developing operations in South-east Asia, and its basic transportation vehicle (the 'Harimu') is produced in Malaysia.

Developments in the Philippines are more predictable. At the moment, they have one of the highest vehicle densities in the region and are comparatively wealthy. The population is large enough to provide a substantial domestic market for the rapidly expanding assembly industry. A number of foreign (particularly Japanese) companies are already established, and rapid growth is virtually assured.

The Philippines has largely followed the South American and Australian models of development. There are five assemblers in the country which, in order of size, are the Delta Motor Corporation (Toyota), Car Company (Mitsubishi), Ford, DMG (VW) and GM. Car Company used to be owned by Chrysler and has now been bought by a local Yulo Group of companies, giving the area a degree of independence which may be sufficient to allow an indigenous industry to develop.

Like the Philippines, Thailand has a large and fairly wealthy population and a sizeable car parc, although the industry is top-heavy: 15 companies assemble nearly 25,000 vehicles (including 16,000 cars) covering a number of different models. Increased government intervention can be expected, but political instability will undoubtedly hinder further development.

Assembly operations in Singapore are small and total assembly is less than 10,000 units per year.

The Indian sub-continent

India has a stagnant but fully-fledged production facility; Pakistan has newer assembly operations only. India has a vast potential domestic market but, compared with China, has not achieved growth, and China's *per capita* GNP is nearly three times that of India. India has a larger vehicle parc than China and has had steadier growth, although the distinctive character of the market should not be ignored. The urban areas are heavily industrialized and the existing car parc is already reasonably large, but car ownership is limited to higher income earners. Despite a comprehensive rail system, road haulage and road use are increasing. The Indian motor industry has received enthusiastic support from government planners, who are anxious to promote the development of an industry with full manufacturing status, but new projects involving foreign ownership are discouraged. Joint technical collaboration, with either royalty payments or a minority stake, is still possible, but usually only for a limited period and only in certain circumstances.

One of the greatest strengths of the Indian motor industry lies in the components industry, which not only met most of the domestic component requirements but in 1973-74 grossed export earnings of over $14 million. The Indian government has encouraged the motor vehicle manufacturers to follow this example, but the producers cannot be expected to show impressive export results until they have improved their product. At the moment, the Indian car is hopelessly outdated in design and engineering. Although the industry has enormous potential, growth will depend not only on improvements in model design but on political and economic factors, all of which make it difficult to predict future expansion with any certainty.

The industry has a total capacity of almost 100,000 units a year, and this capacity has increased steadily. The car producers are Hindustan Motors which produces a derivative of the 1954 Morris Oxford (the 'Ambassador') and Premier Motors (which produces a late 1950s Fiat 1100 under licence).

The CV producers are split between four manufacturers. Jeeps are made under licence by Mahindra and Mahindra. Ashok Leyland produces CVs (having ceased production of the Triumph Herald), Bajai Tempo makes light trucks, and Tata Engineering makes a derivative of a Mercedes-Benz truck. British Leyland owns a 52 per cent stake in Ashok Leyland, and Daimler-Benz owns a small stake in Tata Engineering. Otherwise, following the withdrawal of GM and Ford in 1954, there are no other foreign participants. (MAN and Nissan make trucks exclusively for the huge Indian military machine.) The industry is highly protected, produces high-priced products and has been accused of inefficiency and production of defective parts. Delivery times on cars run into years and supply has never caught up with demand.

Why has India's stagnant car industry not satisfied domestic demand? With a ready market for its products at existing capacity levels and a protected market, expansion simply was not worth the effort. Any expansion would have been confronted with a range of bureaucratic and administrative obstacles which would have taken several years to overcome. Successive governments did not actively encourage expansion, though Indira Gandhi's modernization programme was committed to a 100 per cent indigenously produced people's car. This was an interesting proposition, but never got off the ground; less than 20 cars were ever made and the model failed to meet its design specification. The 'Hindustan' is fuel-inefficient: it is too heavy and has an inefficient engine which uses heavy steel parts. A possible collaborative venture with British Leyland to introduce a lighter, cheaper model with good fuel consumption is being sought.

The Indian industry has some way to go before it satisfies local demand, produces a modern low priced product or begins to export. However, the Indian motor industry is independent and supports a large components industry. The infrastructure is there; if the petty restrictions and bureaucracy could be overcome, India could become a major producer with a high proportion of the product exported, though this is more likely to occur in CVs than cars.

Pakistan has some relatively small-scale CV assembly plant; GM and Toyota are two of the main companies involved.

Future infant markets

Having examined the development of supply in infant industries, we must now consider future demand in these areas. The countries listed in Table 15.1 are used as a basis for projecting population, *per capita* GNP, motor vehicle densities and the projected vehicle parc in 1990.[1] A summary of the projections is shown in Table 15.5, and Table 15.6 gives a detailed breakdown. It should be emphasized that these projections assume that there are sufficient supplies of motor vehicles to meet the projected demand.

The projections for the region embody two sets of assumptions. Scenario 1 assumes realistic growth rates based on experiences in the 1960s and 1970s; the effect of the oil crises has been taken into account in these projected growth rates. However, some observers would argue that the energy crises have so affected the economic system that growth rates of one or 2 per cent will become the norm in growing countries, and the fastest growth achievable will be 3 or 4 per cent.

Scenario 1 suggests that by 1990 these areas will have a combined vehicle parc of over 57 million (assuming the bottom end of the range for China), with an annual demand of some 5-14 million vehicles a year. A central projection predicts the market size to be around 10-12 million vehicles a year, 3-4 million of which would be CVs. This forecast is by no means optimistic and it would be quite possible for demand to exceed these levels, though growth rates will differ widely between regions.

This forecast suggests that all these areas will have significantly increased demand by 1990. Central and East Africa and South Asia (excluding India) will amount to significant markets. North and West Africa (mainly Nigeria) could establish an annual demand in excess of 0.5 million vehicles. Turkey, South Korea, Taiwan and Indonesia may

---

1. See Appendix 3 for an explanation of the methodology and a more detailed breakdown of the statistics of this forecast.

Table 15.5 *Projected vehicle parc and demand for 1990*

	Scenario 1		Scenario 2	
	Motor vehicle parc	Annual demand	Motor vehicle parc	Annual demand
	(millions)		(millions)	
North Africa (Algeria, Morocco, Tunisia)	2.7	0.2-0.6	2.3	0.15-0.5
Turkey	6.0	0.4-1.0	4.0	0.25-0.8
Central and East Africa (Kenya, Zaire, Ethiopia, Sudan, Tanzania, Uganda)	2.3+	0.2-0.5	1.8	0.1 -0.4
West Africa (Nigeria, Ivory Coast, Ghana)	3.9	0.3-0.7	2.8	0.2 -0.5
China	3-16	0.3-3.0	3-11	0.3 -2.0
South Korea	5.5	0.5-1.0	2.8	0.2 -0.8
Taiwan	3.2	0.4-0.8	2.5	0.2 -0.7
Indonesia	4.0	0.5-1.0	3.0	0.4 -0.8
Rest of South-East Asia (Malaysia, Philippines, Thailand, Vietnam, Burma)	7.0	0.7-2.0	4.8	0.5 -1.5
India	7.3	0.5-1.5	4.9	0.3 -1.0
Rest of South Asia (Pakistan, Bangladesh, Afghanistan, Sri Lanka, Nepal)	2.1	0.2-0.4	1.7	0.1 -0.3
Others	10	1.0	5	0.5
	57.0+*	5.2-13.5	38.6+*	3.2 -9.8

* Assumes China's vehicle parc at lowest point in projected range

experience demand up to one million vehicles per year — a viable volume for a cheap labour cost area. India's population growth ensures that demand and vehicle parc will grow over time. China's demand depends on policy decisions and is difficult to predict.

Scenario 2 incorporates pessimistic growth assumptions. It projects a vehicle parc of over 39 million, and annual demand of 3-10 million vehicles, giving a central forecast, would be around 7-8 million vehicles a year.

Whichever scenario is correct, these regions will have an annual demand equivalent to or approaching that of the current (and future) North American or Western European markets, and demand in excess of that predicted for Japan in 1990. Who will supply these regions? This question is discussed in the concluding section.

Table 15.6 *Production and assembly in selected developing countries in 1977 by manufacturer*

	Car	CV
Morocco		
Aetco Lever Maroc-Land Rover (BL)	—	764
Renault	9382	5664
Ford	—	1440
Saida-Bedford (GM)	—	1222
Saida-Volvo	—	739
Jeep (AMC)	—	92
Fiat	6205	—
Opel (GM)	468	—
Simca/Talbot (Peugeot-Citroen)	4771	630
Daf	—	109
	20,826	10,658
Turkey		
British Leyland	—	6772
Celik Montaj (Skoda)	—	655
Chrysler	—	6597
Cifteiler	—	901
Genoto (GM)	—	3828
MAN	—	806
Otobus Karoseri (Magirus)	—	573
Otosan (Otosan cars, Ford CVs)	—	12,536
Otoyol and Tofas (Fiat)	19,212	1892
Oyak (Renault)	33,668	—
TOE (International Harvester)	—	1335
	58,739	41,455
South Korea		
Asia Motors (Fiat cars, Unic trucks)	—	1325
Hyundai Motor	27,466	10,788
Kia Industrial Company (Toyo Kogyo)	10,548	18,936
Saehan Motors (GM)	4270	9667
Shinjin Jeep Company (AMC)	1697	—
	43,981	40,716
Philippines		
Amalgamated Motors (BL)	—	204
Car Company (Mitsubishi)	8494	4338
DMG (VW)	3669	334
Delta Motors (Toyota)	12,801	7674
Ford Philippines	3651	7724
Francisco Motors (Toyo Kogyo and Pinoy)	—	2752
GM	2474	3814
International Harvester	—	336
Pilipinas Hino	—	284
Renault Philippines	178	—
Universal Motors (Nissan)	602	161
	31,869	27,521

Table 15.6 *continued*

	Car	CV
Malaysia		
Associated Motor Industry		
Albion	—	80
Austin/Morris	1783	378
Chrysler	105	—
Commer	—	17
Ford	6543	1394
Leyland	—	17
Asia Automobile Industry		
Mazda	5619	629
Peugeot	1081	—
B G Motors		
Seddon	—	54
Cycle and Carriage		
Mercedes Benz	—	1114
General Motors		
Bedford/Harimau/Luv	—	541
Holden	125	—
Honda	4	282
Opel	3138	—
Kelang Pembena Kereta		
Alfa Romeo	263	—
Fiat	1367	—
Mitsubishi	6695	326
Motor Associates		
Audi	53	—
Bedford	—	1290
Holden	45	—
Land Rover	—	614
Mercedes Benz	1954	—
Renault	249	—
Toyota	11,404	927
Vauxhall	31	—
Volkswagen	302	291
Swedish Motor		
Alfa Romeo	643	—
Daihatsu	121	458
Datsun	1530	291
Volvo	720	18
Tan Chong and Sons Motor		
Datsun	8708	1577
	52,483	10,298
India		
Ashok (Leyland [BL])	—	8083
Bajai Tempo	—	4770
Hindustan Motors (BL)	20,256	969
Mahindra and Mahindra (AMC)	—	10,547
Premier Automobiles (Fiat)	17,481	1881
Standard Motor (BL)	112	1617
Tata Engineering and Locomotive Co (Mercedes)	—	23,419
	37,849	31,556

Source: Automobile International

Part 4: Conclusion

Chapter 16

The Future

General economic background and the energy problem

First, we may list some of the main assumptions about the economic background; many of these, particularly for the mature markets, are already a reality.

1. Higher rates of inflation.
2. Slower economic growth because of:
   - ☐ firmer action by national governments to curtail inflation
   - ☐ a move away from growth objectives *per se* towards environmental considerations and concern for the quality of life
   - ☐ world capital shortage
   - ☐ rising relative cost of primary commodities, suggesting that resource-poor countries may have to allocate a greater proportion of their wealth to pay for them
   - ☐ slower growth in productivity
   - ☐ restrictions on growth in resource-poor countries to cut down imports.
3. Possible trade restrictions.
4. Changing labour attitudes in advanced countries:
   - ☐ increasing worker dissatisfaction with semi-skilled jobs
   - ☐ growing worker concern with the fruits of their labour rather than the 'labour' itself, which may mean a higher real cost of labour
   - ☐ demands for a shorter working week and increased leisure time
   - ☐ realization that labour is not a completely variable unit of production, making it impossible to hire or fire labour at will in line with the movement of the trade cycle
   - ☐ increased labour participation in industrial management.

Increased government intervention — in economic policies, control of design (eg safety regulations, pollution control and limitations on fuel consumption) and consumer legislation — is now firmly established. A new development is direct intervention in the management of the motor industry and competitive bidding by government to attract new motor industry investment.

Energy considerations

Oil reserves are rapidly being depleted, and are unlikely to last beyond 2025.[1] New propulsion systems, new vehicle designs, and new materials may create a more fuel-efficient, vehicle, but this will *not* radically improve the situation. This book has predicted that vehicle ownership will increase in most areas, and will remain more or less static in some of the more mature markets. How can these conflicting trends be reconciled?

Before examining this question in greater detail, a reminder of the experience following the 1973 oil crisis may be useful. The degree to which demand recovered in North America and particularly Western Europe, surprised most observers. Some consider America's apparent unsusceptibility to saturation to be a largely artificial phenomenon, produced by continued government subsidy of oil. Table 16.1 shows the extent to which the US consumer has been protected from world-wide fuel prices.

Table 16.1 *Comparative fuel prices*
(premium petrol in 1977 per US gallon)

	Pump price ($)	Price adjusted for per capita GNP differences ($)
US	0.67	0.67
Western Europe	1.6	2.44
Britain	1.15	2.33
Germany	1.46	1.59
France	1.79	2.15
Italy	2.12	5.54
Spain	1.6	4.44

This, however, ignores one of the main lessons learned since 1973: the recovery in demand throughout the world has been spectacular and cannot be explained purely on cost grounds. Nearly all the forecasters in the industry failed to predict the record vehicle demand levels experienced in France and West Germany in the mid-1970s. The price of oil was not subsidized in either market and the cost of vehicle ownership dramatically increased, yet by 1976 (within three years of the oil crisis), demand had exceeded the 1973 peak. The consumer's preference for motor vehicles is not as price-sensitive as might be imagined and it appears that the Western social system cannot exist without the car.

If oil supplies are exhausted, how will a society dominated by

1. This estimate is based on the consumption of proven *and* projected 'new' reserves.

personalized transport satisfy its demand? The solution appears to be to find an alternative source of power (see Table 16.2). Much publicity has been given to the electric/battery car as the replacement to the internal combustion engine. A battery-powered car might satisfy a limited urban demand in the 1980s, but it is too inflexible a solution to be of general applicability.

Table 16.2 *Some alternatives to petrol*

Alternative fuel	Comments
Synthetic oil from shale	Extremely likely for countries with shale deposits
Synthetic oil from coal by refining extraction	Technology still needs some development
Methanol/Ethanol	Bulky, heavy and expensive to produce
Ammonia	Corrosive, toxic, requires pressure container
Hydrogen	Bulky and requires special handling and storage facilities
Propane developed from coal	Requires pressure container
Electricity	If adopted widely would need extra generating stations. Inflexible and limited range
Powdered carbon	Technology and pollution problems

The most likely solution is to find a fuel (probably a liquid or a gas) which can be substituted for petrol. An intermediate stage may be to extend the amount of energy yielded by a given volume of petrol, since many of the alternatives require massive capital expenditures and would only be feasible if developed on an enormous scale. It seems likely that the future development of alternative fuels will be based on a variety of acceptable alternatives rather than a single 'global' replacement. Individual countries will attempt to become self-sufficient in energy by developing whatever local alternatives are available. Brazil is gradually replacing petrol with hydrated ethyl alcohol produced from sugar cane. Manufacturers, including GM, are gearing up engine production to produce multi-fuel engines capable of accepting petrol, alcohol and other fuels.

Though not as cataclysmic in their impact on demand as might have been imagined, the 1973 and the 1978 oil crises cannot be ignored. The shock to the Western world has registered (with governments if not consumers) and the conclusions on demand in this book have been modified by recent events.

Automation

An important supply consideration is the possible drop in labour productivity, caused by a shorter working week, and the job dissatisfaction inherent in semi-skilled assembly work. The only economic solution to this boring and repetitive process is to automate the process and use the labour force profitably in maintaining the equipment. Either solution has important employment implications: no employment in the car manufacturing industry because of the uncompetitiveness of the industry, or some employment in a competitive industry.

The reduction in employment consequent upon automation is not as great as might be supposed. The mechanical parts of the equipment would need regular servicing. There would also be a new area of electronic maintenance. Each robotic piece of equipment may require a human monitor in case of faulty operation or if the repertoire of programmed instructions did not include the particular set of events which were found to occur. In addition, whenever a new model or operation is introduced, the computerized equipment needs reprogramming. This software development will require substantial manpower. The reduction of the labour force would be of the order of 30-40 per cent, although the nature of the work would change and a substantial retraining programme might be necessary.

The mature markets

The mature markets are dealt with first since this is where the established producers are, and where the greatest pressure on the motor industry will occur.

Product trends

Three factors will constrain product developments for the mature markets in the future. First, environmental awareness is growing: the motor vehicle can no longer be produced without ecology and the environment being considered. Second, the declining growth in demand, coupled with a slowing down in exports and rising import penetration, places enormous pressure to lower costs in a competitive field. This may result in the search for increased standardization to take advantage of the scale savings for a given production volume and on a more easily produced vehicle. Third, these pressures will add $1-2000 per vehicle; consumers will, therefore, demand a product with improved reliability, easier repair and maintenance, and greater comfort. For the North American car, the weight reduction necessarily requires a drastic cut in the length of the vehicle, while preserving the maximum amount of interior room. The mature producer will produce a standardized car which will be front-wheel drive and fairly compact. These new world-wide vehicles will alter the competitiveness of the manufacturers across the mature areas, and increasingly mean that the markets of the mature areas (North America, Western Europe and Japan) will be merged into a single indistinguishable market, in which some 23-33 million vehicles (the upper and lower limits for demand) will be sold annually during the 1980s.

For CVs the tendency in all countries will be for a growth in the demand for linehaul trucks (which are used on motorways) and panel vans. However, there will be less standardization in Japan, where the small CV dominates and is likely to dominate in the medium term. For the US, diesel CVs will become the order of the day, and this will provide the West European CV producers with an opportunity to enter the lucrative US market. The North American phenomenon of RVs will not be followed to the same extent in West Europe or Japan. The increase in leisure time in North America will ensure the continuation of RV ownership, but its growth will, to some extent, be retarded.

Market development

A fundamental conclusion is that, given current events, the growth in demand in the mature markets will not continue indefinitely; the total market must begin to stabilize. The market will then comprise a large element of replacement demand and only a small element of new demand. As well as stagnation in the growth of demand, a feature of a mature market was a cyclical fluctuation in demand: the more mature the market, the greater the amplitude of the cycles. The reasoning behind this observation depends on replacement demand, and the degree to which the replacement decision can be postponed. Table 16.3 shows how demand has evolved since 1955 and its projected future development.[1]

North America's early dominance in demand has been caught up by Western Europe. Japan looked set to catch and pass both mature markets, but the oil crises, the question of energy resources and the impact of environmental considerations have altered this trend. Chapter 9, using a more plausible set of assumptions, postulated that Japan

1. In his foreword to the book, Michael Hinks-Edwards indicated that he felt some of the projections were on the high side. In terms of demand predictions, the 1980 forecast is below the consensus forecast given in the foreword and the 1990 range estimates are consistent with the single demand projection of 45 million cars.

It is on production that the consensus forecast suggested by Michael Hinks-Edwards and the predictions contained in the book disagree most. Whereas the consensus view specifies car production for the mature markets at some 31 million, the forecast contained here puts production considerably lower. This implies that my view of the developing and infant procedures is for their production to be proportionately higher. However, inherent in my forecasts is an element of double counting (ie kits from a mature market counted as well as local assembly in a developing region) and qualitatively the two forecasts may not be that far apart.

Table 16.3 Market demand[1] for motor vehicles (millions)

	1955	1960	1970	1973-78 Peak[2]	1980 Forecast	1985	1990
	Actual					Projection range	
Cars							
North America	8.3	7.0	9.0	12.3	10.5	11-12	8.0-13.5
Western Europe	1.8	3.5	7.9	10.4	9.0	10-12	9.0-13.5
Japan	0.03	0.1	2.4	2.9	2.5	2.3-3.5	2.0-3.8
Total for mature markets	10.13	10.7	19.3	25.6	22.0	23.5-27.5	19.0-30.8
Rest of the world	0.8	1.3	2.6	5.9	6.5	9-16	15-27
Total	10.93	12.0	21.9	31.5	28.5	32.5-43.5	34-57.8
CVs							
North America	1.3	1.0	1.9	4.4	3.0	2.0-3.0	1.5-3.0
Western Europe	0.5	0.7	1.0	1.2	1.0	1.0-1.3	0.9-1.35
Japan	0.1	0.3	1.7	2.0	1.6	1.6-2.1	1.0-2.0
Total for mature markets	1.9	2.0	4.6	7.6	5.6	4.6-6.4	3.4-6.35
Rest of the world	0.8	0.9	1.5	3.1	3.3	4.2-8	7-15
Total	2.7	2.9	6.1	10.7	8.9	8.8-14.4	10.4-21.35

1. Defined as new registrations
2. Peak year for region between 1973-78

would not continue its rapid growth and would probably not be comparable to North America in size or to Western Europe in productive capacity by the 1990s.

For North America a central forecast was made in Chapter 6; however, GM and Ford are predicting an annual car demand of 15 million in the 1980s. If these more optimistic forecasts are correct, by the 1990s vehicle ownership will approach one car per person (ie several cars per household). The lower scenario envisaged in Chapter 6 seems more plausible with an annual demand for cars of 8-13.5 million. Western Europe's demand range offered three scenarios; the one chosen in Chapter 8 was the central forecast, giving growth of car demand of 12-13 million cars a year; superimposed on this demand is the detrimental effect of the two oil crises in the 1970s, which has modified the forecasts downwards. Similarly, a conservative view of events has been predicted for Japan.

The bottom end of the CV projection range appears catastrophic for the CV industry. This range assumes that the troughs of all the producers will occur simultaneously. Except in the case of RVs, evidence from the mature markets suggests that during maturity the number of CVs demanded declines or stagnates, because of a switch to larger and heavier CVs with higher carrying loads. The peculiar North American demand for RVs will not be repeated elsewhere, and in the US RVs will be bought in far fewer numbers.

The mature markets, because of the increased standardization of the motor vehicle across all three markets, will integrate into a single homogeneous market, with a few local or regional variations (eg RVs in North America, extremely small cars in Japan). Annual sales in this market will be 19-31 million cars and 3.4-6.4 million CVs.

Although demand is forecast to grow slightly, the growth will be confined mainly to the newer and developing markets. Newer producers, irrespective of ownership, will emerge as the dominant force behind future growth of demand. Demand by 1990 in the rest of the world will be equal to, if not greater than, that of the three mature markets, though vehicle ownership will be below those found in the West today.

Growth of demand and saturation

Growth of demand in the rest of the world will become a major element in the motor vehicle market, but vehicle ownership rates will not, in general, reach those achieved in the mature markets. Similarly, vehicle ownership in Japan may not be as dense as in Europe, and European ownership will not reach the levels achieved in North America. The reasons are numerous and include the energy crisis, pollution considerations, the degree of available space, lifestyle and lower *per capita* incomes outside the developed countries.

One of the problems with the motor vehicle is that it is part of modern life and yet incompatible with it. We argued in Chapter 3 that demand for cars arises in an urban society in the process of urbanization and industrialization. Cars aid society in the complicated structure inherent in urban society, where specialization and division of labour have occurred. This process creates congestion and congestion requires new roads to be built. Once built, the increased capacity of the new roads leading into the centre of a town (or new parking facilities) tends to be used up as fast as the new capacity is generated. Construction of new roads linking a central business district with a sparsely populated peripheral area usually results in the rapid commercial and residential development of the area adjacent to the new road. The new development attracted by the new road — built to cure an existing congestion problem — increases traffic and adds to the original congestion problem in the central areas. Hence the conclusion that reliance on travel by car as the only form of transport is essentially incompatible with high-density urban development.

The motor vehicle, particularly in North America, has changed the whole style of living. The motor vehicle influences the location of work, home and schooling, and the scope of our leisure. To reduce reliance on the motor vehicle would mean relocating a whole range of services, factories, shops, leisure centres, etc. Some industries or services dependent on customers use of a car would collapse, and the cost to society would be considerable.

Housing has been greatly affected by the motor vehicle. The phenomenon is illustrated by the urban sprawl of Southern California, London, and parts of Japan, which have resulted from the increased accessibility afforded by widespread vehicle ownership and the investment cost of building roads to serve those cars. In Southern California, population density is now too low to be served economically by any other mode, and a public transport service might, in any case, not be effective. To reduce vehicle ownership implies adopting a new lifestyle, building new towns and factories, redesigning the concept of a central business district, and so on. All this may be possible in the long term — with improved telecommunications, viewdata systems, etc — but, given current levels of technology, will be difficult to achieve.

There is no possibility that vehicle ownership will be abandoned in the mature markets; alternative forms of transport may be used more, but the requirement to own a vehicle will still exist. Its convenience and flexibility ensure the survival of the motor vehicle.

Newer developing societies which have not yet built massive urban areas, capable of functioning only through the existence of the motor vehicle, have the opportunity to develop alternative lifestyles, less dependent on the motor vehicle.

Production

Increased competition, huge expenditure on design and production facilities, increased concentration leading to higher economies of scale, declining markets and an uncertain future mean that the mature producers will face a difficult period. Western Europe has recently challenged North America's dominance (see Table 16.4), and Japan's phenomenal growth of production capacity is not far behind Europe, but is unlikely to exceed North America and Western Europe.

Further growth of production facilities for the mature producers as a whole will not occur except at the margin. Stagnation in the growth of demand for motor vehicles is the main reason for this. As the market matures, so labour and other costs (eg land) rise, and newer producers operating from low cost bases are able to undercut the mature producers, especially the demand for cheap basic products. Rising import penetration is thus a standard feature of a mature market. For similar reasons, declining exports, except for specialized vehicles, are also a 'built-in' phenomenon of a mature market.

North America's early dominance in production was overtaken by Western Europe, which was the leading exporter and a net exporter to North America. Japan displaced Western Europe as the leading exporting region, and Europe has followed North America, and now suffers from declining exports (eclipsed by Japan) and rising import penetration (mainly from Japan). But Japan cannot sustain its phenomenal growth rates, will experience the problems inherent in maturity, and, even using optimistic assumptions, will not produce more than 7.5 million cars and 4 million CVs a year in the short to medium term. Japan will thus not be on an equal footing with North America or Western Europe, and its export dominance may be cut back by new producers with lower production costs.

Car capacity

In Western Europe there is now sufficient installed capacity to meet the projected demand for the 1980s. Even so, some manufacturers will reduce capacity (British Leyland, VW and Fiat), while others will expand (GM and Ford). Including RV capacity, North America also has ample capacity. Only Japan may expand car production, since over 50 per cent of car production is exported, but this depends crucially on whether this export level is maintained. In Chapter 9 we concluded that Japan's capacity might reach a peak in 1985.

CV capacity

With demand in most Western European CV markets still at pre-1974

Table 16.4 Supply[1] of motor vehicles (millions)

	1955	1960	1970	1973-78[2]	1980	1985	1990
	Actual				Forecast	Projection range	
Cars							
North America	8.3	7.0	7.5	10.9	9.2	8.5-10.5	6.7-9.7
Western Europe	2.5	5.1	10.4	11.5	11.3	11-13	9-13.5
Japan	0.02	0.2	3.2	5.8	5.7	6.7	5-6.5
Total for mature markets	10.82	12.3	21.1	28.3	26.2	24.5-29.5	20.7-29.7
Rest of the world	0.2	0.6	1.9	4.2	5.0	8-15	13-35
World total	11.02	12.9	23.0	32.5	31.2	32.5-44.5	33.7-54.7
CVs							
North America	1.3	1.3	2.0	4.4	3.0	1.9-2.9	1.4-2.7
Western Europe	0.7	1.0	1.3	1.4	1.3	1.1-1.4	1.0-1.45
Japan	0.05	0.3	2.1	3.3	2.9	2.6-3.0	2-3
Total for mature markets	2.05	2.6	5.4	9.1	7.2	5.6-7.3	2.6-6.15
Rest of the world	0.3	0.7	1.2	1.9	2.8	4-7	6-14
World total	2.35	3.3	6.6	11.0	10.0	9.6-14.3	8.6-20.15

1. Defined as production and/or assembly of vehicles
2. Peak year for region between 1973-78

levels, the outlook for the Western European producers is not good. Indeed, the rationalization of the European producers has been occurring at an accelerating rate. North America, with the switch away from RVs, has excess capacity. Japanese capacity will again depend on the ability to hold on to export markets. The structure of the Japanese CV production will move away from volume CVs to medium and large trucks; hence, in future production figures, no growth may be discernable, although production value will be far higher.

The new growth areas

Figure 16.1 shows production of all motor vehicles and estimates of future production.

Table 16.4 assumes that the future supply of motor vehicles will stagnate and that new growth will occur outside established markets, and might intrude into the mature markets (as imports) causing further problems for the mature producers. This leads to an important question: given that Japan will become more like Western Europe, who will take the place of Japan as a major new producer and exporter of motor vehicles?

Figure 16.1 *Production* by major region 1950-90*

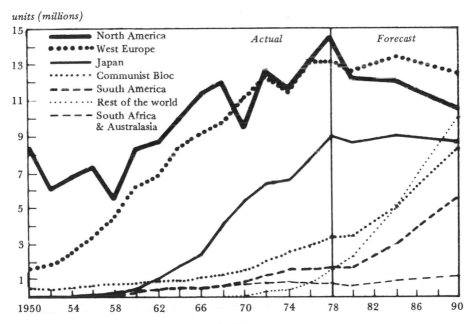

* Defined as production and/or assembly of vehicles

There are three possibilities. First, one particular area, such as the Communist Bloc, could supplant Japan. Second, a number of smaller producers may jointly become the new mass motor vehicle producer. Third, there may be no successor to Japan; instead, the three mature producers may become the core producing regions, with the peripheral areas being developed through subsidiaries of major motor manufacturers based in established areas. There are industries, such as cement and steel production, which are concentrated in certain areas with a wider diffusion across the remainder of the world. The latter theory looks the most plausible.

There are two major arguments against the diffusion theory. First, economies of scale provide an enormous impetus to build up local centres of production. Second, the centre of some industrial production (eg textiles) has shifted dramatically to where the bulk of the world's population is; traditional centres have declined rapidly (the US now ranks as the 26th largest producer). In the production of television sets, Japan, the Communist Bloc, South Korea and Taiwan are increasing production, while US production has declined. An even more striking example is radio set production, and Table 16.5 shows how the fortunes of various producers have changed fairly radically over the years. There is clear evidence that production has been switched from the mature markets to newer producers. Throughout the period about two-thirds of total world production was concentrated in the six countries listed.

Table 16.5 *Radio set production by main producer*
(millions of units)

	1960	1970	1976
Japan	12.9	32.6	16.8
USSR	4.2	7.8	8.4
Taiwan	0	6.2	6.8
South Korea	0	1.1	6.6
USA	10.7	8.3	6.1
West Germany	4.3	6.7	4.4
Total	52	86	66

Source: The Economist: The World in Figures

The newer producers

The 'Old Colonials' were discussed as being relatively unimportant markets. Both Australia and South Africa had no indigenous producer, and supply will probably do little more than keep pace with demand. Of the new production centres, the Communist Bloc has the largest potential demand followed by South America and the Middle East.

The joint estimates provided in Table 16.6 illustrate the range of predictions given in Part 3. All three regions have used Western technology. The South American motor industry is controlled by major US and European companies, and it is, therefore, unlikely to become a major or mature producer unless the US or European companies source sales from production centres in South America to North America.

Table 16.6 *Demand and supply[1] for the new producers (millions)*

	1977	1980	1985	1990
Communist Bloc				
Demand — cars	1.9	2.5	3.6	5.0
— CVs	0.9	1.0	1.7	1.5
Supply[1] — cars	2.1	2.7	4.0	6.0
— CVs	1.0	1.2	2.0	2.3
South America				
Demand — cars	1.5	1.6	2.5	3.0
— CVs	0.5	0.6	1.0	1.3
Supply[1] — cars	1.5	1.6	2.5	3.0
— CVs	0.5	0.6	1.0	1.3
Middle East				
Demand — cars	0.4	0.4	0.9	1.5
— CVs	0.3	0.3	0.5	0.7
Supply[1] — cars	0.2	0.3	0.9	1.3
— CVs	0.2	0.2	0.3	0.6
South Africa and Australasia				
Demand — cars	1.0	0.8	0.8	0.8
— CVs	0.3	0.3	0.3	0.3
Supply[1] cars	1.0	0.8	0.8	0.8
— CVs	0.3	0.3	0.3	0.3

1. Includes assembly only operations

At the moment there is such a political cloud over Iran and other countries in the Middle East, that even the conservative assumptions in Chapter 13 may be too optimistic. On the other hand, the industry in Iran is controlled by the Iranians, rapid growth may occur, and the Iranian motor industry would then benefit from increased economies of scale.

The Communist Bloc, with indigenous control of the industry, is perhaps the only new producer with a chance of being able to follow Japan. This would, however, require active state support of an expansion of private car transport and massive capital expenditure. The Lada and Polski Fiat companies have demonstrated that they can produce new models independently of Fiat (which supplied the original technology). If the projection in 1990 is correct (in Chapter 11 a range of estimates were provided, not just a single point estimate), the

Communist Bloc would be producing about as many motor vehicles as Japan. It is doubtful whether the Communist Bloc would ever wish to promote exports to the same extent as Japan; a more limited objective would include exports to Western Europe and some spheres of Russian influence.

Growth in the future will occur in the newer and infant producers. Production will, however, be far more diffuse than previously, and will spread worldwide with quality production remaining in the mature areas and cheap basic production dominated by the newer producers. Given this greater diffusion, there will, however, be room for some concentration within the newer producing areas. Whether the motor industry will follow textiles and the radio manufacturing industry is largely dependent on the manufacturers' strategy.

The infant producers

If the performance of Taiwan and Korea in electronics is indicative of growth potential in vehicle manufacture, they will certainly establish a major domestic industry. Logically Taiwan, South Korea and Japan should form a single producing area (like Western Europe), but political problems rule this out, at least in the short term. By integrating production, the three countries would have a combined market of some 4-5 million cars a year, which, coupled with some exports, could keep the major motor vehicle manufacturers in this area viable.

China is the largest potential market. No doubt it will eventually establish an enormous industry and produce motor vehicles probably for current consumption only. However, all the regions discussed in the previous chapter have some hope of establishing a motor industry, with North Africa and South-east Asia (including Indonesia and the Philippines) particularly likely prospects for development.

Supply problems

When each region is examined individually, local characteristics and the development history of the area often conspire to produce a unique set of problems facing the motor industry in a particular market. First we return to the mature markets and its problems, especially the enormous sums to be spent on capital investment.

Investment

The search for energy saving devices, attempts to reduce the worst environmental hazards associated with the motor vehicle, and the introduction of new production technology necessitate phenomenal expenditures. GM's investment programme from 1978-83 will be greater

than the cost of landing a man on the moon. The US producers alone
are to spend some $75 billion, and the total worldwide cost could
exceed $200 billion over a 10-year period. These tremendous additional
overheads will tend to increase the minimum viable annual volume for a
motor car manufacturer from one million to 2 million cars. The extra
design and engineering costs involved in preparing for these newer
products involve an additional 5000 staff. Including variable administrative and overhead costs, the additional staff will probably involve an
additional recurrent outlay of some $300-400 million. Ford and GM do
not need to employ any additional staff; they can simply stop design
teams in different parts of the world carrying out duplicate work. GM,
for example, before it rationalized its model policy on a worldwide
basis, had parallel design teams in the US, UK, Germany, Australia,
South Africa and South America.

Regional difficulties

The Western European situation is critical for, although the market is
mature, the industrial structure is not. Despite increasing rationalization,
Western Europe still has too many motor vehicle manufacturers
producing too many low-volume models; this is especially crucial in
car, van and small truck production. However, a feature of all three
mature markets is that the concentration of the industry is increasing,
and more international links and mergers will occur.
    The switch to smaller cars (similar to some European models) in
North America may induce the US manufacturers to try to export to
Western Europe. In Part 2, this was discounted because the profitability
of the US manufacturers' European plants would decline. Rising import
penetration on the home market, coupled with heavy government
control and an anti-car lobby, will make North America a much less
profitable market.
    The two large independent Japanese manufacturers, Toyota and
Nissan, will have to diversify the location of production. Continued
growth of export demand from Japanese assembled motor vehicles
(especially cars) is simply no longer possible on the scale previously
experienced.

Diseconomies of scale

In Chapter 4 doubts were expressed as to whether companies as large as
GM would be sufficiently responsive to market conditions. It would be
easy for organizational and administrative diseconomies to cause
corporate management to underestimate the basic and turbulent nature
of changes in the business environment that will take place on a
global scale during the 1980s. GM seemed insensitive to the business

environment during the late 1960s and early 1970s, but has since demonstrated that it can react correctly and with speed. GM's strategy towards its new US models and its increasing attention to European and world developments cannot be faulted. If GM continues increasing in strength, one must conclude that the supposed organizational diseconomies do not exist, or at least can be overcome.

The manufacturers

In Chapter 5, we identified 10 groupings of companies that might exist in the 1980s, though we were cautious in predicting the way in which groupings might change through mergers, takeovers, etc. Whether mergers actually occur or not, cooperative ventures between manufacturers are likely to increase. Given enormous international pressures, it is inconceivable that the French government would not try to encourage collaboration (if not merger) between Renault and PSA Peugeot-Citroen: fierce competition between the two companies could be extremely expensive for the French government, who might have to provide funds to allow Renault to keep pace with the larger, privately owned company. There can be little doubt that eventually, the common French national interest will force the two companies closer together.

One can identify six major car manufacturers likely to dominate world production — GM, Ford, French group (including Renault, PSA Peugeot-Citroen) and AMC, Volvo and associated companies, Toyota, Nissan and a Communist Bloc grouping centred on Lada (see Table 16.7). The basic criterion for these major groups would be to have production capabilities spread across the world, with a total annual capacity of 6 million or more vehicles. GM, Ford and the French group would produce models in the seven standard car segments, and a range of vehicles covering all segments of the CV market. Toyota, Nissan and Lada would concentrate a far larger proportion of their capacity on the Third World; the USSR may learn that supplying technology and assembly plants is an effective way of providing political propaganda and a 'presence' in the Third World.

China has been excluded from consideration here because the possibilities are numerous. The Lada and Japanese groups are unlikely to get a toe-hold in China, whereas Ford, GM and the French group may.

This leaves various other groups which may experience one of three possibilities: independence, collapse or merger with one of the major groups. It is interesting that the six major groups together have an annual capacity of some 50-60 million vehicles a year. In most realistic scenarios for world demand, this should be ample to service the world's needs during the 1990s, with a shift in the proportion of vehicles produced outside the mature markets. There must be no natural presumption, therefore, that what are by any standards huge companies

Table 16.7 *Manufacturers' motor vehicle capacity* [1]
in 1990-2000 (millions)

	Mature markets	Communist Bloc	South America	Middle East	Other[2]
Major manufacturers					
GM group[3]	9-10	0.1	1.0	0.2	1.0
Ford group[4]	8-9	—	1.0	0.1	1.0
French group[5]	5-6	0.2	0.3	1.0	0.2
Toyota group	4-5	—	0.2	0.1	2.0
Nissan group	3-4	—	0.2	0.1	2.0
Lada group[6]	3-5	3-6	0.2	0.1	3.0
	32-39	3.3-6.3	2.9	1.6	9.2
Unattached group					
Chrysler)	3.0	—	—	—	1.0
Mitsubishi)	1.0	—	—	—	
VW	2.5	0.1	1-2	0.1	0.5
Fiat/IVECO	2.0	0.5	0.5	—	0.5
British Leyland)	1.0	—	—	—	0.2
Honda)	1.0	—	—	—	0.2
Huyundai	—	—	—	—	1.0

1. Includes production and assembly of cars and CVs
2. Excluding China where the possibilities are endless
3. Includes Isuzu
4. Includes Toyo Kogyo
5. Includes Peugeot-Citroen, Chrysler Europe, Renault and AMC
6. Includes Lada, Moskvitch, Zaporzhet, GAZ, Kama River and other Communist Bloc manufacturers

(eg Chrysler, VW, Fiat) will actually survive. One or two of them might exist in the 1990s and remain independent. Some may collapse and others might merge together to make a seventh international grouping. The latter possibility could include a Chrysler/Mitsubishi group merging with VW and/or Fiat, although any of these companies might separately merge with one of the big six companies. It is also possible that a smaller group of VW, Fiat and perhaps Daimler-Benz (though unlikely because of a clash in the CV market) could also make a seventh group. Huyundai by 1990 will also be ripe for merger, being of sufficient size to be important, but too small to be fully competitive.

In playing this 'structural chess' game, one could imagine eight major companies, comprising the big six, Chrysler/Mitsubishi and the VW/Fiat group (or some other combination). While eight companies are possible in a world context, it is unlikely unless GM, Ford or the French group lose market share throughout the world.

In Chapter 4, the possibility of a French group taking over Fiat was mooted, but this is unlikely. The French group would have enough difficulty reorganizing its worldwide activities, and would be advised to concentrate on building up Middle Eastern capacity and starting to develop new facilities elsewhere.

Smaller companies such as BMW, Rolls-Royce and so on might carve a specialist niche for themselves in the marketplace. By 1990 some will have merged, while others will still retain their independence. Collapse for such prestigious companies is less likely, though the very small companies (eg De Lorean, TVR, Lotus, Aston Martin) have had varying fortunes and do not offer such a valuable takeover prize.

The pressures of economies of scale will affect the CV producers but to a lesser extent. The big six manufacturers will all have significant CV capacity across the range, but GM, Ford and the French group will be the specialists in linehaul trucks. Two other significant companies — Daimler-Benz and International Harvester — may remain independent. The smaller independent US companies (eg White and Mack) will either increasingly develop collaborative agreements, or might be taken over by a European-based company. Daimler-Benz, like International Harvester, looks set to diversify out of the pure motor vehicle market into other related areas such as agricultural machinery.

The scenario described here describes the manufacturers as they might appear in the 1990s. A switch of production away from the mature markets will not have occurred by then. Unlike textiles, and radio and TV production, a major increase in capacity cannot be faster than Japan's was, in other words, a 15-20 year span to generate a capacity of some 9 million vehicles. This is a limiting factor and may be conclusive: the mature producers in 1990 will be producing a smaller proportion of the world's output, but control of the world motor industry by the then major companies will be nearly absolute.

Trade

With rising import penetration in the mature markets, a new phenomenon will be established by 1990. The mature markets, as a whole, may suffer import penetration from newer producing areas. The Communist Bloc and an independent South Korea (ie Huyundai) have every motivation to export. The other newer areas have less motivation, since their industry will be controlled by the major manufacturing companies. Nevertheless, the large companies may transfer production away from the mature markets in an attempt to increase economies of scale (and profits) in the newer producing areas, and to take advantage of a cheaper cost base.

Conclusion

Unquestionably, the motor vehicle will still be a major consumer durable by the year 1990. It may be powered by other fuels and it will certainly be more functional than at present. The character of the motor industry will be transformed. As a strategic industry of major economic importance, it must expect greater government intervention. Decisions affecting the industry — how it functions, what it produces, the profits it is permitted (or obliged) to make — will be arrived at in different ways and with different priorities in mind. As profits shrink in the mature markets, producers there will struggle to maintain their lead over the newer producers. Technical innovation and sophistication will be of paramount importance as manufacturers chase after even more elusive profits. By 1990, the pattern of trade in the motor industry will have changed beyond recognition: the established manufacturing companies will, with one or two exceptions, control world motor vehicle production. Through merger, collaboration or collapse, there will be eight or fewer major car manufacturers; we have predicted a concentration of the industry to six companies with a few smaller companies in the CV and specialist fields. Though geographically more diffuse, control will be centralized; a small number of companies, with productive capacity and complex production and distribution networks throughout the world, will dominate the industry.

see pg 360.

Appendices

Appendix 1:
Glossary

AI   Automobile International

AMC   American Motor Corporation

billion   1000 million

BL   British Leyland

BU   Built-up unit (ie complete car or CV assembled and ready to drive)

CAFE   Corporate Average Fuel Economy (US only)

CBU   Completely-built-up

cc   Cubic capacity

CD   Car derived

CKD   Completely knocked-down. This consists of components, power train (engine, gearbox and clutch) pressings and other components

CO   Carbon monoxide

COMECON   Council for Mutual Economic Assistance (Bulgaria, Czechoslovakia, East Germany, Hungary, Mongolia, Poland, Romania and the USSR)

CPRS   Central Policy Review Staff (UK)

CV   Commercial Vehicle

CVCC   Compound Vortex Controlled Combustion

$ US dollars

DCF   Discounted cash flow

Down-size   The US process of taking a car segment and making the car smaller and lighter

EEC   European Economic Community

4 x 4   Four-wheel drive (in a four-wheel drive vehicle)

FSM Douvrin   *Franco-Suedoise des Moteurs*; joint project between PSA Peugeot-Citroen, Renault and Volvo (produced at Douvrin)

GDP   Gross Domestic Product

GM   General Motors

GMC   General Motors Corporation (a division of GM)

GNP   Gross National Product

GVW   Gross Vehicle Weight

HC   Hydrocarbons

HP   Hire purchase or horse-power

IVECO   Industrial Vehicles Corporation

KD   Knocked-down. (KD kits can either be 'counted' as a vehicle in which case the value of the kit must be greater than 50 per cent. If it is less it is non-countable)

KHD   Klockner-Humboldt-Deutz

Kg   Kilograms

MAN   Maschinenfabrik-Augsburg-Nurnberg

MVMA   Motor Vehicle Manufacturers Association (US)

NOx   Nitrogen Oxides

OECD   Organization for Economic Cooperation and Development

OEM   Original Equipment Manufacturer

OPEC   Organization of Petroleum Exporting Countries

Panel   Panel van is a medium-sized van

Parc   Number of vehicles in existence and capable of being used on the road

Power train   Engine, gearbox, clutch and other parts of the transmission

PR   Public Relations

PROCO   Programme-controlled combustion

RV   Recreational Vehicle

SEVEL   Société Européenne des Vehicules Legers

SOFIM   Société Franco-Italienne des Moteurs

SMMT   Society of Motor Manufacturers and Trades (UK)

'T' Car   GM's worldwide concept car that can be tailored to local market conditions but which is based on the Chevette/Kadett model range

Tonnes   One tonne equals 1000 kilograms or 2204.62 pounds or 1.10231 short tons or 0.984207 long tons

UAW   United Automobile Workers Union

V8   An eight-cylinder engine in V formation

VW   Volkswagen

Wheelbase   The distance between the front and back wheel

X Body   GM's new front wheel down-sized car (eg Chevrolet Citation)

Appendix 2:
Statistical Sources

This book provides a considerable amount of statistical information. Problems of definition create many problems in the use of statistics in the study of the motor industry: should a unit, car or CV in kit form be counted as a vehicle or a collection of components; how does one define a region geographically, etc. The motor industry is one of the best documented industries, but the statistics still are inaccurate or difficult to interpret.

The classic example is Ford's assembly plant in Ghenk in Belgium. Components are supplied by Ford's UK, German and Spanish plants. Since the components are less than 50 per cent of the value of the product when leaving Ford's plants they are not counted as a unit of production; since Ford's Belgium assembly plant adds very little value (about 20 per cent), the cars and CVs produced are not counted as car production either. Thus, the statistics show that Ford produces cars in the UK, Spain and West Germany, but not in Belgium; its assembly function is not recognized by the standard counting measures. This tendency is likely to increase in the future as sourcing becomes more difficult as manufacturers attempt to squeeze the last ounce of competitiveness from the scale manufacture of components.

Every attempt has been made to ensure the consistency and accuracy of the data presented in the book. Wherever no source is given, the material will usually comprise data gathered from some or all of the following:

World Motor Vehicle Data the Motor Vehicle Manufacturers Associations (MVMA)
The World Automotive Market Automobile International
Market Data Book Issue Automotive News
The Motor Industry of Great Britain the Society of Manufacturers and Traders (SMMT)
Motor Business the Economist Intelligence Unit
Sewell's Profit Information Unit *Reports* Ronald Sewell & Associates
Motor Industry of Japan Japan Motor Industrial Federation
The Motor Industry of Japan Toyota Motor Sales Company

A number of regular publications include useful motor vehicle statistics. These include *L'Argus, Verband der Automobilindustrie* and *Chambre Syndicale des Constructeurs d'Automobiles.* The annual reports of most of the manufacturers have been most useful (particularly those of Daimler-Benz, VW, Fiat and Peugeot-Citroen). Information has also been gained from various newspapers, particularly the *Financial Times* and the *Economist.* The information services of the Sewell PIU and particularly Eurofinance have been beneficial. The Euroeconomics branch of Eurofinance is arguably the most authoritative specialist on the world motor industry and its reports are always a pleasure to read. It was therefore logical that Michael Hinks-Edwards from Eurofinance should be asked to contribute to this book. A major report by *Business International* (see Preface) has influenced this book. Various UK government reports including the Ryder report, the CPRS (using McKinsey's) report entitled *The Future of the British Car Industry* and the various Expenditure Committee reports were also of some use. Comparative economic data has been taken from UN sources and from figures published by the *Economist.* In addition some confidential data and information from contacts within the motor industry has been used.

Many of the predictions have been supplemented by sophisticated models, including econometric and computer simulation models. It has not been possible to give the results in this book because of space limitations. But the predictions based on a simple forecasting methodology have been modified by numerous runs using more sophisticated (though not necessarily more accurate) models.

Books and other publications which provide some insight into the workings of the motor industry are listed in Appendix 4.

Appendix 3:
The Methodology
of Forecasting

This appendix contains the detailed figures and methodology of forecasting. The steps involved are given below:

1. Project population.
2. Project *per capita* GNP.
3. Project motor vehicle densities on the basis of *per capita* GNP and other local conditions.
4. Using the projected motor vehicle densities and projected population, calculate vehicle parc.
5. Using the vehicle parc as the basis for calculating replacement demand, add subjective estimate of new vehicle demand.

Table A1 lists countries in the $100-3500 *per capita* GNP range and their respective vehicle densities; these densities were used as a basis for projecting the future motor vehicle densities shown in Table A2.

Table A1 *GNP and vehicle density in selected countries (1976)*

	Per capita GNP in 1976 ($)	Vehicles per 1000 people
Burma	110	2
India	130	3
Pakistan	180	4
Sri Lanka	214	10
Kenya	220	12
Ghana	230	11
Indonesia	242	5
Egypt	310	8
Thailand	358	15
Philippines	360	16
Chile	960	43
Taiwan	970	20
Turkey	980	19
Brazil	1100	74
Mexico	1130	59
Jamaica	1296	67
Portugal	1484	127
Argentina	1840	142
Venezuela	2070	119
Greece	2324	81
Ireland	2367	204
Spain	2663	176
Italy	2681	306
UK	3550	459

Table A2 *Projected growth in developing countries*

	Population 1976 (millions)	Projected growth rate (%)	Projected population 1990 (millions)	Per capita GNP 1976 ($)	Scenario 1 Projected growth rate (%)	Scenario 1 Projected per capita GNP 1990 ($)	Scenario 1 Projected motor vehicle density (vehicles per 1000 people)	Scenario 1 Projected vehicle parc in 1990 (millions)	Scenario 2 Projected growth rate (%)	Scenario 2 Projected GNP per capita in 1990 ($)	Scenario 2 Projected vehicles per 1000 people	Scenario 2 Projected vehicle parc in 1990 (millions)
North Africa												
Algeria	17	2.9	25	840	3	1271	65	1.6	2	1108	60	1.5
Morocco	18	3.2	28	360	1.5	443	20	0.6	1	414	19	0.5
Tunisia	6	1.8	8	735	3	1112	60	0.5	2	970	35	0.3
								2.7				2.3
Turkey	41	2.8	60	980	3	1482	100	6.0	2	1293	66	4.0
Central and East Africa												
Kenya	14	3	21	220	3	333	20	0.4	2	290	14	0.3
Zaire	26	3	39	124	3	188	10	0.4	1	143	8	0.3
Ethiopia	29	3	44	108	3	163	8	0.4	1	124	5	0.2
Sudan	19	3	29	230	3	348	17	0.5	1	264	13	0.4
Tanzania	16	3	24	150	3	227	12	0.3	2	198	11	0.3
Uganda	12	3	18	240	3	363	16	0.3	2	317	15	0.3
								2.3				1.8
West Africa												
Nigeria	65	2.7	94	350	6	791	30	2.8	4	606	25	2.4
Ivory Coast	5	2.6	7	730	6	1650	120	0.8	2	963	35	0.2
Ghana	10	3	15	230	3	348	20	0.3	2	303	15	0.2
								3.9				2.8

Table A2 *continued*

	Population 1976 (millions)	Projected growth rate (%)	Projected population 1990 (millions)	Per capita GNP 1976 ($)	Scenario 1 — Projected vehicle parc				Scenario 2 — Projected vehicle parc			
					Projected growth rate (%)	Projected GNP per capita 1990 ($)	Projected motor vehicle density (vehicles per 1000 people)	Projected vehicle parc in 1990 (millions)	Projected growth rate (%)	Projected GNP per capita in 1990 ($)	Projected vehicles per 1000 people	Projected vehicle parc in 1990 (millions)
East Africa												
China	825	1.7	1079	380	4	658	3–15	3.2–16	2	501	3–10	3–11
South Korea	36	1.8	46	641	7	1653	120	5.5	4	1110	60	2.8
Taiwan	16	1.8	21	970	6	2193	150	3.2	4	1680	120	2.5
South-east Asia												
Indonesia	140	2.6	201	242	4	419	20	4.0	3	366	15	3.0
Malaysia	12	2.9	18	840	4	1455	120	2.2	3	1271	75	1.4
Philippines	44	2.9	66	360	2.5	509	30	2.0	1	418	23	1.5
Thailand	43	2.8	63	358	3	541	31	2.0	1	416	21	1.3
Vietnam	47	2.9	70	160	4	277	10	0.7	2	211	7	0.5
Burma	31	2.2	42	110	0.5	118	2	0.1	0	110	2	0.1
								11.0				7.8
South Asia												
India	610	2.1	816	132	2	174	9	7.3	1	153	6	4.9
Pakistan	72	3.3	113	180	2	238	12	1.4	1	209	10	1.1
Bangladesh	79	2.4	110	85	2	112	2	0.2	1	99	2	0.2
Afghanistan	20	2.5	28	110	2	145	7	0.2	1	128	5	0.1
Sri Lanka	14	1.5	17	214	3	282	14	0.2	1	248	11	0.2
Nepal	13	2.3	18	120	2	158	5	0.1	1	139	3	0.1
								9.4				6.6

Appendix 4:
Select Bibliography

ANFIA (annual) *Automobile in Cifre* Turin

L'Argus (annual statistical number in June) *L'Argus de l'Automobile et des Loco-motions* Paris

Armstrong, A G (1967) The motor industry and the British economy. *District Bank Review*

Arrow, K (1962) Economic welfare and the allocation of resources for invention. In *The Rate and Direction of Inventive Activity: Economic and Social Factors* National Bureau for Economic Research, Princeton University Press

Autocar

Automobile International (annual) *The World Automotive Market* New York

Automotive News

Automotive News, *Market Data Book* Detroit

Baranson, J (1971) International transfer of automotive technology to developing countries. United Nations Institute for Training and Research, *Research Reports* New York

Behrman, J (1972) *The Role of International Companies in Latin American Integration: Autos and Petrochemicals* Heath: Lexington

Beynon, H (1973) *Working for Ford* Penguin: London

Bhaskar, K N (1975) *Alternatives Open to the UK Motor Industry* University of Bristol

Bhaskar, K N (1979) *The Future of the UK Motor Industry* Kogan Page: London

Bloomfield, G (1978) *The World Automotive Industry* David and Charles: Newton Abbot

British Leyland *Annual Reports*

Brooke, M Z and Remmers, H L (1970) *The Strategy of Multinational Enterprise: Organisation and Finance* Longman: London

Business International (1975) *The World Automotive Industry to 1995* New York

Car and Driver

Central Policy Review Staff (1975) *The Future of the British Car Industry* HMSO: London

Chambre Syndicate des Constructeurs d'Automobiles *L'Industrie Automobile en Amerique L'Amne* Paris

Consumer Guide (auto bi-monthly) Skohie, Illinois

Counter Information Service (1973) *British Leyland: The Beginning of the End* CIS Anti-Report: London

Counter Information Service *Ford* CIS Anti-Report: London

Cowling, K G and Cubbin, J S (1975) Quality change and pricing behaviour in the UK car industry 1956-68. *Economica*

Cubbin, J S (1978) Impact penetration in the UK passenger car market: a cross section study. *Applied Economics*

Daimler-Benz *Annual Reports*

Department of Trade and Industry (1971) *Sources of Statistics I: The Motor Industry* HMSO: London
Department of Industry (1976) *The British Motor Vehicle Industry* HMSO: London
Donner, F G (1967) *The World-Wide Industrial Enterprise: Its Challenge and Promise* McGraw-Hill: New York
Dunn's Review
Economist (1978) *The World in Figures* London
Economist Intelligence Unit, *Motor Business*, London (see special reports: *Worldwide Automotive Activity 1977, Outlook 1978-79* and *The West European Motor Industry: Where Now?*
Economist Intelligence Unit (quarterly) *Multinational Business* London
Edwards, C E (1965) *Dynamics of the United States Automobile Industry* University of South Carolina Press: Colombia
Ensor, J (1971) *The Motor Industry* Longman: London
Euroeconomics (1974) *Changes in the World Automobile Industry, 1974-85* Eurofinance: Paris
Euroeconomics (1975) *Current European Topics: British Leyland Cars: The Next Twelve Years* Eurofinance: Paris
Euroeconomics (1975) *Current European Topics: Industrial Planning and State Investment, The UK Motor Industry* Eurofinance: Paris
Euroeconomics (1975) *The Communist Bloc Automobile Industry: Implications for Western Manufacturers* Eurofinance: Paris
Euroeconomics (1975) *The Recession in the Automobile Industry: How Deep and How Long?* Eurofinance: Paris
Euroeconomics (1975) *World Vehicle Production and Sales Forecasts to 1985* Eurofinance: Paris
Euroeconomics (1976) *The Middle Eastern Automotive Markets* Eurofinance: Paris
Euroeconomics (1977) *European Motor Industry Conference, Frankfurt 1977* Eurofinance: Paris
Euroeconomics (1978) *The European Car Industry Review, 1978-82* Eurofinance: Paris
Euroeconomics (1978) *The Long Term Environment for Commercial Vehicles in Western Europe* Eurofinance: Paris
Euroeconomics (1979) *Automotive Financial Performance Indicators* Eurofinance: Paris
Euroeconomics (1979) *The European Car Industry Review, 1979-83* Eurofinance: Paris
Expenditure Committee (1976) *Public Expenditure on Chrysler UK* HMSO: London
Expenditure Committee (1975) *The Motor Vehicle Industry* Fourteenth Report of the Expenditure Committee, HMSO: London
Fiat *Annual Reports*
Ford *Annual Reports* (of parent company and subsidiaries)
Fortune
General Motors *Annual Reports* (of parent company and subsidiaries, including Vauxhall, Opel and Holden)
Giles, G E and Worsley, T E (August 1979) Development of methods for forecasting car ownership and use. *Economic Trends* HMSO: London
Hellman, R (1970) *The Challenge to US Dominance of the International Corporation* Dunellen: New York
Hinks-Edwards, M (1979) Les guards problèmes de l'industrie mondiale voitures particulières. *Analyse Financière*
Hirsch, S (1967) *Location of Industry and International Competitiveness* Clarendon Press: Oxford

Hirschman, A O (1968) The political economy of import substituting industrial-isation. *Quarterly Journal of Economics*

Japan Motor Industry Federation (annual) *Guide to the Motor Industry of Japan* Tokyo

Jenkins, R O (1977) *Dependent Industrialization in Latin America: The Automotive Industry in Argentina, Chile and Mexico* Praeger: New York

Karssen, W J (1968) Concentration in the automobile industry of the EEC. In US Congress, Subcommittee on Antitrust and Monopoly *Economic Concentration*

Kitching, J (1974) Winning and losing with European acquisitions. *Harvard Business Review*

Knickerbocker, F T (1973) *Oligopolistic Reaction and Multinational Enterprise* Harvard University Press: Cambridge, Massachusetts

Little, I M D, Scitorsky, T and Scott, M (1970) *Industry and Trade in Some Developing Countries: A Comparative Study* Oxford University Press (OECD)

Marris, R and Wood, A (1971) *The Corporate Economy: Growth, Competition and Innovative Potential* Macmillan: New York

Maxly, G and Seberston, A (1959) *The Motor Industry* Allen and Unwin: London

Motor

Motor Vehicle Manufacturers Association, Canada (annual) *Facts and Figures of the Automotive Industry* Toronto

Motor Vehicle Manufacturers Association, US (annual) *Motor Vehicle Facts and Figures* Detroit

Motor Vehicle Manufacturers Association, US (annual) *World Motor Vehicle Data* Detroit

National Economic Development Office, Motor Manufacturing Economic Development Office (1968) *The Effect of Government Policy on the Motor Industry* HMSO: London

National Economic Development Office, Motor Manufacturing Economic Development Council (1971) *Japan: Its Motor Industry and Market* HMSO: London

Nissan Motor Company (annual) *The Global Datsun Family: A Guide to Nissan Motor Company* Tokyo

Pratten, C (1971) *Economics of Scale in Manufacturing Industry* Cambridge University Press

Predicasts (1975) *World Motor Vehicles*

PSA Peugeot-Citroen *Annual Reports*

Rae, J B (1959) *American Automobile Manufacturers* Chilton: New York

Rae, J B (1971) *The Road and Car in American Life* Harvard University Press; Cambridge, Massachusetts

Renault *Annual Reports*

Rhys, D G (1972) *The Motor Industry: An Economic Survey* Butterworths: London

Rhys, D G (1974) Employment, efficiency and labour relations in the British motor industry. *Industrial Relations Journal*

Rhys, D G (1977) European mass-producing car makers and minimum efficient scale: a note. *Journal of Industrial Economics*

Ryder Report (1975) *British Leyland: The Next Decade* HMSO: London

Saab-Scania *Annual Reports*

Seidler, E (1973) *The Romance of Renault* Edita: Lausanne

Seidler, E (1976) *Let's Call it Fiesta*

Shier, A (1977) *Motor Trade Management* Oxford University Press

Silberston, A (1972) Economics of scale in theory and practice. *Economic Journal*

Sloan, A P (1967) *My Years with General Motors* Pan: London

Society of Motor Manufacturers and Traders *Monthly Statistical Review* London

Society of Motor Manufacturers and Traders (annual) *The Motor Industry of Great Britain* London

Stubbs, P (1972) *The Australian Motor Industry: A Study in Protection and Growth* Melbourne

Toyota Motor Sales Company (annual) *The Motor Industry of Japan* Tokyo

Truck

Turner, G (1971) *Leyland Papers* Eyre and Spottiswood: London

UK Annual Abstract of Statistics

UNCTAD (1972) *Major Issues Arising from the Transfer of Technology to Developing Countries*

UNIDO (1972) *The Motor Vehicle Industry*

US Statistical Abstract

Verband der Automobilindustrie e V (annual) *Tatsachen und Zahlen aus der Kraftverkehrswirtschaft* Frankfurt-am-Main

Vernon, R (1966) International investment and international trade in the product cycle. *Quarterly Journal of Economics*

Volkswagen *Annual Reports*

Volvo *Annual Reports*

Wall Street Journal

White, L J (1971) *The Automobile Industry Since 1945* Harvard University Press: Cambridge, Massachusetts

Young, S and Hood, N (1977) *Chrysler UK: A Corporation in Transition* Praeger: New York

Index